Critical Essays on
Sarah Orne Jewett

Critical Essays on Sarah Orne Jewett

Gwen L. Nagel

G. K. Hall & Co. • Boston, Massachusetts

Library of Congress Cataloging in Publication Data

Main entry under title:

Critical essays on Sarah Orne Jewett.

(Critical essays on American literature)
Includes index.
1. Jewett, Sarah Orne, 1849–1909—Criticism and
interpretation—Addresses, essays, lectures. I. Nagel,
Gwen L. II. Series.
PS2133.C74 1984   813′.4   83-26549
ISBN 0-8161-8422-4

This publication is printed on permanent/durable acid-free paper
MANUFACTURED IN THE UNITED STATES OF AMERICA

CRITICAL ESSAYS ON AMERICAN LITERATURE

This series seeks to anthologize the most important criticism on a wide variety of topics and writers in American literature. Our readers will find in various volumes not only a generous selection of reprinted articles and reviews but original essays, bibliographies, manuscript sections, and other materials brought to public attention for the first time. Gwen L. Nagel's volume on Sarah Orne Jewett is a welcome addition to our list in that it contains nine original essays, including an introduction that provides a detailed bibliographic survey of Jewett scholarship. In addition, Philip B. Eppard's essay includes two recently discovered Jewett stories, not previously listed in the canon, and reprinted here for the first time. There are also original contributions by Richard Cary, the Dean of Jewett criticism, Judith Roman, Jean Carwile Masteller, Barbara A. Johns, Elizabeth Ammons, Rebecca Wall Nail, and Josephine Donovan. We are confident that this collection will make a permanent and significant contribution to American literary study.

James Nagel, GENERAL EDITOR

Northeastern University

for my parents,
Helen and Byron Lindberg

CONTENTS

ORIGINAL ESSAYS

INTRODUCTION

A chronological review of the history of scholarship on Sarah Orne Jewett (1849–1909) and her works reveals a progressive sophistication of insight within a relatively narrow range. Save for recent work by feminist scholars, which has led to a reinterpretation of many of her works, most of the major areas of critical thought on Jewett were established early, soon after the publication of *Deephaven* in 1877 and, interestingly, before the appearance of her most important book, *The Country of the Pointed Firs*, in 1896. That Jewett wrote with considerable artistic control about basically regional subjects; that a persistent theme in her works was the decline of stature of South Berwick, Maine, and the surrounding area; that her characters tend to be elderly, mostly female, and rarely dynamic young men; and that her principal artistic skills are in style and characterization rather than in plot are all matters established well within her lifetime.

Although Jewett wrote verse, numerous works for children, including the early collection of short stories, *Play Days* (1878), an historical romance, *The Tory Lover* (1901), and a history, *The Story of the Normans* (1887), most of the important scholarship has quite properly been biographical, iconographical, or focused on her several volumes of regional realism. There is a running debate as to whether Jewett's serious fiction represents realism, regionalism, or local colorism, but the substance of critical reaction has been much less controversial than the terms of this dispute would seem to suggest.

Serious comment on Jewett begins with William Dean Howells' favorable review of *Deephaven* in the *Atlantic Monthly* in which he lauds the "fresh and delicate quality" of her sketches, her skill in rendering dialect, her control of language, her subtlety of characterization, and the depth of her portrait of life in her region.[1] From his desk as editor of the *Atlantic*, as well as from his position as one of the important novelists in the Realistic movement, Howells was able to give encouragement to this young writer from a Maine village and to help shape critical responses to her work. Although there were some narrow and peevish reviews of Jewett's works (one reviewer of *Deephaven* concluded that "it is by some mistake, doubtless, that it got into print at all"[2]), the preponderance of

1

critical reactions for the next twenty years followed Howells' lead. For example, in reviewing *Play Days* in 1878, Horace E. Scudder praises the "good breeding," "humor," and "refinement" of Jewett's stories for children and compares them favorably with her sketches in *Deephaven*. Scudder also points out what was to be a continuing flaw in much of Jewett's fiction, her difficulties with plot and structure.[3]

The weaknesses as well as the virtues of Jewett's fiction are not especially obscure matters and were recognized by contemporary reviewers. Like Scudder, critics praised Jewett's fine workmanship while they acknowledged her limitations, especially in plotting. Those reviewers who attempted to come to terms with the appeal of Jewett's fiction turned to metaphor. The *Critic* declared that the charm of Jewett's fiction is "flavor rather than shape; essence rather than body." The *Nation* found her unconventional fiction had the restful effect of "a strain of sweet music repeating itself again and again," while the *Atlantic*, which also commented on their "restful" quality, found the works imbued with "all the value and interest of delicately executed watercolors."[4] Though the charm of Jewett's art may have been elusive, its limitations were not. The same *Atlantic* reviewer warns Jewett against confining herself to "too narrow a range" and urges her to try a larger work. When she does attempt her first novel, *A Country Doctor*, one reviewer labels it "an expanded sketch" but delicately finished "within its limitations."[5] Noting the exquisite detail of the landscape in *A Marsh Island*, a reviewer asserts that here the restful effect of her works has become "drowsy": "It is, indeed, because they are so fine that one looks for something more important to happen in them than the eating of apples or the making of pie."[6]

Reviewers continue to note that Jewett's plots are "slight"—the reviewer for *Literary World* boldly declaring Jewett "incapable of constructing a plot"—but her workmanship is exquisite.[7] The stories in *A White Heron*, for example, receive high marks, the *Overland Monthly's* reviewer finding the title story "perfect in its way—a tiny classic."[8] Jewett receives praise for her foray into history and for *Betty Leicester*, her novel written to inspire young girls.[9] Though most reviewers declare the quotidian events of life to be her proper subject, there is a range of response to her portraits of New England. Her works are variously characterized as sunny, fresh, idealistic, charming. A reviewer for the *Independent*, however, finds her New England "dreadfully doleful," and he lauds her masterful portraits of "bleakness and barrenness of soil and life."[10]

Though an English reader in a review of Jewett's masterpiece declared that "a good book was never made of slighter material," *The Country of the Pointed Firs* assured Jewett's place in literary history. She is praised by the *Times* for her "delicate and sympathetic portrayal of nature and of character" and for her "perfect" artistry. The *Independent* concurs and refers to her "perfect sympathetic touch." She is declared a master of her craft, with her book combining "the freshness of *Deephaven* with the mellowness of matured power." Alice Brown celebrates *Pointed Firs* as a beautiful and perfect work, "the acme" of Jewett's career.[11]

Another writer, Octave Thanet, reviews Jewett's last novel, *The Tory Lover*, with as much enthusiasm as Brown evinces for *Pointed Firs*, but Thanet's was a minority opinion. Reviewers for the *Independent* and *Outlook* agree that Jewett's literary craftsmanship is amply displayed in this new work, but they find it "tedious." The *Literary World* regrets that Jewett should ever deviate from her true subject, while the *Outlook* concludes: "she has no need of success in a new field; her own field is ample, and her possession of it complete." This comment is echoed by Henry James when, in a letter, he admonishes Jewett to "Go back to the dear Country of the Pointed Firs. . . ." It is unfortunate that she never did. It was left for a *Times* reviewer of the seven-volume edition of her works who was struck by the completeness of this, her "life work," to declare that Jewett's fiction will "remain a permanent part of our literature."[12]

Beyond the important reviews she received from Howells and Scudder, Jewett had the good fortune to attract early attention from Madame Blanc (Thérèse Bentzon), whose essay in *Revue des Deux Mondes*, "Le roman de la femme-medicin,"[13] was a substantial piece of criticism, exploring Jewett's strengths and weaknesses and stressing the theme of the New Woman in *A Country Doctor*, a matter now receiving renewed attention by feminist critics. Blanc's assessment that Jewett's propensities for reason (rather than emotion), digression, and problems of transition between sketches indicates that she is more suited for the short story than the novel is essentially undisputed throughout the scholarship. This essay, along with Madame Blanc's "Le Naturalisme aux Etats-Unis" in 1887,[14] established the French critic as one of the most perceptive and balanced of Jewett's contemporary reviewers.

Perhaps the outstanding quality of Jewett scholarship over the decades has been its balance, its capacity for enthusiastic appreciation of her works while maintaining an understanding of their limitations and weaknesses, a quality sustained in the single most important scholarly study, Richard Cary's *Sarah Orne Jewett*.[15] Although several contemporary reviewers made reference to Jewett's "perfect" craftsmanship, there was a general tendency to temper praise of Jewett's work, especially with regard to her delineation of New England character, dialect, and scene, with a recognition of her limitations in plotting and in the portrayal of action, passion, and tragedy.

By the time of Jewett's death in 1909, she had received wide recognition as a writer of stories of New England which equal, sometimes surpass, those of Mary E. Wilkins Freeman, with whom she was frequently linked. Jewett had become the foremost writer of her region, had become a member of the literary society of Boston, partly through her intimate relationship with Annie Fields (widow of the publishing mogul James T. Fields), had traveled widely and received acclaim throughout much of the Continent and Eastern United States, and had been awarded an honorary doctorate by Bowdoin College, the first such award the college had ever given to a woman. A year after her death, Simmons College, in Boston, established the Sarah Orne Jewett Scholarship Fund to aid deserving students from Maine. The announcement of the award referred to Jewett's continuing theme of the tragedy of the "narrow life" for women, but it also stressed that Jewett "never lost sight of the humanity that is larger and deeper than sex."[16]

After the tragedy of Jewett's carriage accident in 1902, which terminated her writing career, and the shock of her death in 1909, Jewett's reputation quickly stabilized into a pattern which continues largely unchanged today. For example, in 1904 Brander Matthews expressed his judgment that Freeman and Jewett were the foremost regionalists of New England, an assessment somewhat broadened in 1913 when Edward M. Chapman compared Jewett's local-color writing favorably with that of Thomas Hardy and Jane Austen. This high regard for Jewett's New England portraits, expressed in a variety of critical formulations, has remained virtually constant. Henry James saw Jewett's work on New England as exceeded only by the stories of Nathaniel Hawthorne, and Bliss Perry and F. O. Matthiessen later concurred on essentially the same point. Harry R. Warfel and G. Harrison Orians included several of Jewett's sketches in their important anthology *American Local-Color Stories* and John Eldridge Frost, in the best biography of Jewett, and Carlos Baker, writing in the fourth edition of the *Literary History of the United States*, arrive at basically the same evaluation as Matthews.[17]

Jewett continues to be classified as a local colorist by such critics as Susan Allen Toth, Perry D. Westbrook, Ann Douglas Wood, and Julia Bader,[18] and her works have been examined in a number of dissertations on the local-color phenomenon.[19] Foremost and most recent among the published studies of Jewett and her school is Josephine Donovan's *New England Local Color Literature: A Woman's Tradition*. Donovan traces the sources that gave rise to the New England local-color school, explores the fictional world they created, and concludes that the culmination of what she calls "women's literary realism" may be found in Jewett's *The Country of the Pointed Firs*.[20] Although some critics, namely, Richard Cary, feel that "local colorism" is a delimiting conception of Jewett's contribution to literature, her reputation seems fixed in one dimension as a writer of local-color regionalism who brought to the genre its finest artistic expression in America.

By the 1920s, however, especially through the efforts of Willa Cather, scholarly assessment of Jewett had begun to modify the regionalist approach to her work. To the extent that "regionalism" implied a limitation of the quality of her work, or its significance in American literature, there were voices to argue for a broader context in which to view Jewett's contribution. Willa Cather, in a famous remark, concluded the introduction to her edition on *The Best Short Stories of Sarah Orne Jewett* with the assertion that *Pointed Firs* ranks with *The Scarlet Letter* and *Huckleberry Finn* as three works certain to endure in American literature.[21] Jewett was now in good company, indeed. A writer in *Outlook*, reviewing Cather's edition, observed that Jewett's reputation had changed from that of a New England regionalist to being one of the "accredited masters of the short story."[22] Soon Jewett was regarded as being more "Realist" than "regionalist," and so nearly every modern scholar has described her.

A few readers, however, see Jewett's works as representing a blend of realism with the romanticism still lingering in New England since the days of Hawthorne and the Transcendentalists. Walter Fuller Taylor described her in these terms in his *A History of American Letters* in 1936, and so did Jean Sougnac in a doctoral dissertation at the University of Paris a year later. This rationale is pursued by Richard Cary in his *Sarah Orne Jewett* and by Michael W. Vella in a perceptive article in the *Emerson Society Quarterly*. A. M. Buchan, in *"Our Dear Sarah": An Essay on Sarah Orne Jewett*, takes this line of reasoning to its extreme with his contention that Jewett wrote "with a theory of her craft and a skill in it that were independent of a fashionable new realism."[23]

The most recent commentators on the generic identification of Jewett's fiction do not find her independent of other literary movements. Cynthia Griffin Wolff pronounces Jewett a New England regionalist who portrays the romantic vision, and Priscilla Leder explores how Jewett assimilated the elements of romance in her fiction. Jeri Parker labels Jewett an experimental realist whose works bridge the gap between the genteel sentimentalists and the naturalists. And Josephine Donovan sees the tradition of "women's literary realism," of which Jewett's work represents the powerful and complex culmination, rejecting the romantic and sentimental traditions. Finally, Julia Bader, in a useful new essay on realism, examines how the stable, tangible reality in Jewett's fiction is subverted by her presentation of chaotic, distorted mental states (the clouded vision of Captain Littlepage, for example). Though Bader does not explore this line of thought, Jewett's challenge to the realistic world and, hence, to the reliability of vision might be fruitfully explored in the context of literary impressionism.[24]

Indeed, the extent to which Jewett's works can be made accessible and discursive through the theory of literary impressionism has been referred to briefly by Robin Magowan and others but developed in only two essays. Barton L. St. Armand, in a stimulating article in 1972, argues that Jewett's works are better compared to the impressionism of the American painter John Marin than to standard works of realism, a postulation that was hampered by the lack of a coherent theory of impressionism in American literature. Annis Pratt explores not so much impressionism itself as the related concept of epiphany, comparing epiphanic moments in Jewett's "A White Heron" to those in James Joyce's *A Portrait of the Artist as a Young Man*.[25] This approach, too, would reward a more comprehensive and systematic application to the full scope of Jewett's serious fiction.

Another line of development that has not yet been exhausted is the role of pastoralism in Jewett's works. Robin Magowan has argued provocatively that Jewett turned to Theocritus and the pastoral tradition for her inspiration and that this suppressed tradition in America has its best expression in *The Country of the Pointed Firs*. In 1970, David Stouck explored the temporal implications of pastoralism in Jewett's finest work as well, and pastoralism in New England local color has been investigated in a dissertation by Sister Mary Williams.[26]

One subject which has been the focus of critical comment from the first is the theme of the past, of love for the past and a desire to recapture and preserve it in fiction. This matter was expressed in a review of *Country By-Ways* in the *Nation* in 1881, which described the book as a "loving memorial of a generation that is just passing out of our sight." This theme was given more explicit development in a perceptive essay in Fred Lewis Pattee's *A History of American Literature Since 1870*, published in 1915, in which Pattee commented on Jewett's work as an attempt to preserve the best of New England by writing of the "passing of an old regime." Granville Hicks gave the theme nearly the same formulation in *The Great Tradition* as did Perry D. Westbrook in *Acres of Flint*, a book that has recently been republished in a revised edition. Westbrook characterized Jewett's fiction as a celebration of the American past, of a time when New England was yet unchanged by the influence of the modern, industrial world. Ferman Bishop used the theme of the past to show the coherent development of Jewett's work and to establish a context in which her historical romance, *The Tory Lover*, appears as a consistent part of the canon, as a novel focused entirely on the past, rather than as generic anomaly. Since then it has been difficult to write extensively about Jewett without touching upon some aspects of retrospective time in Jewett's works. Richard Cary explores the subject with prudence in his Twayne book, as does Paul John Eakin in "Sarah Orne Jewett and the Meaning of Country Life" in which he relates the temporal theme to the preservation of traditional village values and customs. In her 1979 dissertation, Gwen L. Nagel explores the variety of means Jewett's heroines use to preserve what they cherish from the past, and, in an essay published in 1981, Charles W. Mayer discusses how the complex nature of Jewett's view of the past is manifested in her fiction.[27]

A familiar motif in contemporary reviews of her fiction was Jewett's accurate delineation of the New England scene. Perry D. Westbrook in

The New England Town in Fact and Fiction argues that Jewett, who was inspired by love of her native village though not blind to rural poverty or the deprivations of Maine life, combined the approaches of the folklorist, social historian, and ethnologist to produce fictional portraits of New England villages. Setting is also the subject of Rebecca Wall Nail's essay "Where Every Prospect Pleases: Sarah Orne Jewett, South Berwick, and the Importance of Place," published here for the first time. Based on her 1981 dissertation, Nail's essay discusses Jewett's ambivalence toward her native village and explores the thematic significance place has in her fiction, including the much maligned *The Tory Lover*. Julia Bader briefly explores how local colorists used landscape and setting to explore their characters' search for identity, and Jennifer Bailey, in an essay appearing in *Revue française d'études américaines* in 1983, finds Jewett used setting symbolically in *Pointed Firs* to portray a female version of nature. Finally, Randall R. Mawer's essay on *A Marsh Island*, examines Jewett's symbolic use of local-color setting in her novel.[28]

Among the recently explored areas in Jewett scholarship are the religious aspects of Jewett's works and her use of folklore. Mary Kraus finds that a humanistic religious vision functions both artistically and thematically in the Jewett canon, while Charles Scott Pugh discusses a symbolic Christian narrative below the local-color surface of *The Country of the Pointed Firs* in his 1979 dissertation, "The Meditative Art of Sarah Orne Jewett." Kraus' "Sarah Orne Jewett and Temporal Continuity," derived from her dissertation, suggests that Jewett's view of time as a single continuum and her belief in a benevolent Providence are subtly manifested in her best work. Elmer Pry discusses Jewett's use of folk materials, including dialect, syntax, proverbs, legends, regional foods, and folk festivals, in an essay published in the *Tennessee Folklore Society Bulletin*, a topic that Susan Joan Martin Fagan also explores in her 1982 dissertation.[29]

Another of the continuing lines of exploration which has received invigorated attention in the last ten years, shaped in large part by feminist studies, is Jewett's representation of women. That Jewett's central fictional interests were with women is hardly new. In an 1880 review, Horace Scudder finds that Jewett eschews the depiction of passionate love for reverent portraits of the old maid.[30] Thirteen years later a reviewer for the *Nation* similarly declares Jewett's subjects are older, reticent women who harbor secret sorrows: "It has been given to Miss Jewett to express these women, to paint their external life and manners, to reveal the secret emotions of the heart and yearnings of the soul."[31] Critics have studied Jewett's women characters for decades, but the recent resurgence of interest in women writers has led to new and promising avenues of reinterpretation. Two essays on Jewett's women characters are published here for the first time. Barbara A. Johns, in "'Mateless and Appealing': Growing into Spinsterhood in Sarah Orne

Jewett," focuses on the "young-maid" heroines in *Deephaven* who pre-figure Jewett's older New England women who have chosen and found the single life fulfilling due, in part, to the "transfiguring power of friendship."[32] Elizabeth Ammons in "Jewett's Witches" discusses how Jewett's fascination with the occult and spirit world is reflected in the variety of herbalists—"white witches"—who serve as spiritual guides for younger, "motherless" women. Ammons examines several central works including "Lady Ferry," *Pointed Firs*, "The Foreigner," and "The Green Bowl," Jewett's last exploration of this theme.

Historically, the concern for the sexual identity of Jewett and her characters gained impetus with the publication of *A Country Doctor* in 1884. The reviews of this provocative book placed stress on the societal norms which restrict a woman's life to domestic duties and on the inherent difficulties for a woman in meeting these expectations and assuming the responsibilities of a profession as well. Most of the review-ers were broadly sympathetic to the plight of Nan in the novel, as well as to the concept of expanding opportunities and roles for women in American culture, but one reviewer in *Lippincott's Magazine* regretted that Jewett had chosen to deal with this theme in her first novel. There are already too many male physicians, he protested, and, besides, women are "not usually considered scientific or endowed with keen, accurate intellectual vision. . . ." Overt, strident sexism has been generally absent from Jewett's scholarship, however, and contemporary comment in par-ticular tended to follow the tone of Horace Scudder's review in which he reflected that the feminism theme in Jewett's work was of a "thor-oughly healthy sort."[33]

Marie Thérèse Blanc's thirty-five-page essay-review of *A Country Doctor* was, in 1885, the most impressive critique of Jewett to date. Madame Blanc's interest in women's issues is reflected here, for she introduced her review of Jewett's works with a survey of the status of women. American reviewers had two other recently published novels about women physicians to compare with *A Country Doctor*: *Doctor Breen's Practice* by Howells and *Doctor Zay* by Elizabeth Stuart Phelps. Jean Carwile Masteller takes a closer look at these novels in "The Women Doctors of Howells, Phelps, and Jewett: The Conflict of Mar-riage and Career"[34] and argues that they represent three different solu-tions to the problems facing a career woman in the late nineteenth century. Masteller's essay appears here for the first time. Recent studies of Jewett have tried to come to terms with Jewett's feminism. Carolyn Forrey, recalling the reviews of ninety years before, discusses *A Country Doctor* in terms of the "New Woman" concept, while Ellen Morgan, in an essay published in the short-lived *Kate Chopin Newsletter*, finds in Jewett's novel both support for and challenges to traditional ideas about the role of women. Elizabeth Dague, on the other hand, labels *A Coun-*

try Doctor a polemic against the traditional submissive and domestic roles for women, an opinion supported by Josephine Donovan in a broad ranging essay, "A Woman's Vision of Transcendence: A New Interpretation of the Works of Sarah Orne Jewett." Donovan finds Jewett's novel so imbued with feminist fervor that it reads like a series of feminist declarations. A recent article by Malinda Snow, which explores the theme of vocation in *A Country Doctor*, suggests that there are still new areas open to critics who wish to explore this, Jewett's most feminist work.[35]

In 1925 Esther Forbes pointed out that Jewett from girlhood on always needed the companionship of other women and wrote frequently of the devotion of one woman for another. This matter, in both its biographical (focusing largely on Jewett's intimate relationship with Annie Fields for three decades) and critical formulations has become an active area of concern. In her youthful diaries, now in the Houghton Library at Harvard, Jewett reveals her close attachment to other young women and her preoccupation with friendship. Her most important adult relationship was of course, with Annie Fields, though during her lifetime she had a wide circle of friends. Josephine Donovan in an essay appearing in *Frontiers* characterizes the Jewett-Fields relationship as a thirty year "affair." Based on evidence in the extant poetry manuscripts and Jewett's letters to Fields, Donovan finds Jewett was far from the "passionless spinster," as she has sometimes been characterized by critics who note the absence of heterosexual passion in Jewett's fiction. Lillian Faderman in *Surpassing the Love of Men: Romantic Friendship and Love Between Women from the Renaissance to the Present* labels Jewett a "conscious, articulate feminist" who illustrated the destructiveness of marriage in "Tom's Husband," finds that "Martha's Lady" depicts "what would be called lesbian love" today, and characterizes Jewett's relationship with Fields as a "Victorian romance."[36] Judith Roman in "A Closer Look at the Jewett-Fields Relationship," a new essay appearing in this volume, explores more fully the nature of this relationship, basing her judgments on a reading of their correspondence and Jewett's fictional works.

Glenda Hobbs, in an essay reprinted here, does not characterize the relationship in "Martha's Lady" as lesbian, as Federman does, but she does focus on the intense friendship depicted in that story, finding that it is both passionate and spiritual and that it meets Thoreau's requirements of true friendship.[37] Hobbs' forthcoming essay "Such Good Friends: Female Intimacies in the Life and Work of Sarah Orne Jewett"[38] is a balanced and insightful discussion of the centrality of female friendships in Jewett's life. Nina Auerbach explores the "miraculous sisterhood" that is created among women in stories like "Miss Tempy's Watchers,"[39] and Josephine Donovan in *Sarah Orne Jewett* points to an

1869 diary as evidence and posits that a real friendship between Jewett and Kate Birckhead was the motivation behind the development of the *Deephaven* sketches.[40]

Donovan's volume, published in 1980 as part of the Ungar modern literature series, is a useful survey of Jewett's writings although it, like Cary's Twayne book, is limited somewhat by the strictures of the series format. Donovan focuses on such themes as the confrontation of city and country, and the individual versus the community, traces their appearance in the canon, and concludes with a useful chapter on Jewett's critical theories. She successfully illustrates in this book how many of Jewett's works concern women's issues. Donovan explores this further in "A Woman's Vision of Transcendence: A New Interpretation of the Works of Sarah Orne Jewett." Here she maintains Jewett's women characters attempt to transcend their sense of alienation through community and a kind of woman's religion of "healing and hospitality."[41]

But there have been other approaches beside the feminist that have given promise of renewed interest in Jewett's works. Two dissertations published in 1976 focus on language; the first, by Gerard John Dullea, is a linguistic study of Jewett's style, while the second, by Evelyn Starr Cutler, is an examination of Jewett's representation of Maine dialect. Two briefer studies focus on Jewett's use of language in "A White Heron." Michael Atkinson finds that Jewett's use of the often criticized authorial voice in that story is justified, and Gayle L. Smith finds that the shifts in tenses and narrative perspectives, rather than fragmenting the story, convey the theme of oneness with nature.[42]

Of all Jewett's shorter fiction, "A White Heron" has received the lion's share of recent critical attention. Jewett's story is given a psychoanalytic reading in 1978 by Theodore Hovet, who, the same year, publishes a study of the fairy-tale structure in "A White Heron." This structure, writes Hovet, allowed Jewett to "explore sexual conflict in a way that a more explicit story could not." James Ellis discovers a complex pattern of sexual symbolism in Jewett's story, as does Richard Brenzo, who suggests that Jewett's tale may present "a provocative satirical image of the condition of late nineteenth century wives." Josephine Donovan sees the story as a repudiation of the Cinderella text, while George Held declares Sylvia a descendant of another Jewett heroine, Nan Prince, and finds that both she and the ornithologist act out for a time "the roles that age and gender have assigned them." Despite the dizzying plethora of commentary on the story [43] "A White Heron" remains as a contemporary reviewer found it: a classic. In 1977 Jane Morrison shot a sensitive film of the story in and around Jewett's home town, South Berwick, Maine, that is available for classroom use.

The Country of the Pointed Firs has also received much recent attention; one of the most perceptive new readings of Jewett's masterwork is Marcia McClintock Folsom's "'Tact is a kind of Mind-Reading':

Empathic Style in Sarah Orne Jewett's *The Country of the Pointed Firs*." Folsom finds that Jewett's characters, who are acutely aware of the world around them, are able to enter the lives of others through the power of empathic imagination. Marjorie Pryse sees the novel as a quest by the narrator for a pastoral world lost to modern women, a world in which women were once united with their mothers and were inheritors of their mother's powers. Pryse pursues this line of thought in a recently published essay on "The Foreigner," a Dunnet Landing sketch that is receiving renewed attention. Josephine Donovan finds the community depicted in Jewett's novel as sustained by Mrs. Todd, "Jewett's great matriarch," and her mother, Mrs. Blackett. This and other Jewett works, writes Donovan, reveal her characters' quest for transcendence through a woman's religion, a kind of "matriarchal Christianity." Jennifer Bailey also gives *Pointed Firs* a feminist reading in her 1983 essay. John Hirsh explores the structure in the novel, which is also the focus of Elizabeth Ammons' "Going in Circles: The Female Geography of Jewett's *Country of the Pointed Firs*."[44] Ammons posits that Jewett's unconventional structure, which she finds "web-like" and cyclical rather than linear, is "outside the masculine mainstream."[45] Finally, critics have long seen Jewett's masterwork as a mature working out of themes set down in *Deephaven*. Ann Romines, who continues this discussion in her study of *Deephaven*, compares the narrator of *Pointed Firs* with the youthful girls in Jewett's first work who through a series of abortive encounters with ritual fail to appreciate the full meaning of life in the village.[46]

This brief survey should suggest that Jewett scholarship has experienced a surge of scholarly activity in recent years, due in large part, though not exclusively, to critical interest in women's studies. There is every reason to expect that feminist criticism will continue to inspire further interpretations, stirring new debate about well-known works, calling renewed attention to Jewett's lesser-known works, and prompting her inclusion in modern anthologies.[47] Indeed, women's studies have altered perceptions of Jewett's works, but this new scholarship, appearing in the last ten years, has its roots in a substantial body of criticism on Jewett and her fiction. No review of the Jewett scholarship would be complete without a survey of this work and of the most significant scholarly documents.

There are two book-length biographies of Sarah Orne Jewett plus numerous essays and notes, which provide data on specific incidents in her life. The most widely known book is F. O. Matthiessen's sympathetic biography in 1929, his first scholarly book and the first important book on Jewett. No study of Jewett will ever be complete without a careful reading of Matthiessen's *Sarah Orne Jewett*[48] as an historically significant volume, but it is essentially a "popular" biography and not a "scholarly" one. It demonstrates no careful searching of the facts of its subject, and it errs in the dates and details of Jewett's life; Matthiessen provides no documentation for the sources of his information, which calls into question the quality and reliability of his evidence; and he equates Jewett's life throughout with characters and situations in her fiction, a practice Jewett herself warned against. Large portions of Jewett's life are covered hastily or not at all, and in general it is clear that Matthiessen did not make the best use of the materials available to him. Two recent assessments of Matthiessen's critical achievement, one by Giles B. Gunn published in 1975 and the other by Frederick C. Stern published in 1981, conclude that *Sarah Orne Jewett* is indeed an inferior work that too often merely evokes a spirit of Maine and Jewett's world at the expense of rigorous analysis. Stern in particular finds Matthiessen ignores the psychological and sexual aspects of Jewett's personal life and speculates he did so because of his own homosexuality.[49] Nevertheless, Matthiessen's book is important in the history of the scholarship, in that it organized dispersed bits of information into a coherent narrative, created a focal point for Jewett scholarship and activity, and because it left a memorable record of the reaction of an important scholar to the life and writings of Jewett.

John Eldridge Frost's biography[50] is a more substantial, if not so widely acclaimed, study. Frost is not the adoring, sympathetic biographer Matthiessen was, but he provides the details and documentation missing in the earlier work. Frost's book is solid in both its personal and critical judgment, at least on the basis of information in the scholarly domain in 1960. He sees her as the finest artist among the regional writers, as writing from a realistic creed, and as best in her descriptive writing. Neither Frost's book nor Matthiessen's are definitive, however, and a thorough study of Jewett's life requires the examination of numerous shorter pieces now on the scholarly record, including the first chapter of Cary's *Sarah Orne Jewett* and Donovan's biographical sketch in her 1980 volume on Jewett.

As there is no definitive biography, there is no definitive edition of Jewett's letters, although there are several ones available. Annie Fields' *Letters of Sarah Orne Jewett*[51] was more the loving tribute to an intimate friend than a work of scholarship, and no modern student of Jewett can rely on this text. Not only are dates and details frequently inaccurate, but the letters have been fused or shortened and are printed without documentation. Josephine Donovan has argued that Fields' extensive editing of the letters was at the urging of Mark Anthony De Wolfe Howe, and that the deliberate deletion of nicknames and other intimacies and the exclusion of extant letters may have been inspired by Howe's discomfort with the Jewett-Fields liaison.[52] Whatever the reasons for the heavy editing, the fact remains that the Fields' volume is unreliable. Carl J. and Clara Weber's edition of 1947 was a professionally edited volume, but it presented only those letters owned by the Colby

College Library.[53] Richard Cary edited a more important collection of the letters in 1956, along with notes and an introduction, but that volume was superseded by the revised and enlarged edition a decade later.[54] Here Cary adds forty-eight additional letters to the ninety-four in the earlier edition. This volume is a significant contribution to Jewett scholarship, done with a great deal of critical discretion and attention to detail, but it represents only a small portion of extant Jewett correspondence.[55] Letter writing was very important to Jewett; she carried on a voluminous correspondence with family and friends, the greatest proportion of which has never been published. Her letters are held in several libraries, but the most extensive collections of unpublished correspondence are at the Houghton Library and the Society for the Preservation of New England Antiquities (SPNEA), Boston.[56] Jewett scholarship would profit by a comprehensive, thoroughly glossed edition of her letters.

There have been too many editions of Jewett primary works to provide full coverage, but a few comments are in order. Jewett scholarship has been hindered from the first by the lack of a comprehensive, professional edition of her works. Not since 1910, when Houghton Mifflin issued *Stories and Tales* in seven volumes, has a large portion of Jewett's works been available in a collected edition. A few other editions deserve comment. Willa Cather's 1925 edition of *The Best Stories of Sarah Orne Jewett* in two volumes will always be remembered for Cather's preface, but it is important for the addition ("A Dunnet Shepherdess," "William's Wedding," "The Queen's Twin") it made to *Pointed Firs* and because it made Jewett's works available during a crucial period in the growth of the scholarship. David Bonnell Green's *The World of Dunnet Landing: A Sarah Orne Jewett Collection*, published in 1962, is significant for its faithfulness to the 1896 edition and its inclusion of "The Foreigner," along with the three other Dunnet Landing sketches. Green's argument for the inclusion of these sketches, pursued in an essay concluding the edition,[57] is a significant statement about Jewett's most important book. The critical essays anthologized in Green's volume are less significant only because they all appeared elsewhere. Until recently, the Doubleday Anchor Books one-volume edition of Cather's collection, which appeared in 1956, has been the most useful for pedagogical purposes. Two paperback editions of *Pointed Firs*, however, have been published that, like the Green collection, are based on the 1896 text. Both Signet's *Short Fiction of Sarah Orne Jewett and Mary Wilkins Freeman*, edited with an introduction by Barbara H. Solomon (1979), and *The Country of the Pointed Firs and Other Stories*, edited by Mary Ellen Chase with an introduction by Marjorie Pryse (1982), include the four additional Dunnet Landing sketches, other Jewett stories, and perceptive introductions. Both are inexpensive and appropriate for classroom use.

An extremely important edition, one unfortunately out of print, is Richard Cary's *The Uncollected Short Stories of Sarah Orne Jewett*,[58] which reprints forty-four of fifty-eight Jewett stories previously uncollected, the remaining fourteen being children's works. This volume is valuable not only for the availability of a substantial portion of Jewett's fiction but also for the scholarly review of criticism which serves as its introduction. Richard Cary also edited *Deephaven and Other Stories*, which College and University Press issued in 1966. The Old Berwick Historical Society, since its publication of *The Tory Lover* in 1975, has issued two pamphlet-sized editions of Jewett's works: "A White Heron" and "The Hiltons' Holiday" in 1979 and, two years later, five of Jewett's *Country By-Ways* sketches describing her ramblings around South Berwick. In 1969 Garrett Press published facsimile editions of *Strangers and Wayfarers* and *The Queen's Twin and Other Stories* followed by *A Country Doctor* in 1970. The announced fourteen-volume edition of Jewett, however, expired with the demise of the company. There is thus still a need for a professional, comprehensive edition which would facilitate serious scholarship.

Richard Cary has provided a major assessment of Jewett scholarship in several essays, most notably in his bibliographic essay on Jewett in the first volume of *American Literary Realism* and in the introduction to his important book *Appreciation of Sarah Orne Jewett*, published in 1973.[59] The list of broadly significant critical articles and books on Jewett, appearing prior to the publication of Cary's *Appreciation*, is too extensive for full review but several studies deserve special mention. Charles Miner Thompson's "The Art of Miss Jewett"[60] is a substantial piece of biographical criticism which explores the influence of Jewett's life and character on her work. It is an informed and judicious essay. Perry D. Westbrook's *Acres of Flint* provides a useful overview of the celebration of the American past as an informing theme in the Jewett canon. A. M. Buchan's *"Our Dear Sarah": An Essay on Sarah Orne Jewett* offers an extended exploration of Jewett's personality and theories of literary creation, touching on both feminist issues and on the romantic tendencies in her work. Warner Berthoff's "The Art of Jewett's *Pointed Firs*" is one of the most important essays, exploring the structure of *Pointed Firs*, its relationship to the local-color movement, and the concept that American life is based on the "pitiless extinction of the past."[61] Hyatt H. Waggoner's "The Unity of *The Country of the Pointed Firs*"[62] explores the structure of the book in terms of its symbolism and finds, as did Berthoff, culturally significant American ideas at the heart of it.

A major scholarly book on Jewett is Richard Cary's *Sarah Orne Jewett* in the Twayne series. It suffers a bit from the Twayne format, which limits its length and demands extensive plot summary. The study is also not without critical problems: a proclivity to biographical and intentional fallacy, and a tendency for summary rather than analysis, but Cary's sprightly prose, his depth of knowledge of Jewett, his wealth of literary background for comparison, and his consistently penetrating intelligence make this essential reading. The book is thorough in its coverage, meticulous in its detail, judicious in its assessments. Aware of the dangers of claiming too much for her works, Cary concludes his study with the assertion that Jewett "is without peer among her contemporaries in the reliable depiction of her chosen time, place, and personalities." Every serious student of Jewett should devote careful attention to this book.

In 1965, when Louis Auchincloss published his *Pioneers and Caretakers: A Study of 9 American Women Novelists,* Jewett was the earliest woman included, and she is discussed in company with Edith Wharton, Willa Cather, and Katherine Anne Porter.[63] Unfortunately, Auchincloss developed only a biographical sketch and did not treat any of Jewett's works in depth. This criticism is also true, albeit to a lesser extent, of Margaret Farrand Thorp's essay for the University of Minnesota Pamphlets on American Writers.[64] Thorp's pamphlet is comprehensive and a good introductory essay for students. It explores Jewett's life and works briefly but with sensitivity. Unfortunately, like so much of Jewett scholarship, it is undocumented despite the fact that it clearly leans heavily on previous work.

Despite the vigor with which Jewett has been studied, the existing scholarship on Jewett is by no means definitive. The same may be said about the existing primary bibliographies, the most extensive of which is still Clara Carter Weber and Carl J. Weber's *A Bibliography of the Published Writings of Sarah Orne Jewett.*[65] The Weber volume, published in 1949, lists the original appearance of Jewett's books and shorter works, reprintings of these in volumes by other authors, and translations, as well as reviews and critical discussions of Jewett. The book is a flawed work of scholarship, however, for there are errors and many lacunae; it needs to be read in connection with more recent bibliographical work.

The first of these is John Eldridge Frost's "Sarah Orne Jewett Bibliography: 1949–1963"[66] which updates the earlier volume for both primary and secondary matters, although without annotation. Richard Cary has done a great deal of bibliographic work in the wake of Carl J. Weber, his predecessor at Colby College, one item of which is his bibliographic essay in *American Literary Realism.* Here Cary reviews Jewett's manuscripts and works, the state of her letters, the biographies and genealogies, and secondary criticism. The following year, in 1968, Cary produced a systematic addenda to the Weber volume in his "Some Bibliographic Ghosts of Sarah Orne Jewett,"[67] which updates both the Weber and Frost listings and provides corrections as well. A standard, primary bibliography of Jewett's work still needs to be done.

Clayton L. Eichelberger's "Sarah Orne Jewett (1849–1909): A Critical Bibliography of Secondary Comment,"[68] was published in 1969 and was valuable for its broad coverage and judicious annotations. It has been superseded by Gwen L. Nagel and James Nagel's *Sarah Orne Jewett: A Reference Guide*,[69] which appeared in 1978. The Nagel volume is a comprehensive annotated listing of commentary on Jewett published between 1873 and 1976. It is chronologically arranged and contains an introductory survey of Jewett criticism and a useful author and subject index. Philip B. Eppard's "Local Colorists: Sarah Orne Jewett, Mary E. Wilkins Freeman, and Mary N. Murfree"[70] is the most recently published bibliographic tool on Jewett. Eppard's survey appeared in 1983 and reviews Jewett bibliography, editions, manuscripts and letters, biography, and secondary criticism. It is a cogent and valuable addition to Jewett bibliography.

Future work on Jewett would benefit enormously by the appearance of a critical biography, a comprehensive edition of letters, a definitive primary bibliography, and scholarly editions of Jewett's works. Jewett's manuscripts also need to be analyzed and described, especially for what they might reveal about her processes of composition. Some areas of Jewett's work have been extensively discussed, while a few others have received scant attention and need further work. The original essays published here for the first time give evidence of a promising future in Jewett scholarship as does the ongoing work of the *Colby Library Quarterly*.

It is rare in scholarship for a single academic institution to have so singly contributed to the growth and knowledge of an important writer as Colby College has to Jewett scholarship. From the early work of the Webers to the production of Richard Cary, scholars associated with Colby have done essential work. The continuing activity of the *Colby Library Quarterly*, edited by John H. Sutherland, in Jewett studies should, as in the past, make an enormous contribution to an understanding of Jewett and her work.

Anyone compiling a collection of this kind is faced with hard choices about what to exclude. I was aided in this particular problem by the existence of Richard Cary's *Appreciation of Sarah Orne Jewett* (1973), which reprinted the most important essays published between 1885 and 1972. Though tempted by some excellent early work, I have made a conscious decision to avoid duplicating Cary's effort here. For historical perspective, I have chosen a number of reviews that reflect the range of contemporary response to Jewett and that have, to lesser or greater extent, shaped critical commentary ever since. Among the pool of essays on Jewett appearing after 1972 were worthy pieces that I have had to exclude because of strictures of space and in the interest of thematic balance. Those gathered here have met a qualitative stan-

dard and reflect a diversity of critical opinion about a wide representation of Jewett's works.

Eight essays are published here for the first time. I have already
briefly described the work by Johns, Ammons, Masteller, Nail, and
Roman in my survey of the major new trends that began this introduc-
tion. It is a special pleasure to be able to publish Richard Cary's "The
Literary Rubrics of Sarah Orne Jewett" here. In this essay Cary gathers
Jewett's scattered and at times contradictory pronouncements of the
craft of fiction. His informed and stylishly written discussion sorts out
the "montage of rules" Jewett employed to fit her diverse fictive needs.
Josephine Donovan's "Sarah Orne Jewett's Critical Theory: Notes
Toward a Feminine Literary Mode" is a provocative study that suggests
Jewett developed seemingly "plotless" structures in her fiction and that
they are consistent with her own expressed critical theory and her
vision of "imaginative realism." Using some recently published feminist
studies, Donovan finds that Jewett's characteristic plots, which are
static or cyclical, are an essentially feminine literary mode. I have
chosen to end this volume with Philip B. Eppard's discovery of two
Jewett stories, "The Player Queen" and "Three Friends." Although
neither ranks among the finest of Jewett's short fiction, they reflect
two of her central themes: the confrontation between city and country
and the importance of female friendships. Both stories are reprinted
here for the first time since their original appearance in short-lived
periodicals in the late 1880s. They conclude this volume in order to
suggest that there may be more Jewett works to be uncovered that will
provide a starting point for new scholarship.

This is an exciting time in Jewett studies. It is my intention that
this collection reflect not only the current directions and trends in
scholarship but, consistent with Jewett's preoccupation with the past
that has shaped us, the earliest critical commentary that Jewett herself
must have read. A full assessment of Jewett as writer will always remain a collaborative effort, demanding the informed and collective wisdom of each generation of scholars. From the early encouraging review
of *Deephaven* by William Dean Howells, to the wide-ranging and solid
contributions made by Richard Cary, and finally, to the current resurgence of work, much of which has followed in the wake of interest
in women's studies, Jewett and her works have inspired a diversity of
intelligent, perceptive, and deeply humane critical attention. In 1929
F. O. Matthiessen wrote of Jewett: "She has withstood the onslaught
of time. . . ."[71] I hope that this volume, published seventy-five years
after her death in 1909, may contribute to the ongoing appreciation of
Sarah Orne Jewett, a writer whose finely wrought fiction recorded and
preserved for all time the essence of life in her country of the pointed firs.

I wish to express my gratitude to the authors whose essays were written for this volume; it was my pleasure to work with them. I especially thank Elizabeth Ammons whose insights and support have meant much to me, much more than I have ever expressed to her. I have been most fortunate having in Linda Micheli a friend whose literary acumen and encouragement I value greatly. But my deepest gratitude goes to my husband, James Nagel, my editor and best critic, who has endured my despairs and shared my joy in writing, who has enriched my work and life.

GWEN L. NAGEL

Notes

1. William Dean Howells, "Recent Literature," *Atlantic Monthly*, 39 (June 1877), 759.

2. Anon., "New Publications," *New York Times*, 28 Apr. 1877, supp., p. 8.

3. Horace E. Scudder, "Recent Literature," *Atlantic Monthly*, 42 (Dec. 1878), 778–79.

4. See Anon., "Country By-Ways," *Critic*, 1 (5 Nov. 1881), 304–05; Anon., "Children's Books," *Nation*, 33 (15 Dec. 1881), 479; Anon., "The Light Literature of Travel," *Atlantic Monthly*, 49 (Mar. 1882), 420–21.

5. Anon., "Miss Jewett's First Novel," *Literary World*, 15 (28 June 1884), 211. See also Anon., "The Bookshelf," *Continent*, 6 (4 Nov. 1884), 127.

6. Anon., "Miss Jewett's 'A Marsh Island,'" *Critic*, 4 (8 Aug. 1885), 64.

7. Anon., [Rev. of *The King of Folly Island*], *Literary World*, 19 (27 Oct. 1888), 365.

8. Anon., "Recent Fiction," *Overland Monthly*, 8 (Oct. 1886), 439–41.

9. See Anon., "Recent Publications," New Orleans *Daily Picayune*, 13 Feb. 1887, p. 10; Anon., "Briefs on New Books," *Dial*, 7 (Mar. 1887), 274; Anon., "The Bookshelf," *Cottage Hearth*, 16 (Jan. 1890), 23.

10. Anon., "A Handful of Fiction," *Independent*, 43 (29 Jan. 1891), 164.

11. See Anon., "From Crowded Shelves," *Academy*, 51 (13 Mar. 1897), 301; *New York Times*, 12 Dec. 1896, supp., p. 2; Anon., [rev. of *Pointed Firs*], *Independent*, 48 (3 Dec. 1896), 1651; Anon., "Recent Novels," *Nation*, 64 (15 Apr. 1897), 288; Anon., "Comment on New Books," *Atlantic Monthly*, 79 (Feb. 1897), 272–73; Alice Brown, "Profitable Tales," *Book Buyer* (New York), 15 (Oct. 1897), 249–50.

12. Octave Thanet, "Fine Portraits by Miss Jewett," *Book Buyer*, 23 (Oct. 1901), 227–28; Anon., "Literature," *Independent*, 53 (14 Nov. 1901), 2717; Anon., "The Fiction of the Early Autumn," *Outlook*, 69 (Oct. 1901), 420; Anon., "Current Fiction," *Literary World*, 32 (1 Dec. 1901), 218; Ferman Bishop, "Henry James Criticizes *The Tory Lover*," *American Literature*, 27 (1955), 262–64; *New York Times*, 19 Nov. 1910, pt. 2, p. 646.

13. Th. Bentzon, "Le roman de la femme-medecin," *Revue des Deux Mondes*, 67 (1 Feb. 1885), 598–632. English translation appeared in *Colby Library Quarterly*, 7 (1967), 488–503, which was reprinted in Richard Cary, *Appreciation of Sarah Orne Jewett: 29 Interpretive Essays* (Waterville: Colby College Press, 1973), pp. 3–15, hereafter cited as Cary, *Appreciation*.

14. Th. Bentzon, "La Naturalisme aux Etats-Unis," *Revue des Deux Mondes*, 83 (15 Sept. 1887), 428–51.

15. Richard Cary, *Sarah Orne Jewett*, Twayne United States Authors Series, No. 19 (New York: Twayne, 1962), hereafter cited as Cary, *Jewett*.

16. A. B. Nichols, "Sarah Orne Jewett and the Simmons College Scholarship," *Simmons Quarterly*, 1, No. 1 (1910), 1–2.

17. See Brander Matthews, "Literature in the New Century," *North American Review*, 179 (Oct. 1904), 513–25; Edward M. Chapman, "The New England of Sarah Orne Jewett," *Yale Review*, 3 (1913), 157–72; Henry James, "Mr. and Mrs. James T. Fields," *Atlantic Monthly*, 116 (July 1915), 21–31; Bliss Perry, *The American Spirit in Literature: A Chronicle of Great Interpreters* (New Haven: Yale Univ. Press), pp. 249–50; F. O. Matthiessen, "New England Stories," in *American Writers on American Literature*, ed. John Macy (New York: Horace Liveright, 1931), pp. 399–413; John Eldridge Frost, *Sarah Orne Jewett* (Kittery Point: Gundalow Club, 1960); Carlos Baker, "Delineation of Life and Character" in *Literary History of the United States*, ed. Robert E. Spiller et al. (New York: Macmillan, 1974), I, 845–48; II, 602–04, 946–47.

18. See Susan Allen Toth, " 'The Rarest and Most Peculiar Grape': Versions of the New England Woman in 19th-Century Local Color Literature," *Kate Chopin Newsletter*, 2, No. 2 (1976), 38–45; Perry D. Westbrook, "Sarah Orne Jewett" in *Novelists and Prose Writers*, ed. James Vinson and D. L. Kirkpatrick (New York: St. Martin's Press, 1979), pp. 653–55; Ann Douglas Wood, "The Literature of Impoverishment: The Women Local Colorists in America 1865–1914," *Women's Studies*, 1 (1972), 3–45; Julia Bader, "The 'Rooted' Landscape and the Woman Writer" in *Teaching Women's Literature from a Regional Perspective*, ed. Lenore Hoffman and Deborah Rosenfelt (New York: Modern Language Association of America, 1982), pp. 23–30, hereafter cited as Bader, "Landscape."

19. See Randall Ray Mawer, "Cosmopolitan Characters in Local Color Fiction," *Dissertation Abstracts International*, 37 (Oct. 1976), 2184A–85A; Raymond L. Neinstein, "Neo-Regionalism in America," *Dissertation Abstracts International*, 38 (Mar. 1978), 548A–83A; Alice Hall Petry, "Local Color Fiction 1870–1900," *Dissertation Abstracts International*, 40 (May 1980), 5867A; Susan Joan Martin Fagan, "Sarah Orne Jewett's Fiction: A Reevaluation from Three Perspectives," *Dissertation Abstracts International*, 43 (Aug. 1982), 445A, hereafter cited as Fagan. See also Alice Hall Petry, "Universal and Particular: The Local-Color Phenomenon Reconsidered," *American Literary Realism*, 12 (1979), 111–26.

20. Josephine Donovan, *New England Local Color Literature: A Women's Tradition* (New York: Ungar, 1983), hereafter cited as Donovan, *Local Color*.

21. Willa Cather, "Preface" to *The Best Short Stories of Sarah Orne Jewett* (Boston: Houghton Mifflin, 1925), I, ix–xix.

22. Anon., "The New Books," *Outlook*, 140 (27 May 1925), 158–59.

23. Walter Fuller Taylor, "Sarah Orne Jewett (1849–1909) and the New England Village" in *A History of American Letters* (Boston: American Book, 1936), pp. 260–61, 544–45; Jean Sougnac, *Sarah Orne Jewett* (Paris: Jouve et Cie, 1937); Michael W. Vella, "Sarah Orne Jewett: A Reading of *The Country of the Pointed Firs*," *ESQ*, 19 (1973), 275–82; A. M. Buchan, *"Our Dear Sarah": An Essay on Sarah Orne Jewett*, Washington Univ. Studies, No. 24 (St. Louis: Washington Univ. Press, 1953), p. 17.

24. Cynthia Griffin Wolff, *A Feast of Words: The Triumph of Edith Wharton* (Oxford: Oxford Univ. Press, 1977), pp. 181–83; Priscilla Leder, "The Gifts of Peace: Sarah Orne Jewett's Vision of Romance," *Gypsy Scholar*, 4 (1977), 27–39; Jeri Parker, *Uneasy Survivors: Five Women Writers* (Santa Barbara: Peregrine

Smith, 1975); Donovan, *Local Color*, pp. 1–3; Julia Bader, "The Dissolving Vision: Realism in Jewett, Freeman, and Gilman" in *American Realism: New Essays*, ed. Eric J. Sundquist (Baltimore and London: Johns Hopkins Univ. Press, 1982), pp. 176–98.

25. Robin Magowan, "Pastoral and the Art of Landscape in *The Country of the Pointed Firs*," *New England Quarterly*, 36 (1963), 229–40, hereafter cited as Magowan, "Pastoral"; Barton L. St. Armand, "Jewett and Marin: The Inner Vision," *Colby Library Quarterly*, 9 (1972), 632–43; Annis Pratt, "Women and Nature in Modern Fiction," *Contemporary Literature*, 13 (1972), 476–90.

26. Magowan, "Pastoral," pp. 229–40; Robin Magowan, "Fromentin and Jewett: Pastoral Narrative in the Nineteenth Century," *Comparative Literature*, 16 (1964), 331–37; David Stouck, "*The Country of the Pointed Firs*: A Pastoral of Innocence," *Colby Library Quarterly*, 9 (1970), 213–20; Sister Mary Williams, "The Pastoral in New England Local Color: Celia Thaxter, Sarah Orne Jewett, Alice Brown," *Dissertation Abstracts International*, 32 (June 1972), 6947A.

27. See Anon., "Children's Books," *Nation*, 33 (15 Dec. 1881), 479; Fred Lewis Pattee, *A History of American Literature Since 1870* (New York: Century, 1915), pp. 231–35; Granville Hicks, *The Great Tradition: An Interpretation of American Literature Since the Civil War* (New York: Macmillan, 1933), pp. 101–05; Perry D. Westbrook, *Acres of Flint: Sarah Orne Jewett and Her Contemporaries*, Rev. ed. (Metuchen: Scarecrow, 1981); Ferman Bishop, "The Sense of the Past in Sarah Orne Jewett," *University of Wichita Bulletin*, Univ. Studies, No. 41 (1959), pp. 3–10; John Paul Eakin, "Sarah Orne Jewett and the Meaning of Country Life," *American Literature*, 38 (1967), 508–31; Gwen L. Nagel, "Women and Preservation in the Works of Sarah Orne Jewett," *Dissertation Abstracts International*, 40 (Sept. 1979), 1471A; Charles W. Mayer, "'The Only Rose': A Central Jewett Story," *Colby Library Quarterly*, 17 (1981), 26–33.

28. See Perry D. Westbrook, *The New England Town in Fact and Fiction* (Madison, N. J.: Fairleigh Dickinson Univ. Press, 1982); Rebecca Wall Nail, "Place and Setting in the Work of Sarah Orne Jewett," *Dissertation Abstracts International*, 42 (Aug. 1981), 705A; Bader, "Landscape," pp. 23–30; Jennifer Bailey, "Female Nature and the Nature of the Female: A Revision of Sarah Orne Jewett's *The Country of the Pointed Firs*," *Revue française d'études américaines*, 17 (1983), 283–94, hereafter cited as Bailey; Randall R. Mawer, "Setting as Symbol in Jewett's *A Marsh Island*," *Colby Library Quarterly*, 12 (1976), 83–90.

29. See Mary Conrad Kraus, "The Unifying Vision of Sarah Orne Jewett," *Dissertation Abstracts International*, 39 (July 1978), 286A–87A; Charles Scott Pugh, "The Meditative Art of Sarah Orne Jewett," *Dissertation Abstracts International*, 39 (May 1979), 6766A; Mary C. Kraus, "Sarah Orne Jewett and Temporal Continuity," *Colby Library Quarterly*, 15 (1979), 157–74; Elmer Pry, "Folk-Literary Aesthetics in *The Country of the Pointed Firs*," *Tennessee Folklore Society Bulletin*, 44 (1978), 7–12; Fagan, p. 445A.

30. Horace E. Scudder, "Recent Novels," *Atlantic Monthly*, 45 (May 1880), 685–86.

31. Anon., "Recent Novels," *Nation*, 57 (14 Dec. 1893), 452.

32. See also Barbara A. Johns, "The Spinster in Five New England Women Regionalists," *Dissertation Abstracts International*, 41 (July 1980), 251A–52A.

33. See Anon., "Recent Novels," *Nation*, 39 (31 July 1884), 96–97; Anon., "Literature: Recent Novels," *New York Evening Post* (2 Aug. 1884), supp., p. 1; Anon., "Recent Fiction," *Lippincott's Magazine*, 34 (Sept. 1884), 319; Horace E. Scudder, "Recent Fiction," *Atlantic Monthly*, 54 (Sept. 1884), 418–20.

34. See also Jean Carwile Masteller, "Marriage or Career, 1880–1914: A Dilemma for American Women Writers and Their Culture," *Dissertation Abstracts International*, 39 (Mar. 1979), 5585A–86A.

35. Carolyn Forrey, "The New Woman Revisited," *Women's Studies*, 2 (1974), 42–44; Ellen Morgan, "The Atypical Woman: Nan Prince in the Literary Transition to Feminism," *Kate Chopin Newsletter*, 2, No. 2 (1976), 33–37; Elizabeth Dague, "Images of Work, Glimpses of Professionalism in Selected Nineteenth- and Twentieth-Century Novels," *Frontiers: A Journal of Women Studies*, 5, No. 1 (1980), 50–55; Josephine Donovan, "A Woman's View of Transcendence: A New Interpretation of the Works of Sarah Orne Jewett," *Massachusetts Review*, 21 (1980), 365–80; Malinda Snow, " 'That One Talent': The Vocation as Theme in Sarah Orne Jewett's *A Country Doctor*," *Colby Library Quarterly*, 16 (1980), 138–47.

36. See Esther Forbes, "Sarah Orne Jewett: The Apostle of New England," *Boston Evening Transcript* (16 May 1925), book section, pt. 6, p. 1; Josephine Donovan, "The Unpublished Love Poems of Sarah Orne Jewett," *Frontiers: A Journal of Women Studies*, 4, No. 3 (1979), 26–31, hereafter cited as Donovan, "Poems"; Lillian Federman, *Surpassing the Love of Men: Romantic Friendship and Love Between Women from the Renaissance to the Present* (New York: William Morrow, 1981), pp. 197–203.

37. Glenda Hobbs, "Pure and Passionate: Female Friendship in Sarah Orne Jewett's 'Martha's Lady,' " *Studies in Short Fiction*, 17 (1980), 21–29.

38. Glenda Hobbs, "Such Good Friends: Female Intimacies in the Life and Work of Sarah Orne Jewett," forthcoming in *New England Quarterly*.

39. Nina Auerbach, *Communities of Women: An Idea in Fiction* (Cambridge: Harvard Univ. Press, 1978), pp. 9–12.

40. Josephine Donovan, *Sarah Orne Jewett* (New York: Ungar, 1980), pp. 6–7, hereafter cited as Donovan, *Jewett*.

41. Donovan, "Transcendence," pp. 365–80.

42. See John Gerard Dullea, "Two New England Voices: Sarah Orne Jewett and Mary Wilkins Freeman," *Dissertation Abstracts International*, 36 (Apr. 1976), 6692A; Evelyn Starr Cutler, "Representation of Main Coast Dialect in the Work of Sarah Orne Jewett," *Dissertation Abstracts International*, 37 (Sept. 1976), 1515A; Michael Atkinson, "The Necessary Extravagance of Sarah Orne Jewett: Voices of Authority in 'A White Heron,' " *Studies in Short Fiction*, 19 (1982), 71–74; Gayle L. Smith, "The Language of Transcendence in Sarah Orne Jewett's 'A White Heron,' " *Colby Library Quarterly*, 19 (1983), 37–44.

43. See Theodore R. Hovet, "America's 'Lonely Country Child': The Theme of Separation in Sarah Orne Jewett's 'A White Heron,' " *Colby Library Quarterly*, 14 (1978), 166–71; Theodore R. Hovet, " 'Once Upon a Time': Sarah Orne Jewett's 'A White Heron' as a Fairy Tale," *Studies in Short Fiction*, 15 (1978), 63–68; James Ellis, "The World of Dreams: Sexual Symbolism in 'A White Heron,' " *Nassau Review*, 3, No. 3 (1977), 3–9; Richard Brenzo, "Free Heron or Dead Sparrow: Sylvia's Choice in Sarah Orne Jewett's 'A White Heron,' " *Colby Library Quarterly*, 14 (1978), 36–41; Donovan, *Local Color*, pp. 107–09; George Held, "Heart to Heart with Nature: Ways of Looking at 'A White Heron,' " *Colby Library Quarterly*, 18 (1982), pp. 55–65.

44. See Marcia McClintock Folsom, " 'Tact is a Kind of Mind-Reading': Emphatic Style in Sarah Orne Jewett's *The Country of the Pointed Firs*," *Colby Library Quarterly*, 18 (1982), 66–78; Marjorie Pryse, "Introduction to the Norton Edition" in *The Country of the Pointed Firs and Other Stories* (New York: Norton, 1982), pp. v–xx; Marjorie Pryse, "Women 'at sea': Feminist Realism in Sarah Orne

Jewett's 'The Foreigner,'" *American Literary Realism*, 15 (1982), 244–52; Donovan, "Transcendence," pp. 365–80; Bailey, pp. 283–94; John Hirsh, "The Non-Narrative Structure of *The Country of the Pointed Firs*," *American Literary Realism*, 14 (1981), 286–88; Elizabeth Ammons, "Going in Circles: The Female Geography of Jewett's *Country of the Pointed Firs*," *Studies in the Literary Imagination*, 16 (Fall 1983), 83–92.

45. See also Josephine Donovan, "Sarah Orne Jewett's Critical Theory: Notes Toward a Feminine Literary Mode," in this volume, pp. 212–25.

46. Ann Romines, "In *Deephaven*: Skirmishes Near the Swamp," *Colby Library Quarterly*, 16 (1980), 205–19.

47. Jewett is represented in the following recent collections of fiction by women writers: Jeri Parker, ed., *Uneasy Survivors: Five Women Writers* (Santa Barbara: Peregrine Smith, 1975); Marcia McClintock Folsom and Linda Heinlein Kirschner, eds., *By Women: An Anthology of Literature* (Boston: Houghton Mifflin, 1976); Ann Reit, ed., *The World Outside: Collected Short Fiction about Women at Work* (New York: Four Winds, 1977); Susan Cahill, ed., *Women and Fiction 2* (New York: New American Library, 1978); Nancy Hoffman and Florence Howe, eds., *Women Working: An Anthology of Stories and Poems* (Old Westbury, N.Y.: Feminist Press, 1979); Barbara H. Solomon, ed., *Short Fiction of Sarah Orne Jewett and Mary Wilkins Freeman* (New York: New American Library Signet, 1979): Cynthia Griffin Wolff, ed., *Classic American Women Writers* (New York: Harper & Row, 1980); Arlen G. R. Westbrook and Perry D. Westbrook, eds., *The Writing Women of New England, 1630–1900: An Anthology* (Metuchen: Scarecrow, 1982).

48. F. O. Matthiessen, *Sarah Orne Jewett* (Boston: Houghton Mifflin, 1929), hereafter cited as Matthiessen, *Jewett*.

49. See Giles B. Gunn, *F. O. Matthiessen: The Critical Achievement* (Seattle: Univ. of Washington Press, 1975), pp. 37–44; Frederick C. Stern, *F. O. Matthiessen: Christian Socialist as Critic* (Chapel Hill: Univ. of North Carolina Press, 1981), pp. 46–62.

50. John Eldridge Frost, *Sarah Orne Jewett* (Kittery Point: Gundalow Club, 1960).

51. Annie Fields, *Letters of Sarah Orne Jewett* (Boston: Houghton Mifflin, 1911).

52. Donovan, "Poems," p. 27.

53. Carl J. Weber, *Letters of Sarah Orne Jewett Now in the Colby College Library* (Waterville: Colby College Press, 1947).

54. Richard Cary, *Sarah Orne Jewett Letters* (Waterville: Colby College Press, 1967).

55. Three Jewett letters are published in James Nagel, "Sarah Orne Jewett Writes to Hamlin Garland," *New England Quarterly*, 54 (1981), 416–23.

56. The SPNEA also maintains the Jewett house in South Berwick, Maine. In 1983 it announced it would sell the Eastman house next door, Jewett's birthplace, to raise needed funds for the repair and maintenance of the Jewett house.

57. David Bonnell Green, "The World of Dunnet Landing" in *The World of Dunnet Landing: A Sarah Orne Jewett Collection* (Lincoln: Univ. of Nebraska Press, 1962), pp. 412–17. For a recent discussion of the text of *Pointed Firs* see Marco A. Portales, "History of a Text: Jewett's *The Country of the Pointed Firs*," *New England Quarterly*, 55 (1982), 586–92.

58. Richard Cary, *The Uncollected Short Stories of Sarah Orne Jewett* (Waterville: Colby College Press, 1971).

59. Richard Cary, "Sarah Orne Jewett (1849–1909)," *American Literary Realism*, 1 (1967), 61–66; Cary, *Appreciation*, pp. ix–xviii.

60. Charles Miner Thompson, "The Art of Miss Jewett," *Atlantic Monthly*, 94 (Oct. 1904), 485–97.

61. Warner Berthoff, "The Art of Jewett's *Pointed Firs*," *New England Quarterly*, 32 (1959), 31–53.

62. Hyatt H. Waggoner, "The Unity of *The Country of the Pointed Firs*," *Twentieth Century Literature*, 5 (1959), 67–73.

63. Louis Auchincloss, *Pioneers and Caretakers: A Study of 9 American Women Novelists* (Minneapolis: Univ. of Minnesota Press, 1965), pp. 6–19.

64. Margaret F. Thorp, *Sarah Orne Jewett*, Univ. of Minnesota Pamphlets on American Writers, No. 61 (Minneapolis: Univ. of Minnesota Press, 1966).

65. Clara C. Weber and Carl J. Weber, *A Bibliography of the Published Writings of Sarah Orne Jewett* (Waterville: Colby College Press, 1949).

66. John Eldridge Frost, "Sarah Orne Jewett Bibliography: 1949–1963," *Colby Library Quarterly*, 6 (1964), 405–17.

67. Richard Cary, "Some Bibliographic Ghosts of Sarah Orne Jewett," *Colby Library Quarterly*, 8 (1968), 139–45.

68. Clayton L. Eichelberger, "Sarah Orne Jewett (1849–1909): A Critical Bibliography of Secondary Comment," *American Literary Realism*, 2 (1969), 189–262.

69. Gwen L. Nagel and James Nagel, *Sarah Orne Jewett: A Reference Guide* (Boston: G. K. Hall, 1978).

70. Philip B. Eppard, "Local Colorists: Sarah Orne Jewett, Mary E. Wilkins Freeman, and Mary N. Murfree," in *American Women Writers: Bibliographical Essays*, ed. Maurice Duke, Jackson R. Bryer, and M. Thomas Inge (Westport: Greenwood Press, 1983), pp. 21–46.

71. Matthiessen, *Jewett*, p. 145.

REVIEWS

[Review of *Deephaven*]   William Dean Howells*

The gentle reader of this magazine cannot fail to have liked, for their very fresh and delicate quality, certain sketches of an old New England sea-port, which have from time to time appeared here during the last four years. The first was Shore House, and then there came Deephaven Cronies, and Deephaven Excursions. These sketches, with many more studies of the same sort of life, as finely and faithfully done, are now collected into a pretty little book called *Deephaven*, which must, we think, find favor with all who appreciate the simple treatment of the near-at-hand quaint and picturesque. No doubt some particular sea-port sat for Deephaven, but the picture is true to a whole class of old shore towns, in any one of which you might confidently look to find the Deephaven types. It is supposed that two young girls—whose young-girlhood charmingly perfumes the thought and observation of the whole book— are spending the summer at Deephaven, Miss Denis, the narrator, being the guest of her adored ideal, Miss Kate Lancaster, whose people have an ancestral house there; but their sojourn is only used as a background on which to paint the local life: the three or four aristocratic families, severally dwindled to three or four old maiden ladies; the numbers of ancient sea-captains cast ashore by the decaying traffic; the queer sailor and fisher folk; the widow and old-wife gossips of the place, and some of the people of the neighboring country. These are all touched with a hand that holds itself far from every trick of exaggeration, and that subtly delights in the very tint and form of reality; we could not express too strongly the sense of conscientious fidelity which the art of the book gives, while over the whole is cast a light of the sweetest and gentlest humor, and of a sympathy as tender as it is intelligent. Danny is one of the best of the sketches; and another is The Circus at Denby, which perhaps shows better than any other the play of the author's observation and fancy, with its glancing lights of fun and pathos. A sombre and touching study is that of the sad, simple life so compassionately depicted

*Reprinted from the *Atlantic Monthly*, 39 (June 1877), 759.

in In Shadow, after which the reader must turn to the brisk vigor and quaintness of Mrs. Bonny. Bits of New England landscape and characteristic marine effects scattered throughout these studies of life vividly localize them, and the talk of the people is rendered with a delicious fidelity.

In fact, Miss Jewett here gives proof of such powers of observation and characterization as we hope will some day be turned to the advantage of all of us in fiction. Meanwhile we are very glad of these studies, so refined, so simple, so exquisitely imbued with a true feeling for the ideal within the real.

[Review of *Play Days*]   Horace E. Scudder*

The qualities which made Miss Jewett's Deephaven so agreeable could not fail to appear in any book which she might write for children, and *Play Days* is characterized by the same temper of gentleness and good-breeding which gave distinction to the earlier book. We are old-fashioned enough to like good breeding, with all that the homely, significant word intends, and we like its mark in *Play Days* because it is so genuine and native. It is, we hasten to say, not modeled upon the type which we recognize instantly in the literature which young English masters and misses receive with apparent docility. There is not a governess in the book. There is no lad there either,—that singular being whom Chauncy Wright so well described as "a boy with a man's hand on his head." There is no slang introduced for the purpose of shocking the governess or older sister, and giving the boy who uses it the reputation of an abandoned swearer and awful example; in effect, that conventional good-breeding which is founded on class distinction, and not on Christian democracy, is refreshingly absent from *Play Days*. The element which we find there is conspicuous also by its contrast with the noisy, ungrammatical, and boisterous type of young America which gets recognition enough in books for young people. The suggestions are of home life and the sweet sanctity of a protected childhood. Even the pathetic and lovely story of Nancy's Doll makes the misery of poverty to be but the dark background on which to sketch one or two golden figures; and The Best China Saucer, which comes as near as any to the conventional type of moral tales, is relieved by a grotesque humor and a charity which never fails. There is a refinement in the book which is very grateful, as we have said, but it does not take the form of a disagreeable fastidiousness. The humor is always spontaneous and simple, and not above a child's enjoyment; The Shipwrecked Buttons shows this

*Reprinted from the *Atlantic Monthly*, 42 (December 1878), 778–79.

in a very charming manner, and is the cleverest story in the book, from the originality of the frame-work, in which a number of little stories are set. There is a facility of writing which possibly misleads the author, for while all the stories are written with apparent ease, the writer does not always distinguish between what is essential to the story and what is mere graceful decoration. If Miss Jewett always had a story to tell, her charm of manner would add to the agreeableness of the story; but her interest in writing sometimes leads her to forget that children want a story, and will be indifferent to many graces which please a writer. A more positive story would add greatly to the pleasure which Miss Jewett's book gives, and we trust that she will cultivate the power of invention. She needs the development of that side of a story-teller's gift to make her work singularly good; it is too good now not to be better.

[Review of *Old Friends and New*]

[Horace E. Scudder*]

Miss Jewett has already begun to appropriate an audience, and may, if she choose, whisper to herself of her readers as a clergyman openly speaks of his people. The womanly kindness which pervades her writings gives her readers a warmer interest in them than the mere weight of their literary quality might command. Yet we shall not be hasty to separate these elements of her work, but accept the pleasure which it gives, and, confessing her claim upon our regard, compare her latest book with her previous one, rather than with an absolute standard.

Deephaven, as our readers will easily remember, was a series of sketches, in which there was no development of plot, but a rambling description of life in a New England fishing-village, caught together by the simple device of bringing into the village two city girls of refinement, who occupy an old mansion, and sally forth from it on their voyages of discovery. The charm lay chiefly in the sympathetic delineation of character, and in the pictures of homely life seen from the side of this fresh, unspoiled, and reverent girlhood. The two young summer visitors at *Deephaven* won upon the fishermen and their families in the real life of their visit, as they do upon readers in the scarcely less real life of the book; and while they call upon us to look on this simple seaside picture they are not conscious that it is they who have most of our thoughts. Nothing could be purer than the relation between young and old which *Deephaven* disclosed.

*Reprinted from the *Atlantic Monthly*, 45 (May 1880), 685–86.

In *Old Friends and New* the same charm reappears. The book is a collection of seven stories, some of which first saw the light in the pages of this magazine. We name the titles that our readers may recall those familiar to them: A Lost Lover, A Sorrowful Guest, A Late Supper, Mr. Bruce, Miss Sydney's Flowers, Lady Ferry, A Bit of Shore Life. One of them, at least, Mr. Bruce, appeared before the *Deephaven* sketches and is a lively piece of girlish fun, refined and agreeable, but immature, and hardly worthy a place in the volume. The stories, written and published at different times, have a singular and apparently unintended agreement in one theme. As in *Deephaven*, so in these disconnected stories, there are two *foci* about which the circle of events are described, the young maid and the old maid. Here, as there, it is the life of the old as seen by young eyes which is delineated, and in nothing is the sweet reverence of youth, as portrayed in Miss Jewett's writings, more profoundly shown than in the frequent and touching pictures of old and lonely age. Miss Horatia Dane in A Lost Lover, Miss Catherine Spring in A Late Supper, Miss Sydney in Miss Sydney's Flowers, Lady Ferry in the story of that name, old Mrs. Wallis in A Bit of Shore Life,—all these are portraits in Miss Jewett's Dream of Old Women, and with womanly chivalry she has taken under her special protection those whom the irreverence of youth has most flouted. Her old maids, moreover, are not pieces of faded sentimentalism; she has shown them in their dignity and homely truthfulness, but she lets us smile quietly with her at their quaintness.

The motive of love as a passion between the young is almost wholly absent from these stories, and as excursions among other emotions and principles they have a certain originality, due in part to this abstemious-ness. Yet since no strong motive of any kind is called in, the stories re-main chiefly sketches, studies, episodes. We shall not quarrel with Miss Jewett for not doing something else than what she has done; she has acquired already a greater firmness of touch in these pencil sketches, and the skill with which the pretty story of A Late Supper is worked up indicates that she may yet succeed in the more difficult art of making her characters act for themselves. At present they cling to her skirts, and she leads them about with her. *Cranford* is often mentioned in com-parison with *Deephaven*, and there are points of likeness: in some re-spects *Deephaven* comes closer to nature, but perhaps that is because it is nearer home; yet *Cranford* has what *Deephaven* lacks, an individ-uality apart from the author. The figures are projected more boldly, because drawn by the hand of one who was primarily a novelist. In *Deephaven* and in these later sketches, the author has not yet felt the confidence which would enable her to withdraw her direct support from her characters. She cautiously holds, for the most part, to the form of the story which permits her to be present during most of the action. We suggest, as a practical experiment in story-telling, that she avail herself of the method which is sometimes used in Mr. James's stories, where one of the characters, not identified with the storyteller, is charged with this duty. If might gradually strengthen her in an ability to conceive of a story which had its own beginning, middle, and end, and was not taken as a desultory chapter of personal experience.

[Review of *Country By-ways*]   Anonymous*

To have known these sketches already in the pages of the *Atlantic* seems to make them only the more welcome for their delicate discrimination, their gentle appreciation of the old New England character. Miss Jewett not only makes us intimate with the roads and lanes, the wide woods and the old farms beyond the Piscataqua, but the sketches read like a loving memorial of a generation that is just passing out of our sight. Such a memorial is needed, for it is so easy to outline in the rough the stern and homely traits of New England life that too many will never know its tenderness and its beauty. That reflex wave from beyond the Hudson River whence comes, as Miss Jewett shows, the typical "American," will soon sweep away the old traditions and the old characteristics. The style of the book befits the subject. Perfectly plain and without pretension, it still never falls from *simplicité* into *simplesse*. If we are sometimes conscious, as in 'River Driftwood,' that the description is something long, for all that we are won to read on with the same restful feeling with which one listens to a strain of sweet music repeating itself again and again.

*Reprinted from the *Nation*, 33 (15 December 1881), 479.

[Review of *Country By-ways*]   Anonymous*

It is perhaps a little forced to call Miss Jewett's sketches a book of travel, yet the reader will find their value to lie chiefly in the skill with which the writer has applied a traveler's art to scenes which lay within easy reach of her own home. Here are the observation of minor incidents, the catching of effects produced by side lights, the rediscovery of the familiar, the looking at a landscape from under one's arm. One is not sure that the sketch which he is reading may not glide gently into a story, or that the story may not forget itself in a sketch. Miss

*Reprinted from the *Atlantic Monthly*, 49 (March 1882), 420–21.

Jewett herself seems sure only of catching and holding some flitting movement of life, some fragment of experience which has demanded her sympathy. One of the stories, indeed, Andrew's Fortune, has a more deliberate intention, and we are led on with some interest to pursue the slight turns of the narrative; yet in this the best work is in the successive pictures of the village groups in the kitchen and at the funeral. It would be difficult to find a formal story which made less draught upon one's curiosity than Miss Becky's Pilgrimage, yet one easily acquires a personal regard for Miss Becky herself. Miss Jewett's sketches have all the value and interest of delicately executed watercolor landscapes; they are restful, they are truthful, and one is never asked to expend criticism upon them, but to take them with their necessary limitations as household pleasures.

Nevertheless, though we cannot persuade ourselves to criticise this work, we are impelled to ask for something more. Miss Jewett has now given us three volumes, besides the one for children, and has shown us how well she can do a certain thing. The sketches and stories which make up these volumes vary in value, but they are all marked by grace and fine feeling; they are thoroughly wholesome; they have a gentle frankness and reverence which are inexpressibly winning, when one thinks of the knowingness and self-consciouess and restlessness which by turns characterize so many of the contributions by women to our literature. It is only when we come to compare Miss Jewett with herself that we become exacting. She has transformed the dull New England landscape into a mossy rural neighborhood; she has brought us into the friendliest acquaintance with people whom we thought we knew and did not know; and now we want her help in knowing other and fuller lives; we are eager to have her interpretation of people who impress us at once as well worth knowing. We are sure that she will bring out what we could not discover by ourselves; but in our impatience we begin to fear that we are to meet the same people and visit the same houses when a new book is offered. Has not Miss Jewett visited all her neighbors, and would not a longer flight of travel give her new types?

That is the way with us. No sooner do we get these charming village scenes, for which we have been asking our writers, than we want something else. Well, our discontent is of Miss Jewett's making. She has opened the eyes of the summer boarder, and when the summer boarder goes back to town it is with a wish to take the friendly Miss Jewett in company. We wish that this light traveler would plume herself for a braver excursion. Possibly we are asking too much, and the skill which executes these short sketches is conditioned upon their very limitations. Yet we heartily wish that this delightful writer would reserve her strength, and essay a larger work. To fail in a long journey may even give one an access of power and dignity when resuming a stroll, and we value the fine moral sense and delicate sympathy of Miss Jewett so highly that we are reluctant to see her gifts possibly diminish in efficacy by too close a confinement and too narrow a range.

Miss Jewett's First Novel   Anonymous*

We do not know whether Miss Jewett has written *A Country Doctor* in obedience to a spontaneous impulse or in compliance with the suggestion of her publishers or of some of her critics. The story is pleasant reading, like everything that we have hitherto had from her hand; but it cannot be said to be the revelation of any new or any greater power. It is simply an expanded sketch, characterized by the same agreeable literary qualities with which we have become familiar in her previous writings. There is not in it the material for a novel proper, and it makes no pretence to being such. It is quite free from "padding" of any sort, and within its limitations it is neatly finished. The young heroine's individuality is defined in lines of simple grace; the character of the elder physician is set before us with the reality of a portrait from the life, while their worthy neighbors, the inhabitants of rustic Oldfields appear in the truth of the mental and moral differences underlying the homely speech and unsophisticated manners common to them all. In Miss Jewett's writings there is always something to be prized beyond a refined and graceful style and a faculty of delicate perception; these are the evident outcome of womanly sentiment, and of a sincere humanity that finds its chief food for thought in the fact of the kinship and mutual dependence of men, high and low, wise and ignorant, strong and weak.

A *Country Doctor* is the third recent fiction by an American author which has had for its heroine a practicing physician. Yet there is little resemblance between the three. Mr. Howells's Dr. Breen is a clever and good young woman whom, the author makes it plain, has mistaken a temporary discontent with life consequent on an unhappy experience for a true calling to the physician's career, and who is lucky enough to discover the error in time to transfer her womanly activities to a strictly domestic sphere. Miss Phelps's Doctor Zay makes up her mind after a distressing mental conflict, that she can contrive to combine matrimony with the exercise of her professional abilities in a more limited area than she originally intended. Miss Jewett's Nan, avoiding sweeping theories and heated argument, and speaking with modest conviction only for

*Reprinted from the *Literary World*, 15 (28 June 1884), 211.

herself and the few who resemble her, declares her decision to follow and abide by the sure prompting of nature.

We cannot leave *A Country Doctor* without one further word. However agreeable the cultured reader may pronounce it to be, he must add the qualification that it is, nevertheless, a less satisfactory literary product than most of the author's shorter works. The book, in spite of its added pages, remains but a sketch, and a sketch is never bettered by being extended beyond its natural limits; its best effect is mainly dependent upon its right proportion. Mr. James's best writing has taken the shape of sketches: *Madame des Mauves* and *A Passionate Pilgrim* are better pieces of work than *The Portrait of a Lady*. An author may no doubt be capable of producing both novels and sketches equally good in their way, but the qualities requisite for the one kind of writing by no means imply possession of those needful for the other. To write a thoroughly good sketch or short story is not an easy task, and it is not to undervalue the literary gift of an author who can do this to say that powers of another and a greater kind go to the making of a novel of the first order.

[Review of *A Country Doctor*]   Anonymous*

We turn from it gladly to the serene and sunny atmosphere of Miss Jewett's first long story, *A Country Doctor*. Here, also, is little or no plot. The story is simply a sketch, and here will be the chief objection to it, even the best disposed critic being obliged to wish that Miss Jewett's constructive ability were larger. But when all this is said, the fact remains that, even as a sketch, it is delightful reading. The life of the little heroine Nan unfolds under our eyes, simply and naturally—at first with her grandmother, in the quiet farmhouse, then in the home of the good doctor, who becomes her guardian, and whose profession she finally adopts. There are stormy tendencies in her blood, for her mother, a petted and only child, had married a young naval surgeon infatuated with her beauty, but finding her in temper and inclination hopelessly incompatible. There is an aunt, of the most sacred caste among New Englanders, who, though she conscientiously aids in her support, refuses to see the child of this disastrous marriage till Nan herself seeks to heal the breach, and does so completely that to break away becomes as hard as to force entrance had been. Nan recognizes her inheritance, and refuses marriage, and the book leaves her at the entrance of her career as a country doctor, content, and even joyous, in the prospect of this

*Reprinted from the *Continent*, 6 (4 November 1884), 127.

future, at work in her own place. But this meagre summary gives no idea of the charm in every page—the old people, whose slow and irrelevant talk we seem to hear; the perfect description of the village life, or the old seaport town, through which we feel the fresh wind blowing; the quaint characters that stand out, each clear and distinct; the atmosphere of high and gentle thought, of noble purpose, under the New England reticence; of lives that hold faith and honor, and all sweet and fine thoughts and actions. The book has even historical value, in its absolute accuracy of rendering the New England life, fast altering, its old characteristics, and must rank first among the notable novels the season has produced.

Miss Jewett's *A Marsh Island*   Anonymous*

Miss Jewett's new book is in many ways very pleasant reading. It is a great advance upon *A Country Doctor*, and exhibits at their best the fine literary traits that have made for Miss Jewett the enviable reputation of one who can interest the public in simple things. Nothing could be better of the kind than the bits of landscape scattered through the book. Inimitable is the description of the marshes, 'looking as if the land had been *raveled out* into the sea,' and of the tide, 'holding itself bravely for a time: it had grasped the land nobly; all that great weight and power were come in and had prevailed; it shone up at the sky, and laughed in the sun's face; then changed its mind, and began to creep away again; it would rise no more that morning, but at night the world should wonder!' So keen and bright and true are these pen-sketches, that if they had been left as landscape painting they would have seemed not only exquisite but spirited. The effort to mingle with them, however, something of a story of life and human nature, has resulted in a drowsy effect upon the reader, which reminds one of Lucretia Mott's saying on entering a room where her husband and brother were together: 'Ah! I thought thee must both be here; it was so quiet!' It is impossible to feel excited, very hard to feel even decently interested, as regards the characters of the story. The *mise en scène* is perfect, but the people are dull. That is, they are not even really dull; they simply do not exist for us. The good housewife does not touch our hearts, even as a frier of doughnuts; Doris is entirely inanimate; and the artist is as quiet as if he knew professionally that he ought to sit still while his portrait was being painted. But it is pleasanter to praise, and for the scenery and settings of the incidents no one could have anything

*Reprinted from the *Critic*, 4 (8 August 1885), 64.

but praise. It is, indeed, because they are so fine that one looks for something more important to happen in them than the eating of apples or the making of a pie.

[Review of *A White Heron* and *Other Stories*]

Anonymous*

Of Miss Jewett's stories little can ever be said, except to remark afresh on their beauty, their straightforward simplicity, and above all, their loving truth to the life of rural New England not merely in its external aspects, but in its very heart and spirit. It needs only to compare such a bit of outside observation as Mr. Howells's picture of Lydia Blood's home with the studies of the same sort of people from the more intimate and sympathetic standpoint of Miss Jewett's stories, to realize how great is the mere historic importance, apart from the purely humane or artistic value, of these stories, and the little "school" of which they, with Rose Terry Cooke's, stand at the head. They constitute the only record for the future of the real motive and temper of life among the latest (and possibly the last) distinct representatives of the English Puritan colonization of New England; as well as very nearly the only one, in any detail, of its manners and customs. In view of the current misconceptions of the Puritan temper, which threaten to fasten themselves upon history, such authentic records of its rugged kindliness, its intensity of personal affections, its capacity for liberality, are invaluable. Nor can one doubt that these *bona fide* Yankees, yet lingering among the remote farms, are the true descendants in character as well as in blood of the original colonists, if he will compare them with George Eliot's studies of the farmer folk from among whom they came. The community of essential character, modified by two hundred years of greater independence, more liberal thought, and harder effort, is unmistakable. *A White Heron* contains two or three stories that are among Miss Jewett's best; the average of the collection is scarcely equal, we think, to previous ones. The first story, "A White Heron," however, is perfect in its way—a tiny classic. One little episode of child life, among birds and woods, makes it up; and the secret soul of a child, the appeal of the bird to its instinctive honor and tenderness, never were interpreted with more beauty and insight. . . .

*Reprinted from the *Overland Monthly*, 8 (October 1886), 439–41.

[Review of *The King of Folly Island and Other People*]

Anonymous*

Miss Jewett's graceful command of the picturesque attributes of humble New England seaboard life is exemplified once more in the collection of studies embraced under the above-quoted title. Stories in the proper sense of the word Miss Jewett does not give us. There is in her pages no evolution of character, she reveals no gradual unfolding of motive, she is incapable of constructing a plot. But how fine and true, within its narrow limits, her work is! Given a situation suited to her peculiar talent, she has no rival in the gentle art of depicting two or three people in certain simplified relations and making them denizens of reality. Her art is photographic in fidelity to general outlines and essential details, while having a softness of tone that bare description could never rival. The whole secret of her success is sympathy. She knows and loves the sterile hillsides and rude coasts where her fancy loves to wander, and the people who inhabit them are with her objects of unfailing interest. Only once in the volume before us does she step aside from her familiar province to enter other fields. "Mère Pochette" is perhaps worthy of a place with Miss Jewett's other productions, but certainly it lacks vitality and is, compared with the rest of the book, a most lame and impotent conclusion.

*Reprinted from the *Literary World*, 19 (27 October 1888), 365.

[Review of *Betty Leicester*]

Anonymous*

Miss Jewett has been known hitherto chiefly as a writer of books—quite unsurpassed in their atmosphere of sweet, pure, New England country life—for the general reader. She now takes her place in the ranks of those women whose works are calculated to elevate and inspire the young; not little children, but young girls who need a true woman's influence and counsel as they step forward to take their places in the busy world. "Betty Leicester" is a girl of fifteen, which she thinks "such a funny age—you seem to perch there, between being a little girl and a young lady, and first you think you are one and then you think you are the other." The story of her simple, natural, sunny life, bringing "a bit of color" into the gray lives of the country people where she spends the summer, is an exquisite bit of helpful writing, worthy of a place beside *Little Women* and *Faith Gartney*. The world seems to us, after we have read this little book, a brighter and better place to live in.

*Reprinted from *Cottage Hearth*, 16 (January 1890), 23.

[Review of *Strangers and Wayfarers*]   Anonymous*

Miss Sarah Orne Jewett's *Strangers and Wayfarers* contains eleven of those delightfully artistic, yet oftentimes depressing and enervating stories of poverty-stricken or ignorance-stricken folk, for which this author has become justly famous. Miss Jewett has genius, and she has literary conscience. We always go to her work sure that she will not disappoint us with it; but her sketches of New England life nearly always leave the impression that New England is a dreadfully doleful and undesirable sort of country. She certainly paints bleakness and barrenness of soil and life with the hand of a master.

*Reprinted from the *Independent*, 23 (29 January 1891), 164.

[Review of *A Native of Winby and Other Tales*]   Anonymous*

Miss Jewett's *Native of Winby* is another example of the natural and proper unity of idea and expression. It would be hard to name stories better from any point of view than are four at least of those included in her latest volume. There was a time when she trembled on the verge of fashionable art, the art of writing a tale wherein no tale is discoverable; but she never went over to the unintelligibles, and is now firmly reëstablished on the old, sure ground of something to tell. One of the most vivid of general impressions about New England is given by those innumerable women very interesting for reasons which have nothing to do with being in love or being made love to. Most of them have passed, happily or unhappily, the years when love-making is very important. They are reticent and inexpressive to the stranger, who can only guess at their sorrows, personal or vicarious, from physical signs and tokens. It has been given to Miss Jewett to express these women, to paint their external life and manners, to reveal the secret emotions of the heart and yearnings of the soul. The dominant tone is sad, but the wail of despair is seldom heard; poverty does not shriek for alms, nor sickness of body or soul for pity. The "Stern Daughter of the Voice of God" compels repression, and the beneficent spirit of national humor in its most delightful mood lightens profoundest misery. A poor-house would not be half bad if one could be sure of the company of a Betsey Lane. Several writers have won success in Miss Jewett's field, but not one has a similar grasp of situation and character, her tenderness or anything

*Reprinted from the *Nation*, 57 (14 December 1893), 452.

like her sense of proportion. So free is she from strain and extravagance, so easy and adequate in expression, that she goes far to remove any doubt about whether great naturalness is or is not the final phase of great literary art.

[Review of *The Country of the Pointed Firs*]   Anonymous*

It has been a pleasure, repeated at intervals the past few years, to have in convenient form collections of Miss Sarah Orne Jewett's stories, but the pleasure is heightened at this time in the appearance of *The Country of the Pointed Firs* (Houghton) by the light thread of identity of place and character on which the stories are strung. Miss Jewett has, in effect, made a seacoast of her own, a mirage lifted just above the horizon of actual land, and peopled it with figures that are images of reality, also. She herself moves among them, and her warm sympathy is the breath of life which animates them. Her art has devised no more enchanted country, or given a more human substance to the creatures of her imagination. The book has the freshness of *Deephaven* with the mellowness of matured power.

*Reprinted from the *Atlantic Monthly*, 79 (February 1897), 272–73.

[Review of *The Country of the Pointed Firs*]   Alice Brown*

The Country of the Pointed Firs is the flower of a sweet, sane knowledge of life, and an art so elusive that it smiles up at you while you pull aside the petals, vainly probing its heart. The title is exacting, prophetic; a little bit of genius of which the book has to be worthy or come very "tardy off." And the book is worthy. Here is the idyllic atmosphere of country life, unbroken by one jarring note; even the attendant sadness and pathos of being are resolved into that larger harmony destined to elude our fustian words. It is a book made to defy the praise ordinarily given to details; it must be regarded *au large*. For it takes hold of the very centre of things. The pointed firs have their roots in the ground of national being; they are index fingers to the stars. A

*Reprinted from the *Book Buyer* (New York), 15 (October 1897), 249–50.

new region unrolls before you like a living map, whereof The Bowden Reunion and Captain Littlepage are twin mountain heights, warm in sunshine and swept by favoring airs. The Reunion indeed bears a larger significance than its name. It stirs in us the dormant clan-spirit; we understand ancestor-worship, the continuity of being. All the delicate humor, the broidery of the day, "like fringe upon a petticoat"—the pictorial pies, the alien guest with her pseudo-likeness to "Cousin Pa'lina Bowden about the forehead," the woman who "wouldn't get back in a day if she was as far out o' town as she was out o' tune"—this thrills you with a fine and delicate pleasure; but meanwhile your mind marches grandly with the Bowdens, you throb like them with pride of race, you acquiesce willingly in the sweet, loyal usages of domesticity. The conception has its tap-root in the solid earth; but Captain Littlepage's story of the unknown country "up north beyond the ice" takes hold on things remote: it breathes the awful chill and mysticism of the Ancient Mariner. Here are the powers of the air portrayed with Miltonic grandeur. Less tangible even than the denizens of the Beleaguered City, they throng and press upon the mind, making void all proven experience. It is as strange and true a page out of the unseen possibilities of being as Kipling's story of the dead sea-snake. It is not, moreover, the only hint of the inter-relations of known and unknown. Even the herbs in Mrs. Todd's garden could not all be classified. There was one that sent "out a penetrating odor late in the evening, after the dew had fallen, and the moon was high, and the cool air came up from the sea." You would not know that herb for a world of science. It is mystical as moly, and so it shall remain.

Mrs. Todd and Mrs. Blackett are as real as the earth. For pure fascination, Mrs. Todd can never expect to vie with her mother; she did "lurch about steppin' into a bo't"; it was not she who put forth the grave axiom that it was scarcely "advisable to maintain cats just on account of their havin' bob tails." But she is the colossal figure of a simple woman dowered with sorrow and loss, who set her feet firmly on the ground—

To crush the snake and spare the worm,

who made personal grief no reason for bickering with the universe, whose moral life went sanely with the stars, and whose nostrils were delighted with sweet savors from the earth which had denied her. Too often we are taught that great grief and finer feeling are the concomitants of revolt; but it is the larger mind which links them to sweetness, serenity, and obedience. Here is quiet revelation of human tragedy, but none of that fierce rebellion through which individual suffering eats its own heart and the heart of the onlooking chorus. Even the self-exiled Joanna, pursued by the phantom of the unpardonable sin, cannot afflict us irremediably; for still was she surrounded, as with a sea, by faulty human love, and still, as we read, the tranquil company of the firs bids us be patient till her affliction shall be overpast.

To pluck the flowers of humor, quaint philosophy, and legend here is as hopeless as to make a Poyser anthology. You are simply bewildered by the richness and life-giving balm of this herby garden. It is the acme of Miss Jewett's fine achievement, blending the humanity of the "Native of Winby" and the fragrance of the "White Heron." No such beautiful and perfect work has been done for many years; perhaps no such beautiful work has ever been done in America.

[Review of *The Tory Lover*]   Anonymous*

Miss Jewett's work has been a long loyalty to art—so delicate, finely wrought, and sincere has it been from the beginning. She has never been diverted from her vocation as a painter of New England traits and life— a painter of sensitive feeling, clear insight, and a finished, reposeful, but individual and vital style. Her quiet fidelity to high standards, wholesome methods, and the realities of character has evidenced that quality in her nature and in her art which stamps her as one of the writers of our time whose place is secure. In *The Tory Lover* she does not leave the field which she knows intimately and with the insight of affection. The larger movement of the story is on the other side of the sea; but the passions and convictions which dominate and shape it are of New England origin, and the air of New England fills the sails of the little craft which bears Paul Jones and his turbulent crew. There is in the story no striving to catch the wind of popular favor which is bearing tales of adventure to such fabulous ports in these days; no attempt to adjust an exquisite art to the taste of the hour. Miss Jewett is beyond the reach of these grosser temptations. Her method is unchanged; her refinement, delicacy, and trained skill are on every page; she has simply varied her material. For any writer of average ability *The Tory Lover* would be an achievement, so admirable is its workmanship. Miss Jewett must be judged by her own standards, however; and by her standards her latest tale cannot be regarded as on a level with her most characteristic work. It is not convincing. The story of incident and adventure is not her vocation. Fortunately, she had no need of success in a new field; her own field is ample, and her possession of it complete.

*Reprinted from the *Outlook*, 69 (19 October 1901), 420.

REPRINTED ESSAYS

Henry James Criticizes
The Tory Lover
Ferman Bishop*

Although Henry James's esteem for the work of Sarah Orne Jewett is well known, none of his actual correspondence with her has ever appeared in print. Their literary friendship, though possibly begun as early as 1881, did not flourish until September, 1898, when Miss Jewett and Mrs. Annie Fields visited James at Lamb House.[1] Soon after, in his notebook entry for February 19, 1899, he acknowledged that her story "A Lost Lover" in the volume *Tales of New England* (which he described as "charming") had provided him with the germ of an idea for a story.[2] But undoubtedly one of the most interesting documents to pass between them is the following unpublished letter from the Sarah Orne Jewett Collection at the Houghton Library, Harvard University:[3]

Lamb House
Rye, Sussex
October 5, 1901

Dear Miss Jewett,

Let me not criminally, or at all events gracelessly, delay to thank you for your charming and generous present of *The Tory Lover*. He has been but 3 or 4 days in the house, yet I have given him an earnest, a pensive, a liberal—yet, a benevolent attention, and the upshot is that I should like to write you a longer letter than I just now—(especially as it's past midnight) see my way to doing. For it would take me some time to disembroil the tangle of saying to you at once how I appreciate the charming touch, tact & taste of this ingenious exercise, & how little I am in sympathy with experiments of its general (to my sense) misguided stamp. There I am!—yet I don't do you the outrage, as a fellow craftsman & a woman of genius and courage, to suppose you not as conscious as I am myself of all that, in these questions of art & taste &

*Reprinted, with permission, from *American Literature*, 27 (1955), 262–64. Copyright 1955 by Duke University Press.

sincerity, is beyond the mere twaddle of graciousness. The "historic" novel is, for me, condemned, even in cases of labour as delicate as yours, to a fatal *cheapness*, for the simple reason that the difficulty of the job is inordinate & that a mere *escamotage*, in the interest of each, & of the abysmal public *naïveté*, becomes inevitable. You may multiply the little facts that can be got from pictures, & documents, relics & prints, as much as you like—*the* real thing is almost impossible to do, & in its essence the whole effect is as nought. I mean the evolution, the representation of the old CONSCIOUSNESS, the soul, the sense, the horizon, the action of individuals, in whose minds half the things that make ours, that make the modern world were non-existent. You have to think with your modern apparatus a man, a woman—or rather fifty—whose own thinking was intensely otherwise conditioned. You have to simplify back by an amazing tour de force—& even then it's all humbug. But there is a shade of the (even then) humbug that *may* amuse. The childish tricks that take the place of any such conception of the real job in the flood of Tales of the Past that seems of late to have been rolling over our devoted country—these ineptitudes have, on a few recent glances, struck me as creditable to no one concerned. You, I hasten to add, seem to me to have steered very clear of them—to have seen your work very bravely & handled it firmly; but even you court disaster by composing the whole thing so much by sequences of speeches. It is when the extinct soul talks, & the earlier consciousness airs itself, that the pitfalls multiply & the "cheap" way has to serve. I speak in general, I needn't keep insisting, & I speak grossly, summarily, by rude & provisional signs, in order to suggest my sentiment at all. I didn't mean to say so much without saying more, now I have touched you with cold water when I only meant just lightly & kindly to sprinkle you as for a new baptism— that is a *re*-dedication to altars but briefly, I trust, forsaken. Go back to the dear Country of the Pointed Firs, *come* back to the palpable present *intimate* that throbs responsive, & that wants, misses, needs you, God knows, & that suffers woefully in your absence. Then I shall feel perhaps—& do it if only for that—that you have magnanimously allowed for the want of gilt on the gingerbread of the but-on-this-occasion—*only* limited sympathy of yours very constantly

HENRY JAMES

P.S. My tender benediction, please, to Mrs. Fields.

Notes

1. M. A. DeWolfe Howe, *Memories of a Hostess* (Boston, 1922), pp. 297–301.
2. F. O. Matthiessen and K. B. Murdock (eds.), *The Notebooks of Henry James* (New York, 1947), p. 286.
3. Printed with permission of the Harvard College Library.

In *Deephaven*: Skirmishes
Near the Swamp   **Ann Romines***

> *Sweet is the swamp with its secrets,*
> *Until we meet a snake;*
> *'Tis then we sigh for houses,*
> *And our departure take*
> *At that enthralling gallop*
> *That only childhood knows.*
> *A snake is summer's treason,*
> *And guile is where it goes.*
>   Emily Dickinson

In *The Country of the Pointed Firs*, Sarah Orne Jewett traces a woman's education by ritual, a coherent education in her connections to and distance from the circular life of a seaport town. Jewett's first book, *Deephaven*, published twenty years earlier, in 1877, is usually viewed as her initial attempt to grapple with the themes of her mature masterpiece, where "every element broached in *Deephaven* is ... augmented and brought to highest pitch."[1] Yet when I look again at this early book, built from sketches which Jewett began publishing in her twentieth year, I discover that *Deephaven*—despite its delicately elegaic tone—records a series of abrupt, abortive encounters with ritual. Again and again, the two young protagonists quietly crash into a transparent, unbreakable partition which protects them from the power, danger, and meaning of life in the village of Deephaven—which protects them, in fact, against fully experiencing their own lives. The older narrator of *The Country of the Pointed Firs*, of course, has an opposite experience: in ritual after ritual (funeral, visit, reunion, departure), partitions fall, and she must claim her kinship to the community of solitaries which she has entered as a visitor and which she must leave as a communicant. Her experience will have shape and meaning that she cannot evade. In *Deephaven*, we see Jewett and her characters moving through an "inchoate"[2] series of false starts, starts which grow from two young women's half-conscious attraction to a ritualized world and from their vague intuitions of the dangers inherent in such a world.

Deephaven's narrator, Helen Denis, begins her account with these words: "It happened that the morning when this story begins I had waked up feeling sorry, and as if something dreadful were going to happen. ... I have never known any explanation for that depression of my spirits, and I hope that the good luck which followed will help some reader to lose fear, and to smile at such shadows if any chance to

*Reprinted from the *Colby Library Quarterly*, 16 (1980), 205–19, with the permission of the author.

come."[3] Immediately we see a sensibility capable of perceiving a "dreadful" darkness—and also capable of a doggedly cheerful determination to ignore that darkness. Even though *Deephaven* will contain one funeral chapter titled "In Shadow," as well as a number of other chapters which might share that title, Helen chooses to recall her Deephaven summer as a streak of sunny good luck. Any troubling dreams are dispelled with smiles.

The Deephaven summer is initiated not by Helen but by her friend Kate Lancaster. Both girls (as they call themselves) are twenty-four, unmarried, genteelly unoccupied; at the edge of an adulthood they are not wholly eager to claim. Helen's family is only her aunt and an absent Naval father; Kate's network of parents, siblings, aunts is spreading, loosing its taut, elastic hold on her life. Understandably, both girls are attracted to the protection of ritual, in the sense described by Ernest Becker: "The whole idea of ritual is the manmade forms of things prevailing over the natural order and taming it, transforming it, and making it safe."[4]

Kate's mother owns a house in a declining port town, Deephaven, inherited from a recently dead aunt, Katharine Brandon. When everyone else in the Lancaster family has present occupations and obligations for the summer—camping in Michigan, business in London—Kate projects an adventure in retreat: she will set up temporary housekeeping in Deephaven.

When Kate summons Helen to invite her along, we can see from her greeting the almost ceremonious seriousness with which she regards her plan: "I hurried to the parlor.... I went up to her, and she turned her head and kissed me solemnly. You need not smile; we are not sentimental girls, and are both much averse to indiscriminate kissing, though I have not the adroit habit of shying in which Kate is proficient. It would sometimes be impolite in any one else, but she shies so affectionately" (pp. 37–38). And we also see that Kate, by "shying," is adept at fending off social conventions which she finds meaningless, at evading dead ritual. Real ritual, as in the kiss of greeting, is something they respect too much to debase. But both are well-schooled in protective conventions, and, as the book proceeds, we will see them receptive to Deephaven life when it intrigues or amuses or charms, but always ready (gracefully) to withdraw a chaste cheek from a too-intrusive touch.

As Kate unfolds her plan to Helen, she emphasizes its *childlike* delights: "For two little girls who were fond of each other and could play in the boats and dig and build houses in the sea sand, and gather shells, and carry their dolls wherever they went, what could be pleasanter?" (p. 38). So the girls plunge into their preparations, much enjoying the domestic bustle of planning provisions and "being housekeepers in earnest" (p. 40). But never do they seem to feel that they are doing more than *playing* house, building a sandcastle. They have each other, and they have two servants from the Boston Lancaster house, so they arrive at Deephaven—significantly, at sunset—in the midst of their own small transplanted and protective community. Never are they fully vulnerable to the buffeting of their environment; never is sexuality an acknowledged fact or problem for either.

The novel's first chapter sets up Kate's plan and transports the girls to Deephaven. Remaining chapters sketch various aspects of the town's life; although we may think we observe a pattern of tentative growth in the visitors, that pattern will never crystallize.

Kate and Helen rapidly discover that Deephaven is dominated by two dwellings: the Brandon house and the lighthouse. The Brandon house is an aristocrat, in which the town's less exalted citizens take a communal pride. It has been a focus for local life; a neighbor says: "I like to see the old place open; it was about as bad as having no meeting. I miss seeing the lights" (pp. 59–60). The Brandon house has been a kind of lighthouse, a beacon to the dignified past. Now that Katharine Brandon is dead, no Brandons remain to preserve her mansion. That task is left to the women of the village, especially a favorite friend of Kate and Helen's, the Widow Jim. She is the woman of faculty, the domestic arbiter, in this book:

> There must be her counterpart in all old New England villages. She sewed, and she made elaborate rugs. . . . and she went to the Carews' and the Lorimers' [local aristocrats] at housecleaning or in seasons of great festivity. She had no equal in sickness, and knew how to brew every old-fashioned dose . . . and when her nursing was put to an end by the patient's death, she was commander-in-chief at the funeral . . . she sometimes even had the immense responsibility of making out the order of the procession, since she had all genealogy and relation-ship at her tongue's end. (p. 61)

A ritual priestess, surely—with a fine nose for propriety. She may not be able to control time, but she has ritualized response to each of its events, from celebration to death.

The bustling, ordering domesticity of Widow Jim and a few women like her is the strongest force in Deephaven; it is they who keep the "moth millers" and most of the rats out of the empty Brandon house. But what they preserve is largely past, not present. We usually see Widow Jim snug in her parlor, recalling bygone ceremonies. When she recalls a recent rite—a ministerial tribute to Katharine Brandon—it is with regret: "There wasn't a blood relation there to hear it. I declare it looked pitiful to see that pew empty that ought to ha' been the mourn-ers' pew. There! . . . p'r'aps nobody thought of it but me" (p. 59). For in Deephaven the cohesive family is breaking and broken, and rituals tend to reveal, not to mend, the fracture. Miss Katharine, the last childless survivor of a large, fragmented family, illustrates this. And from the Widow Jim we learn another crucial fact about Katharine Brandon: she died mad. "Her mind failed her, you know. Great loss to Deephaven, she was" (p. 58).

Childless Widow Jim herself illustrates the pitfalls of committing oneself to matrimony: she bears a dent in her forehead, put there by her alcoholic husband. Having been dealt such an appalling surprise, no wonder she now devotes herself to more certain matters. And she advises Kate and Helen to do likewise: "Don't you run no risks, you're better off as you be, dears" (p. 63). Widow Jim, despite her solidity and her comforting advice—which urges cosy stagnation—has already hinted at the limited power of ritual against human change and has reminded the girls that even the single life which she urges on them can offer no guarantee against a failed mind like that of Katharine Brandon. This is Helen's first knowledge of Miss Brandon's madness. And typically, she does not comment; she only records the Widow's words. It is easy to overlook many of the defeats and disappointments Kate and Helen suffer in this book, for Helen's narrative blithely refuses to acknowledge them with comment.

The other Deephaven beacon is the actual lighthouse, and it is dominated by another priestess, Mrs. Kew, to whom the girls are equally attracted. The lighthouse reminds them of this acute and engaging woman's power to make a workable pattern out of the contradictory facts of her life. Mrs. Kew is Vermont-born, "a real up-country woman. . . . The sea doesn't come natural to me, it kind of worries me" (p. 41). Yet she loved and married a sailor, and was able to keep him ashore only by moving with him to the lighthouse, at land's end. She has paid for the man she wanted by living, for seventeen years, in the midst of the still-disquieting sea. Mrs. Kew has gone as far out to sea as a Deephaven woman can, yet her earnest farewell to the girls from Boston, at summer's end, suggests the stringencies and deprivations of her life: "She told us that she loved us as if we belonged to her, and begged us not to forget her." The girls are amazed—"We had no idea until then how much she cared for us . . ." (p. 42).

This amazement indicates Kate's and Helen's failure to appreciate the full meaning of either Deephaven lighthouse. Although they camp delightedly in the Brandon house, and ransack its corners for diverting relics, they seem determined to reduce Katharine Brandon's long, dignified life to a charmingly pathetic tale.

Although they are constant visitors with Mrs. Kew, their detachment from her world is also indicated when Kate, one day, plays local maiden and gives a guided tour to some city shopgirls who are visiting the lighthouse on holiday.

"But it's such a lonesome place!" said one of the girls. "I should think you would get work away. I live in Boston. Why it's so awful quiet! nothing but the water, and the wind when it blows, and I think either of them is worse than nothing." (p. 51)

Kate, enjoying the charade and probably savoring her superior appreciation of Deephaven's charms, makes no reply, but when the most earnest of the visitors stays behind to entreat her to escape to Boston, she is sufficiently touched to declare her position, as proper Bostonian only playing at lighthouse girl. "And she [Kate] held out her hand to the girl... when she noticed Kate's hand, and a ring of hers, which had been turned round, she looked really frightened" (p. 52). The naïve shopgirl who has taken Kate Lancaster seriously as a person whose life is committed to Deephaven is put firmly in her place by a (perhaps inadvertent) flash of social class. The girls both intermittently use such flashes of "superior" class or sophistication or erudition to stave off Deephaven, when it comes too close.

Yet they enjoy the lighthouse, especially the daily ritual of watching the sunset, with Mrs. Kew: "There was a little black boat in the distance drifting slowly...as if it were bound out into that other world beyond. But presently the sun came out from behind the clouds, and the dazzling golden light changed the look of everything, and it was time then to say one thought it a beautiful sunset; while before one could only keep very still, and watch the boat, and wonder if heaven would not be somehow like that far, faint color, which was neither sea nor sky" (pp. 52–53). But the limitations of the girls at the beginnings of their Deephaven summer are suggested by this passage's near-sentimental prettiness, its sense of a spectacle seen from a safe distance, and its tacit refusal to recognize the potential power and desolation of "the water and the wind, when its blows," which were so real and alarming to that Boston shopgirl. Mrs. Kew's life, also, has daily limitations, subtleties, and complications which her visitors will not acknowledge.

As the summer deepens, Helen and Kate try out local rites. First, church services, where they behave like spectators at a theater, clutching each other's hands in delighted amusement at a particularly antiquated costume, or at the quaint sound of a bass viol. Then tea with an aristocratic local family, the elderly Carews: an unmarried brother and sister, and a sickly widowed sister. They are especially enchanted to be included in the Carew household rite of family prayers, and apparently find nothing sad or ironic in the age or fragility of the family involved. Afterward, "we told each other, as we went home in the moonlight down the quiet street, how much we had enjoyed the evening, for somehow the house and the people had nothing to do with the present, or the hurry of modern life. I have never heard that psalm since without its bringing back that summer night in Deephaven, and the beautiful quaint old room, and Kate and I feel so young and worldly, by contrast, the flickering shaded light of the candles, the old book, and the voices that said Amen" (p. 76). Here is ritual as spectator sport; ritual as a kind of sympathetic voyeurism. By glimpsing and momentarily, partially, sharing the Carew family prayers, Kate and Helen—now out on the dark street, not confined in the old house—have gained self-definition. Free, "worldly," "young," they imagine themselves; able to walk into and out of whatever rituals they choose.

Another value of Deephaven for Kate and Helen is the fact that it provides an escape from the bustling post-war America which Jewett herself sometimes viewed with such alarm. The town "was not in the least American. There was no excitement about anything; there were no manufactories; no body seemed in the least hurry" (p. 84). The equivocal nature of Deephaven's tranquility is especially evident in local men. Most of them have sailed around the world, and most of them, suffering from the decline of their industry, and their aging bodies, now hang around the deserted warehouses and fish for a modest living. The ritual act most typical of these men is the telling and retelling of stories, yarns from their seafaring days.

Kate and Helen, perhaps trying to touch a dimension of freedom in Deephaven beyond the household limitations imposed on women, seek out the old sailors' stories, and provide an avid, if somewhat condescending, audience. But for every tale of lighthearted escapade Helen records, there are two contrasting tales of loss, of abrupt and violent death, of a life without the cushioning compensations of ritual. In one story, for example, an insult provoked a deadly blow, which led to an immediate hanging. The best the hanged man's companions could do for him was to cut his body down and thrust it wordlessly into the sea. This is a far cry from the funerals superintended by Widow Jim, with their prescriptions and processions. Helen does not comment on the disparity—or the horror—implicit in such a tale.

A younger, orphaned ex-sailor, Danny, is used to illustrate the pathos of a man without a domestic anchor; he tells wistful tales of a nun who cared for him in a hospital, and of a lost "kitty" which seems to have been the closest thing he's had to a wife: "I never went into Salem since without hoping that I should see her. I don't know but if I was a-going to begin my life again, I'd settle down ashore and have a snug little house and farm it. But I guess I shall do better at fishing" (p. 91). Women, with their ritual domesticity, may have learned to wrest some satisfaction and meaning from a landlocked life; men cannot.

Stories from another beached sailor, old Captain Sands, reveal that he has developed a special, compensatory sensitivity to the supernatural. His accounts of feats of prediction and divination, of dream-omens, especially fascinate the girls, and back in the Brandon house, they drift "into a long talk about the captain's stories and those mysterious powers of which we know so little" (p. 129). Their conversation vacillates between admitting the possible influence of such uncontrollable powers in their own lives, and placing them at a safe and interesting distance. Kate makes scholarly references to Greek mythology; Helen connects such forces with "simple country people" (which she and Kate assuredly are not) who "believe in dreams, and . . . supernatural causes" (p. 130). Remember that Helen began the book with an account of a dream-omen which she has not been able to forget, but will not believe. The conversation ends with Kate's equivocal comment: "The more one lives out of doors [as they have been doing] the more personality there seems to be in what we call inanimate things." She tries to attribute this "personality," this animate meaning, to the hand of God writing in "the book of Nature." But the trite and pious explanation does not really touch the mysteries of the old captains' tales, and the girls retreat to a cautious and reflective silence—ending as they bar "the great hall door," shutting out the inexplicable "out of doors," and go "upstairs to bed" (p. 131). They are always shutting themselves into or out of a house, or a story, or a world—never can they risk staying inside or outside Deephaven's various shelters, for long.

During their visit, Kate and Helen observe two attempts from outside to revitalize Deephaven with ritual. But both end by illustrating the community's frailty. First, a circus comes to the area, and Deephaven turns out in force. Kate and Helen take as their special guest Mrs. Kew, who devotes "her whole mind to enjoyment" (p. 100). It is not really the circus which most pleasures Mrs. Kew; it is the assembled company, the communal nature of the occasion. Both she and Kate reminisce about circuses in their pasts: this ritual both confirms and denies the passage of time and change. Kate says to Helen: "Doesn't it seem as if you were a child again? . . . I am sure this is just the same as the first circus I ever saw. It grows more and more familiar, and it puzzles me to think they should not have altered in the least while I have changed so much, and even had time to grow up" (p. 104). This reflective comment indicates the considerable capacity for sympathy and understanding which Kate *does* possess; it also indicates the puzzlement which the girls have been unable to escape even in Deephaven: what is the relation of their changing lives to the seemingly unchanging patterns of rituals?

But grotesque incidents qualify the pleasure of the circus day, especially the three women's parting stop at a sideshow, to see "The Kentucky Giantess." The fat woman, who has never seen Kentucky, turns out to be an old neighbor of Mrs. Kew's, Marilly, who "used to be spare." Her husband, she tells them,

> "took to drink and it killed him after awhile, and then I began to grow worse, till I couldn't do nothing to earn a dollar, and everybody was a-coming to see me, till at last I used to ask 'em ten cents apiece, and I scratched along somehow till this man came around and heard of me, and he offered me my keep and good pay to go along with

him. . . . [her married son's] wife don't want me. I don't know's I
blame her either. It would be something like if I had a daughter. . . .
I believe I'd rather die than grow any bigger. I do lose heart sometimes, and wish I was a smart woman and could keep house. I'd be
smarter than ever I was when I had the chance, I tell you that!"
(pp. 106–107)

Here we see, in the midst of the circus gaiety, another house and family
shattered by weakness, and are forcibly reminded of the formidable
power of domestic discipline which has kept a woman like the Widow
Jim (who also had an alcoholic husband) from being reduced (or in-
flated) to this woman's state. The Giantess illustrates the helpless vul-
nerability to change which Kate earlier hinted at in her own life. She
cannot even control her huge, traitorous body. And by the chance of
having borne a son and not a daughter, she is cut off from the imagined
comfort of a daughter's female household. Even the competent Mrs.
Kew is powerless now to do anything for her old neighbor. She considers inviting her out for a visit—but "'she'd sink the dory in a minute.
There! seeing her has took away all the fun,' said Mrs. Kew ruefully"
(p. 108). The hard-won domestic equilibrium of the lighthouse is not
accessible to the likes of a Kentucky Giantess.

But by the time they arrive back in Deephaven, Mrs. Kew has regained her cheerfulness, and parting, tells the girls that "she should
have enough to think of for a year, she had enjoyed the day so much"
(p. 109). A successful ritual, as the circus has partially been, has an
echoing power: memory. And memory is especially crucial to a life as
isolated as Mrs. Kew's.

The other ritual of this chapter is a temperance lecture for young
men—"On the Elements of True Manhood"—delivered at great and
boring length by an obliviously enthusiastic travelling orator, to a tiny
audience composed of women, small children, and a few doddering
graybeards. The situation may suggest the desperation of some Deephaven women, who will attend *any* gathering, and the paucity or weakness or indifference of local men. No one goes so far as to put a contribution in the lecturer's collection plate, and for Kate and Helen, the
whole affair first seems a fiasco and a laugh. But next morning, they
grow "suddenly conscious of the pitiful side of it all," and dispatch an
anonymous contribution to the lecturer, "anxious that everyone should
have the highest opinion of Deephaven" (p. 111). They have become the
dutiful preservers of properties which no one else in Deephaven finds it
necessary to defend; they are protecting their chosen retreat against
complicating truths which they themselves have already, reluctantly
glimpsed.

Perhaps it is these confounding complications which, in the three
chapters which precede the book's conclusion, push Kate and Helen to
range out beyond the town itself, and to discover some of the desolation

of the surrounding hill country, almost impossible to farm profitably. We have seen the girls becoming slightly and cautiously more reflective as the book has proceeded; now Helen cannot close her eyes to the cramping, lethal narrowness of such country lives. "It is all very well to say that they knew nothing better, that it was the only life of which they knew anything; there was too often a look of disappointment in their faces, and sooner or later we heard or guessed many stories." But she is still careful to detach herself and Kate from the implications of such lives: "We used to pity the young girls so much. It was plain that those who knew how much easier and pleasanter our lives were could not help envying us" (p. 153).

Widowed Mrs. Bonny, the first countrywoman Kate and Helen meet, is a sturdy survivor. Her tiny upcountry house is cluttered with poultry and dusty oddments; she is most definitely *not* an immaculate housekeeper. The Boston girls, with their ladylike ways, are rather taken aback by the Bonny menage. Perhaps housewifely niceties do not apply in the stringencies of upcountry life? But Mrs. Bonny proves her worth, and indicates some of the spirit which has preserved her, when she condemns the sham of a revival meeting. No dishonest ritual for her:

> "I wa'n't a-goin' to set there and hear him [a histrionic testifier] makin' b'lieve to the Lord. If anbody's heart is in it, I ain't a' goin' to hender 'em; I'm a professor, and I ain't ashamed of it, weekdays nor Sundays neither. I can't bear to see folks so pious to meeting, and cheat yer eyeteeth out Monday morning. Well, there! we ain't none of us perfect; even old Parson Moody [her alltime favorite] was round-shouldered, they say." (p. 137)

This woman's unsentimental, wholehearted consistency abandons the rigid distinctions (between town and country, between Deephaven and themselves) which Kate and Helen are trying to enforce. Outdoors and indoors mingle in her life, just as the chickens amble through her kitchen. She's willing to allow human inconsistencies: "ain't none of us perfect." And the girls are fascinated—but they tend to see her as an undomesticated "character," a comic figure. "There was something so wild and unconventional about Mrs. Bonny that it was like taking an afternoon walk with a good-natured Indian" (p. 139). They may admire and accept her knowledge of the woods, but they can't quite come to terms with the unconventionality of her household, and they manage to avoid ever tasting Mrs. Bonny's cooking! For Mrs. Bonny cannot be shut into or out of a house or a sex-determined pattern. The "good-natured Indian," at home in forest and in kitchen, bears no sexual designation.

We encounter another upcountry household in "In Shadow," the finest sketch in *Deephaven*. In early summer, Kate and Helen met a frail farm family, quite lacking in Mrs. Bonny's obdurate strength, with appealingly "thin and pitiful" (p. 141) children, and hard-working, honest parents. When the girls return in late October, with gifts for the children, they find that both parents have died. First the wife. Then, without the necessary female anchor, the husband "was sore afflicted, and . . . didn't know what to do or what was going to become of 'em with winter comin' on, and . . . he took to drink and it killed him right off" (p. 147). Kate and Helen arrive just before this man's sparse funeral; both are "more startled than I can tell" (p. 143). Startled, because they have almost blundered into real and present shadows: "We wondered how we should have felt if we had gone further into the room and found the dead man in his coffin, all alone in the house" (p. 146).

For Kate and Helen, the most affecting thing about this family's situation (a situation not entirely unlike their own, although they do not say so) is that it is now "broken up, and the children to be half strangers to each other" (p. 146). Kate sees the dead farmer as a pitiable victim: "like a boat adrift at sea, the waves of his misery brought him in against the rocks, and his simple life was wrecked" (p. 146). In Helen's earlier description of the sunset, the "little black boat" was an anonymous fleck in the composition of a seascape; now, months later, when Kate uses the same boat figure, it is tied to a *particular* (although still seen in terms of her own stereotype of "simplicity"), helpless human life.

The girls climb the rocks above the farmhouse, to have a good view of the walking funeral procession: "We said how much we should like to go to that funeral . . . but we gave up the idea: we had no right there, and it would seem as if we were merely curious, and we were afraid our presence would make the people ill at ease, the minister especially. It would be an intrusion" (p. 145). This statement, though much qualified by Helen's self-conscious awareness of the class difference between herself and Kate and these farm people, is probably the clearest evidence of growth in *Deephaven*. The funeral has a power of its own; participation is a *right* earned by caring and connection. To waltz in and out of it, as they have done with so many Deephaven rituals, *would* "be an intrusion."

So, from a distance, Kate and Helen hear the funeral music, and see the transforming power of the ritual: "Before the people had entered the house, there had been, I am sure, an indifferent, business-like look, but when they came out, all that was changed; their faces were awed by the presence of death, and the indifference had given place to uncertainty" (p. 148). Helen and Kate, as they watch and talk, try to fend off that uncertainty: they quote Shakespeare; they contrast their own comfortable financial situation with the precariousness of up-country life; they extol the necessity of Christianity. But the funeral itself, the uncertain reality, continues to compel their attention: "there was something piteous about this; the mourners looked so few, and we could hear the rattle of the wagon wheels. 'He's gone, ain't he?' said some one near us.

That was it,—*gone*" (p. 148). All of Helen's cultivated observations have somehow missed the mark—this passing stranger, who belongs to the upcountry world, has made the essential observation. Helen's role, as spectator, is but to recognize and to affirm it.

Back in Boston a year later, Helen still cannot shake the memory of that country funeral. And typically, her last thought of it is in terms of the house, a shelter abandoned, locked and empty and riteless as the Brandon house will soon be, again: "I think today of that fireless, empty, forsaken house, where the winter sun shines in and creeps slowly along the floor; the bitter cold is in and around the house, and the snow has sifted in at every crack; outside it is untrodden by any living creature's footstep. The wind blows and rushes and shakes the loose window sashes in their frames, while the padlock knocks—knocks against the door" (p. 149).

Mrs. Bonny may have endured because she is a "professor"; the unnamed farmer of "In Shadow," lacking her powers, could not finally summon up the strength to "profess." And the third, last native of the Deephaven environs whom Kate and Helen meet, Miss Sally Chauncey, has survived only by a negative profession. " 'Ah, they say everyone is "dead" nowadays. I do not [and will not] comprehend the silly idea!' said the old lady, impatiently" (p. 154). Family, fortune, and position gone, Miss Sally has no defense but denial.

Rituals are one means by which Miss Chauncey feeds her disbelief. She reassures herself by recounting past rites, by maintaining old forms, entertaining callers to her tumbledown house in her former elegant manner. As Kate and Helen wait for their hostess, they furtively investigate her house:

> So we went into the great hall with its wide staircase and handsome cornices and panelling and then went into the large parlor on the right, and through it to a smaller room looking out on the garden, which sloped down to the river. Both rooms had fine carved mantels . . . and in the cornices we saw the fastenings where pictures had hung,—old portraits, perhaps. . . . The [servant] girl did not remember, only it would all fall through into the cellar soon. But the old lady was proud as Lucifer, and wouldn't hear of moving out.
>
> The floor in the room toward the river was so broken that it was not safe. . . . Three old hens and a rooster marched toward us with great solemnity when we looked in. The cobwebs hung in the room, as they often did in old barns, in long, gray festoons; the lilacs outside grew close against the two windows where the shutters were not drawn, and the light in the room was greenish and dim. (p. 153)

Into this shadowy space, where solemn chickens and festooned cobwebs mock the house's past of ceremony and civility, where lilacs, once part of an ordered garden, have gone wild and threaten the rooms with their rank green, comes Miss Chauncey, "an elegant woman still" (p.

152). Unconscious of the decay around her, she entertains her young guests with tales of her coming-out party in this house, and urges them to stay for a tea which does not exist. When her guests ask her to read from the Bible for them, Miss Sally Chauncey "opened the great book at random and read slowly, 'in my father's house are many mansions'; and then, looking off for a moment at a leaf which had drifted into the window recess, she repeated it: 'In my father's house are many mansions; if it were not so I should have told you' " (p. 157).

Miss Chauncey's house is much like the Brandon house in style. It also resembles Mrs. Bonny's house in its dilapidation and its closeness to the world outdoors—even its indoor chickens. But Mrs. Bonny accepts and thrives on the mix; Miss Chauncey denies and defies it, living now in the "many mansions" of her memory. In some ways, her house has remained her "father's"; she has never summoned up the rigorous female power (like Mrs. Kew's) which would allow her to see, to order and to possess this dwelling as it really is. For Sally Chauncey, ritual is compounded with evasion, not the truth-telling which gave the up-country funeral its force and value. Her holy text locates human rich-ness and possibility *within* mansions, but does not indicate that the time is the present, the house is crumbling, and its legal owner is not her father but her female self.

No character speaks more directly to the situation of Kate and Helen, themselves inhabiting an inherited house, than Sally Chauncey. And her story is the only one which Helen continues beyond the boundaries of the Deephaven summer. In winter, news reaches Boston of Miss Chaun-cey's death. A well-meaning neighbor finally induced her to leave her "uninhabitable" house. "But her fondness for her old house was too strong, and one day she stole away . . . and crept in through the cellar, where she had to wade through half-frozen water, and then went up-stairs, where she seated herself at a front window and called joyfully to the people who went by, asking them to come in and see her, as she had got home again" (p. 157). She never recovered from the illness induced by this excursion. Miss Chauncey had nowhere to turn but back: to the shelter and the rituals of her youth, to a denial of change which was itself denied by that change she refused to admit: death. Kate and Helen came to Deephaven in a similar spirit, imagining they could again be "two little girls," playing with their dolls on the shifting sea sand.

The shelters which Kate and Helen have observed in their outland forays have all seemed somehow flawed, and have made Deephaven community, which contains both lighthouse and Brandon house, an even more precious haven. In the final chapter, "Last Days in Deep-haven," Helen attempts to catalog all the various details of the summer which she has not mentioned elsewhere. But she does not acknowledge that all the outland extremities they have observed are also present, in embryo or fully grown, in Deephaven. Although Katharine Brandon's house still stands, its fate is uncertain: Kate's family may sell it. And Miss Katharine, when she died, was as mad as her friend Sally Chauncey. The Widow Jim, sans house and inheritance, could be sturdy but slipshod Mrs. Bonny. The alcoholism and spiritless displacement of the dead farmer are seen in any number of Deephaven men. Rituals—calls, circus, storytelling etcetera—may have helped to preserve Deephaven's strength, but they have also revealed its human weaknesses.

Nevertheless, Kate and Helen depart charmed: "we said over and over again how happy we had been, and that it was such a satisfactory summer" (p. 160). They are delighted with their efforts at domestic rite—at playing house—and think they've made considerable progress. On their arrival at Brandon house, Kate showed Helen "a great square figure" in the carpet, where as a child-visitor she "used to keep house . . . with her dolls for lack of a better playhouse" (p. 44). But by summer's end, Helen assures her, she has expanded into the mistress of the whole house, not just a circumscribed carpet-square: "It used to seem to me that Miss Brandon was its mistress; but now it belongs to you" (p. 162). For Kate and Helen this is a crucial statement, for they tend to see a woman's house, her domestic structure, as an essential part of her identity: "we always like to see our friends in their own houses" (p. 61). (Male friends, by contrast, are usually visited outside their houses.)

But the reader may not be so willing to grant that Kate Lancaster *is* mistress of Brandon house. Winter is coming, the winter which the dead farmer could not bear to face; the sea more and more frequently flashes treachery. And Helen and Kate retreat (or advance?) to the conventions of the city; they are "willing to admit that we could be as comfortable in town, and it was almost time for sealskin jackets" (p. 165). Kate will never be committed to, imprisoned in, defined by Brandon house as her dead aunt was. (And Helen, of course, has never been more than a sympathetic guest.)

On a final round of goodbye calls, the girls try to pretend they will return next year. But they know they won't. The evanescence, the limited demands of Deephaven's ceremonies have been among the summer's charms. They've savored the sense of being "placed" in this definable community, if only by virtue of Kate's ancestry. Yet Boston has always been only a train ride away, and they've had a constant stream of city visitors, to admire their rustic discoveries.

When they arrived, they felt that the past of Brandon house could *never* have been as complex or as vital as their own present lives; one of Kate's final comments (on parties with city visitors) sounds the same arrogantly elegaic note: "I think there had never been such picnics in Deephaven before, and I fear there never will be again" (p. 162). When they leave for Boston, the girls carry among their vacation souvenirs a youthful portrait of one of Kate's ancestors, who seemed to them "solitary and forlorn" and "imploring" among the staid elders of the surrounding portraits. "She was soon afterward boxed up, and now enjoys society after her own heart in Kate's room in Boston" (p. 47). Youth, including their own, must be rescued. (Although note that Kate's Boston world is diminished from a house to a room.) Kate and Helen have learned the art of escape (to Boston, to Deephaven, to and from the rituals of both places), but they have not yet begun to master the arts which the lives and rituals of Mrs. Bonny, Widow Jim, and Mrs. Kew might have taught them—acceptance, and endurance.

The "simple" rituals and routines of Deephaven, which Kate and Helen thought would be a retreat from change and uncertainty, have instead offered an education in the stringencies, complications, and constant demands, as well as satisfactions, of being human *anywhere*. But the visitors have not really accepted or admitted the offer of this knowledge. Self-protected, and self-insulated to the last, they return to Boston in the same mood of naïve delight in which they arrived. The transparent partition has not shattered. Or perhaps it is more accurate to say that the partition has sustained a few cracks, which Kate and Helen refuse to acknowledge. In the words which end the book, Helen, in Boston, imagines a return to Deephaven in some distant, probably impossible future. Typically, she visualizes a sunset:

> I should like to walk along the beach at sunset and watch the color of the marshes and the sea change as the light of the sky goes out. It would make the old days come back vividly. We should see the roofs and the black chimneys of the village, and the great Chantrey elms look black against the sky. . . . Turning, we should see the lighthouse lamp shine out over the water, and the great sea should move and speak to us lazily in its idle, high-tide sleep. (p. 166)

Town houses: lighthouse: trees: sea (which, Helen now knows, does not always sleep). All the elements are there. But, even in this imagined landscape, all Helen Denis can do is observe from the edge, and walk by. Like Miss Chauncey, she inhabits an imagined Deephaven, a remembered mansion. The last word we heard from Miss Chauncey was death. The last word from Helen is not too dissimilar: "sleep."

Jewett reread *Deephaven* in the nineties, when she was working on the "Pointed Fir sketches." She did not then disown Helen Denis, but felt very far removed from her—although still related by blood: "I felt as if I had come to be the writer's grandmother. I liked it better than I expected. It is the girlishness that gives it value. . . . It is curious to find how certain conditions under which I wrote it are already outgrown."[5]

And in *The Country of the Pointed Firs*, she strips her new, nameless narrator of the conditions which allowed Kate and Helen to reject much of what Deephaven offered: their youth, their companionship, their proximity, their self-conscious condescension, their family house. Deephaven and the village of the Pointed Firs, Dunnet Landing, are similar.

But this new, older woman, like her creator, has learned not to be Helen Denis. She shares Helen's attraction to and suspicion of rituals. But she must walk directly into and out of them; she cannot, like Helen, walk *by*. Late in *The Country of the Pointed Firs*, Mrs. Todd, the wise woman of Dunnet Landing, says to the narrator, her guest and friend: "Dear . . . how you do understand poor human natur'!"[6] Helen and Kate are not without the potential for such understanding, as their tentative sympathies show. But they refuse the risks and rewards offered them in Deephaven's rituals; they refuse to acknowledge both the sustaining power and the crippling sexual dualism perpetuated in the houses where they have been visitors. The lessons implicit in their refusal are surely a part of the material from which Jewett later built her most moving and most fully realized book. For Helen Denis, awakened, could well become the woman who narrates *The Country of the Pointed Firs*.

Notes

1. Richard Cary, "Introduction," in Sarah Orne Jewett, *Deephaven and Other Stories*, ed. Richard Cary (New Haven: College and University Press, 1966), p. 15.

2. Cary uses this term, p. 18.

3. *Deephaven and Other Stories*, p. 37. All further references to this work appear in the text.

4. *The Denial of Death* (New York: The Free Press, 1973), p. 238.

5. Richard Cary, "Jewett to Dresel: 33 Letters," *CLQ*, XI (March 1975), 38.

6. Sarah Orne Jewett, *The Country of the Pointed Firs and Other Stories*, ed. Willa Cather (Garden City, N.Y.: Doubleday, 1956), p. 155.

Heart to Heart with Nature:
Ways of Looking at "A White Heron"   George Held*

Though " A White Heron" has been among Sarah Orne Jewett's most admired stories since its publication in 1886, its richness and strength may appear even greater today in the light of a feminist perspective. This tale of nine-year-old Sylvia's encounter with a young male ornithologist, reverberates with meaning for such issues as the socialization of girls, the balance of power between the sexes, and the need for a woman to be true to her nature. In the heroine's conflict over revealing the heron to the young man, the story also concerns the need for mankind to resist the erosion of our integrity with the natural world.

Jewett herself claimed to "love" this fiction, though she despaired that it was too romantic to appeal to many readers in an age of literary realism. In fact an earlier story, "The Shore House," had drawn praise from the champion of realism, William Dean Howells, who had "urged her to do more, for he thought that she had found her true bent in realism."[1] Thus after having written the romantic "A White Heron," Jewett refrained from trying to publish it in a magazine, as was her practice, and instead withheld it to appear first as the title story of a new collection of her work. Her reasons for this strategy she explained in a letter to her dearest friend, Annie Fields: "Mr. Howells thinks that this age frowns upon the romantic, that it is no use to write romance any more; but dear me, how much of it there is left in every-day life after all. It must be the fault of the writers that such writing is dull, but what shall I do with my "White Heron" now she is written? She isn't a very good magazine story, but I love her, and I mean to keep her for the beginning of my next book. . . ."[2]

Despite its admitted romanticism, "A White Heron" reflects some of the tough-minded independence that Sarah Jewett had developed from childhood and displayed particularly in the years following her father's death. The story dates from the end of that transitional period in her life when she was transferring her deepest human affection from her deceased father to Annie Fields, widow of the publisher James T. Fields. Dr. Theodore Herman Jewett, after whom his daughter had been named Theodora Sarah Orne, died in 1878, causing her first deep sorrow, "and soon after began the correspondence," "a diary in truth,"[3] with Mrs. Fields. After her husband died in 1881, Annie Fields's friendship with Sarah Jewett grew intimate: "the two women were absorbed into a union that endured as long as their lives."[4] Though fifteen years older than Sarah Jewett (1849–1909), Annie Fields (1834–1915) shared with her, among other things, a similar relationship to the most important

*Reprinted from the *Colby Library Quarterly*, 18 (1982), 55–65, with the permission of the author.

man in each woman's life: James T. Fields (1817–1881) was, after all, born only two years after Theodore Herman Jewett (1815–1878); Annie had been a teen-aged bride, her husband a man practically old enough to be her father. Thus when both women suffered, within the span of three years, the loss of the older man to whom each was emotionally committed, the fruition of their own attachment became natural and inevitable. And one of the significant fruits of that union was the volume to which "A White Heron" gave its title.[5]

This volume marked "the first time [Jewett] far transcended 'Deephaven,'"[6] her first, very successful, published book. Earlier, however, Jewett had dedicated *The Mate of the Daylight* (1883), her fourth collection of stories, to Annie Fields, with whom she had made an extended tour of Europe in 1882. And then, in *A Country Doctor* (1884), Jewett had given a fictionalized account of her life with her father. This book is usually cited for its early descriptions of the delighted company little Nan Prince, Jewett's alter ego, keeps with Dr. Leslie, her guardian, the same sort of pleasurable companionship that little Sarah had known with Dr. Jewett. But more important for understanding the course of Jewett's life and art are the final two chapters. In the first of these the now grown-up Nan rejects the marriage proposal of the attractive young lawyer George Gerry in order to pursue singlemindedly her plan of being a doctor. For "she had long ago made up her mind that she must not marry. . . . It would be no real love for another person, and no justice to herself, to give up her work, even though holding it fast would bring weariness and pain and reproach, and the loss of many things that other women held dearest and best."[7] In Jewett's own case, though she had once considered becoming a doctor, "her work" was writing, and the firm resolve to stay unmarried was clearly autobiographical.

In the final chapter of *A Country Doctor* Jewett offers, through the thoughts of the understanding Dr. Leslie, a sensitive, reasoned defense of a woman's right to choose both to pursue a career and to remain free from wedlock. Dr. Leslie is allowed to perceive what Jewett had perceived about herself, that some women "are set apart by nature for other uses and conditions than marriage."[8] Jewett was set apart by nature to be a writer and to be the companion of first her father and then another woman. In the three or four years prior to writing "A White Heron," then, she had secured her union with Annie Fields, had paid homage to her late father, and had openly declared, for anyone willing to read *A Country Doctor* plainly, her independence from matrimony.

It was against this background that Jewett wrote "A White Heron." As its main character she chose a nine-year-old girl very like herself at that age and equally like little Nan Prince, of *A Country Doctor*, though children are rare in her fiction, which mainly concerns old people. "This lonely country child" (p. 171)[9] Jewett named Sylvia, in reference to the girl's affinity for the forest. Like little Sarah and little Nan, "this little woods-girl" (p. 163) is at home among the trees and animal life of the "New England wilderness" (p. 164). Describing herself as a child, Jewett once wrote Whittier that in "the country out of which I grew, . . . every bush and tree seem like my cousins."[10] And Annie Fields called her friend "a true lover of nature and . . . one accustomed to tender communings with woods and streams, with the garden and the bright air."[11] In a similar vein, Dr. Leslie says of Nan Prince that "she has grown up as naturally as a plant grows, not having been clipped back or forced in any unnatural direction."[12] Sylvia, then, clearly descends from Jewett and the autobiographical Nan Prince.

Also like Nan, Sylvia, through family misfortune, has come to live with her grandmother; Nan, based more explicitly on Sarah Jewett, soon proceeds to live with a doctor, her guardian Dr. Leslie. But for Sylvia it's crucial that she be isolate on her grandmother's farm, with no males about, because the conflict in this story occurs with the sudden, unexpected arrival of the ornithologist. The farmhouse is "lonely" (p. 162)[13] and Sylvia's only "companion" is a prankish milch cow: "a plodding, dilatory, provoking creature in her behavior, but a valued companion for all that" (p. 161). Thus with an economy of detail that F. O. Matthiessen found new to her work in A White Heron and Other Stories,[14] Jewett establishes the aloneness of her heroine.

Though alone—"the child had no playmates" (p. 161)—Sylvia is not lonesome; indeed she is incomparably happier in the country than she was during the first eight years of her life, spent "in a crowded manufacturing town" (p. 162). Released in the environs of the farm, Sylvia seems almost mythically at home: "there never was such a child for straying about out-of-doors since the world was made!" (p. 162), thinks her grandmother. And "as for Sylvia herself, it seemed as if she never had been alive at all before she came to live at the farm" (p. 162). The key to her vivacity is that she is utterly in harmony with nature. As her grandmother tells the ornithologist, "There ain't a foot o' ground she don't know her way over, and the wild creatur's counts her one o' themselves" (pp. 164–65).

The town-country antithesis indicated by the contrast between Sylvia's earlier life in "the noisy town" (p. 163) and her previous year on the "beautiful" (p. 162) farm introduces part of the underlying dialectic of this story. Its next increment appears in the ornithologist, whose presence Sylvia first becomes aware of through his whistle: "suddenly this little woods-girl is horror-stricken to hear a clear whistle not very far away. Not a bird's whistle, which would have a sort of friendliness, but a boy's whistle, determined, and somewhat aggressive" (p. 163). Jewett underscores the intrusion of this foreign sound into Sylvia's world by shifting, in these two sentences, into the present tense, a device she will use significantly twice more in the story. The comparison be-

tween a bird's whistle and a boy's helps to emphasize the antithesis between the forest creatures with whom Sylvia is friendly and "the great
red-faced boy who used to chase and frighten her" (p. 163) in her home-
town, about whom she has been thinking uneasily just before she hears
the whistle. Thus when Jewett first introduces the ornithologist himself, she labels him "the enemy" and Sylvia responds "trembling,"
"alarmed," "awed" (p. 163). There seems, then, to be something
threatening in his very "boyness" that makes Sylvia fearful and that
perhaps psychologically predisposes her to reject him in the climax. Her
awe of the ornithologist may in part be caused by his being the first
grown-up boy she has seen in her woodland isolation. When he first appears to the girl she is practically unable to speak, and "she did not dare
to look boldly at the tall young man, who carried a gun over his shoulder..." (p. 163). A gun, to paraphrase Freud, is sometimes only a
gun, but in "A White Heron" the ornithologist's weapon may be a symbolic as well as a real threat. Later, her initial fear of him having abated,
"Sylvia would have liked him vastly better without his gun..." (p.
166), for whether deadly weapon or symbolic phallus, his hunting piece
makes her uncomfortable.[15]

No description of "the tall young man" (p. 163) or his dress is given;
he is simply identified by the accoutrements of his profession, a gun and
a game-bag heavy with the birds he has killed and collected. Mainly, the
ornithologist is characterized by his voice. Toward Sylvia, whom he
hails as "little girl" (p. 163), he adopts the superior tone of one older,
more cosmopolitan, and maler, but he also speaks to her "kindly" and
"gallantly" (p. 163), trying to calm her fears and win her assistance. By
the time he has supped, the recipient of the grandmother's hospitality,
the young man and his hosts have become "new-made friends" (p. 164).
Yet we sense exploitation in the relationship: in exchange for supper and
lodging, the guest provides merely the entertainment of a stranger to the
isolated and his charm, while all the time plotting to use his hosts in his
quest to collect the white heron.

That Jewett sees the ornithologist as an outsider inimical to the farmstead is illustrated by Mrs. Tilley the grandmother's reference to her son
Dan, who "was a great hand to go gunning" (p. 164), but who hunted
only for food. By contrast, her guest goes gunning in the interest of an
abstraction, the science of ornithology, and of his egoistic desire to complete his bird collection. He self-importantly tells Mrs. Tilley, "I am
making a collection of birds myself. I have been at it ever since I was a
boy." Then in response to her question whether he cages them, he says,
"Oh, no, they're stuffed and preserved, dozens and dozens of them,...
and I have shot or snared every one myself" (p. 165). His pride in his
expertise allies him with those characters in Hawthorne who have sacri-
ficed warm humanity on the chill altar of science; but Jewett's ornithologist is less evil than banal, for his cheery egoism reflects the optimism

of the nineteenth-century despoilers of nature who deforested the woods where she grew up.

In his overriding self-interest the young man adds to the story's dialectic the contrast between the egoist and the altruist, a conflict often dramatized by W. D. Howells, Jewett's mentor. Thus, in response to the stranger's plea for lodging, Mrs. Tilley immediately and altruistically proffers her hospitality, saying, "You're welcome to what we've got. I'll milk right off, and you make yourself at home" (p. 164). Furthermore, she and her granddaughter live with the kind of modest self-sufficiency that Howells's Silas Lapham, bankrupt after his fall, gratefully settles for on his Vermont farm. Mrs. Tilley's housekeeping Jewett characterizes as "the best thrift of an old-fashioned farmstead" (p. 164). The author here salutes the homely economy of her own girlhood, even then "a fashion of life already on the wane, . . . that subsistence on sea and forest which was already a forgotten thing in New England when she was grown."[16]

During the ornithologist's conversation with his aged hostess, he listens insensitively yet selectively: he "did not notice [the] hint of family sorrows [in Mrs. Tilley's discourse] in his eager interest in something else" (p. 165), but he grasps alertly the useful information that Sylvy knows all about birds. And at this point he brings up a white heron he has spotted and pursued to the vicinity of the farm. He calls the bird a little white heron, a species unknown to that area. In ornithological fact, such a bird was never more than a casual visitor as far north as southern Maine. It is usually known as the snowy egret, but also as the little white egret and the snowy heron, among several other names. Around the time Jewett wrote her story the snowy egret was being extirpated to fill the need of the millinery industry. By 1900 it was almost extinct, and in 1913 it was completely protected by the federal government.[17] Thus its rareness may have prompted Jewett to select the little white heron for her story in order to give her bird unusual value. In addition, she depicts the creature as odd: the ornithologist describes it as "a queer tall bird," and Sylvia instantly knows it as "that strange white bird" (p. 165). Strangeness and whiteness in a wild creature recall Moby Dick. Does Jewett hope to probe the skies with her bird as Melville tries to sound the depths with his whale? On her decidedly smaller scale, "A White Heron" does involve a hunt that focuses on a white prey valuable for both material and symbolic reasons and that causes a conflict in values between its pursuers such as we find in *Moby Dick or, The White Whale*. Of course, the ornithologist is no Ahab, Sylvia no Starbuck; but saving the white heron is the rough equivalent of Starbuck's humane policy's winning out in *Moby Dick*.

In order to induce Sylvia to lead him to the sought-after bird, the ornithologist offers a reward of ten dollars. In the moral and dialectical scheme of the story, this offer amounts to a bribe of the poor by the rich, the seduction of good by evil. Its impact on the girl is so great that "no amount of thought, that night, could decide how many wished-for treasures the ten dollars, so lightly spoken of, could buy" (p. 166). By offering to pay for a favor that would otherwise be done as but a gesture of country hospitality, the ornithologist introduces into a subsistence economy the instrumentality of money. Perhaps no other element of his determination to secure the heron as a specimen more bespeaks his alien presence at the farm and suggests the possibility of corruption from without than his proffer of the ten dollars. Thus at the climax Sylvia, dearly tempted to please the young man, reasons, "He can make them rich with money; he has promised it, and they are poor now" (p. 170). Despite his attractive qualities, there is something insidious about his attempt to bribe the girl in effect to betray her world. Yes, he represents the broader, more cosmopolitan world beyond the New England wilderness, the man of science and technique, and the rich, in contradistinction to the poor but homely people on the farmstead. But he also suggests a sort of blithe Satan tempting a naïve Eve to eat of the fruit of the Tree of Knowledge. From this point of view the Maine woods parallels the Garden of Eden, and the early label of "the enemy"[18] for the ornithologist becomes recognizable as a traditional term for Satan.

It should also be noted that the introduction of money into the story has the effect of interfering with Sylvia's instinctive harmony with the natural world. As the ornithologist tells of his quest for the heron, the girl has been watching a hop-toad and disguising her recognition of the white bird he has referred to. But after the ten dollars has been mentioned, "Sylvia still watched the toad, not divining, *as she might have done at some calmer time*, that the creature wishes to get to its hole under the doorstep, and was much hindered by the unusual spectators at that hour in the evening" (p. 166; my emphasis). Her mind on the "treasures" his money could buy, she loses her usual sympathy for the wild.

The next day, however, Sylvia is tempted less by the young sportsman's money than by his masculine appeal. Though he "hovered about the woods" like the bird of prey he speculates may have chased the heron out of its home region, Sylvia finds him "friendly," "most kind and sympathetic" (p. 166). In a gesture with possible phallic significance, "he gave her a jack-knife, which she thought as great a treasure as if she were a desert-islander" (p. 166), though the gift also has the aspect of a trinket for the natives. Despite her discomfort over his gun and the birds he brings down with it, "Sylvia still watched the young man with loving admiration. She had never seen anybody so charming and delightful; the woman's heart, asleep in the child, was vaguely thrilled by a dream of love" (p. 166).[19] If this romantic response seems a strange turn for a story about a nine-year-old to take, it nevertheless has a certain psychological validity. Though originally frightened by her association of the ornithologist with the town boy, Sylvy now sees only the superficial charm and attractiveness of the young sportsman; he also impresses her with his knowledge of birds, though this is not so great as to lead him to perceive that they should be preserved, not collected.[20] Moreover, many a nine-year-old girl feels attracted to or develops a crush on an older boy or a man, especially one who might drop unique from the sky like our ornithologist *ex machina*. If the young girl has no one to warn her of the possible consequent dangers, she is quite liable to go on, as Sylvia does, in a kind of thrall to him. At this point Jewett's alliterative style enhances the romantic aura of the situation: "Some premonition of that great power [love] stirred and swayed these young foresters who traversed the solemn woodlands with soft-footed silent care" (pp. 166–67)—a twenty-one word sentence containing twelve sibilants, including six initial *s*'s.

True to the roles that age and gender have assigned them, the young man leads the way and the girl follows. In other words, even though she knows these woods better than he, expertise leads instinct, male leads female. Nevertheless, Sylvia's feelings are ambivalent: "She grieved because the longed-for white heron was elusive, but she did not lead the guest, she only followed, and there was no such thing as speaking first" (p. 167). In this sentence Jewett implies that if the girl would, she could take the lead; she could speak up and say she's seen the heron and will show the way to it. But her socialization as a girl, ironically, saves her from revealing the bird and therefore betraying her world to this intruder. For if Sylvia were a boy or if the element of romantic attraction were eliminated, she could quite readily speak up and take the lead.

Given the situation as it is, however, Sylvia feels extraordinary tension: "The sound of her own unquestioned voice would have terrified her—it was hard enough to answer yes or no when there was need of that" (p. 167). The tone has now, within the space of a few sentences, shifted from sensuously romantic to threateningly gothic. What does "her own unquestioned voice" mean? That she has not been asked a question that would allow her to voice a response? Or that she herself daren't make a sound without questioning her motivation? In any case, this sentence depicts a girl in peril. This is also the climax of the first part of the story, which ends a sentence later in a tone of pastoral serenity as Sylvy and the sportsman drive home the cow together, and the "pleasure" (p. 162) that she felt the previous evening over listening to the thrushes is replaced by the "pleasure" of coming "to the place where she heard the whistle and was afraid only the night before" (p. 167). A day's outing has thus brought the girl closer in sympathy to the young man than to the natural world.

Part 2 of "A White Heron" relates Sylvia's quest for the sought-after bird and focuses on a giant pine tree, "the last of its generation" (p. 167) to remain standing in the wake of the woodchoppers. No doubt the tree is based on Jewett's memory of a childhood favorite of hers that did not survive the lumbermen, and about which she wrote to Annie Fields, "Alas, when I went to see my beloved big pitch-pine tree that I loved best of all the wild trees that lived in Berwick, I found only the broad stump of it beside the spring, and the top boughs of it scattered far and wide. It was a real affliction. . . ."[21] The "excitement" (p. 167) that Sylvia felt while walking behind the ornithologist the previous day has been superseded by "a new excitement" as she thinks of climbing the tree to enable her to "see all the world, and easily discover whence the white heron flew, and mark the place, and find the hidden nest" (p. 167).[22]

At this point in the story the narrator formulates its crux: "Alas, if the great wave of human interest which flooded for the first time this dull life should sweep away the satisfactions of an existence heart to heart with nature and the dumb life of the forest!" (p. 168). This didactic rendering of the threat to Sylvia's innocence is both condescending and supererogatory. To call the girl's romantic excitement over the young sportsman a "great wave of human interest" generalizes and diminishes what has earlier been "a dream of love" (p. 166); to speak of her "dull little life" unnecessarily belittles the charming, if not charmed, existence that has earlier been characterized as making Sylvia feel "as if she had never been alive at all before she came to live at the farm" (p. 162). Still, this authorial intrusion does express nicely the substance of Sylvia's quiet strength: living "heart to heart with nature." It is this wholly integrated existence that the ornithologist, and all that he represents, ultimately threatens. We have seen how the lure of his money put Sylvia out of sympathy with the hop-toad. Now, as she climbs the great pine tree at dawn, she disturbs a bird in its nest, and a red squirrel scolds her; she has become a "harmless housebreaker" (p. 168) to the very creatures among whom she'd walked at the beginning of the story "as if she were a part of the gray shadows and the moving leaves" (p. 162) of the forest. But the "little birds and beasts" were then "in the great boughs overhead' (p. 162), and Sylvia was on the ground. Once she is aloft in the pine tree, "the sharp dry twigs caught and held her and scratched her like angry talons, the pitch made her little fingers clumsy and stiff" (p. 168), as though nature itself sought to keep her from succeeding in her project and thereby breaching their heart-to-heart relationship.

The higher Sylvia climbs, however, the more her harmony with nature seems restored. Jewett personifies the great tree as in a fairy tale: "The old pine tree must have loved his new dependent" (p. 169), supporting and lifting her along the way to his summit. Purified in the heights she has reached, Sylvia becomes metaphorically at one with the universe: her face is "like a pale star," and she feels "as if she . . . could go flying among the clouds" (p. 169) with a pair of hawks. Despite the wonder of the view from atop the tree, the girl resolutely wants to discover the white heron's nest: "was this wonderful sight and pageant of the world the only reward for having climbed to such a giddy height?" (p. 169). Would she who has lived so contentedly in the natural world have thought about a "reward" previous to the ornithologist's offer of ten dollars? At this point the narrator shifts into the imperative mood and the present tense, pointing out to Sylvia the white heron rising in flight from a dead hemlock far below, directing her to remain motionless and unconscious lest she reveal herself and deflect the bird from reaching the perch he assumes on a pine bough close to her. "Well satisfied" by knowing the secret of the heron's nesting place, Sylvia painfully "makes her perilous way down again" (p. 170), filled with thoughts of the ornithologist's response to her news of the bird's location.

The present tense works well to create a sense of immediacy and heighten the drama of Sylvia's discovery. In contrast, back at the farm her grandmother and the guest awake in the past tense, removed in time, place, and sense of wonder from the girl's experience. But as she enters their presence, with the young man determined that she tell what she knows of the heron, Jewett once more shifts into the present tense: "Here she comes now, paler than ever, and her worn old frock is torn and tattered, and smeared with pine pitch" (p. 170). "Paler," she approximates the whiteness of the heron, while the pitiful condition of her frock emphasizes her poverty and her need of the ten dollars; "smeared with pine pitch," she wears the shameful sign of her enterprise to find the bird but also the badge of her identity as a "dependent" of the tree. The shift in tense here increases the suspense at the climactic moment, "the splendid moment [that] has come to speak of the dead hemlock-tree . . ." (p. 170). In this instant Sylvia balances the desire to earn the ten dollars and to please the attractive stranger against her unspoken fidelity to nature. As Jewett formulates it, "Has she been nine years growing, and now, when the great world for the first time puts out a hand to her, must she thrust it aside for a bird's sake?" (pp. 170–71). But how can "the great world" that the ornithologist represents compensate her for the world that she has seen from atop the pine tree, a world in which she recalls having achieved a union, with the white heron as it "came flying through the golden air and . . . *they* watched the sea and the morning *together*" (p. 171; my emphasis)? Her heart stirred for a bird, "Sylvia cannot speak; she cannot tell the heron's secret and give its life away" (p. 171).

Most readers will find that "A White Heron" would better end here. They will regret the didactic final paragraph, with its apostrophes, its needless question, and its mixed tone. But it also contains some pertinent material. In its first sentence Jewett addresses Sylvia as "Dear loyalty" and rather satirically suggests that, had things been otherwise with the guest, "she could have served and followed him and loved him as a

dog loves" (p. 171).[23] Though Sylvy has earlier followed the ornithologist in the woods, Jewett's principled opposition to such subservience,
as expressed in *A Country Doctor*, makes it clear that no heroine of hers
could be allowed such a fate. The final paragraph also contains this
vivid picture of the fate that would have awaited the white heron had
Sylvia revealed its nest to the collector: "the sharp report of his gun and
the piteous sight of thrushes and sparrows dropping silent to the ground,
their songs hushed and their pretty feathers stained and wet with
blood" (p. 171).

As the story concludes, all woodland and summertime secrets are,
like the heron's, safe with "this lonely country child" (p. 171). For in the
end the heron's life has become the equivalent of the girl's life, at least
of her existence heart to heart with nature. In addition, the heron signi-
fies the solemnity and beauty of the natural world that human beings
relinquish at the cost of impoverishing their existence. For Sylvia, to surrender the bird would be to surrender her integrity with the natural
world as well as with herself, since the heron has come to represent anything precious that a girl might yield for the sake of a man, but only at
her peril. Resistant to masculine allure, and the offer of monetary profit, Sylvia, can grow into a woman like Nan Prince or Sarah Jewett, a
woman committed to values that will allow her to be her natural self
and lead a life heart to heart with her own nature.

Notes

1. Francis Otto Matthiessen, *Sarah Orne Jewett* (Boston: Houghton Mifflin, 1929),
p. 48.

2. *The Letters of Sarah Orne Jewett*, ed. Annie Fields (Boston: Houghton Mifflin,
1911), pp. 59–60.

3. Fields, p. 5.

4. Matthiessen, p. 71.

5. *A White Heron and Other Stories* (Boston: Houghton Mifflin, 1886).

6. Matthiessen, p. 82. *Deephaven* (Boston: Houghton Mifflin, 1877).

7. Sarah Orne Jewett, *A Country Doctor* (Boston: Houghton Mifflin, 1884),
pp. 307–08.

8. Jewett, p. 336.

9. Sarah Orne Jewett, *The Country of the Pointed Firs and Other Stories* (Garden
City, N.Y.: Doubleday Anchor, 1956). Parenthetical references to "A White Heron"
are to this, most readily accessible, edition.

10. Cited in Matthiessen, p. 22.

11. Fields, p. 6.

12. *A Country Doctor*, p. 102.

13. Jewett uses "lonely," as in "this lonely country child" (p. 171), to mean
"solitary," in the sense of Wordsworth. Sylvia is akin to his rural solitary figures.

14. Matthiessen, p. 82.

15. In *A Country Doctor* Nan Prince's suitor George Gerry is introduced as "Friend and Lover," the title of Chapter XIX. But George is so nice and genteel that he poses no phallic threat; Nan's conviction that she should remain unmarried easily carries the day against his gentlemanly proposal.

16. Matthiessen p, 12.

17. John Bull, *Birds of the New York Area* (New York: Dover, 1964), p. 99.

18. In *A Country Doctor* Jewett uses the word "enemy" in describing Nan Prince's fearful reaction to the probability that George Gerry wants to be her lover: "she had been suddenly confronted by a new enemy, a strange power, which seemed so dangerous that she was at first overwhelmed by a sense of her own defenselessness" (p. 299). Since Sylvy is only nine, her fear of "the enemy" is less radical than Nan's. To stave off the threat of George's suit, Nan converts him from prospective lover to friend, thereby deftly desexualizing their relationship: "I will always be your friend," she tells him, "but if I married you I might seem by and by to be your enemy" (p. 325). A neat transference of roles.

19. In this respect "A White Heron" is the forerunner of such stories as Anne Warner's "The New Woman and the Old" (1914) and Flannery O'Connor's "Good Country People" (1955), in which an unmarried woman living alone with her mother is courted by an unsuitable man. The main difference between Jewett's heroine and the other two, of course is their age: Warner's Emily and O'Connor's Hulga are both in their early thirties, women old enough to be vulnerable to a man's romantic entreaties. Make Sylvia eighteen instead of nine, and you have a very different story. Jewett, however, was probably incapable of and uninterested in writing a romance in which libido is an express reality—Matthiessen notes "her inability to portray passion in her books" (*Sarah Orne Jewett*, p. 144); nor would she have been able to call her male intruder Manley Pointer, as O'Connor does, although the name is apt for her unnamed ornithologist with his gun.

20. Even J. J. Audubon, of course, shot birds and mounted them in order better to paint them from close observation. But, then, birds were plentiful in the earlier nineteenth century, and Audubon's paintings brought pleasure to the many who saw them. But compare Thoreau: "As for fowling, during the last years that I carried a gun my excuse was that I was studying ornithology, and sought only new or rare birds. But I confess that I am now inclined to think that there is a finer way of studying ornithology than this. It requires so much close attention to the habits of the birds, that, if for that reason only, I have been willing to omit the gun" ("Higher Laws," *Walden*).

21. Fields, p. 24.

22. Sylvia's excitement as she begins her climb has a sexual resonance: "There was the huge tree asleep yet in the paling moonlight, and small and hopeful Sylvia began with utmost bravery to mount to the top of it, with tingling, eager blood coursing the channels of her whole frame . . ." (p. 168). A Freudian critic might find it tempting to call the great pine tree the largest phallic symbol in American literature.

23. Curiously, Jewett uses the simile of a faithful dog in a positive way to describe young Nan Prince "every day by the doctor's side, . . . following him like a little dog . . ." (*A Country Doctor*, p. 85). This is no doubt the source of Matthiessen's remark that young Sarah Jewett "used to follow her father about silently, like an undemanding little dog, content to be at his side" (*Sarah Orne Jewett*, p. 13).

The Language of Transcendence in Sarah Orne Jewett's "A White Heron"

Gayle L. Smith*

While virtually every modern critic of Sarah Orne Jewett's work is moved to comment on the close connection she depicts between man and nature, few have investigated just how this connection is forged in her language and how it informs the overall effectiveness of her fiction. In "A White Heron" it is especially clear that this connection is but part of a larger, truly transcendental vision uniting man not only with green nature but with animal life as well, the past with the present, and one human sensibility with another.

Richard Cary, speaking of Jewett's work in general, observes her thematic use of nature, her use of analogy and symbol, and adds that she "does not hesitate to commit the pathetic fallacy when she wishes to emphasize the oneness of man and nature."[1] Robin Magowan, speaking primarily about *The Country of the Pointed Firs*, sees a strong link between Jewett's work and the pastoral tradition in which nature figures as "a transparent medium, a psychic mirror reflecting a one-to-one correspondence between the person and the setting in which he is imaged."[2] This critic goes on to observe Jewett's "knack of placing, situating her objects in relation to the total background or world that they evoke in such a manner that their situation will carry a maximum of symbolic suggestion within the narrative frame."[3] Robert Rhode goes further still, stating that "man and environment merge," the people becoming "immersed into" landscape and the settings becoming "vitalized by a vague sense of humanity." He notes too that this personification is "often exercised at the subliminal level."[4] He defends her use of personification as more than the product of "figurative speech" and cites references in "A Winter Drive" to "Hylozoism, which appeals to my far from Pagan sympathies ... the doctrine that life and matter are inseparable."[5] While Rhode fails to distinguish clearly between the voice of the writer herself and of her created persona and seems not to note the qualification in the passage itself, he is accurate in observing that such expressions are indeed part of a world view and not mere accidents or embellishments. In a fine article on *The Country of the Pointed Firs*, Michael Vella connects such unions with the theme of the work, showing how "a unity of vision . . . reached through simile, allusion, and descriptive detail bordering on the inherently metaphoric" functions as a kind of index to the narrator's growing ability to comprehend the profound unity of life revealed by Dunnet Landing culture.[6] Vella too defends the narrator's habit of seeing correspondences between individ-

*Reprinted from the *Colby Library Quarterly*, 19 (1983), 37–44, with the permission of the author.

uals and various plants as more than "quaint literary technique," as part of the transcendental vision the narrator gains during her summer stay.[7]

Jewett's transcendental, even mystical, vision of reality is at least as important to the theme of "A White Heron" as it is to the theme of *The Country of the Pointed Firs*, and it is crucially important to the structure of the story. A closer look at Jewett's linguistic choices reveals an underlying strategy for the rich variety of ways in which she projects her vision. The surprising correspondences and unities she forges between plant, animal, and human life, between past and present, and between the consciousnesses of different human beings, are basic to the dilemma of the tale. Briefly, Sylvia, the nine-year-old heroine who lives in the country with her grandmother and an assortment of wild and tame animals, is tempted by an engaging young man to tell him where the white heron nests that he might shoot and stuff the bird, a particularly coveted specimen. When the time comes to tell the secret she has worked hard to learn, "Sylvia cannot speak; she cannot tell the heron's secret and give its life away."[8] Jewett's narrator refrains from explicitly applauding or criticizing the girl's decision and makes it clear that long afterward Sylvia misses the handsome young man; perhaps she has lost her one opportunity to experience love in the wider world.

Do most of us feel that Sylvy has done the right thing simply because of our preconceptions? Richard Brenzo argues that between being a "free heron" and a "dead sparrow," which is what Sylvy would symbolically become, "allow[ing] herself to be caught, raped, killed, stuffed, and put on display in a man's house," Sylvy makes the only choice that can preserve her independence and integrity.[9] In addition to this, however, Jewett's linguistic choices, even before the entrance of the young hunter, who is also described as "most kind and sympathetic," argue a great oneness between human and non-human life that powerfully affirms the girl's choice, whatever sacrifices we may suspect it involves (p. 12). Jewett's position is radical, as radical as Emerson's when he declares in *Nature*, "The greatest delight which the fields and woods minister, is the suggestion of an occult relation between man and the vegetable. I am not alone and unacknowledged. They nod to me and I to them."[10] Were she to make such a bold assertion early in the story, she would probably lose any reader demanding a sense of realism. In fact, there are several statements entirely comparable to Emerson's in the story, statements such as "the tree stood still and frowned away the winds," but Jewett builds up to them with a subtlety that deserves our attention (p. 17).

Jewett begins to build her world of equals in the very first paragraph of the story as we are urged to consider animals our equals. It is no surprise to find a cow described as a "plodding, dilatory, provoking creature in her behavior," but it may come as a small surprise to find her called "a valued companion for all that," since "companion" usually refers to another human being (p. 1). The gulf narrows again, in the very next sentence, when the narrator says, "They were going away from whatever light there was," and refers to "their eyes" and "their feet" (p. 1). While the plural pronouns cannot be said to be deviant, they do encourage the reader to think of the girl and the cow as a pair now. Our linguistic awareness that the sentence could just as easily refer to a pair of equals probably helps us to impute some of that equality to these two. Such instances, taken collectively, create the "subliminal" effect observed but unexplained by Rhode.

In the next paragraph we learn that it is the cow's "greatest pleasure to hide herself away among the huckleberry bushes," displaying a sense of play we usually associate primarily with human intelligence (p. 1). At this point we learn the girl's emblematic name, Sylvia. We learn the cow's name, Mistress Mooly, just before we learn Sylvia's grandmother's, Mrs. Tilley, and the similarity between the names makes for a humorous connection between them. Perhaps it is precisely because the reader need not take the connection too seriously at this point that it does indeed register. Nor is it long before we learn of Sylvia's attachment to green nature. It seems to Sylvia "as if she never had been alive at all before she came to live at the farm. She thought often with wistful compassion of a wretched geranium that belonged to a town neighbor" (p. 3). Jewett's simple juxtaposition of the girl's thoughts suggests the deeper connection between human and plant life as does the word "compassion," normally reserved for human or animal objects. In these opening paragraphs we are gently led to accept the idea that there is more that unites human and non-human sensibilities than divides them. We have yet to learn what this means in terms of choices and loyalties.

Sylvia and the cow are now simply "the companions," a phrase that might have seemed considerably stranger had we not been prepared for it by less forthright assertions (p. 4). Having brought one union to this degree of stability and simplicity, it is as though Jewett steps back and begins to work on effecting another, even more crucial to the plot of the story. In beginning over, she assumes a more tentative and therefore acceptable voice. When she speaks of "little birds and beasts that seemed to be wide awake, and going about their world, or else saying good-night to each other in sleepy twitters," she qualifies their human behavior with a cautious "seemed" (p. 4). The connection is enough for Sylvia, who "herself felt sleepy as she walked along" and is made to "feel as if she were a part of the gray shadows and the moving leaves" (pp. 4–5). The subjunctive mood here keeps the statement plausible and unobtrusive while it hints at a harmony that will prove basic to the tale. A few paragraphs later, not knowing how to respond to the young hunter's questions, she hangs her head "as if the stem of it were broken" (p. 6). Here the subjunctive in no way mutes the fact that here she is indeed spoken of as a plant, a step nearer identification than was her own compassionate thought for the dying geranium.

As the ornithologist takes his place in the story, he too participates in this pattern, though to a lesser degree than Sylvia. We are told that he hopes to find that the white heron is one of Sylvia's "acquaintances," a word that makes his hope sound positively murderous (p. 10). The union enlarges as Sylvia thinks of the sea, "whose great voice could sometimes be heard above the noise of the woods on stormy nights" (p. 11). The choice of the relative clause construction, requiring the use of "whose," normally restricted to use with animate subjects, helps us accept the "voice" of the sea as more than a casual figure of speech, as one more claim that the entire universe possesses what are conventionally regarded as solely "human" characteristics. Before the first section of the action concludes, we learn that the intruder himself fits into this scheme. He is identified with the very creatures he studies and kills as we are told that he "hovered about the woods" (p. 12). He and Sylvia are joined and joined again with the entire animal world when they are referred to as "those young creatures," just after we hear how Sylvy is afraid of him only when he brings down "some unsuspecting singing creature from its bough" (p. 13, p. 12). The fact that Jewett's language links the hunter himself with all of nature is crucial. Were Sylvy alone so described, we could see her as a rare case; as it is, we must admit a much broader vision to be implied by her linguistic pattern.

In the second section of the story, Sylvy searches for the heron's nest, half eager to give the man the information he seeks, and finally keeps that knowledge to herself. The narrator seems to pose the choice in starkly contrary terms: "Alas, if the great wave of human interest which flooded for the first time this dull little life should sweep away the satisfactions of an existence heart to heart with nature and the dumb life of the forest!" (p. 15). At this point, however, the polarization between human values and nature is already proving to be an over-simplification. We have already met "the great pine-tree" Sylvy will climb to locate the heron's nest and learned that it is "the last of its generation" and that its "mates" have been felled long ago (p. 14). The tree is "asleep yet" when Sylvy begins to climb the tree next to it with feet and fingers "that pinched and held like bird's claws" (p. 16). The tree's twigs "caught and held her and scratched her like angry talons," suggesting now that both she and the tree are bird-like (pp. 16–17). This similarity will outweigh all others.

Jewett now takes her thesis a step further and has her narrator speak of the tree itself in decidedly human terms. Within a rather remarkable paragraph in which the tree is the focusing sensibility, we see Jewett making progressively more surprising statements. She tempers the agent status assigned to the tree with a "seemed" that reminds us that we are reading of Sylvy's impression when she describes how the tree "seemed to lengthen itself out as she went up, and to reach farther and farther upward" (p. 17). It is a different voice, more insistent and irreducible, that we hear in the observation that the tree "must truly have been amazed that morning through all its ponderous frame as it felt this determined spark of human spirit wending its way from higher branch to branch" (p. 17). The tree's role becomes more active, at least by implication, when the narrator asks, "Who knows how steadily the least twigs held themselves to advantage this light, weak creature on her way!" (p. 17). As the tree takes on more and more human characteristics, once again Sylvy is called a "creature." Most surprising perhaps, "The old pine must have loved his new dependent" (p. 17). And in a superhuman effort, the tree "stood still and frowned away the winds" (p. 17). It is testimony to the consistency of the transcendental vision Jewett unfolds throughout the story and the care with which she does so that these passages seem far more reasonable in the context of "A White Heron" than they may here.

Nor has she neglected the dimensions of Sylvy's being through this passage: "More than all the hawks, and bats, and even the sweet voiced thrushes, was the brave, beating heart of the solitary gray-eyed child" (p. 17). While she is distinglished from the creatures named, the basis of comparison assumed and in part created by such a statement is vitally important here. And the evaluation, of course, is that of the amazed, loving, helpful tree. When Sylvia climbs high, she feels "as if she too could go flying away among the clouds" (p. 18). When she spies the heron, the narrator urges her to make no move "for the heron has perched on a pine bough not far beyond yours, and cries back to his mate on the nest and plumes his feathers for the new day!" (p. 19). The economical use of pronouns here reminds us that Sylvia is perching on her bough, a kind of mirror image of the endangered heron. Finally, though urged, tempted, even bribed, Sylvia "remembers how the white heron came flying through the golden air and how they watched the sea and the morning together," and cannot give away the secret (p. 21). Their watching "together" can be so simply mentioned, and seems so natural yet poignant, because it is but a dramatically enriched version of the companionship established earlier with the cow, the sea, the forest, and all the birds of the forest.

An awareness of how this fusing impulse pervades the story helps us to recognize as further manifestations of her transcendental vision structural features sometimes dismissed as flaws. Cary, for instance, questions Jewett's "manipulation of point of view," observing that she "plays several tricks with perspective and violates the detachment of her stance too frequently."[11] As she systematically transcends the usual distinctions between orders of life and sensibility, so she reflects Emerson's assertion that the soul "abolishes time and space."[12] Her use of mixed narrative perspectives and tenses, rather than fragmenting the story, argues the radical oneness she perceives binding persons, feelings, and events together, making a whole that is greater than the sum of its parts.

The first shift, from past to present tense narration, is appropriate in more ways than one:

> She was just thinking how long it seemed since she first came to the farm a year ago, and wondering if everything went on in the noisy town just the same as when she was there; the thought of the great red-faced boy who used to chase and frighten her made her hurry along the path to escape from the shadow of the trees.
>
> Suddenly this little woods-girl is horror-stricken to hear a clear whistle not very far away. Not a bird's whistle, which would have a sort of friendliness, but a boy's whistle, determined, and somewhat aggressive. (p. 5)

In addition to being appropriate to the subject of Sylvy's musing, the passage of time and how it feels to her, this shift to the dramatic present tense can be seen as mimetic, surprising the reader as Sylvy herself is surprised. Moreover, the shift argues the oneness of, or at least the absence of a distinct boundary between, past and present, as does the action, the sudden reappearance of the somewhat threatening figure. The "past" experience is still very present in Sylvy's consciousness and continues to influence this "present" experience.

The narrative continues in the past tense until near the conclusion, where past and present intermingle rather freely. In addition, the narrator turns from a detached and omniscient observer-creator addressing the reader to an involved party, accompanying and even advising Sylvy as she searches for the elusive heron. She leads up to this direct address as she has led up to other departures from our expectations. "Where was the white heron's nest in the sea of green branches, and was this wonderful sight and pageant of the world the only reward for having climbed to such a giddy height?" the narrator asks, leaving open the possibility that she no longer knows what will happen (pp. 18–19). If the tense were merely changed to the present, it could be Sylvy herself asking this question; this question serves as a kind of bridge between the sensibility of the girl and that of the narrator.

Immediately after, as though answering Sylvy's would-be question, the narrator speaks directly to her: "Now look down again, Sylvia . . ." (p. 19). The entire revelation from the treetop continues in the present tense, and even Sylvy's return home, in possession of her secret, is narrated in the present. She concludes this incident with the only fragment of its kind in the story, a form that focuses intensely on Sylvy's mental state: "Wondering over and over again what the stranger would say to her, and what he would think when she told him how to find his way straight to the heron's nest" (p. 20). To say that Sylvy "wonders" or even that she "is wondering" would put stricter bounds on her activity;

the participal fragment suggests the indeterminate nature of her wondering, the fact that it is associated with more than one action, more than one time in the narrative.

After a brief return to the past tense to describe the reactions of her puzzled grandmother and the man who intends to extract the answer from Sylvia: "Here she comes now, paler than ever, and her worn old frock is torn and tattered, and smeared with pine pitch. The grandmother and the sportsman stand in the door together and question her, and the splendid moment has come to speak of the dead hemlock-tree by the green marsh" (p. 20). It is in this "splendid moment" that all culminates, and the present tense conveys its drama and fragility at the same time that, along with the impersonal sounding definite articles modifying "grandmother" and "sportsman," it suggests its eternal, archetypal significance. It is of course memory, memory of experience that is still alive and with her, that prevents Sylvy from accommodating the young man's wishes: "The murmur of the pine's green branches is in her ears, she remembers how the white heron came flying through the golden air and how they watched the sea and the morning together, and Sylvia cannot speak; she cannot tell the heron's secret and give its life away" (p. 21). Both the presence of the "past" and the "human" qualities of the heron prevent her from doing so.

Finally, nature is addressed as just another character or sensibility in the story: "Whatever treasures were lost to her, woodlands and summertime, remember! Bring your gifts and graces and tell your secrets to this lonely country child!" (p. 22). The fact that it has been unfashionable for a long time to address woodlands and summer-time, and ask favors of them, ought not prevent us from recognizing the philosophical and even aesthetic appropriateness of such an apostrophe here. In the context of a story in which persons, sensibilities, and times have been permuted and blended again and again, an address to the forces of nature has a logic and coherence of its own.

Notes

1. Cary, *Sarah Orne Jewett* (New York: Twayne Publishers, 1962), p. 55.

2. Magowan, "Pastoral and the Art of Landscape in *The Country of the Pointed Firs*," *New England Quarterly*, XXXVI (June 1963), rpt. in *Appreciation of Sarah Orne Jewett: 29 Interpretive Essays*, ed. Richard Cary (Waterville, Me.: Colby College Press, 1973), p. 188.

3. Magowan, p. 192.

4. Rhode, "Sarah Orne Jewett and 'The Palpable Present Intimate,'" *Colby Library Quarterly*, VIII (September 1968), rpt. in *Appreciation of Sarah Orne Jewett*, p. 231.

5. Rhode, pp. 234–35.

6. Vella, "Sarah Orne Jewett: A Reading of *The Country of the Pointed Firs*," *ESQ: A Journal of the American Renaissance*, XIX (4th Quarter 1973), 276.

7. Vella, pp. 277 and 280.

8. *A White Heron and Other Stories* (Boston: Houghton Mifflin, 1886), p. 21. Subsequent references to "A White Heron" are to this edition and are cited in the text by page numbers.

9. Brenzo, "Free Heron or Dead Sparrow: Sylvia's Choice in Sarah Orne Jewett's 'A White Heron,'" *Colby Library Quarterly*, XIV (1978), 41.

10. *The Collected Works of Ralph Waldo Emerson*, ed. Alfred R. Ferguson and Robert E. Spiller (Cambridge, Mass.: Belknap of Harvard Univ. Press, 1971), I, 10.

11. Cary, p. 101.

12. *The Complete Works of Ralph Waldo Emerson*, Centenary Edition, ed. Edward Waldo Emerson (Boston: Houghton Mifflin, 1903–04), II, 272.

"Tact is a Kind of Mind-Reading": Empathic Style in Sarah Orne Jewett's *The Country of the Pointed Firs*

Marcia McClintock Folsom*

A chief source of the enduring appeal of Sarah Orne Jewett's *The Country of the Pointed Firs* is its presentation of a world which seems to us touchingly coherent. Unlike the fragmented, incongruous worlds we find in modern literature (and in our own experience), in this work Jewett presents a world which seems mythic in its stability, integration, and consequent warmth. However, the book does not seem sentimental, because of Jewett's unflinching presentation of decay, loss, and imminent death in the coastal Maine town she calls Dunnet Landing. Numerous characters remark that things have been going down-hill there in recent years; Captain Littlepage calls it "a low-water mark here in Dunnet" since the port lost its commercial significance. Irritation, thwarted potential, unresolved grief, eccentricity bordering on madness, are all explicitly part of the book's emotional atmosphere. Nonetheless, the book achieves a poignant elegiac quality while preserving a social and natural world which Jewett plainly felt was lost to her, as certainly we feel it is lost to us.

What is it in Jewett's writing that enables her to offer so convincing a celebration of the coherence of this world, and yet to avoid treating it condescendingly, as quaint, simple, byegone? A pattern in Jewett's management of narrative and dialogue, which can be called "empathic style," partly accounts for her singular achievement of unsentimental celebration of the country of the pointed firs.

*Reprinted from the *Colby Library Quarterly*, 18 (1982), 66–78, with the permission of the author.

The two main characters in *The Country of the Pointed Firs* are women who are able to read nature, the physical world, and the minds of other people. Mrs. Todd and the narrator are both acute observers who habitually penetrate and interpret external facts, and both are able to reconstruct the whole through active interpretation of details. Different in their knowledge of Dunnet Landing, the two women are alike in their impulse to see into and beyond casual conversation, gesture, and expression, or details of houses, weather, and landscape, to identify the larger human significance of each small outer sign.

In her preface to the 1925 edition of Jewett's *Country of the Pointed Firs and Other Stories*, Willa Cather claimed that "sympathy" was the source of Jewett's greatness.[1] If the artist achieves "anything noble, anything enduring," she wrote, "it must be by giving himself absolutely to his material. And this gift of sympathy is his great gift. . . . He fades away into the land and people of his heart, he dies of love only to be born again. The artist spends a life-time in loving the things that haunt him. . . ."[2] This is very perceptive praise of Jewett, despite the masculine pronouns. Cather's idea of the artist "giving himself absolutely to his material" implies that the artist relinquishes a personal point of view in order to enter into the spirit of the other people or even of objects. The clearest illustration of the artist's "fading away into the land and people of his heart" is the way Jewett's anonymous narrator remains nearly invisible while she observes and sees into the world of Dunnet Landing.

In terms similar to Cather's, the narrator of *The Country of the Pointed Firs* describes and praises Mrs. Todd's mother, Mrs. Blackett: "Tact is after all a kind of mind-reading, and my hostess held the golden gift. Sympathy is of the mind as well as the heart. . . . Besides, she had that final, that highest gift of heaven, a perfect self-forgetfulness."[3] This capacity to anticipate and grasp another's feelings which the narrator values in Mrs. Blackett is exactly what distinguishes her own style and approach to Dunnet Landing. Mind-reading requires intelligent curiosity, mental activity, specific knowledge; sympathy depends on thinking as well as feeling. "Self-forgetfulness" allows the narrator freedom to enter other lives even as it denies her full fictional presence in the book.

The counterpart of the narrator's "tact" is Cather's idea that the objects which an artist loves actively "haunt him." This implies a reciprocity of feeling between the artist and a congenial landscape or society, which is repeatedly demonstrated in *Pointed Firs* by the accessibility of the natural and social world to reliable interpretation. The narrator's extraordinary responsiveness to what she sees and hears is the corollary of the expressiveness of the world in Jewett's work. Empathic style is what creates the atmosphere of trust, familiarity, and coherence in this book, as intelligent observers—mainly women—move in a comprehensible world.

In the section called "Green Island," the narrator accompanies Mrs. Todd on a sail to one of the outer islands to visit Mrs. Todd's eighty-six year old mother, Mrs. Blackett. In this trip to Green Island, as in many of the visiting scenes in *Pointed Firs*, isolated people seem to be connected across water and countryside not only because of the web of visits and messages sent and delivered, but because of the tremendous power of empathy which binds distant people to each other and informs them of particulars in lives they do not see.

The chapter opens with the narrator remarking that "One morning, very early, I heard Mrs. Todd in the garden outside my window" (p 34). Noting the "unusual loudness" of Mrs. Todd's remarks to a passerby, the narrator "knew that she wished I would wake up and come and speak to her" (p. 35). The trip to Green Island is thus set in motion by the narrator's perception that Mrs. Todd's loud talking is a signal to her sleeping lodger. "In a few minutes she responded to a morning voice from behind the blinds." The "morning voice" is all the presence the narrator grants to her own sleepy mumble, but it nonetheless represents a fully conscious tactfulness, an awareness of Mrs. Todd's unspoken request.

Without explaining herself, Mrs. Todd remarks despairingly that probably the narrator will be busy all day. Attempting to fathom the purpose behind Mrs. Todd's indirection, the narrator replies with kindly indecision, parenthetically explaining her hunch about Mrs. Todd's intentions:

> "Perhaps not," said I. "Why, what's going to be the matter with you, Mrs. Todd?" For I supposed that she was tempted by the fine weather to take one of her favorite expeditions along shore pastures to gather herbs and simples, and would like to have me keep house.
> "No, I don't want to go nowhere by land," she answered gayly,— "no, not by land; but I don't knows we shall have a better day all the rest of the summer to go out to Green Island an' see mother." (p. 35)

The reader may easily fail to notice here that Mrs. Todd replies to the narrator's thought, to her presumably unstated guess that Mrs. Todd intended to go herb-gathering. But Mrs. Todd reads the narrator's mind— "No, I don't want to go nowhere by land," she says, as if contradicting the narrator's mistaken surmise.

This kind of attention to hints and unspoken conversation is also reflected in both women's facility in reading other signals. As they sail together out to the island, from far off they can see its landscape, and slight details can be interpreted from a distance.

> A long time before we landed at Green Island we could see the small white house, standing high like a beacon. . . . There were crops in the fields, which we presently distinguished from one another. Mrs. Todd examined them while we were still far at sea. "Mother's late

potatoes looks backward; ain't had rain enough so far," she pronounced her opinion. "They look weedier than what they call Front Street down to Cowper Centre. I expect brother William is so occupied with his herrin' weirs an' servin' out bait to the schooners that he don't think once a day of the land." (pp. 37–38)

The image of the beacon calls attention to the house's distinct outline and sharp whiteness against the green, which make it an aid to navigation as well as a house. When the passengers can discern crops growing in the lower field, Mrs. Todd's acute observation proceeds to particulars. She readily distinguishes between potato crops, knows how mature each should be by mid-July, and why the late crop is not as far along as it should be. She also pointedly observes that the potatoes need weeding, and immediately surmises why. Her distant reading of the ragweed in the garden is thus weighted with her usual criticism of what she considers her brother's lack of ambition or "snap."

These prompt translations demonstrate Mrs. Todd's grasp of the human meaning of details of the landscape. The importance of potatoes as a staple to Mrs. Blackett and William comes clear a few pages later, when the narrator is sent out to dig some for lunch. She cannot tarry over the enjoyable job, however, for even as she works she imagines her hostess awaiting her return: "I was sure Mrs. Blackett must be waiting impatiently to slice the potatoes into the chowder, layer after layer, with the fish" (p. 44). The unexpected guests fortunately have foreseen the need and brought along a fresh-caught haddock and an onion.

In this way, Jewett succinctly indicates the power of empathic imagination, in a world without telephones, when families are separated by water as well as distance. Mrs. Todd's bringing along an onion and a fish, and the narrator's concrete image of how the potatoes will be layered into the chowder with the haddock, demonstrate both women's uncanny accuracy in imagining the needs, feelings, and intentions of an absent person. This accuracy is the result of the familiarity of the other's routines, and of an affectionate desire to know and visualize someone else's life, however islanded and far from ordinary communication it may be.

Following Mrs. Todd's reading of the garden from at sea, the narrator notices a pennant waving on Green Island. "What's the flag for, up above the spruces there behind the house?" she asks eagerly (p. 38). Mrs. Todd explains that when her brother has caught enough herring in the weirs to warrant a stop by the larger fishing vessels, he flies the flag. When the catch is poor, the signal is lowered, and then only the small "bo'ts" come in to get bait for their trawls. Dwellers on isolated islands and sea-farers, Jewett shows, must accustom themselves to reading signals from afar and to providing such signals.

Mrs. Todd, who certainly has the sea-farer's keen sensitivity to distant signals, now notices another kind of flag, one whose meaning is less idiosyncratic than William's signal to the fishing boats, but still nearly obscure to the narrator:

> "There, look! there she is: mother sees us; she's wavin' somethin' out o' the fore door! She'll be to the landin' place quicks we are."
> I looked, and could see a tiny flutter in the doorway, but a quicker signal had made its way from the heart on shore to the heart on the sea.
> "How do you suppose she knows it's me?" said Mrs. Todd with a tender smile on her broad face. . . . "Look at the chimney, now; she's gone right in an' brightened up the fire. Well, there, I'm glad mother's well; you'll enjoy seein' her very much." (p. 38)

A "tiny flutter in the doorway" is all we or the narrator can see, but a "quicker signal" is telegraphed between the "heart on shore" and the "heart on the sea." Mrs. Todd's quick discernment and almost telepathic reading of her mother's activity around the distant house informs her that Mrs. Blackett sees the approaching dory, knows who is coming, and will reach the dock as soon as the boat does. When the flutter disappears, Mrs. Todd can interpret its absence as well: Mrs. Blackett will be inside brightening up the fire. Relishing her clairvoyance, Mrs. Todd instructs the narrator to watch the chimney: in a moment, evidence that the fire has been freshened will curl out of the chimney and into the air above the house. These little signs—the flutter at the door, the fresh smoke at the chimney—are open to further interpretation: they prove that "mother's well." Mrs. Todd's ability to grasp a whole situation through intense and active interpretation of a glimpse or a detail indicates her complete familiarity with her world, and also the unbroken wholeness and integrated expressiveness of that world.

The brief chapter "Shell-heap Island" offers a rich instance of the narrator's reconstructing someone else's feelings by actively interpreting a few outer facts. Practically nothing happens in this chapter except the narrator's landing on an empty island where she walks to an old house site. Yet her ability to read the meaning of a visible path and a distant view of the mainland affords her a complete and imaginative understanding of a woman who died nearly twenty-two years before.

In the two chapters just preceding this one, the narrator hears Mrs. Todd and her friend Mrs. Fosdick recount the story of "poor Joanna" who exiled herself to Shell-heap Island after being disappointed in love. These two women work through the story in the narrator's presence, as if trying to sort out together the meaning of Joanna's apparently sad, eccentric life. Mrs. Todd likens Joanna to "one of the saints of the desert," and this image finally organizes the narrator's understanding of Joanna's story. Mrs. Fosdick mentions that Shell-heap Island had a history as a sacred place from before Joanna's exile: "'T was 'counted a great place in old Indian times; you can pick up their stone tools 'most any time if you hunt about. There's a beautiful spring o' water, too. Yes, I remember when they used to tell queer stories about Shell-heap Island. Some said 't was a great bangeing place for the Indians, and an old chief resided there once that ruled the winds" (p. 59).

Out sailing one day, the narrator decides to visit this noted place. Without difficulty, she locates the path to Joanna's grave, and she immediately grasps the significance of its evident use. "I found the path; it was touching to discover that this lonely spot was not without its pilgrims. Later generations will know less and less of Joanna herself, but there are paths trodden to the shrines of solitude the world over,—the world cannot forget them, try as it may; the feet of the young find them out because of curiosity and dim foreboding, while the old bring hearts full of remembrance" (p. 75). The worn path testifies that "pilgrims" still visit this "shrine," and the religious diction connects the recent and remote past with a distant future; "later generations" will still visit this island even if they know little of Joanna.

The narrator walks through the fields, making tame birds flutter up out of the grass, to the place where Joanna's house had stood, finding there only foundation stones and scant trace of the old flower garden. Still, an Edenic atmosphere of undamaged goodwill pervades the hot afternoon. "I drank at the spring, and thought that now and then someone would follow me from the busy, hard-worked, and simple-thoughted countryside of the mainland, which lay dim and dream-like in the August haze, as Joanna must have watched it many a day" (p. 75).

This superbly evocative sentence epitomizes Jewett's empathic style. It begins with concrete action, drinking at the famous spring, an action which is sacramental and also demonstrates the enduring benignity of the island. The narrator's thought moves naturally to other people, future pilgrims who will now and then follow her to this island. She deftly summarizes the contrasting existence most people live over in the "countryside of the mainland": "busy, hard-worked, and simple-thoughted." Theirs are lives of farming, fishing, raising families, falling into bed sleepy and unreflective at night, and the narrator's sympathy fully extends to such lives. Yet she describes them as they appear in the eye of eternity, from the vantage point of the saint in the desert. She glances across the bay to the mainland which seems "dim and dream-like in the August haze," as though from Joanna's hermitage the real world itself seems hazy and unreal. The narrator sees the distant shore "as Joanna must have watched it many a day," and her use of the word "watched" indicates how fully she imagines Joanna's isolation and continuing interest in the world she had left.

Shell-heap Island, like Green Island, like the ghostly northern town in Captain Littlepage's story, like Dunnet Landing itself in some ways, is a "kind of waiting place between this world and the next," a place of melancholy isolation, which yet provides a permanent outlook on ordinary life. Joanna's persistence in living alone with her "poor insistent human nature and the calms and passions of the sea and sky" made her a kind of *sentinelle perdue*, a distant watcher of human life from a transitional place between this world and the next. As the narrator puts it, "there was the world, and here was she with eternity well begun," for eternity began for Joanna years before she died.

The narrator expresses her insight into all the pilgrims to Shell-heap Island in a sentence saturated with memories of Melville's prose: "In the life of each of us, I said to myself, there is a place remote and islanded, and given to endless regret or secret happiness; we are each the uncompanioned hermit and recluse of an hour or a day; we understand our fellows of the cell to whatever age of history they may belong" (p. 75). The empathic perception that in every life there is a "place remote and islanded" places Joanna firmly within the human community, from which she seemed to have been isolated. Confirming this shift in understanding, sounds of distant voices now reach the solitary listener, and instantly she knows how Joanna felt when she heard the same.

> But as I stood alone on the island, in the sea-breeze, suddenly there came a sound of distant voices; gay voices and laughter from a pleasure-boat that was going sea-ward full of boys and girls. I knew, as if she had told me, that poor Joanna must have heard the like on many and many a summer afternoon, and must have welcomed the good cheer in spite of hopelessness and winter weather, and all the sorrow and disappointment in the world. (p. 75)

Alone on the island as Joanna had been, the narrator experiences Joanna's life from inside Joanna's perspective, for her imagination fully penetrates the heart of the solitary, and she realizes that Joanna could hear, receive, and welcome distant voices which reminded her of her unrenounceable fellowship in the human world. The impulse which drove Joanna to Shell-heap Island is akin to the impulse which brings the narrator there, the same impulse for all the pilgrims and the Indians before them; Shell-heap Island satisfies a common human longing for a place of solitude, a detached vantage point from which to look at ordinary life.

The chapter "Along Shore" offers the richest and most compounded instances of empathic dialogue and narration in *Pointed Firs*. The chapter concerns the narrator's discovery of the emotional self of an apparently wooden old fisherman, a coastal Maine "character," whose silent preoccupation with boats and nets and fish makes him appear inaccessible, inexpressive. Yet this very appearance of woodenness and elemental silence has made the narrator speculate about what human feelings might lie within: "I often wondered a great deal about the inner life and thought of these self-contained old fishermen."

Her chance to find out comes when she walks along shore one day, and one of the ancient fishermen, Mr. Elijah Tilley, emerges "softly out of his dark fish house, as if it were a burrow."

> Elijah Tilley was such an evasive, discouraged-looking person, heavy-headed, and stooping so that one could never look him in the face, that even after his friendly exclamation . . . I did not venture at once to speak again. Mr. Tilley was carrying a small haddock in one hand, and presently shifted it to the other hand lest it might touch my skirt. I knew that my company was accepted, and we walked together a little way. (p. 103)

The fisherman's adjustment of moving the haddock from one hand to the other suggests that he wishes to make it easy for the two to walk together, and the narrator, ever sensitive to such hints, finds that she has suddenly "come into a smooth little harbor of friendship." Tilley invites the narrator to visit him, she accepts, and then looks keenly at the old fisherman, whom she knows to be a widower. "There was a new patch high on the shoulder of his old waistcoat, . . . and I wondered if his own fingers, clumsy with much deep-sea fishing, had set it in" (p. 103).

The habit of precise observation and active interpretation yields remarkable insight here. The narrator seems to see through the patch on the fisherman's jacket into an imaginative creation of the scene when his work-worn fingers fumble with needle and thread by lamplight. Her desire to penetrate the fisherman's brusqueness and leathery exterior leads the narrator to seize upon a detail of his appearance which must have a history of effort and activity. Later in this same day, she visits Tilley's house, and she finds him knitting a sock—almost as though her mental image of the man at home sewing on a patch is corroborated by finding him at home knitting.

The narrator's visit with Elijah Tilley is punctuated by his elegiac speeches about his much-loved wife, "poor dear," who died eight years before, and this conversation surpasses all others in the book in its delicacy of mind-reading and empathic listening. The narrator finds a conversational opening by commenting on Tilley's comfortable kitchen: "I ventured to say that somebody must be a very good housekeeper" (p. 105). The old fisherman replies, "that's me," and explains that he keeps everything looking just as "poor dear left 'em." Since he knows so well how she liked things to be, he does all the housekeeping rather than have anyone help him and disturb the order she created. As a result, the kitchen reminds him so much of her that "I get so some days it feels as

if poor dear might step right back into this kitchen. I keep a-watchin'
them doors as if she might step in to ary one. . . . I can't get over losin'
of her no way nor no how" (p. 106).

The old fisherman's grief, his colorful images of his life before and
after poor dear's death, begin to work upon the narrator's imagination:

> The visible tribute of his careful housekeeping, and the clean bright
> room which had once enshrined his wife, and now enshrined her mem-
> ory, was very moving to me; he had no thought for any one else or
> for any other place. I began to see her myself in her home,—a
> delicate-looking, faded little woman, who leaned upon his rough
> strength and affectionate heart, who was always watching for his boat
> out of this very window, and who always opened the door and wel-
> comed him when he came home. (p. 107)

The narrator correctly reads the careful housekeeping as a "visible tribute," and so active is her reading that she actually begins to see the
"delicate-looking, faded little woman." Well can the narrator imagine
what it would have been like for such a woman to watch for the boat
"out of this very window," for she so fully identifies with the waiting
wife that she experiences the interior of the house, the window's outlook
on the water, and the path winding through the field where the fisherman would walk home, as it must have felt to the anxious woman making supper and standing by the door.

> "I used to laugh at her, poor dear," said Elijah, as if he read my
> thought. "I used to make light of her timid notions. She used to be
> fearful when I was out in bad weather or baffled about gettin' ashore.
> She used to say the time seemed long to her, but I've found out all
> about it now." (p. 107)

The narrator's empathic grasp of Mrs. Tilley's point of view is communicated to Elijah, who also experiences the interior from his wife's
vantage point of lonely waiting and anxiety as she stood "right there
watchin' from the door." As if "he read my thought," Tilley turns his
talk to the emotions of the young woman, at whom he used to laugh
for her "timid notions." His poignant statement, "I've found out all
about it now," suggests that their places have been reversed now that he
keeps watching the doors "as if she might step in to ary one": now he
knows what it is to wait for a beloved footstep, to look wistfully to sea
for a boat that doesn't come. Through empathic imagination, the narrator and Elijah are taking part in the inner life of a person who is long
gone, the *young* Mrs. Tilley.

The kitchen seems almost saturated with this reciprocal reading of
feelings between Elijah, the narrator and the absent Mrs. Tilley, when
the fisherman takes the narrator to see the "best room," yet another
moment when the mute details of the domestic interior—and these de-

tails are particularly inert—manage to express a richly emotional human meaning.

> The best room seemed to me a much sadder and more empty place than the kitchen; its conventionalities lacked the simple perfection of the humbler room and failed on the side of poor ambition; it was only when one remembered what patient saving, and what high respect for society in the abstract go to such furnishing that the little parlor was interesting at all. I could imagine the great day of certain purchases, the bewildering shops of the next large town, the aspiring anxious woman, the clumsy sea-tanned man in his best clothes, so eager to be pleased, but at ease only when they were safe back in the sailboat again, going down the bay with their precious freight, the hoarded money all spent and nothing to think of but tiller and sail. I looked at the unworn carpet, the glass vases on the mantle piece with their prim bunches of bleached swamp grass and dusty marsh rosemary, and I could read the history of Mrs. Tilley's best room from its very beginning. (p. 107–8)

The store-bought impersonality of this furniture, the surfaces lacking in patches or hand-work, the "parlor suite" veneer, would seem to defy the narrator's capacity to find a pathway or crack into the meaning behind its appearance. Yet this very quality of dumb, catalogue perfection reminds her of the "patient saving" necessary to make such a purchase. From this reminder springs the richly developed tale of buying such furnishings, complete with a vision of the uncomfortably dressed-up couple sailing to the next large town with their hoarded money and back with their "precious freight." The prim bunches of native grass and wildflower tell all: in them "I could read the history of Mrs. Tilley's best room from its very beginning."

Like the narrator, Elijah finds imperfection easier to read than perfection: in the best room he comes to a shelf which had held a hidden accident. For years, he tells the narrator, he and Mrs. Tilley liked to boast that the set of china he bought in the port of Bordeaux had never had a piece broken, but when women were arranging supper things for Mrs. Tilley's funeral they found a broken cup wrapped in paper and pushed back in a corner of the shelf.

> "Poor dear! I had to put right out o' the house when I see that. I knowed in one minute how 't was. We'd got so used to sayin' 't was all there just's I fetched it home, an' so when she broke that cup somehow or 'nother, she couldn't frame no words to come an' tell me. She couldn't think 't would vex me, 't was her own hurt pride. I guess there wa'n't no other secret ever lay between us." (p. 108)

The poignancy of this interpretation lies in Elijah's complete understanding of his wife's feelings, so the broken china wrapped in paper occasions an instantaneous revelation to him of his wife's unshared regret.

This chapter begins in the outdoors, along the shore, and moves into a richly presented domestic interior; and it begins viewing Elijah Tilley from the outside, whence he appears mute and inexpressive, and moves into a discovery of his inner self, which is surprisingly tender and articulate about his own feelings and those of his wife. Without belaboring the point, Jewett shows that the narrator's habitual empathic curiosity about what lies beneath a mute exterior sometimes yields a world of Vermeer-like color, light, and feeling.

The chapter closes with an effective reversal of mood; after all Elijah's speeches of mourning, Mrs. Todd offers a tart aspersion which allows the reader to admit that he is a bit long-winded. But Mrs. Todd's comments offer another instance of accurate prediction, another version of empathic style. Upon hearing that the narrator has been "visitin' with 'Lijah," she immediately perceives as far as the narrator's initial perception of Tilley: "I expect you had kind of a dull session; he ain't the talkin' kind; dwellin' so much long o' fish seems to make 'em lose the gift o' speech." With typical succinctness, Mrs. Todd sums up the narrator's first impression of Elijah. However, when Mrs. Todd finds out that Tilley "had been talking," she instantly knows what the conversation was about:

> "Then 't was all about his wife, an' he can't say nothin' too pleasant neither [can't exaggerate her goodness]. She was modest with strangers, but there ain't one o' her old friends can ever make up the loss . . . there ain't hardly a day I don't think o' dear Sarah Tilley. She was always right there; yes, you knew just where to find her like a plain flower. 'Lijah's worthy enough; I do esteem 'Lijah, but he's a ploddin' man." (p. 111)

The visit to Elijah's house is an intense instance of empathic style, of experiencing the feelings of apparently mute people (the silent Elijah and his dead wife), and of finding meaning invested in scenes, images, clothing, furniture, windows, doorways, rooms, everyday life. The mournfulness in this episode is the result of the scrapbook quality of the visit, of Elijah's and the narrator's impulse to make the most of every detail, so each fact is an avenue to images of human activity and to memory. The tenderness toward objects and emphasis on the power of imagination, more than the fact of Mrs. Tilley's death, give the chapter its poignancy, for certainly it is possible to imagine treating this kind of scene differently.

A contrary example from a novel by Jane Austen may clarify this point and help illustrate both the strengths of Jewett's empathic style and its natural limitations. Austen's novels are a relevant point of comparison, because she too wrote about knowable, coherent, tightly-knit communities, and because Jewett particularly admired Austen's writing. In a letter to Annie Fields, for example, Jewett wrote, "Yesterday afternoon I amused myself with Miss Austen's 'Persuasion.' Dear me, how like her people are to the people we knew years ago! It is just as much New England before the war—that is, in provincial towns—as it ever was old England."[4] *Persuasion*, with its respect for the Navy and sea farers, and its setting in provincial towns like Lyme and Bath, must have seemed especially congenial to Jewett, and it contains a scene which Jewett may have remembered as she wrote "Along Shore."

In *Persuasion*, Anne Elliot finds herself "placed rather apart" in the company of the bereaved Captain Benwick, whose fiancée, Fanny Harville, died while he was at sea.[5] So placed, "a very good impulse of her nature obliged her to begin an acquaintance with him," for from her own unhappiness she can empathize with his. Here, as in the scene in *Pointed Firs*, a sensitive woman listens to the outpourings of a grieving man (in both cases a mariner). The scenes have some inherent differences: Captain Benwick is a young man, he lost his beloved before they married, and he is eventually reconciled to another wife. Captain Tilley, on the other hand, was married many years and is still inconsolable eight years after his wife's death. Still, the differences in style between these scenes are instructive.

Unlike the apparently uncommunicative Elijah Tilley, Captain Benwick appears from the first ready to speak: "he shewed himself so intimately acquainted with all the tenderest songs of the one poet, and all the impassioned descriptions of hopeless agony of the other; he repeated, with such tremulous feeling, the various lines which imaged a broken heart, or a mind destroyed by wretchedness, and looked so entirely as if he meant to be understood, that she ventured to hope that he did not always read only poetry."[6] It is impossible here not to see Jane Austen smile, indeed, not to hear her laugh.

Instead of giving Benwick's talk in direct discourse, so his suffering would be experienced first-hand, or in plaintive dialect as in the case of Elijah Tilley, Austen *describes* Benwick's speeches, his significant indirection, his lavish quotation from the poetry of hopeless agony. Austen's amusement is directed at his naked ploy for sympathy, at the excesses in the poetry he reads, and probably at the social procedures which keep Benwick from openly mentioning his grief. Her amusement is also directed at Anne Elliot, whose solution to the problem posed by Benwick's affliction (and to the accumulating force of so many incomplete comparisons in one sentence) is to recommend some change in reading matter: "she ventured to hope that he did not always read only poetry." Further, "she ventured to recommend a larger allowance of prose in his daily study."

In *Persuasion*, the narrator is a third party, a spectator to the interaction between Anne Elliot and Captain Benwick, and therefore able to see differences between them, the blind spots of each, and the irony of their similarities. Anne is aware of the irony of her attempt to fortify

Benwick against his pain—she "could not but be amused at the idea of her coming to Lyme to preach patience and resignation," and she reflects that she may have been "eloquent on a point in which her own conduct would ill bear examination"—but she is certainly unaware of the narrator's and reader's amusement at her recommendation that prose be substituted for poetry for effective consolation. The narrator's removal from the action, her position as observer, not only distances her from the characters but also distances the characters from each other.

In Jewett, the narrator is part of the scene, and her impulse to see into Elijah's words, to grasp his feelings and the relationship he is describing, makes her nearly disappear, melt into the two Tilleys and their kitchen. In *Persuasion*, Anne Elliot's attempt to help Benwick grapple with his grief makes the two characters more distinct, more separate. They do not melt together, for they represent two struggling points of view—Anne trying to help Benwick find consolation, and Benwick trying to make her sympathize with him. In this way, empathic style is the opposite of dramatic or ironic style, for the distances between characters are reduced in Jewett when the narrator effaces herself to enter the spirit of other characters.

Two further differences between these scenes emerge, which help define Jewett's achievement. The first is that Austen's construction of the scene where the grief-stricken man is comforted by a perceptive woman implies and indeed assures that future change is possible. The two characters—however slightly—push against each other, represent different points of view, feel each other's pressure. Out of such pressure, action may come, and it does come when another young woman accepts Benwick's melancholy temperament and situation, allowing him to fall in love again. Benwick recovers, and his recovery is instrumental in freeing Frederick Wentworth to propose again to Anne Elliot, retrieving the lost opportunity for which they have paid so dearly. In Jewett, no change is contemplated or even possible. "He had no thought for any one else or any other place." The very completeness of the narrator's identification with Elijah Tilley and his wife precludes any possibility that she may serve as a catalyst for change—she would consider it a travesty to suggest that he change his housekeeping habits or seek a new wife. Empathic style allows full expression to what is, but implies stasis. Ironic style makes future action possible.

But a strength of Jewett's mode is that it allows her to show Tilley and the narrator in the process of recreating Sarah Tilley, bringing her back to life. Fanny Harville is utterly absent from Benwick's grief and Anne's sympathy—she is completely dead and gone. But Sarah Tilley seems to come alive, to haunt her own familiar kitchen, to sail once again to buy new furnishings, to feel pained regret at breaking a piece of the Bordeaux china, to fret by the door for her young husband. You *still* know just where to find her like a plain flower. Thus Jewett's empathic style, though it tends away from action, change, and the future, through the power of imagination can bring the dead to life, preserve forever moments of deep and comprehensible feeling, and make powerful connections across water and time, between the present and a past which only seemed to be irretrievably lost.

Notes

1. Although Cather and Jewett both use the word "sympathy" to designate the power of entering into the feelings of another, the word "empathy" has greater usefulness because it not only suggests entering mentally into the feelings of someone else, but also appreciative perception of another person or object, the quality Cather described as the artist's "loving the things that haunt him." Since "empathy" does not carry the suggestions of compassion for another's sorrow that "sympathy" does, it seems the more general term.

2. Willa Cather, "Preface," *The Country of the Pointed Firs and Other Stories,* by Sarah Orne Jewett (Doubleday Anchor reprint, 1956), p. 7.

3. Sarah Orne Jewett, *The Country of the Pointed Firs and Other Stories,* ed. Willa Cather (Doubleday Anchor reprint, 1956), p. 46. Subsequent page references given in the text are to this edition.

4. Sarah Orne Jewett to Annie Fields, not dated. *Letters of Sarah Orne Jewett,* ed. Annie Fields (Boston, 1911), p. 185.

5. Jane Austen, *Persuasion,* ed. D. W. Harding (Penguin Edition, 1965), ch. 11, p. 121.

6, *Persuasion,* pp. 121–22.

Women "at Sea": Feminist Realism in Sarah Orne Jewett's "The Foreigner"   Marjorie Pryse*

Sarah Orne Jewett's "The Foreigner" (1900) appeared four years after the publication of *The Country of The Pointed Firs,* yet it was not until David Bonnell Green included the story in his collection of Jewett's Dunnet Landing tales that it became available to contemporary readers.[1] And, indeed, much of Jewett's relative "availability" is a recent phenomenon, as major anthologies of American literature, those destined for inclusion in undergraduate courses, have included Jewett for the first time only in their more recent editions.[2] "The Foreigner" continues to be omitted from at least one edition of *The Country of the Pointed Firs* and related stories in print at this writing.[3]

Usually grouped with the three related sketches—"A Dunnet Shepherdess," "The Queen's Twin," and "William's Wedding"—and briefly

*Reprinted from *American Literary Realism,* 15 (1982), 244–52, with permission.

discussed (if at all) in the context of *The Country of the Pointed Firs*, "The Foreigner" has never been subjected to the scrutiny of close analysis. Warner Berthoff describes "The Foreigner" as "extraordinary . . . one of the mislaid treasures of American writing" and yet limits his discussion of the story to a paragraph.[4] Bert Bender gives the story its fullest treatment (four pages), yet includes this commentary within his more general treatment of Jewett's "lyric narratives."[5]

While it is helpful to place "The Foreigner" within the context of Dunnet Landing and read it in light of *The Country of the Pointed Firs*, it is not necessary to do so. Richard Cary, who has done more than any other editor and scholar to preserve Jewett's work and make it accessible, considers that the story "assumes prior knowledge of the Dunnet Landing ambience."[6] Yet an independent reading of the story does much to illuminate character, theme, and narrative method in Jewett's larger work, even though *The Country of the Pointed Firs* antedates "The Foreigner." In the work of William Faulkner, readers of American literature have witnessed an author returning at a later date to alter facts of earlier narratives (as he does in the "Appendix" to *The Sound and the Fury*) and to retell earlier stories (in the note with which he opens *The Mansion*, he actually claims that "he knows the characters in this chronicle better than he did" three decades earlier, when he first began to write about Snopeses[7]). Nothing of the magnitude of Faulkner's later revisions of his Yoknapatawpha County material appears in the Dunnet Landing stories which Jewett published after 1896, yet "The Foreigner" more than the other three provides evidence that Jewett herself may have known her own characters "better" as a result of completing *Pointed Firs*.

With the understanding that criticism itself often functions as hindsight, an occasion for a culture to revise its evaluation of a writer and to confess that we know the characters in a writer's world (just as we know ourselves) better than we once did, I take this opportunity to redress the neglect we have accorded one of Jewett's finest stories and to place it within a context of the growing body of criticism which finds in the fictions of women writers what Warner Berthoff has been the first—and only—critic of this Jewett story to describe as "peculiarly American" resonances.[8] In giving the reader Jewett's revision, a second comprehensive "view," of Mrs. Todd, "The Foreigner" effectively offers an introduction to *The Country of the Pointed Firs* and to Jewett's finest work.

Like *Pointed Firs* itself and many of Jewett's stories, "The Foreigner" appears to rely heavily on setting. However, from the opening paragraphs, particularly for the reader who approaches the story apart from *Pointed Firs*, the apparent setting serves immediately to bring out the inner anxieties of the women present. The story opens as "The first cold northeasterly storm of the season was blowing hard outside" (p. 307) and Mrs. Todd arrives to pay the narrator a visit. For the narrator, the storm possesses significance even before Mrs. Todd enters her room: "I could hear that the sea was already stirred to its dark depths, and the great rollers were coming in heavily against the shore. One might well believe that Summer was coming to a sad end that night.... It seemed as if there must be danger offshore among the outer islands" (p. 307).

For Mrs. Todd, the storm evokes fears which may appear initially unrelated to her actual story about "the foreigner." She tells the narrator, "'I know nothing ain't ever happened out to Green Island since the world began, but I always do worry about mother in these great gales'" (p. 307). She dwells on imagined dangers: tidal waves, an accident to her brother William's boat, that the August storm might have caught them unprepared. As she and the narrator sit before the fire, "we could feel the small wooden house rock and hear it creak as if it were a ship at sea" (p. 308). The two women might be the wives of seagoing men from the days when Dunnet Landing was an active port, except that neither woman is worried about a man. Both join in worrying about "mother" out on Green Island.

The narrator sympathizes with the "families of sailors and coastwise adventurers by sea." They "must always be worrying about somebody, this side of the world or the other. There was hardly one of Mrs. Todd's elder acquaintances, men or women, who had not at some time or other made a sea voyage, and there was often no news until the voyagers themselves came back to bring it" (p. 308). Some women, Mrs. Todd comments, go to sleep in order to forget, "'but 't ain't my way.'" Her way is to sit and worry, preferably not alone. The narrator's initial function, for Mrs. Todd, seems not that of mere listener to the story the older woman eventually relates, but rather that of an intimate who can share Mrs. Todd's anxieties.

"'You have never told me any ghost stories,'" says our narrator by way of suggestion (p. 308), and as "The Foreigner" unfolds, it is easy to disregard the storm as merely an introduction to what does seem to be a ghost story. Like the narrative frame of James's "The Turn of the Screw," the opening section of "The Foreigner" appears to set the stage for the tale; yet this tale comments on the narrative frame itself in much more subtle ways than does James's novella. "The Foreigner" is no mere ghost story.

As is the case with many of Jewett's stories and sketches, a story within a story creates the narrative design and a visit provides the narrative occasion for "The Foreigner." Both of these elements in the work remain apparent throughout. At no point does our narrator move directly into the story Mrs. Todd tells; at every point she allows Mrs. Todd to tell her own story. The effects are several. For one, the device makes Mrs. Todd herself as much the focus of the story as the story she tells. Second, both that story and our narrator's experience with Mrs. Todd are

clearly mediated, even translated, for the reader by means of the narrative within a narrative. And finally, because our narrator is conspicu-
ously present throughout the telling, the story creates a Jamesian
"personal, direct impression"[9] in the reader by portraying the impression
Mrs. Todd herself makes on the narrator. For some readers unaccustomed
to Jewett's method, the result may be an apparent loss of suspense. Most
of us, after all, may have been trained by Henry James in the art of
telling a good ghost story. For James, the ghosts in "The Turn of the
Screw" must make their own direct impressions on their readers/hearers.
For Jewett, the final appearance of the ghost is anticlimactic; the story
dramatizes not the appearance of the ghost but rather Mrs. Todd's
attempt to translate the experience of being "foreign" for her listener,
our narrator.

Both Mrs. Todd and the narrator are trying to understand an experience which has been "foreign" to them. In Mrs. Todd's case, both her
character and her listener are foreign. She becomes an interpreter for
her listener, who is a guest in her house and at Dunnet Landing. For our
narrator, the reader is also a foreigner; in creating the world of Dunnet
Landing by means of local speech rhythms and details of weather,
history, and topography (all in self-conscious use of the stylistic conventions of "local color" writing), our narrator becomes Mrs. Todd's
interpreter for her own "listener"—the reader. In a sense, the impulse to
"translate" or to "interpret" life for listeners and readers explains the
realist's intention, as Howells implied when he wrote that a writer's
business "is to make you understand the real world through his [or her]
faithful effigy of it."[10] But the unexamined question which runs through
Jewett's work involves the nature of the world itself which Jewett's
"effigies" portray. In this particular story, the nature of foreign experience is the central concern. What is "foreign" about Mrs. Todd? What
does the narrator need to "translate" about her in order for the reader
to understand her?

There is, of course, the experience she had with Mrs. Tolland, the
main character in Mrs. Todd's own narrative. Mrs. Tolland was herself a
foreigner, alienated from the community of women in Dunnet Landing
by religion (she was Catholic) and cultural heritage (she was French).
Her manners and customs differed from theirs—she felt alone in the
meeting house and danced in the vestry; she was isolated for her strangeness. She was hard to feel close to; she died of solitude and grief just
a few months after hearing the news that her husband had died at sea.
But she has given Mrs. Todd more than the money she eventually left
her: she has shown Mrs. Todd a great deal about herbs, plants, and cooking. Hearing about Mrs. Tolland therefore helps our narrator understand
Mrs. Todd better. Some of this understanding seems superficial—she
knows why Mrs. Todd makes good omelettes. But some of it goes deeper
—Mrs. Todd herself is different from the other women in the community.

At her mother's urging she initially befriended Mrs. Tolland, even though she remained aware of their distance. "'I never gave her a kiss till the day she laid in her coffin and it came to my heart there wa'n't no one else to do it'" (p. 315).

Mrs. Todd thinks that she has gained from Mrs. Tolland a knowledge of death. She describes sitting with Mrs. Tolland in the last moments of her life, when "'All of a sudden she set right up in bed with her eyes wide open. . . . And she reached out both arms toward the door, an' I looked the way she was lookin', an' I see some one was standin' there against the dark'" (p. 322). This is the moment in which "The Foreigner" becomes a ghost story. At first Mrs. Todd was uncertain: "'I felt dreadful cold and my head begun to swim. . . .'" But she carried on: "'I did try to act calm, an' I laid Mis' Tolland down on her pillow, an' I was a-shakin' as I done it.'" But Mrs. Tolland was consoled: "'You saw her, didn't you?' she says to me, speakin' pefectly reasonable. "T is my mother,' she says again. . . .'" Mrs. Todd's uncertainty passed and she, too, felt relieved: "'I felt calm then, an' lifted to somethin' different as I never was since.'" Mrs. Tolland opened her eyes in the moment of death and asked Mrs. Todd a second time, "'You saw her, did n't you?'" And Mrs. Todd tells how she said, "*Yes, dear, I did; you ain't never goin' to feel strange and lonesome no more'*" (p. 323).

What is unexpected for the reader, and probably for the narrator as well, about Mrs. Todd's response to seeing Mrs. Tolland's mother is that no one is frightened. We know that the narrator initially expected to be frightened—she states, at the beginning of "The Foreigner," that after she had suggested to Mrs. Todd that she tell a ghost story, "I was instantly filled with reluctance to have this suggestion followed. . . . I was really afraid that she was going to tell me something that would haunt my thoughts on every dark stormy night as long as I lived" (p. 308). In the moment of Mrs. Tolland's death, the James reader might feel most strongly the apparent anticlimax—the ghost, when it finally does arrive, does not appall. Rather, the appearance of the ghost allows Mrs. Todd to console her dying friend: "'you ain't never goin' to feel strange and lonesome no more.'" Death, the one experience to which all living narrators and readers feel foreign, is stripped of its strangeness and its lonesomeness.

Mrs. Todd, then, becomes a figure very much like the speaker in Emily Dickinson's poem "Just lost, when I was saved!"—someone who has caught a glimpse of death and returns to tell about it. The real foreigner now seems to be not Mrs. Tolland but her mother—the ghost. But the experience of having seen the ghost makes Mrs. Todd an equal foreigner. Her story is about the glimpse she once had of another world, and as she translates that glimpse, she sits knitting, and the storm rages. We have moved back into the narrative frame. She expresses her opinion that "'You know plain enough there's somethin' beyond this world; the doors stand wide open. "There's somethin' of us that must still live on; we've got to join both worlds together an' live in one but for the other." The doctor said that to me one day, an' I never could forget it . . .'" (p. 323). In the process of telling her ghost story, ghost stories have ceased to create anxiety. In relating the sense of calm she felt when Mrs. Tolland's mother appeared to her daughter, she calms those other anxieties with which the story opened, and as the weather returns to normal ("the sea still roared, but the high wind had done blowing"), Mrs. Todd's worry about her own mother has implicitly calmed: " 'Yes, there goes the boat; they'll find it rough at sea, but the storm's all over' " (p. 324).

For the narrator, Mrs. Todd is like someone who has journeyed to another world and come back to tell the story. Making a "sea voyage" takes on the resonance of exploring "this side of the world or the other," like those "sailors and coastwise adventurers by sea" whose families the narrator had sympathized with earlier; and this is precisely what Mrs. Todd has done by the time she finishes her narrative: she has described the time *she* explored "the other" side of the world in the moment in which she saw the "foreigner," the ghost of Mrs. Tolland's mother. Again like those "adventures by sea," about whom "there was often no news until the voyagers themselves came back to bring it," Mrs. Todd has told the circumstances of Mrs. Tolland's death "to but very few" (p. 323). The effect is that she has "come back" from a voyage bringing news.

What is ultimately "foreign" for the reader about this story may be that Mrs. Todd's "sea voyage" has no real ship, and that her "news" is so well disguised as ghost story that we miss its greater import. Her "ship" and the "news" with which she returns are intertwined. It is her anxieties, her fears and her memories, which are tossed about as she and the narrator sit indoors while the season's first "nor'easter" rages outside. In earlier nineteenth-century American fiction, we are accustomed to seeing real battles with the elements (in *Moby Dick*, for example) as metaphors for experience; in "The Foreigner," Mrs. Todd's experience seems at first to be only a metaphoric "sea voyage"—yet it is as real a battle as women in her circumstances can have. It is a story about a woman's anxieties and the way she tries to calm them; it concerns Mrs. Todd's inner life in more detail than even the sketches in *The Country of the Pointed Firs*; and it illustrates the way in which Mrs. Todd tries to "join both worlds together an' live in one but for the other." It is too easy to identify one of those "worlds" as the world of men and of action and the other as the world of the women who stay home knitting while the men enact the "real" battles. Rather, "The Foreigner" suggests that while the women's experience of the storm may have nothing to do with the immediate effects of battling it (they sit indoors knitting), the real storm for the women is the one anxiety creates. And the real anxiety for women is not that of being cut off from the physical elements but of feeling separated from that "other world" where "mother" resides, and therefore where it is not necessary to feel "strange an' lonesome."

Eased anxiety and a sense of being "at home" rather than being "at sea," for both Mrs. Tolland and Mrs. Todd, are the result of becoming reunited with their mothers. What initially seems "foreign" about the story becomes quite commonplace indeed, very much an effigy of real life: the story is about the anxiety Mrs. Todd feels at being separated from her mother; she is "at sea" until the storm passes. While Mrs. Tolland lived, Mrs. Todd's mother served to unite the younger women; in the moment of her death, her own mother appears to unite the two friends. Mrs. Todd is left with her memory of the moment in which Mrs. Tolland's mother eased her daughter's way into that most foreign of human experiences, death—and, therefore, telling Mrs. Tolland's story brings her into close contact with her own mother, in spite of the danger she feels on her mother's behalf from the "great gales."

The story which our narrator "composes" (in the Howellsian sense[11]) involves the juxtaposition of the dead Mrs. Tolland and her mother, and the living Mrs. Todd and *her* mother; but the pattern comes to include the narrator as well. By her very presence as a" foreigner," a summer visitor, in Dunnet Landing, she is either trying to escape urban turmoil or, more accurately, to find inner peace. Her presence there suggests that she, too, feels cut off from that "other world." At the beginning of the story, then, it is the narrator who appears as Jewett's foreigner. Mrs. Todd is her friend but also her hostess; when the older woman enters the narrator's room, she becomes her "guest" as well (p. 307). Despite the "harmony" of their "fellowship" (p. 307), a conventional and formal distance separates the two women—until Mrs. Todd tells her story. Mrs. Todd's description of the woman she came to feel close sympathy with (Mrs. Tolland) parallels the unspoken experience of the narrator, who is encountering the inner life of a woman she has become acquainted with, and encountering it directly and deeply for the first time. In the Jamesian sense, then, our narrator comes to have a "personal, direct impression" of Mrs. Todd's "other world," her inner life.

By implication, telling the story about Mrs. Todd allows the narrator to become reunited with her own inner life, just as Mrs. Todd has had a consoling experience of the "other world" and has "come back" to tell about it. Just as the narrator stated at the beginning when she became aware of Mrs. Todd's worries about her mother, by the story's end she has also "thought as [she] had never thought before of such anxieties" (p. 308). Yet in thinking about them, and particularly by telling her story, she is also able to ease them. Mrs. Todd's story, far from telling her "something that would haunt [her] thoughts on every dark stormy night" (p. 308), gives her something to mitigate those thoughts. For Mrs. Todd, in her stance not simply as storyteller but as the older woman and a "sea-goer," becomes a figure of the narrator's mother. More is at stake than the relationship between storyteller and listener; and by extension, more is also at stake between the story's narrator and her own reader, if that reader happens to be female. Women sit together around the home fire on a stormy night not merely to entertain each other, as they ostensibly do in James's "The Turn of the Screw," but to teach each other, to pass down from mother to daughter the ability to "live in one world but for the other."

Jewett's story seems foreign to us, perhaps, because we are unaccustomed to fiction which transforms into art not simply the lives of women but their inner lives. If Jewett's reader happens to be female, the experience of reading her fiction can be revolutionary. The process—described by Judith Fetterley in her book *The Resisting Reader*—by which women have to defeminize themselves in order to read most of American fiction's portraits of women without wincing at their unreality, is not necessary in Jewett.[12] Like Jewett's own narrator, her female readers are permitted to think as we have not thought before "of such anxieties." What appears initially foreign turns out to be familiar; what seems terrifying becomes a consolation; and what seems to be beyond human experience becomes, in Mrs. Todd's phrase, "all natural." "'You know plain enough there's somethin' beyond this world; the doors stand wide open. 'There's somethin' of us that must still live on. . . .'''" In Sophocles, open doors signify new vision, when Oedipus twists the bolts out of their hinges and bursts into Jocasta's bedroom. In Jewett, vision is not Oedipal. Despite the decline of the sad sea captains of *Pointed Firs*, her New England women discover new resources and inner strength. Mrs. Todd's narrative opens "the doors" for her narrator, who finds in the "old prophetess" (p. 321) new reasons for telling stories. The doors that "stand wide open" depict the sibyl-storyteller in the process of giving birth. "'There's somethin' of us that must still live on'"—in daughters, and in stories.

But what of Jewett's male readers? In teaching this story to a group of male undergraduates, I have witnessed firsthand that male readers may feel themselves to be the ultimate foreigners in the story. Yet the image of the open doors invites male readers as well to identify childbirth with storytelling. Giving birth has long been a metaphor of the writing process for male writers as well. A man's book is his "child." The narrator of this story, though female, is not herself a mother. She therefore shares a man's relative ignorance of the experience of actual childbirth. The search of daughters for mothers, like that more familiar (because more frequently examined in literature) search of sons for fathers, is a common paradigm of the human condition. Despite the widely accepted generalization about late nineteenth-century New England fiction, that it portrays a region in decline and is itself the mark of that decline (written as it is predominantly by local-color writers and by women at that),[13] Jewett's story at least creates a world where neither male nor female readers must "resist" the reading. Captain Tolland, before he left home for the last time, understood that his wife, in his absence, would have her own voyage to make, and he "had left his house well provisioned as if his wife was goin' to put to sea same's himself . . .'" (p. 318).

Mrs. Todd understands that much as the lives of women, like the lives of men, may furnish metaphors for vision, she is not a separatist and Dunnet Landing, though populated by many women alone, is no mere sisterhood. In describing the "'old part of the buryin' ground'" to Jewett's narrator, Mrs. Todd remarks, "'All their women folks lies there; the sea's got most o' the men'" (p. 309). Those great foreign experiences of death and human anxiety in the face of the unknown know no gender. It is significant that Mrs. Todd's closing advice to the narrator ("we've got to join both worlds together") comes not out of her own experience but from one of the "'old doctor's books'" (p. 323). This may be the only moment in "The Foreigner" which assumes prior knowledge of *The Country of the Pointed Firs*, for the doctor is a familiar figure for the readers of that novel: he is Mrs. Todd's rival. He with his medicines and the herbalist with her lore have learned to work together to heal the sick and comfort the lonely in Dunnet Landing. In creating a fictional world which, though not devoid of men, seems unconcerned with relationships between men and women, Jewett lends even greater significance to Mrs. Todd's advice. "We've got to join both worlds together"—the world of men at sea and women, at home but equally "at sea"—in order to comprehend fully not just New England regional literature but the entire canon of American fiction. Literary critics have a lot to learn from those women writers (like Harriet Beecher Stowe, Mary E. Wilkins Freeman, Rose Terry Cooke, Alice Brown, and others including Jewett) whom they have for so long described as "limited in scope." Mrs. Todd's mother, speaking through her own daughter's narrative, offers the best advice of all to readers both male and female who would re-examine the work of our women writers with the goal of understanding more than the male half of the American experience:

> "'What consequence is my supper?' says she to me; mother can be very stern,—'or your comfort or mine, beside letting a foreign person an' a stranger feel so desolate; she's done the best a woman could do in her lonesome place, and she asks nothing of anybody except a little common kindness. Think if 't was you in a foreign land!'" (p. 314)

Let us provision the house of American criticism, like Captain Tolland, as if our women were going to put to sea the same as our men. Only then will the inner lives of women cease to be foreign, and women themselves cease to be foreigners.

Notes

1. First published in *Atlantic Monthly*, 86 (Aug. 1900), the story was reprinted for the first time in David Bonnell Green, ed. *The World of Dunnet Landing* (Lincoln: Univ. of Nebraska Press, 1962). Page references in the text are to Richard Cary's edition of "The Foreigner" in *The Uncollected Short Stories of Sarah Orne Jewett* (Waterville, Me.: Colby College Press, 1971), pp. 307–24.

2. I am referring here to *The Norton Anthology of American Literature*, 2 vols., eds. Ronald Gottesman et al. (New York: W. W. Norton, 1979), and to *Anthology of American Literature*, 2 vols., ed. George McMichael (New York: Macmillan Publishing Co., 1980).

3. The Doubleday Anchor edition reprints Willa Cather's 1925 arrangement of *The Country of the Pointed Firs*, which omits "The Foreigner."

4. Warner Berthoff, *The Ferment of Realism: American Literature 1884–1919* (New York: Free Press, 1965), p. 98.

5. Bert Bender, "To Calm and Uplift 'Against the Dark': Sarah Orne Jewett's Lyric Narratives," *Colby Library Quarterly*, 11 (1975), pp. 219–229.

6. Richard Cary, "The Uncollected Short Stories of Sarah Orne Jewett," reprinted in Richard Cary, ed., *Appreciation of Sarah Orne Jewett: 29 Interpretive Essays* (Waterville, Me.: Colby College Press, 1973), p. 275.

7. William Faulkner, *The Mansion* (New York: Random House, 1959).

8. Berthoff, p. 99.

9. This phrase is James's "broad definition" of the novel, from "The Art of Fiction," in *Partial Portraits* (London: Macmillan & Co., 1888), p. 384.

10. William D. Howells, "Novel-Writing and Novel-Reading: An Impersonal Explanation," in William M. Gibson, ed., *Howells and James: A Double Billing* (New York: New York Public Library, 1958), p. 24; reprinted in *A Selected Edition of William Dean Howells* (Bloomington: Indiana Univ. Press, 1978).

11. Ibid., p. 9.

12. Judith Fetterley, *The Resisting Reader: A Feminist Approach to American Fiction* (Bloomington: Indiana Univ. Press, 1978).

13. Major proponents of the "New England in decline" theory are V. L. Parrington, *Main Currents in American Thought*, Vol. III: *The Beginnings of Critical Realism in American*, 1860–1920 (New York: Harcourt, Brace, 1930), and Van Wyck Brooks, *New England: Indian Summer*, 1865–1915 (New York: Dutton, 1940).

Pure and Passionate: Female Friendship in Sarah Orne Jewett's "Martha's Lady"

Glenda Hobbs*

Though much of Sarah Orne Jewett's short fiction describes women befriending one another in nineteenth-century rural New England, these friendships have been seen usually as backdrops for other, more "important" subjects. Jewett's portraits of Maine villagers' closeness to nature, the humiliation of threatened destitution and the good works that usually prevent it, her characters' lament for their more prosperous past, and the pathos of wasted, if endearing lives that have been cited among her central concerns. Yet in many of her stories—"The Flight of Betsey Lane," "The Town Poor," and "Miss Tempy's Watchers" to name a few— Jewett is as intent on depicting the nature and importance of female friendships as she is on dramatizing these other themes.

"Martha's Lady," (1897) one of her best and most frequently anthologized short stories, focuses on one of these intense female friendships, which were, as Henry James noted, "so common in New England."[1] Unique among Jewett's stories for depicting both the passion (itself rare in her fiction) and the spirituality that marked many of these friendships, "Martha's Lady" also provides a fictional counterpart to the many historical friendships recent scholarship has unearthed.[2] Jewett's story testifies to their singular importance in women's lives and helps to clarify their nature.

"Martha's Lady" is one of the few Jewett stories to focus on women before they reach old age. It describes the burgeoning friendship between two women in their twenties: Helena, a beauty from Boston, and Martha, the ungainly maid she meets while visiting her cousin Harriet for a summer in the country. After their summer of shared companionship, they separate for forty years; Helena marries and has children, but Martha remains in Harriet's household, treasuring her memories and thinking of Helena, as she promises when Helena departs. They rekindle their friendship when they are elderly.

This friendship must be viewed in the context of the nineteenth century's elevated perception of friendship.[3] Because it presumably excluded carnality, friendship was believed to be the highest form of love, with love between two women the most perfect possible because women were thought morally superior to men.[4] While their husbands and brothers became tarnished competing in the marketplace, women remained aloof and pure, protecting home and religion. In "Martha's Lady" Jewett employs "transcendental" concepts to convey the spiritual roots of Helena's and Martha's friendship; her perceptions and descriptions resemble Thoreau's as stated in his paean to friendship in the

*Reprinted from *Studies in Short Fiction*, 17 (1980), 21–29, with permission.

"Wednesday" section of *A Week on the Concord and Merrimack Rivers,*
a book in Jewett's home library.

Helena and Martha are drawn to each other in a way not entirely
explainable; each feels the natural and inevitable "affinity"[5] Thoreau
posits as the basis for true friendship. Although Harriet complains of
Martha's ineptness, Helena thinks her a "dear good girl" and begs Harriet to give her a chance to improve. And Martha, whom Jewett describes
as "dull and indifferent to everyone else, showed a surprising willingness
and allegiance to the young guest."[6]

In this story Jewett demonstrates a sympathy with Thoreau's belief
that "no such affront can be offered to a Friend, as a conscious good will,
a friendliness which is not a necessity of the Friend's nature" (p. 286).
Although Helena teaches Martha how to execute her household duties,
and on her wedding day sends Martha some trifles when she recalls the
maid's "plain and dull" life, this is not the story of a sanctimonious bene-
factor and a grateful recipient. Helena is not motivated by a do-gooding
Christianity, an intentional good will; her actions are the natural out-
growth of her affection for Martha rather than expressions of pity.

Both women bloom in an atmosphere of mutual affection; each expresses herself as she expresses love for the other. Buoyed in part by
Martha's love and admiration, Helena exhibits her intrinsic exuberance,
helping Martha to manage Harriet's household graciously and tastefully.
She creates an affectionate, even inspiring atmosphere wherein Martha
discovers and develops dormant talents. As Martha strives to earn Helena's approval she also unfolds a latent artistry, flowering inwardly as
she masters the skills. After performing a task impeccably, she "looked
for once almost pretty and quite as young as she was" (p. 146). As she
learns to command her art, Jewett describes her as growing "unconsci-
ously beautiful like a saint" (pp. 160–161), a phrase echoing Thoreau's
when describing the "hero" or "saint" who achieves true friendship.

Helena and Martha also flourish because each strives to embody her
friend's image of her own ideal self. Both meet Thoreau's requirement
for a true Friend, "one who incessantly pays us the compliment of ex-
pecting from us all the virtues, and who can appreciate them in us"
(p. 283). Martha's perception of Helena as "exquisite"—a perfect embodiment of the mischief, brightness and ebullience she lacks—helps
Helena thrive in Ashford; she even rids residents of their "unnecessary
provincialism and prejudice" and gives them "wider outlooks upon the
world" (pp. 149–159). Likewise, Helena's faith that Martha can become
a model hostess prompts the maid to do everything exactly right, "all
for love's sake" (p. 151), a phrase recalling Jewett's own in a letter to a
close friend, Sarah Whitman. "The only thing that really helps any of
us," she wrote, "is love and doing things for love's sake."[7]

Martha's continued devotion to perfecting her art, even after Helena
departs, confounds some twentieth-century critics. One is troubled by

Martha's unawareness of "the pathos of sustaining this love for a lifetime on the basis of a summer's visit."[8] But in the nineteenth century, friendships were believed to be indisputably deep and true only if they could withstand prolonged absence. The more high-minded, like the Transcendentalists, deemed them truly worthy only if the friends didn't require each other's presence.[9] Thoreau explains this willingness to forsake companionship when he says that true friendship "takes place on a level higher than the actual characters of the parties would seem to warrant" (pp. 287–288). "Our actual Friends are but distant relations of those to whom we are pledged" (p. 281). Jewett shares Thoreau's belief in the value of absent, silent friendship, though not his apparent preference for it.[10] To him, the friend is elevated by the purest vision of his ideal, one untainted by the flaws unavoidable in its earthly embodiment. Jewett depicts the joy of companionship and Martha's despondency when it is over. But "if love is true," she interjects, "there comes presently a higher joy of pleasing the ideal, that is to say, the perfect friend" (p. 153). As Martha seeks to "conform to an ideal," which she sees as a "saint's vision," she has the "ineffable satisfaction of trying to please one whom she truly loved" (p. 153).

Both women benefit from the friendship because they are equal, as Thoreau required, in "all that respects or affects their Friendship" (p. 287). Although Helena is a lady and Martha a servant, their need for the other's love is commensurate. "All difficulties appeared to vanish" every time Martha ponders how much Helena "believed in her" (p. 146). Remembering Helena's support sustains her through forty years of a life outwardly uneventful, but one Jewett describes as a "passion and happiness of service" (p. 161). Helena's need for Martha's faith is expressed only once, at an anomalous moment, when perhaps feeling a portent of future affliction, she confesses to difficulties and pleads for Martha's remembrance. On the eve of her departure Helena suddenly exclaims: "'Martha! I wish you would think of me sometimes after I go away. Won't you promise?' and the bright young face suddenly grew grave. 'I have hard times myself; I don't always learn things I ought to learn, I don't always put things straight. I wish you wouldn't forget me ever, and would just believe in me. I think it does help more than anything'" (p. 152). Although as she speaks Helena may not fully realize the value of Martha's faith, the story's ending illustrates the truth of her declaration that belief in a friend means "more than anything." During the forty year interval before the friends reunite, Helena suffers "a great deal of trouble" and apparently loses sight of Martha's supporting love. When Martha learns of Helena's visit, she becomes pale and hears a ringing in her ears. She looks "wistfully" at Helena's telegram, discerning that Harriet "knew nothing of the love that had been in her heart all these years; it was half a pain and half a golden joy to keep such a secret; she could hardly bear this moment of surprise" (p.

167). That evening Martha exhibits her flawless housekeeping, remembering even to serve Helena's favorite dish. As Martha attends Helena, performing "the old unforgotten loving services," Helena "suddenly knew the whole story and could hardly speak. 'Oh, my dear Martha!' she cried, 'won't you kiss me good night? Oh, Martha, have you remembered like this, all these long years!'" (p. 169). Helena's surprise gives way to a relief and an ecstasy that somewhat compensate for her sorrow; having endured the vicissitudes of marriage, children, and travel, she at last faces constancy and abiding love.

The story's ending highlights the passion that characterizes the women's friendship from its inception to its reawakening decades later when they are "past sixty;" it also intimates the romance that imbued actual female friendships at that time.[11] The amorousness of these attachments in no way undermined their spirituality; Helena, Martha, and their historical counterparts could reconcile as Thoreau could not, passion with idealism. Passion was too "human" for many of the lofty Transcendentalists, who often scorned anything Reason could not contain.

Jewett's suggestions of romantic love between Helena and Martha pervade the story. Throughout she describes Helena as a seductress, a Helen of Troy, a "siren in India muslin" (p. 148). Adorned with red ribbons or a crimson silk shawl, she has "mischievous appealing eyes" (p. 139) and sings "enchanting" old songs on a guitar. She regards Ashford's minister as a "conquest," but invests her emotions in Martha. The language Jewett uses to describe their first shared experience is sensuous, suggesting an earthiness and a vibrancy that are as characteristic of the friendship as the transcendental ideals the women envision. They go to a "large sunshiny garden" where there is a "fragrance of the old garden's inmost life and soul blowing from the honeysuckle blossoms on a long trellis" (p. 142). Responding to Helena's plea for help in reaching the treetop's highest cherries, the tall Martha "began to climb the cherry-tree like a boy. Down came the scarlet fruit like bright rain into the green grass" (p. 144). The encounter is marked with the joy and affection of first love: when Helena shouts up to her friend, "oh, you're a duck, Martha!", the maid, "flushed with delight," "came rustling down to earth again" (p. 145). Jewett implies that Martha is the captivated and seduced "boy," descending from heights higher than the tree.

The romantic undercurrent intensifies when Martha learns of Helena's approaching marriage; she begins to feel like a jealous lover. Although class differences prevent the women from corresponding personally, Helena asks Harriet to show Martha her letters, especially the one describing her "dear Jack." Martha cries after reading that "there never was such a lad to reach for cherries with his six-foot-two" (p. 156). She feels "a strange sense of loss and pain; it hurt her heart a little to read about the cherry-picking. Her idol seemed to be less her own since she had become the idol of a stranger." Although Martha feels replaced by Helena's husband, her sorrow is only momentary. Jewett boasts that "love at last prevailed" (p. 157) when Martha realizes that Helena is happy. Martha's love and passion are again apparent as she lays down Helena's letter: "feeling overbold," she "kissed the last page where her name was written" (p. 157).

Martha's and Helena's friendship is undoubtedly passionate, but not necessarily erotic. Jewett's own remarks about the story insinuate her intentions. Her friend Sarah Whitman had read the story and sent her comments to Jewett. Jewett's response begins:

> It is impossible to say how your letter has heartened me. I send you love and thanks,—it is one more unbreakable bond that holds fast between me and you. You bring something to the reading of a story that the story would go very lame without; but it is those unwritable things that the story holds in its heart, if it has any, that make the true soul of it, and these must be understood, and yet how many a story goes lame for lack of that understanding. In France there is such a code, such recognitions, such richness of allusions; but here we confuse our scaffoldings with our buildings, and—and *so!*[12]

An admirer of French literature, notably George Sand, Jewett may have been referring to a code she believed French fiction writers used for depicting lesbian encounters. Such subjects were certainly "unwritable" in Howells's America. Jewett may have been expressing the wish that she, like French writers, had a way of revealing same-sex physicality, but more likely she was wishing for an improved reciprocal communication between author and reader, so she could be assured that readers would appreciate the depth of Martha's love. These "unwritable" things at the story's core are likely its extraordinary emotional intensity: in the nineteenth century feelings were often described as inexpressive or unwritable—too overpowering or transcendent to be conveyed in words.

In her letter to Whitman, Jewett elaborates on these "unwritable things," confiding her thoughts about Martha:

> I thought that most of us had begun to grow in just such a way as she did, and so could read joyfully between the lines of her plain story, but I wonder if most people will not call her a dull story. That would be all my fault, and sets me the harder at work; the stone ought to be made a lovely statue. Nobody must say that Martha was dull, it is only I.

Rather than calling for her audience to read a physical relationship "between the lines," Jewett is probably again stressing the depth of Martha's love. Her reference to how "most of us grow" suggests that she believed most adolescent women learn about caring from a "best" friend of the same sex. We need to read "between the lines," or to recall our own memories, to appreciate the intensity of Martha's attachment to Helena. This reminiscence and Martha's similar experience should allow us to see "joyfully" a beautiful building evolve from Jewett's plain scaffolding.[13]

The unpublished Whitman letter Jewett is answering further suggests that the story's "heart" is Martha's passionate devotion. Mrs. Whitman says that Jewett's searching "Heaven and Hell" for the exact word leads to the story's "revelations," which she feels are focused in the words "it was forty years."[14] The exact wording of the section Whitman alludes to reads: "It seemed like yesterday that Helena Vernon had gone away, and it was more than forty years" (p. 154). Whitman says that in using this phrase Jewett makes "that swift appeal to the imagination which only genius can make and to which the whole human heart responds." It is unlikely that she is praising Jewett for making a physical relationship implicit and inviting readers to imagine the "revelations" she could not delineate. Mrs. Whitman is applauding Jewett's telescoping the forty years, thereby forcing readers to use their imaginations to supply what happens to each in the interim; she is also suggesting that readers need their imaginations to envision a love intense enough to survive a forty year absence as though it were a day. Elsewhere Jewett stresses the women's love defying time: though Martha's hands are work-worn, her "face still shone" (p. 154), and Helena's "young eyes" and smile belie her "changed face" and "tired, bent little figure" (p. 168).

Perhaps twentieth-century readers must take even a larger imaginative leap than Jewett and Whitman invite. As recent scholarship has demonstrated, intense emotional and sensual attachments between women were permitted, even encouraged, at a time when courtship was so strictly formalized. In a society unhampered by a heterosexual-homosexual dichotomy or by a Freudian model of normalcy, women could express their love freely, without a fear of violating taboos. They could feel comfortable, as do Helena and Martha, sharing an amatory relationship, and could perceive no paradox in a friendship both idealistic and passionate.[15] This alliance is the most valuable contribution of "Martha's Lady" to the study of nineteenth-century female friendships; it is crucial to an understanding of an intriguing, overlooked element in Jewett's fiction. Helena's and Martha's friendship confutes critics who descry the absence of passionate love in Jewett's fiction.

From her own experience Jewett knew that friendships between women could be as deep as the bond between husband and wife.[16] In a letter to Willa Cather the seasoned author suggests to the novice that she substitute a woman for the husband in her story ("On the Gull's Road") because it's always a "masquerade" "when a woman writes in a man's character." She cautions Cather not to "try to be he!" Jewett adds, "you could almost have done it as yourself—a woman could love her in that same protecting way—a woman could even care enough to wish to take her away from such a life, by some means or other."[17] At this writing Jewett had already published "Martha's Lady," her story describing a woman loving another in that "protecting way." Martha regards Helena as her "sympathetic ally and defender" (p. 146) against Harriet's criticism. Jewett even implies in "Martha's Lady" that such a friendship is superior to marriage. Martha, who never marries, achieves a full flowering of her talents while Helena suffers gravely (though she also knows joy) after her marriage. Jewett seems to share Harriet's "protest" against Helena's marriage: "Helena was so equal to happy independence . . . that it was hard to let her sink her personality in the affairs of another" (p. 156). When Helena participates in Martha's affairs, Jewett portrays her involvement as a soaring of self-expression rather than a self-abnegating submersion. In friendship, not in marriage, she seems to say, caring and autonomy can co-exist.

In many of Jewett's stories women befriend each other because loneliness or Christian charity compels them to become their sister's keeper. Frequently these stories provide blueprints of good behavior rather than dramatize the power of love; they lack the ardor, rooted in the fusion of fervent affection and high ideals, that distinguishes "Martha's Lady." This full-bodied transcendental attraction sustained scores of women in nineteenth-century New England. "Martha's Lady" reveals Jewett's kinship with her compatriots: at once high-minded and passionate, she here demonstrates her assurance that female friendships merit a lifetime of devotion.

Notes

1. *The Notebooks of Henry James*, 8 April 1883, ed. F. O. Matthiessen and Kenneth B. Murdock (New York: Oxford University Press, Inc., 1947), p. 47.

2. For the best description of and commentary on these friendships, see Carroll Smith-Rosenberg, "The Female World of Love and Ritual: Relations Between Women in Nineteenth Cenutry America," *Signs: A Journal of Women in Culture and Society*, 1 (1975), 1–29. She views these eighteenth- and nineteenth-century friendships in their cultural and social setting, exploring the social structure and world view that made these deep and at times sensual friendships socially acceptable and emotionally satisfying.

An earlier article that provides a case study of the friendship between Luella Case and Sarah Edgarton is William R. Taylor and Christopher Lasch, "Two 'Kindred Spirits': Sorority and Family in New England, 1839–1846," *New England Quarterly*, 36 (1963), 23–41.

In the "Sisterhood" chapter of *The Bonds of Womanhood: 'Woman's Sphere' in New England, 1780–1835* (New Haven: Yale University Press, 1977), pp. 160–97, Nancy F. Cott offers an excellent analysis of how the changing social structure affected these friendships.

3. This self-conscious and idealized concept of friendship actually emerged in the late eighteenth century. See H. Clay Trumbull, *Friendship the Master-Passion* (Philadelphia: John D. Wattles & Co., 1894) for a description of the importance attached to friendship.

4. See Norton Mezvinsky, "An Idea of Female Superiority," *Midcontinent American Studies Journal*, 2 (1961), 27–37.

For a discussion of the nineteenth-century woman's alignment with the clergy and her assumed responsibility for society's moral improvement, see Ann Douglas, *The Feminization of American Culture* (New York: Alfred A. Knopf, 1977).

For an analysis of the development of this belief in women's superiority, see *The Bonds of Womanhood*, esp. "Religion," pp. 126–60.

5. Henry David Thoreau, *A Week on the Concord and Merrimack Rivers* (Boston: Houghton, Mifflin & Co., 1883), p. 285. All further references to this work appear in the text.

6. Sarah Orne Jewett, "Martha's Lady," *The Queen's Twin and Other Stories* (Boston: Houghton, Mifflin & Co., 1899), p. 142. All further references to this work appear in the text. "Martha's Lady" first appeared in the *Atlantic Monthly*.

7. "Dearest S.W.," n.d., *Letters of Sarah Orne Jewett*, ed. Annie Fields (Boston: Houghton, Mifflin & Co., 1911), p. 130.

8. Michele Murray, ed., *A House of Good Proportion: Images of Women in Literature* (New York: Simon & Schuster, 1973), pp. 106–07.

9. Emerson wrote: "It is sublime to feel and say of another, I need never meet, or speak, or write to him, we need not reinforce ourselves, or send tokens of remembrance." Quoted in Trumbull, pp. 60–61. Trumbull also cites an example of friends who shared only three days before being separated; but "the friendship then awakened was maintained unswervingly during twenty-six years of absence, and of silence, which followed that meeting" (p. 61).

10. Perry Miller discusses Thoreau's almost perverse tendency to become disenchanted with actual friends in "The Strategems of Consciousness—Woman and Men," *Consciousness in Concord* (Boston: Houghton, Mifflin & Co., 1958), pp. 80–103.

11. Smith-Rosenberg and Cott discuss the romantic aspect of actual female friendships at that time; often a woman became anxious over news of her friend's marriage, but usually the friendship was sustained. Jewett herself experienced anxiety when a close friend, her "Dear darling cousin Nelly" was about to marry. In her diary entry for 21 September 1867 she wrote: "I hate to have her married for which I can give no definite reason . . . . I nearly broke my heart over having to say goodbye." MS diary, Sarah Orne Jewett Collection, Houghton Library, Harvard University, quoted by permission of Houghton Library.

12. "Dear Friend," n. d., *Letters of Sarah Orne Jewett*, pp. 112–13.

13. In " 'Our Dear Sarah': An Essay on Sarah Orne Jewett," *Washington University Studies*, No. 24 (St. Louis, 1953), pp. 3–48; reprinted in *Appreciation of Sarah Orne Jewett*, ed. Richard Cary (Waterville, Maine: Colby College Press, 1973), pp. 86–111, A. M. Buchan asserts that Martha and "most of us" grow towards "dignity of character by means of a loyalty that has strength to endure through the years." Martha is loyal, Buchan says, to a woman who "brought a flash of brightness and understanding into her duties as a maid" (p. 102). It seems to me that loyalty is only one aspect of Martha's love for Helena, and that Helena gives her much more than help with her "duties as a maid."

14. Sarah Whitman to Sarah Orne Jewett, 26 September 1897, SOJ Collection, Houghton Library, Harvard University, quoted by permission of Houghton Library.

15. Smith-Rosenberg proposes that in the nineteenth century Americans viewed sexual and emotional impulses on a "continuum or spectrum of affect gradations" (p. 8). She describes many of these women's friendships as "sensual and platonic" (p. 4). She argues persuasively that these friendships cannot be explained by the romantic rhetoric that surrounded the concept of friendship at that time; the friendships were too emotionally intense and physically explicit.

16. Jewett's thirty year friendship with Annie Fields is an obvious source of such knowledge; the two women had strong emotional and spiritual ties. But throughout her life Jewett had similarly intense friendships with a dozen other women.

17. "My Dear Willa," 27 November 1908, *Letters of Sarah Orne Jewett*, pp. 246–47.

The Unpublished Love Poems of
Sarah Orne Jewett   Josephine Donovan*

Sarah Orne Jewett is not known as a poet; it is safe to say that she did not think of herself primarily as a poet. She published thirty-six poems in her lifetime.[1] Most of these were printed in her early years— before 1884. The only collection of her poetic works, *Verses*, which contains nineteen poems (twelve of which had been previously published), was published posthumously. Nevertheless, among unpublished Jewett materials,[2] there are 140 verse compositions, seventy-three of which are complete or nearly finished poems. The rest are fragments or unfinished, heavily reworked verses. Thirty of these compositions are love poems, or fragments thereof, and appear to have been written to women.

It is upon these love poems that I wish to concentrate, for they, together with early diaries, provide important new biographical information about this distinguished writer.[3] They should lead us to reevaluate the ongoing critical image of Jewett as a passionless "spinster," an image upon which much mistaken critical evaluation has been founded. They also provide us with yet another illustration of the complex nature of female-female liaisons in the nineteenth century.[4] As information such as this is acknowledged and integrated into our critical awareness, our understanding of the variety and quality of female experience expands, and the sophistication of our critical insights into work by women is thereby refined.

The realization that Jewett's emotional orientation was lesbian should make us look at her writing in a new light.[5] By "lesbian" I choose to use the definition developed by Blanche Wiesen Cook: "Women who love women, who choose women to nurture and support and to create a living environment in which to work creatively and independently, are lesbians."[6]

Many of Jewett's works are structured upon relationships between women. *Deephaven* (1877), her first major work, and *The Country of the Pointed Firs* (1896), considered her masterpiece, are framed upon intense friendships. Even in the most recent criticism, scholars are unclear as to what to make of these relationships. Their comments reveal their

*Reprinted from *Frontiers: A Journal of Women Studies*, 4, No. 3 (1979), 26–31, with permission.

discomfort. Writing on *Deephaven* in 1972, Robert L. Horn complains that the narrator, Helen Denis, "spends too much time . . . trying to get the reader to love and admire her friend Kate Lancaster. . . ."[7] Eugene Hillhouse Pool, in an article entitled "The Child in Sarah Orne Jewett," goes to tortuous lengths to explain away these relationships and to reduce them to a puerile, "undeveloped" level.[8]

Pool argues that Jewett's female characters' rejection of male suitors in "A White Heron" and *A Country Doctor* express their author's "repudiation" of "mature, passionate love," and her decision to remain in a state of childlike dependence upon her father. Indeed, he goes so far as to assert that the female friends in *The Country of the Pointed Firs* and *Deephaven* really represent Jewett's father. The reason the father is fictionally cast in female form, according to Pool, is because for Jewett "to travel about with a man . . . would be socially indecent."

This interpretation is erroneous. In fact, Jewett was quite aware of the temptation to fictionally disguise female-female relationships as heterosexual love stories, and consciously rejected it. One of her most pointed critical comments to the young Willa Cather was to advise her against doing this kind of "masquerading" in her future work. (See further discussion of Jewett's advice to Cather later in this article.)

While it is true that Jewett had a strong relationship with her father, it is clear from the poems and the diaries that Jewett's primary relationships were with women. These unpublished poems help to document once and for all the intensity of those ties, and to show that they were of primary significance in her life. Jewett's thirty-year liaison with Annie Adams Fields is well known and alluded to in every Jewett biography. Not so well known is the character of that relationship. Several of the poems appear to relate to their affair—for affair it was—and can therefore help us to understand its nature.

A perennial problem for scholars is reading the past through the meanings and significances of the present. To some degree, this is of course inevitable. Recent analyses of female relationships in the nineteenth century have acknowledged this problem. Carroll Smith-Rosenberg warned against the twentieth-century tendency to see everything in terms of dichotomies—in this case, between heterosexual and homosexual. "The essential question is not whether these women had genital contact and can therefore be defined as heterosexual or homosexual. . . ." The question is really to enlarge our understanding of these intimate female couples by neither denying their "emotional intensity and [their] sensual and physical explicitness," nor forcing them into twentieth-century definitions.[9]

Most Jewett scholars have erred in the former way by omitting material or by ignoring the significance of her relationships with women. The first to commit this error was Annie Fields herself in her edition of the Jewett letters published in 1911. The decision to edit out intimate material was made, however, only at the urging of Mark Anthony DeWolfe Howe, an eminent but genteel Boston scholar, who later put forth a heavily edited version of Fields' journals (*Memoirs of a Hostess*).

According to Howe's daughter Helen, "Father laid a restraining editorial hand across [Fields'] enthusiasm . . ."[10] in publishing the Jewett letters. He particularly urged her to delete nicknames, an obvious sign of intimacy, arguing that otherwise "all sorts of people [will read] them wrong . . ." (p. 84). Helen Howe quotes a typical letter from Jewett to Fields which she found, and which had been penciled through in the editing process. ("One sees the gentle pencil has been obediently at work. Miss Jewett's nickname for Mrs. Fields has been obliterated throughout" (p. 85). The original letter, as cited by Howe, reads:

> Good night dear dear Fuff—
> if you could only dream how
> I want to see you!
>
> . . .
>
> Your own P[inney] L[awson—a Jewett nickname]
> (p. 85)

This and one other letter which Helen Howe found "tucked" in her father's presentation copy of the Jewett letters were probably written in 1881, because in one of them Jewett mentions having received a copy of Fields' book, *Under the Olive*, which came out in 1881. Yet these letters were not included in the Fields edition of the Jewett letters; indeed Fields claims in that volume that there exist no extant letters between 1880 and 1882.[11] This was patently not the case, and Fields must have known it. Indeed there are several letters, most of them intimate, written from Jewett to Fields between 1877 and 1882.

I elaborate this because it shows deliberate falsification, for whatever reasons, on the part of Mark Anthony DeWolfe Howe and Annie Adams Fields. This raises questions as to how Jewett and Fields saw their relationship—whether each saw it differently, how contemporaries saw it, and whether such views were changing in 1911 when Annie Fields was editing her volume.

"Boston marriages,"—female couples living in a union similar to marriage—were relatively common in nineteenth-century Boston. Helen Howe notes that there were several such "marriages" in her father's circle, and that the Jewett-Fields liaison was one of them. In addition to her father's discomfort with the relationship, Helen Howe suggests that Henry James was similarly unnerved by the pair. "What Henry James, whose *The Bostonians* was published in 1888, found to 'catch at' in the friendship between the Charles Street ladies we can only guess" (p. 83).

The implication here is that the latent lesbian relationship between the characters Olive Chancellor and Verena Tarrant which James satirized in the novel was based on the Jewett-Fields liaison. There are in fact some parallels between the two couples: Olive was older than Verena, more aristocratic; Fields was also older and more urbane than Jewett, a native of rural Maine. Without commenting on this possibility, Leon Edel claims that James was merely reflecting the attitudes of his time in depicting the women so harshly.[12]

Nan Bauer Maglin argues that *The Bostonians* was an attempt to discredit the suffrage movement "with the charge of 'lesbianism' or perhaps only intense relationshipism.'"[13] Jewett in fact knew of the intense relationship that existed between Henry's sister Alice and Katherine Loring, commenting in a letter how "Alice James' going has made a great empty place in [Katherine's] life."[14]

The bulk of the commentaries, including the Frost and the Matthiessen biographies, and Laura Richards' and Willa Cather's remembrances, focus on the two women in the drawing room setting of Fields' 148 Charles Street home.[15] All are in a genteel vein, including Cather's, and none undertakes a critical analysis of the relationship.

Interestingly enough, however, in the mentor relationship which developed between Jewett and Cather in the latter months of Jewett's life, Jewett strongly suggested to Cather that her writing was weakened by the use of male personae. In criticizing one of Cather's early stories, she notes:

> The lover is as well done as he could be when a woman writes in the man's character,—it must always, I believe, be something of a masquerade. I think it is safer to write about him as you did about the others, and not try to be he! And you could almost have done it as yourself— a woman could love her in that same protecting way—a woman could even care enough to wish to take her away from such a life, by some means or other.[16]

It is instructive to compare Cather's *My Antonia* (1918) with Jewett's *The Country of the Pointed Firs* (1898) in this regard. Both deal with a strong female protagonist and both stories are told by an emotional, nostalgic narrator who was once in love with the central character. In Jewett's book the narrator is a woman; in Cather's, it is a man. The relationship in Jewett's work is far more credible than the awkward bond between Jim Burden and Antonia in the Cather novel. Cather chose to masquerade or encode what was a relationship between two women whereas Jewett did not.

Jewett never sought to deny the feminine in literary point of view as Cather did, and as did Gertrude Stein, a contemporary of Cather's. Catharine R. Stimpson has pointed out that Stein, too, seems to have moved toward a male identification in the early years of the twentieth century and a denial of the female.[17] Like Cather she also encoded or "masqueraded" her own lesbian relationships as she transposed them into her fiction.

Jewett did have, or at least was sensitive to, female role identity problems. The struggle of adopting a male profession but remaining "feminine" is manifest in her autobiographical novel, *The Country Doctor* (1884). But the struggle seems to have been less intense than with Cather and Stein, and it seems to have been more possible for her to do "male" things while "being" female than it was for her successors. One reason for this, I suppose, is that Jewett lived in a society which was "feminized," a process which was being reversed by the early twentieth century.[18]

The evidence of the following Jewett poems suggests that a world of female behavior existed in nineteenth-century America which has for the most part remained hidden. These poems have been available to researchers for more than forty years; none has chosen to pay them any attention. They come out of a lost world of female behavior that we now re-enter.

I would like to begin with a poem dated "23 Aug. 1880," on the theory that it is addressed to Annie Adams Fields and that it indicates the beginning of their relationship. It is possible, however, that the "girl" in this poem refers to an earlier romance, Cora Lee Rice. If it is referrent to the Jewett-Fields relationship, the 1880 date comes after the death of Jewett's father (September 20, 1878) and before the death of Annie Fields' husband, James T. Fields (April 23, 1881). These losses were severe emotional blows to each of them and are referred to in another poem. The 1880 poem was written to commemorate the first anniversary of the inception of a relationship between two women. It begins:

> Do you remember, darling
>   A year ago today
> When we gave ourselves to each other
>   Before you went away
> At the end of that pleasant summer weather
> Which we had spent by the sea together?
>
> How little we knew, my darling,
>   All that the year would bring!
> Did I think of the wretched mornings
>   When I should kiss my ring
> And long with all my heart to see
> The girl who gave the ring to me?
>
>   . . .
>
> We have not been sorry darling
>   We loved each other so—
> We will not take back the promises
>   We made a year ago—
>
>   . . .

> And so again, my darling
> I give myself to you,
> With graver thought than a year ago
> With love that is deep and true. (25)[19]

A surer documentation of the developing relationship between Jewett and Fields exists in early letters from Jewett to Fields, some of which Helen Howe mentions, and almost all of which were omitted from the 1911 edition of the Jewett letters. The earliest extant letter is a rather formal note dated "4 Dec 1877"; in the next letter, dated "8 Sept 1880," the tone has become warmer and somewhat coy. The next letter, dated "12 Jan 1881," is addressed, "Dear Mrs. Fields," and is again relatively formal. However, the next extant letter, which is undated except for the annotation "1881" penciled at the top (presumably by Annie Fields as she prepared her edition of the Jewett letters), is a letter of intimate friendship. It is addressed "Dearest Fuff" and signed "Pin," both familiar nicknames used by Jewett and Fields for one another.

Following chronologically are a series of letters, dated 1882 in pencil, which express the passionate love of Jewett for Fields. One addresses her "darling":

> Are you sure you know how much
> I love you? If you don't know,
> I cannot tell you! but I think of
> you and think of you and I am always
> being reminded of you . . .
> I am yours most lovingly—
>
> S.O.J.

Another early letter, dated in pencil "June 1882," reads in part:

> . . . Oh my dear darling I had
> forgotten that we loved each other
> so much a year ago—for it all seems
> so new to me every day—there is so much
> for us to remember already—
> But a year ago last winter seems
> a great way off for we have lived
> so much since . . .[20]

In a (probably) later poem Jewett laments that (presumably) Annie Fields spends more time in charity work than she does with her. Fields was heavily involved in social welfare work in Boston, and founded the Associated Charities of Boston, which she directed from 1879–94.

> No time for love! Because your way
> Goes all up hill; and every day
> Brings beggars for your thought, your time
> Until you hear the midnight chime.

However the poet comes to an appreciation of the loving nature of her friend and concludes, "Because you live so lovingly / Must I your constant lover be" (85).

Another poem appears to refer to the deaths of their father and husband and attempts to justify their relationship as a compensation for those losses. The reference to "summer days beside the sea" and "winter days when busy city life / Had caught us in its whirl and made us gay" ties the poem to the Jewett-Fields pattern of spending part of the year at the shore and part at Annie Fields' home in Boston. The poet comments on how, during the seasonal cycle, they have

> kept fast hold and could not stray
> Out of each other's sight, and could not take
> One step or thought but for each other's sake—
> In all this time in which we grew more dear
> Each to the other, there was nothing missed,
> No shadow chilled us and we felt no fear
> We were so happy while we loved and kissed.

After this honeymoon-like interlude, the couple fell upon more difficult days: "God took all other pleasure from us then—/ And when we found each others love alone / was left . . ." (line much reworked)—an apparent reference to the recent deaths. The poet realizes, however, that out of these adversities their love has grown more secure, concluding, "Our new love is the old love glorified" (64).

Another fragment reveals that the poet feels inadequate towards her beloved:

> For she should have the best of love
> And I must all my faults remove
> To love her fitly. Pity me
> That I always myself must be.

One poem speaks of the sense of comfort her lover's arms give her, and laments the time they must spend apart.

> My darling when you hold me in your arms
>   fills
> So sweet a sense of comfort thrills my heart
>
>   . . .
> Your love rewards me for all pain I bore
> One kiss you give me takes away regret (79).

She concludes on an interesting but mildly theological note,

> I think we soon should falter by the way
> And grow discouraged oh my dear true
> If we must wait for heaven till we died
> Or miss its glory till we reached the End (79).

The final verses are much reworked but the gist is that God has blessed them with their mutual love. Jewett had broached this idea in her diary of 1872[21] wherein she described at length her intense feelings for Kate (presumably Kate Birckhead), concluding, finally. "I know that it all comes from God, but I am so glad the 'way' is Kate."

Several of these unpublished lyrics are on general love themes, and cannot be linked to any specific relationship. A typical complete poem follows:

> Shall I ever tire of your kisses?
>   I asked myself today:
> When your arms had been around me
>   And you had gone away
>
> Will the pine-tree tire of the wind that blows
>   Through its branches from the sea
> And stirs within it its bravest life
>   As you do mine in me?
>
> Will the flower that the storm has beaten
>   Be tired of the summer sun
> That shines out clear and bright and warm
>   After the rain is done?
>
> Oh, no, my love, my darling
>   You always grow more dear
> Our hearts are one heart always now
>   And I need never fear (104).

Many of Jewett's poems read like song lyrics. A good example is a fragment that begins: "Between two nights between two days / I love I love my love always" (17). Jewett did indeed publish one song in her lifetime,[22] and it seems possible that some of these love verses were written to be sung. One describes the lovers in "the moorland" by the sea.

> Because I am your lover
> I kissed you lovingly.—
>
>   And no one knew I kissed you
> But the white gulls and the sea (76).

Another describes the loved one wandering in the fields, gathering roses.

> Oh come again my true love
>   Nor wander far from me
> I never loved another girl
>   As I do love thee (81).

In "Together," a published poem,[23] Jewett imagines that the dreams of her friend have been sent telepathically. Jewett's interest in dreams and spiritualism has not been thoroughly examined; testimony to its strength may be seen in a very moving letter Annie Adams Fields wrote shortly after Jewett's death in 1909. Fields noted: "She used to say we must learn not to be so dependent upon bodily presence . . . it is indeed true that having laid aside her beautiful body she now seems very near to me in many loving ways which are all her own and feel greatly comforted & companioned by her."[24]

It is clear that some of the unpublished poems refer to individuals other than Annie Adams Fields. Some poems are addressed to "C.L.R." (33), probably Cora Lee Rice, an early friend, and to Ellen Francis Mason (138). In addition, a poem entitled "A Flower's Namesake" (32) speaks to a "Julie"; one slightly amended version of this manuscript has "J.M.S." notated at the top of the page. An unfinished scrap which begins, "I saw her first beside the sea" identifies the "her" as "Beautiful Maud" (57).

Beyond the evidence of the poems, we know from letters and diaries that as a young woman Jewett had close relationships with several women. These included Grace Gordon, Kate Birckhead, Georgie Halliburton, Ella Walworth, and Ellen Mason, the first five names on a list of thirty-one close friends and relatives inserted in her 1874 diary.[25]

The diary itself records her personal feelings about the friends noted above, especially about Kate on whom she clearly had an intense crush:

24 May [1871—written after two days spent with Kate in Boston] . . . when I heard her voice on the stairs . . . it gave me the queerest feeling. I have longed to see her, to be with her, for so many months that I could not believe it was real. My dear dear darling Kate!

January 14 [1872—written after a four-day visit with Kate in Newport] . . . I think she cared more for me than she used . . . How I wish I could *do* something for you to show that I love you Kate! When I try to talk about it the only words I can think of, seem such weak silly meaningless ones, & just the same ones which people used when they do not mean half that I do![26]

Jewett's desire to express her feelings for Kate may have been a primary motivation for her first major composition, *Deephaven*: the first sketches which were later included in the *Deephaven* collection were published in the September, 1873 issue of the *Atlantic Monthly* less than a year after Jewett wrote the above entries in her diary. There seems little doubt that the fictional Kate Lancaster is based upon the Kate of the diaries. *Deephaven*, then, may well be Sarah Orne Jewett's *Orlando*.

We may conclude that beginning as a young woman[27] and continuing through her life Jewett was involved in several intimate relationships with women. At times these reached a level of passionate intensity.

An understanding of the emotional life of a writer gives a critic a better sense of the author's motivations and intentions. And while these insights should not perhaps be controlling in a critical assessment of an author's work, they should at least prevent patently erroneous judgments.

Notes

1. Carl J. Weber, *A Bibliography of the Published Writings of Sarah Orne Jewett* (Waterville, Maine: Colby College Press, 1949). Subsequent bibliographies list no further poems.

2. I am restricting myself in this article to the unpublished poems in The Houghton Library, Harvard University. There are a few unpublished verses in other manuscript collections, as follows: Boston Public Library, University of Virginia, Colby College, Massachusetts Historical Society. These are, however, largely duplicates of those in the Houghton collection.

3. I do not know why previous biographers and critics have ignored this material, as it has been available to researchers for more than forty years. One can only assume, following Thomas S. Kuhn (*The Structure of Scientific Revolutions*, 2nd ed., enl. [Chicago: Univ. of Chicago Press, 1970]), that critics, like scientists, use paradigms which do not allow them to see anomalous "facts" or to recognize their significance.

4. Several excellent articles have initiated this investigation. They include: William R. Taylor and Christopher Lasch, "Two 'Kindred Spirits': Sorority and Family in New England, 1839–1846," *New England Quarterly*, 36, 1 (March, 1963), 23–41; Carroll Smith-Rosenberg, "The Female World of Love and Ritual: Relations between Women in Nineteenth-Century America," *Signs*, 1, 1 (Autumn 1975), 1–29; Catharine R. Stimpson, "The Mind, the Body, and Gertrude Stein," *Critical Inquiry*, 3, 3 (Spring 1977), 489–506. Glenda Hobbs, working independently of me, has also analyzed the nature of Jewett's female friendships in her article "Pure and Passionate: Female Friendship in Sarah Orne Jewett's 'Martha's Lady,'" *Studies in Short Fiction* (forthcoming, Winter 1980).

5. For revised interpretations along these lines, see Josephine Donovan, "A Woman's Vision of Transcendence: A New Interpretation of the Works of Sarah Orne Jewett," *The Massachusetts Review* (forthcoming Winter 1979), and Josephine Donovan, *Sarah Orne Jewett* (New York: Frederick Ungar, forthcoming 1980).

6. Blanche Wiesen Cook, "Female Support Networks and Political Activism: Lillian Wald, Crystal Eastman, Emma Goldman," *Chrysalis*, No. 3 (1977), p. 48.

7. "The Power of Jewett's *Deephaven*," *Colby Literary Quarterly*, 9, 12 (December 1972), 617.

8. *Colby Literary Quarterly*, 7, 11 (September 1967), 506, 508.

9. Smith-Rosenberg, 8.

10. Helen Howe, *The Gentle Americans, 1864–1960, Biography of a Breed* (New York: Harper, 1965), p. 84. All further references to this work are cited by page number in the text.

11. *Letters of Sarah Orne Jewett*, ed. Annie Fields (Boston: Houghton Mifflin, 1911), p. 12.

12. As reported in Nan Bauer Maglin, "Fictional Feminists in *The Bostonians* and *The Odd Women*," in *Images of Women in Fiction: Feminist Perspectives*, ed. Susan Koppelman Cornillon (Bowling Green: Bowling Green Popular Press, 1972), p. 220.

Of course there have been numerous attempts to read the *The Bostonians* as a roman à clef.

13. Maglin, p. 220.

14. John Eldridge Frost, *Sarah Orne Jewett* (Kittery Point, Maine: The Gundalow Club, Inc., 1960), p. 95.

15. Frost; F. O. Matthiessen, *Sarah Orne Jewett* (Boston: Houghton Mifflin, 1929); Laura Richards, *Stepping Westward* (New York: Appleton, 1931); Willa Cather, "148 Charles Street" and "Miss Jewett," in *Not Under Forty* (New York: Knopf, 1936).

16. *Letters of Sarah Orne Jewett*, pp. 246–47. Cather's story is "On the Gull's Road" published in the December 1908 issue of *McClure's Magazine*.

17. Stimpson, cited in note 4, above.

18. An excellent theoretical discussion of the transition in women's relationships at the end of the nineteenth century is provided by Nancy Sahli, "Smashing: Women's Relationships Before the Fall," *Chrysalis*, No. 8 (1979), pp. 17–27.

19. All poems cited, unless otherwise indicated, are from the Houghton Library MS. Am 1743.25. Subsequently, numerals following excerpts indicate the specific item in the verse collection. These works are quoted by permission of The Houghton Library, Harvard University.

20. All these letters are Houghton bMS. Am 1743(255). They are quoted by permission of The Houghton Library, Harvard University.

21. MS. Diary 1871–1879, Houghton MS. Am 1743.1 (341), entry for Jan 14 [1872]. Published by permission of The Houghton Library, Harvard University.

22. "Boat Song," set to music by Richard Hoffman, published in New York by G. Schirmer, c. 1879. See John Austin Parker, "Sarah Orne Jewett's 'Boat Song,'" *American Literature*, 23, 1 (March 1951), 133–36.

23. *Atlantic Monthly*, 35 (May 1875), 590.

24. ALS from Annie Adams Fields to Mrs. Charles Fairchild, August 20, 1909. Boston Public Library MS. 605. Cited by courtesy of the Trustees of the Boston Public Library.

25. Houghton MS. Am 1743.1 (341). The list is not dated but is inserted in the 1874 section. Another letter list dated 1872 holds twenty names, including these five close friends (Houghton bMS. Am 1743.26 [7a]).

26. Houghton MS. Am 1743.1 (341). Cited by permission of The Houghton Library, Harvard University.

27. In an earlier diary (1 Jan–31 Dec 1869) Jewett's intense attachment to several other friends is documented. These include Cicely Burt, Grace Gordon, Minnie Fiske, and especially Ella Walworth (Houghton bMS. Am 1743.26 [4]).

ORIGINAL ESSAYS

A Closer Look at the Jewett-Fields Relationship

Judith Roman*

In 1886 Sarah Orne Jewett wrote to Annie Fields:

> Dearest Fuff—I am sorry that this letter will not get into the morning post and so you will not have a word from your affectionate and lazy Pinny this rainy day. I long to see you and say all sorts of foolish things, and to be as bold a Pinny as can be! and to kiss you ever so many times and watch you going about and to be your own P. L.[1]

This note contains the elements which have puzzled or irritated some readers and led others to make incomplete interpretations of this fascinating relationship. The nicknames (Fuff, Pinny, and P. L. for Pinny Lawson), the private and apparently childish language, and the expression of physical affection, have led some critics, notably Ernest Hillhouse Pool, to conclude that Jewett remained a child in her emotional relationships.[2] These critics see Annie Fields as an older, parental figure in Jewett's life. Recent feminist critics, such as Lilian Faderman and Josephine Donovan, have focused on the emotional intensity of this relationship and considered it essentially lesbian in nature.[3] A closer look at the lesser known member of this couple, Annie Fields, and a careful reading of the Jewett-Fields correspondence, reveals a complex relationship in which there was an easy exchange of roles that fostered both freedom and security for the two women. A reading of two of Jewett's works, the short story "Tom's Husband" and *The Country of the Pointed Firs*, shows how Jewett used her life with Fields, or what she learned from it, to create some of her most interesting fictional relationships.

Annie Adams entered public life by marrying James T. Fields in 1854 when she was twenty and he was thirty-seven.[4] Annie's father, like Jewett's, was a doctor, as well as a member of Boston's school board. Annie received an excellent education at the George B. Emerson School

*This essay was written especially for this volume and is included here by permission of the author.

119

for Girls in Boston, one of the few schools where young women could study such subjects as mathematics, science, English literature, and French. Emerson also inculcated in his students a belief in healthful exercise and in responsibility toward the less fortunate members of society.[5] Strictly in terms of formal education, Annie was better educated than her husband. She could read and translate from French, Italian, and German, and when she and James traveled abroad she became their spokesperson since he knew no languages except English. An avid reader of the classics, Annie also had a working knowledge of Greek.

Although some writers have assumed that Annie was molded by her husband into the confident, intelligent hostess who was capable of handling several delicate egos at a time, it is far likelier that she already possessed these qualities when she was married.[6] James was friendly and enjoyed company, but he had a shy side. Annie, however, in addition to being a good conversationalist and an appreciative listener, possessed a gift for organization which she used both in her work as a hostess and later in her charity activities. Willa Cather, who knew Mrs. Fields well when the latter was in her eighties, perceptively observed: "No woman could have been so great a hostess, could have made so many highly developed personalities happy under her roof, could have blended so many strongly specialized and keenly sensitive people in her drawing-room, without having a great power to control and organize."[7] It is this power which makes Annie's remarkable position in the literary world comprehensible. Annie Fields's principal talents lay in areas not ordinarily studied by scholars, perhaps because they were in the traditional "feminine" areas of entertaining, conversing, advising, and organizing. Even her literary achievements were in nontraditional genres, such as memoir and biography. Her most interesting writing is in her often-quoted, but still unpublished, diaries.[8]

During the 1860s Fields began keeping the literary diaries which have been mined so successfully by biographers for their anecdotes about Holmes, Longfellow, Lowell, Emerson, Whittier, Stowe, Hawthorne, and many other writers. Her diaries sometimes moved into more personal matters, however, and she recorded there her own desire to write poetry and to study languages.[9] Annie's household responsibilities constantly frustrated her efforts to write, for, in addition to supervising a large staff, she was frequently called upon to entertain visiting writers, often several times a day. James relied on her judgment about manuscripts as well as about social matters; their childlessness made it possible for Annie to be a real partner in her husband's work. As a result of her involvement, Annie was hurt by business-related quarrels with two women she cared about, Mary Abigail Dodge (Gail Hamilton), and Sophia Hawthorne, who thought Ticknor & Fields, James's firm, was cheating them on royalties. Dodge eventually filed a lawsuit.[10]

In 1867, Annie and James were distracted from this lawsuit, which was imminent, by the second American lecture tour of Dickens. Dickens is important to an understanding of Annie Fields for two reasons: he appears to be the second of the three passions of her life, and he encouraged the interest in charity work which gave her a successful career completely apart from the lives of either James or Sarah.[11] Partly because of Dickens' influence, partly because of her frustration with her writing, and partly because of natural inclination, Annie began to devote her energy to the improvement of social services for the poor in Boston.

In the 1870s she worked toward the foundation of what eventually became the Associated Charities of Boston. She held a variety of offices including director and vice-president for the rest of her life.[12] Her organizational skill and ability to handle people served her and the community well. She continued to write poetry and to translate, to travel with her husband as he gave lectures, and to entertain, but when James became ill in the late 1870s the activities of both were severely curtailed. He died unexpectedly in 1881, leaving Annie a well-off and comparatively youthful widow at forty-seven. This is the point at which Sarah, fifteen years younger and a promising author of three books, became Annie's lifelong companion.

Jewett had met the Fieldses sometime after "Mr. Bruce," her first story to be accepted by the *Atlantic*, was taken in 1869 by William Dean Howells who succeeded Fields as editor. It is not known exactly when the friendship between Annie and Sarah became intimate, but Sarah visited the Fieldses at their summer home in Manchester, Massachusetts, in 1870. In her article, "The Love Poetry of Sarah Orne Jewett," Josephine Donovan suggests that Jewett may have already been writing love poems to Annie Fields at this time.[13] Jewett had published only three books, including *Deephaven*, before 1880 and was still a relatively new member of the Boston literary circle. Perhaps the single most important thing to understand about the Jewett-Fields relationship and Annie's importance to Sarah's life and career is that in 1881 Fields held a far more prominent position in Boston literary life than Jewett; this is, of course, contrary to their relative importance today. The advantages of this relationship for Sarah were numerous. The preeminent literary hostess of the day, Annie was in a position to introduce Sarah to all the writers she admired, including Tennyson, who disliked American literary tourists. By living with Fields, Jewett enjoyed the advantage of conversation with and exposure to the best creative minds of the time. She also benefitted from the advice, both editorial and practical, of a woman who was extremely knowledgeable about many aspects of both magazine and book publishing. Annie knew about such matters as how and when to ask for more money, better book formats, more favorable contracts. In addition, by living much of the year in a household under Annie's experienced supervision, Sarah enjoyed a home similar to those in fairy tales where meals were magically cooked and served, clothes were picked up, paper appeared on the desk, and ink pots were silently refilled. All of this must have increased Jewett's confidence and decreased any anxiety she had about the practical matters of authorship, making it possible for her to devote herself single-mindedly to the writing itself.

Although she had a strong emotional attachment to her South Berwick home, Boston was very attractive to a young writer who had always lived in a small village. Her life with Fields expanded her horizons in other ways as well, and Jewett took her first trip to Europe in Annie's company in 1882. When they returned, the women settled down to the pattern of visits which lasted with little alteration for the next twenty years.[14] Jewett spent most of the winter with Fields in Boston, typically going to Berwick to visit her family sometime in late spring or early summer. Annie would visit her briefly there, usually on her way to Manchester-by-the-Sea, as she preferred to call Manchester, Massachusetts. Jewett accompanied Fields to the summer house and spent the remainder of the summer there with her friend. In September Fields returned to Boston to reopen the Charles Street house.

The letters exchanged between Sarah and Annie during their time apart tell a great deal about the dynamics of their relationship, including its reciprocity and lack of fixed roles. The letters establish that while Sarah appears to have been more emotionally dependent on Annie—at least on her physical presence—she became the senior partner when their writing was discussed. In 1882 Sarah wrote Annie:

> I have not been getting on very well without you, and I *had* to hear from you just as often as I could. . . . I wanted an armful of little books[15] dreadfully sometimes and I thinked and thinked about them! and I am sure you know just as well this minute, as if I could really put my head in your lap and tease you as you set [*sic*] at your desk— It is just like being with you still—I believe every thing of me but my boots and clothes, and the five little stones and the rest of the things in my pocket, and the hairpin—all goes back to Charles St. and stays with you half a day at a time.[16]

Fields's replies to Jewett's letters suggest that Sarah often pleaded with her friend to come stay with her during her visits home. But after spending twenty-five years giving someone else's interests precedence, Fields clung to her independence. She spent time daily at the Associated Charities, enlisting volunteer visitors, raising money, and lecturing at small meetings as well as conventions. She also used her literary talent for the cause, writing one book, *How to Help the Poor* (1883), and many articles on the improved methods of assisting the needy and solving the problems of the city.[17] Fields staunchly refused to give up any of her work for Jewett. As she wrote in an undated letter, probably written in the early 1880s: "My dearest dearest child; Your dear letters & urgings are hard to resist but I really have too much to do to be able to get away. My Boston business is enough for one person but added to that comes all my private affairs—you see I have the work of two people to do in the world while I stay now—"[18] In an 1888 letter, responding to a gift of claret from Sarah, Annie wrote: "Of course I wish we were together, but I feel as if my life were here and my *purpose*. By and by I will come to you O so gladly—"[19] Unlike Jewett's, Annie's expressions of love do not seem to have included requests for Sarah's prompt return, and she did not dwell on their separation for long in her letters: "My dearest child: How I wish for you all the time! I get quite tired sometimes making decisions and looking about things when you are not here. But this cold and changing weather has been rather difficult to bear."[20] When Sarah expressed guilt over her absence, Annie reassured her that she understood: "O it is quite worth-while for you to be at home; entirely the thing to do just now. I am really very little alone; and when there is other company there are often steps to be taken and talk to be carried on at greater length than I can always manage alone and I am grateful for the assistance."[21] Although neither of the women enjoyed their separations, Annie seems to have approached them more philosophically.

While Fields was the more experienced member of their relationship in most respects, Jewett clearly had greater authority when it came to writing itself. Annie recognized her friend's superior gifts. Although Jewett sometimes looked to Annie for moral support, she was confident about her writing. Annie, however, was insecure about her writing; prior to 1881 she had published only three long poems, all privately printed, and a single volume of classically inspired poems.[22] Annie's poetry was received with respect by her friends and the press, but she was not taken seriously as a writer. In a number of letters Jewett reassured Fields about the success of her work and urged her to new tasks. Thus, the imbalance that could have resulted from the disparity in age and social position was offset by Jewett's skill as a writer.

In 1883, early in their life together, Fields published her first essay, "Mr. Emerson in the Lecture Room," in the *Atlantic*.[23] In the same issue were act 3 of Henry James's dramatization of *Daisy Miller* and Jewett's story "A Landless Farmer." Jewett wrote Fields to compliment her on the appearance of the article and to reassure her about payment and future use of the material:

> I have been looking over the Atlantic and liking it very much—only I think it was an outrage to have filled so much space in three numbers with Daisy Miller's Dramatization—and I don't see how Mr. James could bear to waste his time over it—Oh, dear Fuff, the cheque for your article will not come until the first day of June, so don't be looking for it in vain before that time. . . . Don't you think the Emerson article looks well? I was thinking about there being any trouble about your doing it, but I think there couldn't be for they could use it in a book if they liked just as well as ever. I should never have a fear of it. Pin always said so[.][24]

In another letter, Jewett expressed her enthusiasm about a piece by Fields, probably one of the memoirs she wrote in the 1880s. This note, from a fragment dated 1883, contains one of the most extravagant uses of Jewett's nickname, Pinny: "My dear little Fuff I am so glad about it— Didn't I always say you would have more lovely things to say? Not to be a keeping-still Fuff—but I know the thing—that Pintoe bursted its dear self with pride—it hoped you would excuse it, but it could not contain even one of Pin's feets when she was so proud."[25] In another letter of reassurance, Jewett called Fields, "Mouse," another favorite nickname, and used a different dialect: "Dear Mouse So you are a-writing too! Good luck to you then—and Pinny to be there to hear the paper please Ladies—and to tell Fuff it is good because she will think it isn't, she always does, you know—Now be like Pinny—a-bragging of her success as a historian."[26]

Those familiar with Jewett's correspondence or recent articles about her are already aware that she frequently used nicknames in referring to herself and to Fields as well as to other friends.[27] A careful reading of the letters shows that Jewett's use of these nicknames is important in analyzing the nature of the Jewett-Fields relationship. Sarah primarily uses one nickname for herself—Pinny—which was a childhood nickname referring to the smallness of her head in proportion to her height and broad shoulders. There is an important variation of this name, however, Pinny Lawson or P. L. for short, which is a reference to Sam Lawson, a character in Harriet Beecher Stowe's *Oldtown Folks and Sam Lawson's Oldtown Fireside Tales*. Sam Lawson is the "village do-nothing" in the books, a lazy, talkative, shiftless storyteller and much-beloved rebel against Oldtown's puritanical ways. Annie, Sarah, or both noticed a resemblance (or a playfully attributed resemblance) between Sarah (in certain moods) and Sam Lawson, and so the nickname was born.[28] Annie became T. L., who functions in Jewett's letters as a more responsible member of the Lawson family, and is perhaps even modeled on Hepsy, Sam's waspish wife.[29]

What the letters make clear is that Jewett used these nicknames to correspond to different roles in which she saw herself and Annie. But instead of identifying each woman with one consistent role, such as parent/child or male/female, Jewett used the nicknames to create two different sets of almost diametrically opposed roles. The different names thus imply a relationship in which the women's roles were highly flexible and interchangeable. Pinny Lawson is, in fact, a well-developed character, an irresponsible scamp who needs to be prodded to work and cannot resist leaning out of the window in Charles Street to watch the fireworks. When Sarah is P. L., Annie is T. L., a foil to Sarah's scamp who encourages her to settle down and get to work. In one letter, Sarah refers to T. L. as P. L.'s "doctor." An early letter shows Sarah talking quite seriously about her lack of industriousness, then moving playfully into her "Lawson" self:

> I have had a hard time of worry and hard work since you went away on Monday. I wish I could be idle all the rest of June, that is not feel forced to do things. But I suppose it cannot be and the only thing possible in a busy life is to rest *in* one's work since one cannot rest *from* it. I think a good deal about the long story but it has not really taken hold of me yet—I do feel so impatient with myself dear Fuffy, I'm always straying off on wrong roads and I am so wicked about things This is one of the time's [*sic*] when I think despairingly about my faults and see little chance of their ever being mended—But Fuffy to have patience with Pin and Please to love her!— . . . [(]Oh Pinny to go to work! An idle and thriftless Pinny to whom the rest of the Lawsons are industrious)[.][30]

Another letter further illustrates the child/adult, patient/doctor dynamic which is operating in this set of nicknames:

> Pin wasn't going to tell this, but can't keep anything from T. L.—she runned against a door in the dark last night and banged her head shameful! She was so frightened of T. L., afterward because T. L. scolds she for banging she's head—It was on her eyebrow the blow fell, and after that recovered itself, and Pin composed herself to sleep, her dear nose suddenly began to ache worse than the other and she confidently expected a black eye but she is not at all out of repair this morning.[31]

Jewett's use of nicknames is invariably accompanied by the frequent use of childish diction, a kind of dialect that sounds fearfully close to baby talk; it is illustrated in several of the letters quoted above. Sarah's use of such language is a problem because Jewett scholars of an earlier generation declared that Jewett had no mature sexual relationships in her life and assumed that the Jewett-Fields relationship was like that of a parent and child.[32] Sarah's declaration when she was forty-eight to her friend Sara Norton that "This is my birthday and I am nine years old"[33] lends support to those who would argue that Sarah functioned as a child in her relationships. While it is undeniable, on the evidence of the letters, that Sarah enjoyed playing the role of a naughty child or a tomboy in her relationship with Annie, it is equally true, on the same evidence, that this was not the only role she played.

Sarah had a variety of nicknames for Annie in addition to T. L.: Fuff, Fuffy, Fuffatee, Mouse, and Mousatee. Mouse and Fuffy are not names one would normally associate with a stern parental figure. From the context in which these nicknames appear, it is evident that Sarah used them when she was taking a protective role toward Annie, a role which is often in direct contradiction to her role as P. L., although Sarah is still, confusingly, called Pinny. The protective (and adult) Pinny uses childish diction at least as much as the scamp P. L., which seems strange until it is remembered that it is the parent who uses baby talk to the child, thus aligning Jewett with the role of parent. Annie showed that she understood Sarah's use of this language in her introduction to her edition of Sarah's letters; alluding to the letters that Swift wrote to Stella, she said: "The same handling of 'the little language' is here; the same joy and repose in friendship. This 'little language,' the private 'cuddling' of lovers, of mothers, and children, since the world began, was native also to her."[34]

Sarah's letters to Annie reflected this variety of roles. When she wrote to her as Mouse, she sometimes took a playfully superior tone: "I remind myself constantly how good all this work is in every way—and how thankful I shall be to have done it when I go to England again—I shall be able to improve an ignorant [in tiny writing] mouse's Mind."[35] Many of the letters reflect a picture of Annie as a cute, diminutive, cuddly creature who required the protection of a tougher, more worldly Sarah. In a letter from Jewett to Fields following a big storm, she wrote: "I hope my darling Fuff didn't go blowing along Charley St and get lodged poor little thing! in one of the trees or telegraph wires. Oh I *must* go and tend to her! I am her most loving and anxious Pinny."[36] Sarah's characterization of Annie as "mouse" makes her seem not only weak but also frivolous: "I hope now that you will have a quiet Sunday I think such a giddy mousatee must need it."[37] Sarah was not above using her nickname for Annie as the occasion for a pun reminiscent of Annie's earlier nickname, given her by the Hawthornes, of Mrs. Meadows: "Deep snows are hard on the mice—poor little field mice—(cousins of a dear friend!)."[38]

Once these roles are discerned, it becomes clear that some of the most charming letters contain sudden shifts or at first confusing juxtapositions. The following letter begins, for example, with Jewett encouraging Annie as Mouse, but by the end Jewett has become the rebellious (though obedient) P. L.:

> Dear Mouse, I do hate to have you so tired—Are you having a good full glass of claret twice a day? . . . My dear Fuff you are so good about the verses but when I get thinking about your Orpheus[39] as I did today—*I* think that is the top thing and I am so proud of it and so thankful that we went to Richfield for the writing of that if for nothing else—I want to hear it again when I come, if we get time, and we *will* you know! So we are to see the President and Mrs. C——[40] but hang us if we will go to their reception unless you say so, then a meek Pinny will take hold of hands and say yes Fuff if you please and "tag on"—This letter is just written to send you a kiss in— from your P. L.[41]

The next letter changes from one persona to another so quickly the shifts are dizzying:

> What a Fuff to say that I must destroy the Pearl St—Fuffy poem!! I *won't!* so you may expect vast naughtiness on that point. I love them

very much and you are not to be low about them or about your work or your own dear self—I wonder if you are skipping your claret for lunch or misbehaving yourself any way—Pinny to come and tend to you awfil [sic]![42]

Although the letters reveal the intensity and eccentricity of the Jewett-Fields relationship, they cannot reveal its positive effect on both women's work. The two decades between 1881, when they began living together, and 1902, when Sarah suffered the disabling accident which kept her in Maine, were their most productive years. Sarah published virtually all her best work in these years, as did Annie, and both of their careers peaked in 1896, when Sarah published *The Country of the Pointed Firs* and Annie published her best book, *Authors and Friends*. The secret of the success of this relationship for both their personal and their professional lives lay in its complete reciprocity and in their ability to create for themselves a form of marriage in which all roles were interchangeable and neither partner was limited by the relationship. The fitness of their relationship extended beyond a conventional use of the term "marriage," with its implied roles of husband and wife, or "Boston marriage," which simply refers to a congenial arrangement of two women joining households. Both women brought to their union an understanding of how to make a relationship both intimate and unconfining. Annie had firsthand knowledge of the perils of traditional marriage because of her life with James T. Fields, which had been happy but kept her from pursuing her personal goals.[43] Sarah also understood the danger posed by any assignment of roles; in a conversation with Whittier, Sarah is reported to have said that she had no intention of marrying, and had more need of a wife than a husband.[44] In her book *A Country Doctor*, Sarah rejected marriage for her heroine, Nan Prince, because being a wife precluded the possibility of simultaneously pursuing a career.[45] In addition, one of Jewett's most interesting but little known stories, "Tom's Husband," published in 1883 in the volume dedicated to Annie, provides concrete evidence of Jewett's insight into marriage and the drawbacks of inflexible roles.[46]

In "Tom's Husband" Tom and Mary fall in love and marry despite Mary's unusually independent nature and Tom's lack of interest in the male world of work. Since both had independent incomes prior to their marriage, both stay at home and Mary takes over the housekeeping while Tom pursuses his various hobbies. After a goading letter from Tom's sister, who lives in Japan, Mary persuades Tom to allow her to reopen a factory which he has inherited but has no wish to run. Although Tom thinks people will call him a fool, he admits that he enjoyed running the house before his marriage, thinks he can do it better than Mary, and has no interest in the factory himself. With Tom's somewhat grudging permission, Mary makes a success of the business. But while this open-mindedness pays off at first, eventually it causes problems. Tom and Mary find themselves lapsing into the stereotypical roles associated with the role and sex they have adopted: Mary becomes distant and condescending, brings people home for dinner without warning, and is too tired to be companionable with Tom in the evenings. Tom becomes obsessed with household details and feels humiliated when a neighbor calls to borrow some yeast at a bad moment. In the story, their difficulties are resolved first, by their becoming aware of them, and second, by Mary's agreeing to set aside the business for six months so they can take a trip to Europe together and renew their relationship. Presumably, they will return to the jobs they prefer but their new understanding of the limits and dangers of any fixed role will bring them greater success. In the story, Jewett makes it clear that role *reversal* is not in itself a solution to the role problem. In a successful relationship, both partners must refuse to be limited to *any* single role, whether conventional or not.

This story can be loosely read as a description of the Jewett-Fields relationship, with its situation springing from Sarah's belief in the necessity of flexible roles in any intimate arrangement. The radical nature of their partnership (radical in a sense other than lesbian) has been overlooked because of inadequate, or, in Annie's case, nonexistent biographical studies. Both Annie and Sarah possessed the experience and insight necessary to make their partnership work. Annie's successful, though limiting, twenty-five year marriage, her intelligence, her skill with people, and her insistence upon her own career were her main contributions, while Sarah had observed closely different kinds of marriages and households, including those involving two women, and she moved easily from one role to another. Their correspondence, especially Sarah's letters with their initially puzzling private language, documents the complete reciprocity and successful transcendence of stereotypes they achieved. Jewett's life with Annie led to the writing of Sarah's masterpiece, *The Country of the Pointed Firs*, which contains several relationships, notably that between the narrator and Mrs. Todd, which are strengthened by an ability to be flexible.

Jewett illustrates her characters' flexibility by showing their ability to change themselves in a variety of ways, especially in their relationships to others. There are numerous passages in the book which describe the ability of the older characters to be youthful, especially Mrs. Todd, Mrs. Blackett, William, and Esther. These references to girlishness or boyishness are not evidence of Jewett's clinging to childhood, but reveal an ability to be what one is not, to change roles. The reason the characters always become more youthful rather than older is simply a result of the age of the characters. Both Jewett and Fields had the experience of living with a member of an older generation, and both had many younger friends. Annie Fields turned sixty in 1894, two years before *The Country of the Pointed Firs* came out, and she was as energetic and more productive then than she had been at thirty. When Mrs. Todd says, "Keep me movin' enough, an' I'm twenty year old summer an' winter both,"[47] she is describing agelessness and adaptability, not a longing for childhood. When Jewett's narrator says about William that "Once I wondered how he had come to be so curiously wrinkled, forgetting, absent-mindedly, to recognize the effects of time" (118), she was reflecting a natural indifference to aging in a person one loves.

The inhabitants of Dunnet Landing have the ability to play different roles in their relationships with others as well. The most notable examples of this are Mrs. Blackett and Mrs. Todd, who regularly exchange the roles of mother and child. There are numerous examples of role exchange or reversal: William is both "son and daughter" to Mrs. Blackett (42); Mrs. Todd sends the doctor on vacation; Elijah Tilley in some sense "becomes" his wife after her death by keeping the house just as she left it; when Mrs. Todd goes to visit poor Joanna, she mothers the older woman, who then reverses the situation and comforts Mrs. Todd. Mrs. Todd says that William resembles Mrs. Blackett, while she herself takes after their father, and on several occasions she proves to be a better man than the man; for example, she has to knock down the minister to keep him from capsizing her sailboat. Although role reversal is Jewett's topic in several short stories, such as "Tom's Husband," "Hallowell's Pretty Sister," and "Autumn Holiday," as well as in the novel *A Country Doctor*, role flexibility is a continuous thread in *The Country of the Pointed Firs*, appearing in nearly every characterization and in many incidents.

The bond between Jewett and Fields appears in more definite form in the relationship between the narrator and Mrs Todd. Although the intensity of feeling between the two women has been evident to feminist critics for some time, the obvious lack of resemblance between Mrs. Todd and Annie Fields has deterred anyone from attempting to compare the two relationships in any specific way. However, when the obvious disparities in appearance and occupation are set aside, there are a number of remarkable parallels between the relationships of Jewett and Fields and the narrator and Mrs. Todd. First of all, Mrs. Todd is repeatedly compared to classical images, such as the sibyl and the caryatide; at one point the narrator says of Mrs. Todd, "She might belong to any age, like an idyl of Theocritus" (56). While Jewett might certainly be expected to have knowledge of classical Greek images, critics have overlooked the fact that Annie Fields was a student of classical Greek and that the majority of her poetry was based on classical myths and historical figures. Her first long book of poetry, *Under the Olive*, is composed entirely of poems on Greek subjects, including a tribute to Theocritus, one of her favorite poets. Jewett refers to her admiration of this volume more than once in her letters to Fields. Thus, Mrs. Todd and Annie Fields are linked by classical allusion at the outset.

The first key to the parallels between Jewett and Fields and the narrator and Mrs. Todd appears in the first sentence of the second section, when the narrator says of Mrs. Todd's house, "There was only one fault to find with this choice of a summer lodging place, and that was its complete lack of seclusion" (13–14). There follow a number of parallels between Mrs. Todd and her house and Annie and 148 Charles Street. Jewett, like the narrator, is a writer who intellectually desires seclusion so she can write, but both found themselves drawn to a house that was constantly flooded by visitors. In the case of the narrator, these are Mrs. Todd's customers, seeking herbs and spruce beer, while in the case of 148 Charles Street, they are the throngs of friends and writers who called at the "waterside museum," as Henry James called it. The narrator becomes a "business partner" in Mrs. Todd's absences (16); Jewett became Fields's co-hostess at Charles Street. Mrs. Todd went "afield" every day to gather herbs; Annie went to work at the Chardon Street headquarters of the Associated Charities, leaving Sarah to deal with callers. Like the narrator of her story, Jewett needed resolution to withdraw to get her writing done. Although she did write while in Boston, going home to South Berwick was Jewett's self-imposed exile from Fields and sociability. But, just as in the novel, "Mrs. Todd and I were not separated or estranged by the change in our business relations; on the contrary, a deeper intimacy seemed to begin," so, too, Annie and Sarah were never distanced emotionally by their separations, but carried on an intimate correspondence. Like the narrator, who does not truly belong in Dunnet Landing, Jewett does not truly belong in Boston, but both find their adoptive homes and companions more than congenial. The narrator trudging off to the schoolhouse to write is a reflection of Sarah in her Pinny Lawson role: the narrator says, "I walked away with a dull supply of writing-paper and these provisions, feeling like a reluctant child who hopes to be called back at every step" (114). However, Mrs. Todd, like Annie, was seldom the agent of distraction; in the above example, the narrator was taken fishing by William. And as Dunnet Landing represented a larger world for Almira Todd, compared to Green Island where she grew up, so Boston gave Jewett "a large place [to live] where more things grew" (51). There is even a comparison of Mrs. Todd to a mouse, recalling one of Jewett's nicknames for Fields. Mrs. Todd rose earlier than the narrator, as Annie rose before Sarah; the narrator says of Mrs. Todd, "Long before I was fairly awake I used to hear a rustle and knocking like a great mouse in the walls, and an impatient tread on the steep garret stairs that led to Mrs. Todd's chief place of storage" (76). This passage, with its "great mouse" and reference to Mrs. Todd's large size, may have been a private joke, since Annie was small.

Other parallels exist in the nature of the real and fictional relationships, especially in the mutual protectiveness that exists not only between Mrs. Todd and the narrator but also between Mrs. Todd and Mrs. Blackett, Mrs. Todd and Joanna, and, extraordinarily, between Mrs. Abby Martin and Queen Victoria in the story "The Queen's Twin." As their correspondence shows, Jewett and Fields acted as self-appointed caretakers of each other's health. Jewett called Fields her doctor: "[(] Dear little T. L. to send the medicine—T. L. is Pinny's doctor and she means to have no other whatever)."[48] In the novel, Mrs. Todd "practices" on the narrator against her protest, slipping camomile into her spruce beer (34). Jewett also took care of Fields's health, though, frequently reminding her to drink claret daily and not to overwork, telling her before an imminent visit: "Pinny not to tease Fuff anymore to come but to long for the 29th to be here and to have her dearest Fuff all safe under the green trees and not to let her do much but play and read good little books and pull two weeds a day in the garden."[49] Similarly, the narrator showed her concern over Mrs. Todd after her rough climb to Mrs. Martin's house: "I showed the solicitation that I felt. Mrs. Todd was no longer young, and in spite of her strong, great frame and spirited behavior, I knew that certain ills were apt to seize upon her, and would end some day by leaving her lame and ailing" (131). In another passage, Mrs. Todd reflects Jewett's opinion about Annie's tendency to overwork; Jewett writes: "Mrs. Todd made the apt suggestion that city persons were prone to run themselves to death, and advised me to stay and get properly rested now that I had taken the trouble to come [to Dunnet Landing]" (149). The fact that in this case, Mrs. Todd has Jewett's role rather than Fields's merely emphasizes the essential interchangeableness of their roles.

Although the relationship between the narrator and Mrs. Todd is the most extensive reflection of the Jewett-Fields relationship, the most unusual example of reciprocity occurs later in "The Queen's Twin," when Abby Martin describes her bond with Queen Victoria. At one point Mrs. Martin says: "I sometimes seem to have her all my own, as if we'd lived right together. I've often walked out into the woods alone and told her what my troubles was, and it always seemed as if she told me 't was all right, an' we must have patience" (144). Here, even in a case where one of the members of the couple is completely unaware of the tie, the one who feels it benefits from the relationship. But Abby Martin is not convinced that Queen Victoria is ignorant of their bond, for she says, transforming the queen into just another old lady like her:

> When I think how few old friends anybody has left at our age, I suppose it may be just the same with her as it is with me. . . . But I've had a great advantage in seeing her, an' I can always fancy her goin' on, while she don't know nothin' yet about me, *except she may feel my love stayin' her heart sometimes an' not know just where it comes from* [my italics]. An' I dream about our being together out in some pretty fields, young as we ever was, and holdin' hands as we walk along." (144)

Ironically, this vision of a friendship which transcended physical presence foreshadowed, at least to some degree, the course of its real-life inspiration. After Jewett's 1902 accident, which limited her ability to

travel even short distances, Jewett and Fields lived apart for most of the
rest of Jewett's remaining years. The letters exchanged between the two
increasingly came to reflect a communion that depended less heavily on
physical presence than it had before. For example, one of Jewett's notes
to Fields reminds Annie of the spoken bond between them: "Good night
dearest Annie with so many things left unsaid, or rather all said but not
written—"[50] After Jewett's stroke in 1908, which occurred during the first
winter she had spent in Boston since 1901, Annie was often not allowed
in the sickroom for fear of exciting Sarah too much. Shortly before her
death, Jewett, back in Maine, wrote to Annie to delay her visit: "It is
wise for you not to come quite so soon as my eager heart planned it is still
so cold and bleak—and a fortnight later it will be better for both of us—I
have not got into the my [sic] room yet and we would not do anything
that we don't think and do now[.]"[51] For Annie, at least, their unusual
communication extended beyond Sarah's death, for she confided to her
diary, as well as to at least one old friend, that she could feel Sarah near
her throughout the day.[52] Thus, "The Queen's Twin," one of Jewett's last
and finest stories, occupied a pivotal position in her life, for it both reflected and predicted the course of Jewett's important relationship with
Annie Fields.

Notes

1. Jewett to Annie Fields, MS, Sarah Orne Jewett collection, quoted by permission of the Houghton Library. All manuscript letters cited are from the Jewett
Collection at the Houghton Library bMS. Am. 1743, item 255, or bMS. Am. 1743.1,
items 33 and 117. Neither Jewett nor Fields wrote complete dates on letters,
often writing only a day of the week or nothing at all. When Fields compiled her edition
of Jewett's letters between 1909 and 1911, she penciled dates on many of the
letters, but these dates are unreliable. I give Fields's date, if there is one, or my own
guess, if there is enough evidence to base one on. Most of the letters quoted are
from the period 1881–1902 prior to Jewett's accident, and many are from the
earlier part of that period.

2. Ernest H. Pool, "The Child in Sarah Orne Jewett," in *Appreciation of Sarah
Orne Jewett*, ed. Richard Cary (Waterville: Colby College Press, 1973), pp. 223–28.

3. Faderman discusses the Jewett-Fields relationship in the chapter "Boston
Marriage," in *Surpassing the Love of Men: Romantic Friendship and Love Between
Women from the Renaissance to the Present* (New York: William Morrow, 1981),
pp. 197–203. Donovan discusses the nature of the relationship in her article "The
Unpublished Love Poems of Sarah Orne Jewett," *Frontiers*, 4, No. 3 (1979), 26–31.
Both writers qualify their use of the word "lesbian," and, although incomplete,
these are the best discussions of the relationship to date. See also Donovan's excellent
study, *Sarah Orne Jewett* (New York: Ungar, 1980), pp. 12–18.

4. For detailed accounts of Annie's life with James T. Fields, see W. S. Tryon,
Parnassus Corner: A Life of James T. Fields, Publisher to the Victorians (Boston:
Houghton Mifflin, 1963), chaps. 10–17, and James C. Austin, *Fields of the Atlantic*

Monthly: Letters to an Editor, 1861–1870 (San Marino: Huntington Library, 1953). Both writers note Mrs. Fields's influence but see her as essentially adjunctive and secondary to Fields.

5. For descriptions of the history and curriculum of Emerson's school, see George B. Emerson, *Reminiscences of an Old Teacher* (Boston: Alfred Mudge, 1878) and Thomas Woody, *A History of Women's Education in the United States* (New York: Science Press, 1929).

6. Barbara Ruth Rotundo and W. S. Tryon stress Annie's youth and worshipful love of her husband. See Tryon, *Parnassus Corner*, pp. 216–17, 238, and Rotundo, "Mrs. James T. Fields, Hostess and Biographer," Diss. Syracuse Univ. 1968, p. 39.

7. Willa Cather, "148 Charles Street," in *Not Under Forty* (New York: Knopf, 1936), p. 58.

8. M. A. DeWolfe Howe published heavily edited excerpts of Fields's diaries in *Memories of a Hostess: A Chronicle of Eminent Friendships Drawn Chiefly from the Diaries of Mrs. James T. Fields* (Boston: Atlantic Monthly Press, 1922). However, the published version leaves out some of the most interesting sections about the subjects as well as nearly all passages about Mrs. Fields herself.

9. Annie's inner life as revealed in her diaries will be a subject for discussion in my dissertation which will be submitted to Indiana University in 1984.

10. For accounts of the Dodge and Hawthorne quarrels, see Tryon and Austin and a series of articles by Randall Stewart, including " 'Pestiferous Gail Hamilton,' James T. Fields and the Hawthornes," *New England Quarterly*, 17 (1944), 418–23; "Selections from Mrs. Hawthorne's Letters to James T. Fields, 1865–1868," *More Books* (Boston Public Library), 21 (1946), 43–52, 254–63; and "Selections from Mrs. Hawthorne's Letters to Mr. and Mrs. James T. Fields," *More Books*, 19 (1944), 263–79, 303–13; 20 (1945), 299–315.

11. The best accounts of the relationship between Annie Fields and Dickens are in Arthur A. Adrian, *Georgina Hogarth and the Dickens Circle* (London: Oxford Univ. Press, 1957), and an expurgated version of Annie's diary about Dickens in Howe, *Memories of a Hostess*, pp. 135–95.

12. The best account of Annie's charitable work is in Nathan Irvin Huggins, *Protestants Against Poverty: Boston's Charities, 1870–1900*, foreward Oscar Handlin, Contributions in American History, No. 9 (Westport; Greenwood, 1971). According to a memorial placed on Associated Charities records, Mrs. Fields served as director from 1879 to 1894, as vice-president from 1894 to 1906, and as honorary vice-president from 1906 to 1915. She was also corresponding secretary of the executive committee of her district.

13. Donovan, "The Unpublished Love Poems of Sarah Orne Jewett," p. 28.

14. See accounts of Jewett's life in Francis Otto Matthiessen, *Sarah Orne Jewett* (Boston: Houghton Mifflin, 1929), John Eldridge Frost, *Sarah Orne Jewett* (Kittery Point: Gundalow Club, 1960), and Donovan, *Sarah Orne Jewett.*

15. Little books" is a reference to Annie's having published several of the small-format volumes favored by publishing companies at the time. She also undoubtedly had a house full of such books.

16. Jewett to Fields, quoted by permission of Houghton Library.

17. Boston: Houghton Mifflin, 1881.

18. Jewett to Fields, n.d., quoted by permission of the Houghton Library.

19. Jewett to Fields, quoted by permission of the Houghton Library.

20. Fields to Jewett, n.d., MS, Sarah Orne Jewett collection, quoted by permission of the Houghton Library.

21. Fields to Jewett, n.d., MS, Sarah Orne Jewett collection, quoted by permission of the Houghton Library.

22. *Ode at the inauguration of the great organ in Boston, Nov. 2, 1863* (Cambridge: privately printed, 1863); *The Children of Lebanon* (Boston: privately printed, 1877); *Under the Olive* (Boston: Houghton Mifflin, 1881).

23. "Mr. Emerson in the Lecture Room," *Atlantic Monthly*, 51 (1883), 818–32.

24. Jewett to Fields, n.d., quoted by permission of the Houghton Library.

25. Jewett to Fields, quoted by permission of the Houghton Library.

26. Jewett to Fields, n.d., quoted by permission of the Houghton Library.

27. See Richard Cary's explication of the nicknames in *Sarah Orne Jewett Letters* (Waterville: Colby College Press, 1967), pp. 96–97n.

28. Frost says that Annie Fields gave Jewett the nickname, but I have not seen the letter he refers to. See Frost, *Sarah Orne Jewett*, p. 69.

29. No one seems to know what the "T" of "T. L." stands for. A personal guess is "Tom," because of Jewett's story "Tom's Husband," which will be discussed later.

30. Jewett to Fields, n.d., quoted by permission of the Houghton Library.

31. Jewett to Fields, n.d., quoted by permission of Houghton Library.

32. See Pool, "The Child"; see also Richard Cary, *Sarah Orne Jewett* (New York: Twayne, 1962), pp. 19–20.

33. *Letters of Sarah Orne Jewett*, ed. Annie Fields (Boston: Houghton Mifflin, 1911), p. 125.

34. *Letters*, p. 6.

35. Jewett to Fields, 1885, quoted by permission of the Houghton Library.

36. Jewett to Fields, n.d., quoted by permission of the Houghton Library.

37. Jewett to Fields, 1889?, quoted by permission of the Houghton Library.

38. Jewett to Fields, 1884, quoted by permission of the Houghton Library.

39. *Orpheus: A Masque* (Boston: Houghton Mifflin, 1900).

40. Grover Cleveland was president of the United States during 1885–89 and 1893–97.

41. Jewett to Fields, n.d., quoted by permission of the Houghton Library.

42. Jewett to Fields, 1889, quoted by permission of the Houghton Library.

43. See the Annie Fields diaries in the collection of the Massachusetts Historical Society.

44. Matthiessen, *Sarah Orne Jewett*, p. 72.

45. For a discussion of *A Country Doctor*, see Donovan, *Sarah Orne Jewett*, pp. 64–69; see also Ellen Morgan, "The Atypical Woman: Nan Prince in the Literary Transition to Feminism," *Kate Chopin Newsletter*, 2 (Fall 1976), 33–37.

46. *The Mate of the Daylight and Friends Ashore* (Boston: Houghton Mifflin, 1884), pp. 210–33. See discussion in Donovan, *Sarah Orne Jewett*, pp. 52–53.

47. All page references are to the following edition: New York: Doubleday, 1956; hereafter cited in the text.

48. Jewett to Fields, n.d., quoted by permission of the Houghton Library.

49. Jewett to Fields, n.d., quoted by permission of the Houghton Library.

50. Jewett to Fields, n.d., quoted by permission of the Houghton Library.

51. Jewett to Fields, 1909, quoted by permission of the Houghton Library. Fields dates this letter 3 May 1909.

52. See Fields diary in the Massachusetts Historical Society and Annie Fields's letters to Lily Fairchild in the collection of the Boston Public Library.

The Women Doctors of Howells, Phelps, and Jewett: The Conflict of Marriage and Career

Jean Carwile Masteller*

After W. D. Howells finished his *Dr. Breen's Practice*, he learned to his surprise that he had several female "rivals" also writing about the problems of the woman doctor. Yet when he listened with a "mixture of amusement and anxiety" to Elizabeth Stuart Phelps' plans for a novel about a woman doctor, he was in an advantageous position,[1] for he had written his *Dr. Breen's Practice* and already had part of his novel in print. He thus felt safe in encouraging Phelps to finish her story; indeed, his experience as editor of the *Atlantic* led him to believe that their co-incidental treatment of a common issue would appeal to readers.[2] As he explained to Thomas Bailey Aldrich, his successor at the *Atlantic*, it would be a "card for her to follow on the same subject."[3] He did, however, have two important suggestions: the readers—and Phelps—would have to wait until his serialization reached its conclusion. And when Phelps' novel did begin its run in the *Atlantic*, he felt it necessary that he write a preface to the first installment explaining that she had not borrowed from him even though they dealt with "the same situations and the same characters in a certain degree."[4]

Elizabeth Stuart Phelps was not convinced any comment was necessary. Nor did she think highly of his Dr. Breen. As she bluntly wrote him in 1881, "I don't feel that Dr. Breen is a fair example of professional women; indeed, I know she is not for I know the class thoroughly from long personal observation under unusual opportunities." The preface was printed nevertheless, Phelps' assenting perhaps because she hoped the audience, being reminded of Breen, would favor her heroine. The contrast, she wrote, "may be all the better for my doctor"; indeed, she thought, it may even be "glorious."[5]

Less than three years later, reviewers of Sarah Orne Jewett's *A Country Doctor* noted the curious coincidence that three well-known authors had recently published novels in which the central character was a woman doctor. Howells' *Dr. Breen's Practice* was published in 1881, Phelps' *Doctor Zay* was issued in book form in 1882, and Jewett's *A Country Doctor* followed in 1884. Not all reviewers approved of the subject matter, but as the reviewer in the *Nation* observed, "The fact that such writers as Mr. Howells, Miss Phelps, and Miss Jewett should within four years so carefully study what is practically the same subject, makes it worth while to compare their stories closely."[6]

Most significantly, all three novels depict the woman doctor as the

*This essay was written especially for this volume and is included here by permission of the author.

central character, not a minor character as did Harriet Beecher Stowe in *My Wife and I* (1871) or as Louisa May Alcott was to do in *Jo's Boys* (1886). In novels which allow several role choices for female characters, Stowe's Ida prepares to travel to Europe to study medicine and Alcott's Nan avoids a love-struck suitor so she can become a doctor; each woman freely follows her chosen career. Because they are minor characters, however, the unconventionality of their choice and the problems attending it never receive extended examination.

But for Howells, Phelps, and Jewett, the choice and the problems are central. Is the woman strong enough to be a doctor? Can she combine her career with a marriage? If she must choose between marriage or career, which will she choose? Despite the similarity of their subject matter, Howells, Phelps, and Jewett each offer a different solution to the woman doctor facing the conflict between marriage and career. Both women writers realize that the woman doctor faces special conflicts that the male professional does not, and both explore these complexities in detail, while Howells chooses simply to dismiss them. As contemporary reviewers recognized, however, Jewett's novel was significantly different from the other two.[7] While Howells' Dr. Breen rejects her career in order to marry and Phelps' Dr. Zay marries only on the condition that she continue her career, Jewett's doctor retains her independence: she refuses to marry.

Howells depicts his female physician unsympathetically. Grace Breen should never have become a physician, since she lacked both the necessary education and temperament to succeed in her rigorous career. She even chose medicine for inappropriate reasons. She was neither interested in it, nor did she wish to help others; instead, she responded to an unhappy love affair in which her lover married her best friend. As she admits to her mother, "I wished to be a physician because—because—I had failed where—other women's hopes are."[8] And she rejects any suggestion that she wished to benefit her sex. Her only motive was her failure in love, a motive so stereotyped it became a target for ridicule by some female critics.[9]

If her motives are stereotyped, so is her behavior: she seems a lady pretending to be a doctor. When she is first introduced, she is reviewing her croquet game, laughing at her blunders, and pleading with her patient to take care of herself during their croquet practice. She is a genteel lady, not a professional physician. Nor does she have the independence necessary for a physician. Rather, she accepts her dependence on men. As she explains to her mother, "A woman is reminded of her insufficiency to herself every hour of the day. And it's always a man that comes to her help." Thus, when she gets caught in some spools of thread and is gallantly rescued by the young and handsome Mr. Libby, she admits to her mother, "I could have done it myself, but it seemed right and natural that he should do it" (43–44). She accurately equates this experience with her insufficiency and her timidity about beginning her medical practice: she is simply too weak and too dependent.

These social incidents of stereotypical dependence do in fact foreshadow her ineptitude in her brief practice of medicine. When Grace's treatments fail, her first patient distrusts her skills and asks for a real doctor, meaning a male doctor. Complying with her patient's demand, the ineffective Dr. Breen desperately surrenders her case to an experienced male doctor and consents to continue in the case as his nurse. Fortunately, Grace Breen's first patient is also her last, for she is rescued from her ill-fated career by marriage to a good man. At her husband's insistence, she treats the sick children among his factory operatives but insists that her work is an act of charity, not a career. The former Dr. Breen, now Mrs. Libby, "coldly" rejects praise for her good work, responding, "that was my husband's idea" (269). Even her charity work is done "under the shelter of her husband's name" (271). For Grace, marriage is the appropriate conclusion: she needs a man for guidance. The result of Howells' examination of the female doctor, then, is a hardly subtle reinforcement of the view that women are unsuited for the rigors of medicine. A contemporary biographer of Elizabeth Stuart Phelps accurately analyzed Howells' depiction of Grace Breen: "She was, after all, only the old sort of woman he knows so well, masquerading with a medicine-case."[10]

It is not surprising that Phelps and others who envisioned a different sort of female doctor did not think highly of Howells' lady. Those interested in the advancement of women in medicine did not appreciate a stereotypic portrayal of a woman too weak to pursue her career. One reviewer, herself a woman doctor, could understand from an artistic viewpoint Howells' choice of what to her was an exceptional figure in Grace Breen, but she nonetheless wished he had chosen one of those "hard-headed, cool, and capable medical women of America" for his portrait of the woman doctor.[11]

Proponents of opportunities for women found Elizabeth Stuart Phelps' depiction of the woman more positive. Phelps wished choices to be available for women and especially supported the entry of women into medical careers. Phelps first introduces the theme of the woman doctor in 1872 in "Our Little Woman," a story for children in *Our Young Folks*. When Lois McQuentin's mother is dying, she wishes there had been women doctors in the hospital and wishes she could give Lois her rich cousin's opportunities in order to make a doctor of her. After her mother's death, Lois continues to work in the Lynn shoe factory, but, eventually remembering her mother's dying wish, she decides to become a doctor. She saves enough money to start high school and determines to work weekends and summers to pay for her education, certain that she is strong enough—and has enough Scotch blood—to survive the demands she will face. She is similarly undaunted by her cousin's concern that "nobody believes in women doctors!" As Lois responds, "somebody must be *made* to."[12]

"Our little woman," then, is not weak, but determined and energetic. In fact, Lois thinks to be a little woman means "to be the most, and the best, and the noblest, and the most needed thing that you can get or make the chance to be" (736). And she is not afraid even if, as she laughingly states, she must "cut off a museumful of legs and arms!" (736). Despite its simplified plot and melodramatic prose, the story is important in part because of its intended audience: Phelps gives her impressionable young readers an adventure story populated totally by females, in which the central character is a strong-willed working girl, determined to rise in the world from factory operative to professional physician.

In *Doctor Zay* the protagonist and the audience are adults: Phelps depicts situations the female doctor might encounter, especially situations forcing her ultimately to consider the conflict between marriage and career. By creating a strong young woman doctor who marries only after she has been assured that she can continue her medical practice, Phelps challenges the assumption that the woman must choose between marriage and career, a choice assumed by both Howells and Jewett.

She also challenges the prevailing stereotypes by reversing gender roles. Dr. Zay is a strong, skillful, committed professional who takes control of her cases and works unceasingly for her patients in rural Maine. In contrast, young Waldo Yorke, her suitor, has led an idle upper-class life in Boston under his mother's control. Though a lawyer, he does not practice his profession, and in his idleness he has become a "nervous young man."[13] After his buggy wreck in the Maine woods, his nervousness intensifies, and he begins to resemble prevalent descriptions of the nineteenth-century female hysteric.[14] In this condition, he is placed under Dr. Zay's care, thereby heightening their reversal of roles and their conflict. While he helplessly watches Dr. Zay or faints in precisely those stressful situations where a woman would stereotypically faint, Dr. Zay acts competently, bravely, and forcefully as a physician.[15]

The reversal in roles is intensified as the professional relationship of patient and doctor begins to evolve into a romantic relationship of lover and beloved. Like the woman rebuffed by the busy man who has no time to notice her or to be admired by her, Yorke—in the feminine role—realizes that Dr. Zay—in her masculine role—has no time for his admiration. Yet he confesses his love, only to be rebuffed even more devastatingly. She warns him that he is not strong enough to love and that what he thinks is love is only nervousness. He confuses love with his dependence on her for saving his life. If he goes away and rests, she warns, he will recover and realize his mistake. Even in this developing romantic relationship, in other words, he acts the role of the fond and foolish woman while she remains composed and analytical.

He follows her advice, but returns twice to propose. The first time

he insists he is proud of her and wants her to continue with her profession, since her profession is part of her strength and he wants all of
her. As he argues, "what kind of a fellow should I be, if I could approach
a woman like you, and propose to drink down her power and precious-
ness into my one little thirsty life,—absorb her, annihilate her,—and
offer her nothing but myself in exchange for a freedom so fine, an influence so important as yours?" (239). She is more receptive this time,
but again she reminds him that she is not like others. Despite her love
for him, she is not convinced she can make him happy. When he returns
a second time to propose, she gives in and agrees to marry him, but asks
if he is sure he wants her as she is—"a strong-minded doctor" (254).

A close examination of the conclusion reveals that it is not nearly
so triumphant a victory for women in a new role as the rest of the novel
appears to foreshadow. Although Yorke has been weak, pale, and faint
while Dr. Zay has been strong, healthy, and competent, at the end of the
novel conditions are reversed; he is well and self-confident while she is
weak and drained after a hard winter of illness and overwork. When she
again confronts the confident Yorke, not only is she still weak from
diphtheria, but she has been up the night before with one case and has
just left a delirium tremens case in which the man had been firing a
revolver. She is pale and trembling, although she still retains enough
self-control to keep from fainting when she finds Yorke waiting in her
buggy: "I shall not faint, I never did in my life" (253). Nevertheless, she
is no longer able to resist his pursuit: "she did not protest and battle;
nor, indeed, did she answer him just then, at all. She was worn out,
poor girl" (254). As Yorke senses "the first fumes from the incense of
her surrender" (254), he realizes he is winning her in her weakness.

Admittedly, even as she surrenders to his proposal, she is not the
clinging vine. She still insists she will remain a strong-minded doctor.
And as she rides in the buggy, "she [does] not lean against anything. She
[does] not speak nor turn her face toward him." He even feels a "vague
jealousy of the strong withdrawal which nature had set between her
strength and his tenderness, as if he had found a rival in it" (256).

But he is still winning her. In a comic, but symbolic, exchange she
takes the buggy reins from him when he heads toward a ditch: "Give me
the reins! If you don't mind—please." As he laughingly responds, " 'I don't
care who has the reins,' he cried, with a boyish laugh, 'as long as I have
the driver!' " (256). He does have the driver, and as if to underscore his
victory he confidently accompanies her "without hesitation" to her room:
"his manner . . . was that of a man who belonged there, and who intended
to be where he belonged" (257). When the strong Yorke asks her to come
into his arms, it is because, he says, "you have had your way long enough.
My turn has come" (258). To his request for proof of her love, "with a
swift and splendid motion she glided across the little distance that lay
between them" (258) and the novel ends.

Dr. Zay's name, Atalanta, becomes especially significant in relation to this ending. In Greek mythology Atalanta fended off suitors by promising to marry only the man who could beat her in a foot race. Since she knew no living man could beat her, she felt safe. Time after time she outraced the suitors until Melanion obtained three irresistible golden apples from Aphrodite, who wished to subdue the maiden who despised love. During the race, he dropped the apples along the path and won only because Atalanta could not resist stopping to pick them up. In other words, he won the race and Atalanta—and she lost her freedom—not because of his own strength or quickness, but because of his ability to compensate for her strength and beat her in a moment of weakness. On his final visit after her battle with the delirium tremens case, Yorke recognizes the parallel to the myth. He realizes he has caught her exhausted and has her in a moment of weakness when he says, "I have overtaken Atalanta this time. She stopped for a leaden apple,—for a revolver ball,—and I got the start. Do you suppose I am going to forego my advantage so soon? Do you think you are going to send me off again, after all we have gone through?" (254).

In the myth Atalanta's days of freedom, of athletic contests, of archery, of racing, and of wrestling end with her marriage: one wonders if the new Atalanta will be any more successful than her mythical counterpart. Though she wants to create a perfect marriage in which she can happily combine her marriage and her career, her happiness depends on Yorke's willingness to accept her as she is—with all the demands of her career. She once forewarned him of a probable scene in which he would return home only to find her out on a case instead of waiting to serve him. During the pursuit Yorke is willing to accept her career as a condition of their marriage, but will he so readily assent when her career does in fact conflict with his comfort? To Dr. Zay, his willingness to accept her will depend on his willingness to be the "new man" in a "new marriage." Yet, Yorke's shift from the weak invalid to the strong lover willing to be the "new man" is not convincing; even more suspicious are Dr. Zay's sudden signs of weakness at the end.[16] One contemporary reviewer pursued the implications: "If Miss Phelps, in a sequel, would give us the true history of these two people in their after life, might there not prove to be a confirmation of the Doctor's worst fears?"[17]

Despite the ending, Dr. Zay is a strong woman who, for the bulk of the novel, seriously pursues her career. As Elizabeth Stuart Phelps anticipated, her doctor shines "gloriously" in contrast to Howells' Dr. Breen. It is not surprising that Phelps thought it unnecessary for Howells to preface her Doctor Zay explaining she did not borrow her material from him. Though they both deal with the woman doctor who marries at the end, few other similarities exist.

Nor is there any possibility that Jewett imitated either Howells or Phelps in her depiction of the woman doctor. Jewett created a sympathetic portrait of a strong, capable woman doctor genuinely dedicated to her profession, but, like many reviewers of *A Country Doctor*, Jewett questions the possibility of a woman's combining her medical profession with married life. Furthermore, she argues that not all women, apparently including herself, are suited for marriage. She does not suggest that just any woman should reject marriage and become a professional; but for those women like Nan Prince, whose exceptional talents are repeatedly emphasized, a career is the more appropriate choice.

Throughout the novel, Jewett justifies Nan's choice of her life's work by reference to her exceptional character, a product of both her nurture and her nature. Dr. Leslie, who raises the orphaned Nan, insists that she be allowed to grow up naturally, "not having been clipped back or forced in any unnatural direction."[18] His concern is to help her "to work with nature and not against it" (106). The result, he expects, will be an untrammeled being different from the rest of the village children. Correspondingly, he does not care whether she chooses "a man's work or a woman's work" (106) so long as she chooses what is right for her.

Quite clearly, Nan is not only reared differently, she is also naturally different from other children. To the adults, she seems a wild creature who in a most unfeminine fashion enjoys the impish tricks she plays on others. With mischievous energy she chases squirrels, falls out of trees, and makes a raft from her neighbor's fence. Not surprisingly, her grandmother does not quite know how to raise such an unusual child and defers to the judgment of Dr. Leslie, who is so fascinated by this natural child that he agrees to raise her after her grandmother's death. Even after she becomes a well-mannered young lady, observers note an "untamed wildness" and self-dependence that distinguish her from others and give her special motivation and power.

Given her special character, it follows that "a nature like Nan's must and could make and keep certain laws of its own." Specifically, she would not be bound by the old idea that the home is the place for all women. As she tells her critics, not all women are fit for marriage and motherhood. Yet Nan also insists that she is not saying medicine is proper for women, but that it is proper for her. Dr. Leslie sees Nan's situation as a sign of an advancing civilization that stresses the welfare of the individual. As society progresses, more people realize that not all women are fit for the same role. Given this progression and variation, some individual women will inevitably find their roles in duties outside the home.[19]

Yet Nan is more than a symbol of the future; she is also, as the novel stresses, a special being with a "gift" or "talent" from God. Thus she is not defying the traditional woman's place in society, but instead fulfilling her own God-given possibilities. As she rejects Gerry's proposal, she stresses that she is accepting God's will: "It isn't for us to choose again, or wonder and dispute, but just work in our own places, and leave the rest to God" (327). She is not selfishly choosing her own direction; she is following God's plan.[20] Such a justification for a woman's career very much resembles that of mid-nineteenth-century women authors who insisted they were not intruding on man's activities but were following God's inspiration and transcribing God's messages. Such an argument lends powerful support for an otherwise potentially deviant act.

But as Nan learns, even a gift is not pursued easily or without crises if that gift conflicts with social expectations. Her first crisis occurs after she returns from boarding school and tries to lead a domestic life caring for Dr. Leslie's home. Discontented with this role, she spends many restless and troubled hours wishing she were of some use to the world. In essence, her crisis involves the conflict between a world that forbids her to become a doctor and her own desire to be of use; in other words, she must resolve the conflict between a conventional definition of woman's role in the home and her own unhappiness in that role. Only after a return to her childhood natural setting and a communion with nature—including a long run in the woods—does she acknowledge the naturalness of her call to medicine and announce her decision to Dr. Leslie. She must move from the conventional setting to the natural setting before she can master the crisis and accept her decision to use her own gift.

Dr. Leslie supports her decision to become a doctor, but when she visits her wealthy aunt, she has to face the opposition of those who expect her to fulfill the traditional female role. In fact, her aunt and friends cannot believe that a beautiful and gracious young woman would consider entering medical practice. Once again Nan relies on her God-given fitness for medicine and criticizes a society that shames the woman who pursues her talents in a profession while it honors the man who follows his own direction. As she repeats, she is not arguing that women should be doctors, but that she should. She will practice her belief that "people ought to work with the great laws of nature and not against them" (283). And she does not shrink from a corollary to her belief: since marriage would not allow her to continue her career, she will not marry.

A theoretical proclamation before her aunt, this resolution is soon tested in a practical way when George Gerry falls in love with her. The result is a second crisis, a particularly female crisis, as she confronts the choice between her career and a possible marriage. New to the social pleasures of her aunt's world, she temporarily rests from the work of medical school and enjoys the companionship of new friends. Away from her work and in the presence of young Gerry, she is shocked to recognize how strongly she cares for him. She even foresees the possible happiness ahead if she enters "a quiet life that should centre itself in one man's love, and within the walls of his home" (326). Her crisis culminates during a restless night in which images of love and marriage make "her great profession" seem "all like a fading dream" (307). Her sense of duty, however, wins again. She realizes, "she might be happy, it was true, and make other people so, but her duty was not this, and a certainty that satisfaction and the blessing of God would not follow her into these reverenced and honored limits came to her distinctly" (308). So she resists the "temptation" of marriage. As she explains her decision to a shaken Gerry, she stresses, "I could not marry the whole of myself as most women can; there is a great share of my life which could not have its way and could only hide itself and be sorry" (326–27). In her refusal she repeats the essential reasons for her choice: she is unlike most women who are suited for domestic life; she is using her God-given gift; she cannot give her entire self to a man because she has a duty "to make many homes happy instead of one." At no point are her ambitions presented as selfish. She is not defiant; she is not pursuing personal gain. Rather, she is following her nature unselfishly even though she will suffer "weariness and pain and reproach, and the loss of many things that other women held dearest and best" (308).

In many respects, Jewett's female doctor challenges the social world depicted in W. D. Howells' *Dr. Breen's Practice*. Nan Prince, unlike Dr. Grace Breen, is not frivolous and unsuited for her profession. Nor does she fly to medicine after failure in love. Instead, she is a young woman who follows her true vocation even though it violates the social expectation that she marry and raise a family. Though Nan gives up what most women cherish, she suggests that the single woman can still be useful without a husband and can be happy outside of marriage as she pursues her higher calling. And though she gives up the love of a man in her efforts, she does not give up friendships. She returns to help Dr. Leslie and continues her friendship with the old women in the neighborhood. Nan is certain that she has made the right choice, a choice affirmed in the last line of the novel: " 'O God,' she said, 'I thank thee for my future' " (351).

In a sense Nan Prince resembles that first generation of college women, like Jane Addams, who chose to be of service to the larger society rather than to be wives and mothers in a home world. Because these were exceptional women pursuing a special calling, even the *Ladies' Home Journal*, which supported the rewards of domestic life and criticized the journey away from home, did not usually view them as a threat: the large majority of women would not follow their lead. Likewise, Nan Prince in the end is largely immune from criticism: she is not a threat to society because she too is the exceptional, the unusual woman.

Sarah Orne Jewett was also the exceptional woman who pursued a profession rather than marriage. Like Nan who rode with Dr. Leslie on calls, Jewett as a child rode with her father, a country doctor, and at one point hoped to become a doctor herself.[21] But she was too weak physically and instead chose to write about the scenes she observed. Moreover, the depiction of Nan's preference for a career over marriage bore, as John Eldridge Frost theorized, "a strong kinship to Sarah's own thinking at twenty-eight."[22] Jewett, like Nan, chose a career rather than marriage. And she insisted such a choice was appropriate since "some women have an instinct toward marriage—others have not—these are more useful and make more of themselves if they live single lives."[23] *A Country Doctor* works out the implications of that choice. She "did not mean to say that the practice of medicine was the ultimatum of a woman's career" but rather that if a girl was destined "by nature and by inspiration for any special vocation she has a divine right and obligation to follow it at all cost. . . . To grow in knowledge and practical efficiency and to make the most of her gift and surrounding" were the goals both she and her heroine Nan chose to pursue.[24] *A Country Doctor* celebrates that choice.

All three depictions of the woman doctor echo the themes and values of their authors' other writings. Howells depicted individuals as he saw them, not as they should be. This tendency frustrated Elizabeth Cady Stanton who found "a lamentable want of common sense in all his women." She admitted that "They may be true to nature, but as it is nature under false conditions, I should rather have some pen portray the ideal woman, and paint a type worthy of our imitation."[25]

Elizabeth Stuart Phelps portrays in some respects this ideal woman. Dr. Zay is exceptional, but she need not therefore reject marriage; indeed, since a woman can be strong, she may be able to form a new kind of marriage including a career. Phelps' depiction reinforces her feminist approach. In what she called her life's creed, she proclaimed, "I believe in women; and in their right to their own best possibilities in every department of life."[26] Though she rejected participation on platforms and in conventions, she wrote on women's health, dress reform, economic independence, suffrage, and education. Her defense of the woman doctor was part of her larger support of nineteenth-century women's issues, a support that was unwavering, whether in her refutation of Dr. Edward Clarke's medical views in *Sex in Education*, or in her fictional depiction of the woman doctor in *Doctor Zay*.[27] But her commitment to ideals did not blind her to the difficulty of realizing them. The ambiguous ending of *Doctor Zay*—inverting the power relationships that had operated in the bulk of the novel—hints at the dangers she foresees. If Jewett's solution requires a special woman, Phelps' solution requires a special man as well, one who is willing to lose some of his old privileges and to accept a woman who will not always be waiting to serve him. And it is here that Phelps hesitates: given Yorke's unnatural victory by surprise, their union may be only the beginning of Dr. Zay's defeat. As Dr. Zay warns Yorke, "it is a problem that we have undertaken" (258).

The conclusion of Jewett's *A Country Doctor* is unambiguous, consistent with the character of Nan Prince as it develops throughout the novel. Nan has made the right choice; she has accepted her God-given calling. A recent critic refers to Jewett's "personal advocacy of a kind of individualistic feminism."[28] To another critic, she is a "part of the literary transition to feminism"; as a transitional writer, Jewett presents Nan as the atypical heroine who chooses a career even though most women would not.[29] Whatever the label used to describe Jewett, Nan is, like other Jewett characters, independent and strong. In *A Country Doctor* Nan exerts that independence by pursuing a career despite the objections of her society. Yet even as she challenges its expectations, she returns to the village of Oldfields and dedicates her life to serving the old people, especially all those old women, in the community.

Though Jewett and Phelps both support the woman doctor, they nonetheless represent two strongly opposing views toward the career woman in the late nineteenth century. To Jewett, the special, gifted woman could choose to pursue a career, and in that career she could be useful. But she must also face the reality that in her society, she could not also have a marriage and a family. Though the choice was unfair and was not required of men, it was nonetheless necesssary in a society that assumed that marriage and family were a woman's responsibility. If she chose a career, then, she had to remain single. Many reviewers of *A Country Doctor* agreed: they praised Nan's profession on the very grounds that she was special and that most women would not make her decision. Her choice of career over marriage was acceptable, in other words, precisely because it was exceptional.

Jewett does not propose to change the world. As one long familiar with Howells' theory of realism, she depicts the world as she sees it, not as it should be. But she and Howells see different women. Strong, independent, and useful in their rural worlds, her heroines may not be able to change the nature of relations between the sexes, but they can find ways to be of service to themselves and others, even though the comforts of marriage must yield to this greater personal and public good.

Notes

1. From a draft of W. D. Howells' letter to Elizabeth Stuart Phelps, 28 Oct. 1881, cited by permission of the Houghton Library, Harvard University. The letter, without the clause "I listened with a mixture of amusement and anxiety," appeared as a preface to the first installment of *Doctor Zay* in the *Atlantic*, 49 (Apr. 1882), 518.

2. W. D. Howells to Elizabeth Stuart Phelps, 28 Oct. 1881.

3. "To Thomas Bailey Aldrich," 24 Aug. 1881, *Life in Letters of William Dean Howells,* ed. Mildred Howells (Garden City: Doubleday, Doran, 1928), I, 299.

4. W. D. Howells, Letter to Elizabeth Stuart Phelps, 28 Oct. 1881. As if the incident with Phelps were not surprising enough, Howells also received a story from a younger and less well-known woman author with an outline similar to his and Phelps.' Taking along the proofs for *Dr. Breen's Practice,* he visited the young author to show her his novel and to prevent, he said, "suspicion among our friends that I stole your plot." This young woman never published her story. See *Life in Letters of William Dean Howells,* I, 299. Then Howells encountered a third woman, herself a doctor, writing about the woman doctor at the same time. As he explained to Samuel Clemens, "You know I had two rivals in the celebration of a doctress; now comes a pretty young doctress who had written out her own adventures!" See "To Samuel L. Clemens," 11 Sept. 1881, in *Life in Letters of William Dean Howells,* I, 300.

5. Elizabeth Stuart Phelps, Letter to W. D. Howells, 2 Nov. 1881, by permission of the Houghton Library, Harvard University.

6. "Recent Novels," rev. of *A Country Doctor,* by Sarah Orne Jewett, *Nation,* 31 July 1884, p. 96.

7. For abstracts of reviews of *A Country Doctor,* see Gwen L. Nagel and James Nagel, *Sarah Orne Jewett: A Reference Guide* (Boston: G. K. Hall, 1978), pp. 7–11.

8. W. D. Howells, *Dr. Breen's Practice* (Boston: Houghton Mifflin, 1881), p. 43; hereafter cited in the text.

9. Dr. Sophia Jex-Blake, in reviewing an Englishman's novel about a woman doctor, observed that "The heroine commences with the time-honoured 'disappointment,' which most masculine minds seem to consider the essential preliminary to the study of medicine by a woman" (Sophia Jex-Blake, "Medical Women in Fiction," *Nineteenth Century,* 33 [Feb. 1893], 265).

10. Elizabeth T. Spring, "Elizabeth Stuart Phelps," in *Our Famous Women* (Hartford, Conn.: A. D. Worthington, 1884), p. 579.

11. Jex-Blake, "Medical Women," p. 266.

12. Elizabeth Stuart Phelps, "Our Little Woman," *Our Young Folks,* 8 (Nov.–Dec. 1872), 734; hereafter cited in the text.

13. Elizabeth Stuart Phelps, *Doctor Zay* (Boston: Houghton Mifflin, 1882), pp. 6–7; hereafter cited in the text.

14. For a discussion of the female hysteric see Carroll Smith-Rosenberg, "The Hysterical Woman: Sex Roles and Role Conflict in Nineteenth-Century America," *Social Research,* 39 (1972), 652–78.

15. Yorke, for example, faints when Dr. Zay ligates his bleeding artery, when she uses ether on another patient, and when he is sent for help while she works to revive a drowning man. A similar reversal occurs in Jewett's *A Country Doctor* when Nan sets a separated shoulder while the onlooking Gerry nearly faints. In *A Country Doctor* the suitor is also a young lawyer who is not committed to his profession and who is waiting to inherit his fortune—in this case from Nan's wealthy aunt. In both cases the women are strong and committed; the men are weak and idle.

16. Several critics refer to the novel as wish-fulfillment. See Ann Douglas Wood, " 'The Fashinable Diseases': Women's Complaints and Their Treatment in Nineteenth-Century America," *Journal of Interdisciplinary History,* 4 (1973), 25–52; and Gail Thain Parker, "William Dean Howells: Realism and Feminism," in *Uses of Literature,* ed. Monroe Engel, Harvard English Studies, No. 4 (Cambridge: Harvard Univ. Press, 1973), pp. 133–61.

17. "Doctor Zay," rev. of *Doctor Zay*, by Elizabeth Stuart Phelps, *Literary World* (Boston), 4 Nov. 1882, p. 371.

18. Sarah Orne Jewett, *A Country Doctor* (Boston: Houghton Mifflin, 1884), p. 102; hereafter cited in the text.

19. Jewett expresses the same views about civilization and the special woman in a draft of a response to S. S. McClure's letter of 7 June 1889. Jewett writes: "Now that civilization permits the development of individuality as never before any woman may follow her natural career." Sarah Orne Jewett Papers by permission of the Houghton Library, Harvard University.

20. A recent critic who recognizes the importance of "calling" in the novel is Malinda Snow, " 'That One Talent': The Vocation as Theme in Sarah Orne Jewett's *A Country Doctor*," *Colby Literary Quarterly*, 16 (1980), 138–47.

21. John Eldridge Frost, *Sarah Orne Jewett* (Kittery Point: Gundalow, 1960), p. 24. Richard Cary, *Sarah Orne Jewett* (New York: Twayne, 1962), pp. 21, 160, cites Jewett to suggest that her father was the model for Dr. Leslie.

22. Frost, *Sarah Orne Jewett*, p. 150.

23. Miscellaneous manuscript notes for *A Country Doctor*, Sarah Orne Jewett Papers, by permission of the Houghton Library, Harvard University.

24. Sarah Orne Jewett, draft of a response to S. S. McClure's letter of 7 June 1889, by permission of the Houghton Library, Harvard University.

25. Theodore Stanton and Harriot Stanton Blatch, eds., *Elizabeth Cady Stanton As Revealed in Her Letters, Diary, and Reminiscences* (New York: Harper, 1922), II, 213.

26. Elizabeth Stuart Phelps, *Chapters from a Life* (Boston: Houghton Mifflin, 1896), p. 250.

27. Elizabeth Stuart Phelps, in *Sex and Education: A Reply to Dr. E. H. Clarke's "Sex in Education,"* ed. Julia Ward Howe (Boston: Roberts Brothers, 1874), pp. 126–38.

28. Josephine Donovan, *Sarah Orne Jewett* (New York: Ungar, 1980), p. 74.

29. Ellen Morgan, "The Atypical Woman:' Nan Prince in the Literary Transition to Feminism," *Kate Chopin Newsletter*, 2 (1976), 33–37.

"Mateless and Appealing": Growing into Spinsterhood in Sarah Orne Jewett

Barbara A. Johns*

During her lifetime Sarah Orne Jewett enjoyed the appreciation of writers as renowned as William Dean Howells and Henry James, but nearly twenty-five years after her death in 1909, an influential and representative critic excluded her from the great tradition of American letters, calling her a minor writer whose "delicate powers of perception" had been used to create a "tiny realm" that was little more than an

*This essay was written especially for this volume and is included here by permission of the author.

artistic and personal "refuge."[1] While granting that readers could briefly yield to her artistry, especially as seen in *The Country of the Pointed Firs*, Granville Hicks nonetheless complained that her work grew out of a life just as minor, as disappointing, as her talent. "[S]he was," he wrote, "merely a New England old maid . . ." (104).

Her dismissal here is swift and sure, but Jewett turned out to be not so easily diminished, even in the remainder of Hicks' sentence. She was, he continued, an old maid "who had a private income, traveled abroad, read the *Atlantic Monthly*, and believed in piety, progress, and propriety" (104). A depression-era contemporary of Hicks' might have agreed that both piety and propriety were best relegated to the lives of nineteenth-century spinsters and the beliefs of minor writers. Yet, as Virginia Woolf had pointed out four years earlier, the money, time, and room in which to work which Jewett had clearly possessed were still desperately needed by twentieth-century women artists, married or single.[2] If such liberty of life as Hicks assigned to Jewett came from being "merely a New England old maid," there might indeed be something to be said for both New England and the single state.

Sarah Orne Jewett thought so, and fifty years after the Hicks appraisal, critics have found in her life and work much more than a "tiny realm." Women readers especially have discovered that her farmers, herb-gatherers, aristocrats, widows, dressmakers, and spinsters "tell all the truth but tell it slant."[3] In particular, the truth Jewett tells through her New England old maids is that women need not be trapped by the popular fictions of either wifehood or spinsterhood. On one level, by having her spinsters craft productive, rich, self-affirming lives for themselves, Jewett gently subverts the cultural piety that women's fulfillment depended on the presence of men. On another level, her old maids resist the conventional image of the spinster: they are not angular, excessively plain, or "sharp-set"; they do not wear black dresses or keep their hair tied up in neat buns; they are not housebound or possessed of a rage for order; they are neither cruel witches nor pitifully weak, childish figures.[4] Rather, most of Jewett's spinsters are both "mateless" and "appealing" because they are able to find emotional satisfaction and integrity in nature, in each other, in their homes, and in a female tradition of productive work. At the same time, Jewett recognizes that single women can become grotesque, but they become so not when they adventure beyond the broad, common path (spinsters do this by definition), but when they fail to explore the boundaries of their own freedom. In Jewett, the growth into true spinsterhood and the growth into true adulthood are synonymous: both are lifelong tasks whose rewards transcend the limited expectations inherent in the phrase "merely a New England old maid."

Though deeply flawed in several ways, Jewett's first published book, *Deephaven* (1877), retains importance beyond simply serving as a youthful prelude to the sophistication of *The Country of the Pointed Firs*, for in it Jewett presents two young girls poised on the verge of adulthood whose stories may be read as rehearsals for the lives of all her single women. The intense friendship between Kate Lancaster and Helen Denis, their identification with the natural world, their mutual discovery of the legacy of gracious spinsterhood left by Kate's Aunt Katharine Brandon, their sense of place embodied in the solid objects of the Brandon house, the cautions contained in the stories of the isolated Miss Chauncey and the abused Widow Jim—all are Jewett's first attempts to illuminate the features of New England spinsterhood.

Helen Denis' breathless descriptions of "dear Kate Lancaster"[5] are certainly cloying and even obtrusive in her narrative, but the relationship between the two women reflects Jewett's own belief that there was "something transfiguring in the best of friendship."[6] Like Jewett herself, whose friendships with women "occupied perhaps the first place in her life,"[7] Kate and Helen share a common interest in books, the outdoors, and local history, and more importantly, they share moments of physical affection, comfortable silences, and a deepening sense of place. At the beginning of their stay together, Helen remarks, "I think I should be happy in any town if I were living there with Kate Lancaster" (54) and, indeed, after a summer of early morning fishing expeditions, quiet evenings spent reading, moonlit boat rides, and nightlong conversations, they grew "well and brown and strong" and "did not get tired of each other at all . . ." (164). There is little suggestion of young men in *Deephaven*, except for a reference to a visit by Kate's brothers and a revelation that at the circus the two girls had spent a great deal of time watching "countless pairs of country lovers . . ." (104). But they remain spectators of romantic love, and on one occasion refuse even that opportunity when they deliberately neglect to read Aunt Katharine's old love letters from a young sailor.[8] Rather, the letters which seem to speak more directly to their own lives are those that Miss Brandon had received from her girlhood friend, Dolly McAllister, letters which Kate and Helen recognize had been untied and read many times. One letter serves as a kind of mirror for the younger women: it reflects the affectionate nicknames, the longed-for visits, the delight in each other that Kate and Helen share.

Katharine Brandon's fidelity to her friend's memory hints at the anticipated permanence of Kate's and Helen's relationship. At the end of the book, the two girls laugh at Kate's suggestion that they could choose to become like the Ladies of Llangollen, a female couple who had eloped in order to devote themselves to "romantic friendship."[9] Kate admits that she had lately felt a new "sympathy and friendliness" (160) for the clearly independent Ladies, and that perhaps she and Helen could also spend their future days entertaining guests, studying, and growing wise together. The proposal that Deephaven become a New England Llangollen is whimsical, but in a more serious way, Helen wonders if some day she and Kate will return to Deephaven "for the sake of old times" and "look out to sea, and talk quietly about the girls who were so happy there one summer long before" (165). Notable by its absence in this reverie is any mention of husbands or children; it is as if there is an unspoken inevitability about their shared spinsterhood.

It is not an inevitability, however, that is bleak or without reward, for there is also a natural (and sensual) New England benediction about the scene Helen imagines. She thinks that she and Kate would walk at sunset, and a marsh fog would fall "deliciously cold and wet" against their hands and faces, and "the great sea would move and speak" (166) to them. The sea, of course, has already provided the girls with occasions for wisdom. They have watched the emblematic sea when it was magnificently stormy and wild, or wicked and treacherous, and they have seen it transfigured into a place "quiet and smooth and blue again" (159). In the same way, they have discovered during their short summer the human turbulence and sadness hidden among the inhabitants of Deephaven, but they have also spoken their discoveries to each other within the supportive quiet of their own friendship. As young as they are, their relationship has already begun to transfigure them into wise and understanding women.

Kate's and Helen's communion with the sea at the conclusion of *Deephaven* is part of a pattern of identification with nature that occurs throughout the sketches. Kate and Helen are never held inside by either external or internal strictures; with no thought of being merely decorative, passive, or dependent on men for adventuresome lives, they presume their mobility and they presume that they are free to gather experience, to move in a rhythm of visits that will enlarge their knowledge. The women spend a great deal of time in what Annis Pratt has called "the green world," the physical and psychic place where young women experience a sense of autonomy, freedom, and possibility in the presence of nature.[10] They ride the countryside and become intimately familiar with the woods, fields, cliffs, and coves of Deephaven. "As gay as bobolinks . . ." (162), they watch the seabirds and the stars and are "out of doors so much that there was little time for anything else" (163). Untamed by any notion that they ought not be at such liberty, they sometimes rest among wild-looking pines that, in a sense, are like themselves, "a band of outlaws . . ." (141). The particularity with which Helen describes such moments attests to the girls' rootedness in the Deephaven country, to their sense of belonging, and to their ability to see what is real and sustaining.[11]

The two women keep the vision of the natural world in front of them even when they are indoors. From the landing of the Brandon house, they have a view of "garden and village, the hills far inland, and the sunset beyond all" (45), but this is a position from which they gain perspective on life, not simply view it as outsiders. It is from here that they "wish for wings," and it is from here that they depart on the journeys that will satisfy their curiosity about what they have seen from above.[12] The journeys into nature that Kate and Helen take are features of a spinster's freedom, a freedom that yields a knowledge of decay and loss, of storm and fury, as well as beauty and delicacy. One senses that when older Jewett spinsters hear the earth speak a message they already know, it is because they have continually sought knowledge in moments of communion with nature such as Kate and Helen seek out in *Deephaven*.

In this early work, Jewett also links together single women with their homes: this is seen positively in Katharine Brandon and tragically in Miss Chauncey. What Kate and Helen discover by examining · the Brandon home and by receiving guests within it is that spinsterhood could be a traditional way of graceful living. Miss Brandon's house and its inhabitants are linked to nature by the poplars, lilacs, elms, and rosebushes which surround it, but it is also a museum of sorts "where nothing seems to have been thrown away" (47). Yet the china figures, carvings, and seashells from all over the world and the books and magazines in the library speak of a wide intellectual and aesthetic life inside. The Widow Patton remembers that Miss Brandon did live an expansive life, that when she first knew her, Miss Brandon went to Boston to visit and shop, dressed elegantly, traveled among friends, and entertained in her home. Katharine Brandon also extended herself beyond her own social class, for when Mrs. Patton became ill, the spinster took care of her in such a way that Mrs. Patton grew to love her as a sister. The closeness between the two women is captured in the revelation that only Mrs. Patton was allowed to care for the good Brandon china. In the same way, Miss Brandon's keepsakes which Kate and Helen discover—old copy books, withered flowers, pebbles, love letters—speak not of a narrow, possessive life but of what Adrienne Rich has called "a universe of humble things" without which there is "no memory / no faithfulness, no purpose for the future / no honor to the past."[13]

A true gentlewoman in the best New England tradition, Katharine Brandon's grace and kindness are legacies to the next generation of women. Indeed, Jewett seems to establish a matrilineal tradition of spinsterhood in this work, in the sense that young women see rich lives and therefore possibilities for themselves in the histories of their maiden aunts. Jewett even provides hints that Kate Lancaster will assume the honored position of the aunt whose name she shares. When Mrs. Patton first meets Kate, she remarks that "it seemed as if you had stepped into her place, and you look some as she used to when she was young" (63). Kate carries off cat-o'-nine-tails to preserve in her Boston bedroom, just as her aunt had kept her own "queer little keepsakes . . ." (49), and Helen observes that she and Kate seem to have taken the place of the girls who grew up in the house, that they have "inherited their pleasures, and perhaps have carried on work which they began" (161). Finally, Helen notices just how much Kate seems at home in her aunt's house: "It used to seem to me that it was still under her management, that she was its mistress; but now it belongs to you, and if I were ever to come back without you I should find you here" (162). In Katharine Brandon and her lovingly preserved home, then, Jewett offers not only memory and faithfulness but an example from which Kate Lancaster herself might fashion her own purposeful single adulthood.

But if Jewett creates an aura of fulfillment about the single women in *Deephaven*, she also presents some cautions, most notably in the haunting portrait of Miss Sally Chauncey, a figure trapped by her past who reveals the horrible underside of the single life. The last survivor of an aristocratic family, Miss Chauncey re-creates in her own mind her glory days, but she actually lives in a house where the floors are unsafe, where old hens walk among cobwebs, where lilac bushes grow so closely against the windows that a greenish light is cast inside. She goes about her house in "a rusty black satin gown" and "great black bonnet . . . which came far out over her face" (151). In this outfit, her own face and self obscured, she has no comprehension that her father and brothers have long since fallen into insanity and suicide, that the suitors are all gone, that her place as a belle is forever usurped. Miss Chauncey is a lesson for Kate and Helen. Stripped of her possessions and friends, self-exiled in a barren house, separated from the natural world, she is a woman without the inner resources to create order in her universe.[14] A New England madwoman in the attic, she is hardly a stereotypical "mere old maid," as Hicks would have it, nor a revered "Aunt" in the Harriet Beecher Stowe tradition. She is Sarah Orne Jewett's nightmare moment of spinsterhood.

Jewett's warning about the emotional starvation possible in the single life is matched by her description of the violence possible in marriage. If Kate and Helen seem to have no interest in men, they nonetheless have an opportunity to learn about a disappointing marriage from Widow Patton. Mrs. Patton's husband had been a man of "good prospects" (67) when she married him, but he turned out to be "but small satisfaction" (62), for he lived and died drunk and in debt. Mrs. Dockum tells the girls that the scar on Mrs. Patton's forehead marked where Mr. Patton "liked to have killed her; slung a stone bottle at her" (66). Widow Jim understandably warns Helen and Kate, "Don't you run no risks, you're better off as you be, dears" (63). Mrs. Patton's advice is not an endorsement of a safe life without emotional attachments, but it is her recognition that women's friendships could contain more possibilities than dissatisfying, even dangerous, marriage.[15] The girls' risks, whatever form they might take, were better run elsewhere than in the confines of a traditional marriage.

In *Deephaven*, then, Jewett establishes patterns of spinsterhood that will occur throughout her work. Frequently juxtaposed with women who suffer from the inadequacies of fathers or husbands, or with single women trapped in isolation, and often presented in images of earth, sea, and sky, Jewett's healthy single women create an alternative "woman's place" marked by a deep appreciation of nature, of other women, of women's houses, and of physical and emotional liberty. It is a place where "women full grown" can live.

Although Jewett rarely presents young women at the actual moment of choosing spinsterhood, there are several characters in whom the choice is given more explicit definition than in *Deephaven*. Like Kate and Helen, they prefigure and, in a way, provide the youthful histories of the many middle-aged and elderly Jewett spinsters who have long since elected the satisfactions of the adult single state. It may seem unwise to include a nine year old in this group, or to put much emphasis on the choice of solitariness over romance made by Sylvia in "A White Heron," except that Jewett particularly calls attention to "the woman's heart, asleep in the child," which a young man awakens into vague dreams of love.[16] When Sylvy must then weigh the claims of romance, she can be read as a kind of gloss on the experiences of such older Jewett heroines as Polly Finch of "Farmer Finch" and Nan Prince of *A Country Doctor*.

None of the three young girls are spinsters *ab ova*. They do not, for example, possess the physical characteristics that would make them instantly recognizable old maids in the popular imagination. Jewett, in fact, takes pains to point out that they are not "unwomanly," or "mannish," or "rough," and she calls attention to Sylvy's "shining eyes" (8), Polly's uncommon good looks, and Nan's "bright eyes" and "well-poised" head.[17] Her emphasis, however, is on how their experiences in the green world of nature offer them an illumination into the work they must do and the terms on which they must define their relationships with men.

Sylvia's grandmother recognizes that "there never was such a child for straying out-of-doors since the world was made!" (3) She is so at home with nature that "the wild creatures counts her one o' themselves" (9), birds particularly. Polly Finch is never happier than when "working out-doors and handling a piece of land."[18] Nan Prince is delighted when she can "lie down beside the anemones and watch them move in the wind . . . and afterward look up into the blue sky to watch the great gulls above the river . . . (51). Nan, too, like Sylvy, "belongs with wild creatur's" (61) and has a nature "as wild as a hawk . . ." (60). This sympathetic identification with nature prepares each of the three women for an intense, mystical experience which carries them beyond the strictures of woman's place. In each case, they find that the world and their own possibilities within it are larger than they had ever imagined, and once that discovery is made, Jewett suggests that celibacy may be the seal by which they remain true to their visions and thus to themselves.

For Sylvy and Polly, the consecration may be only temporary; for Nan Prince, it is a part of her vocation.[19]

Sylvy's epiphany, of course, occurs when she climbs the pine tree from which she hopes to sight the white heron. She had looked forward with "a spirit of adventure" and "wild ambition" (15) to making known the heron's nesting place, but in the midst of the awakening birds and a magnificent sunrise, she sees the ocean to the east and the woodlands to the west and knows for the first time that "truly it was a vast and awesome world!" (18). She and the heron watch "the sea and the morning together" (21) and Sylvy has an experience of being "heart to heart with nature . . ." (15). Like Jane Eyre yearning for a wider life, and like Helen and Kate holding both sea and woods within their vision, Sylvy becomes one with herself at the moment her horizon is enlarged. Polly Finch's revelatory moment occurs when she sees a barberry bush on the road. It looks "gray and winterish" from one side, but from the other, "it seemed to be glowing with rubies" and "had taken on a great splendor" (40). This "sudden transformation" of the bush is emblematic of Polly's own insight and will, for she realizes that "There are two ways of looking at more things than barberry bushes . . ." (41). Nan Prince's sense that the world and her place within it are charged with meaning occurs first in Dr. Leslie's garden, where she feels so at one with nature that the garden itself seemed to be a church, the plants parishioners, and she the preacher. Later the same day, she sees her grandmother's farmhouse in the distance. The garden and the house together become almost a sacred text, a word that she preaches to herself, for in their presence, "Life had suddenly grown much larger, and her familiar horizon had vanished and she discovered a great distance stretching far beyond the old limits" (54).

When the familiar horizons vanish, each young woman is compelled to an action which turns her away from women's traditional way of inhabiting the universe. When it comes time for Sylvy to assume her woman's voice, to surrender the hunted to the hunter, she "cannot speak; she cannot tell the heron's secret and give its life away" (21). Her silence causes her to lose the affection of the charming young sportsman for whom she had felt a "loving admiration" (12), but however much his kind, appealing eyes represent the "great world" putting out a hand to her, she has already seen a greater world yet to be explored. Even at nine, she has a vision that cannot be betrayed, and not even her grandmother's strong rebukes will dissuade her. She may, as Jewett suggests, someday forget the dead birds in favor of the romantic memory of the young hunter, but nature nonetheless still promises her "gifts" and "graces" and "secrets" (22), just as Helen and Kate would one day wait for the sea to speak new secrets to them. For Jewett, the woman's heart cannot betray nature's heart; if, in consequence, she must then remain a solitary figure, a woman alone, her integrity and freedom will sustain her.[20]

When Polly Finch is enlightened by nature, she determines to take over the family farm from her sickly and ineffective father, to help him "same as if I were a boy" (51). She becomes renowned as Farmer Finch, taking heart from a neighbor's story of a woman who could plow "as well as a man" (75) and who had so prospered that she earned the title Farmer. Jewett calls attention to Polly's liberty of spirit, observing that "there never was a young man . . . rejoicing in his freedom, who went to work more diligently and eagerly than Polly Finch, and few have set their wits at work on a New England farm half so intelligently" (79). Polly, too, loses a young man but she is the one who ends the romance because she is angered at his condescending attitude toward her family. Though her mother warns her that she ought not to reject a possible husband since "a woman's better to have a home of her own" (71), Polly's reply is a firm, "This is my home, and I wouldn't marry Jerry Minton if he were the President" (72). Jewett later suggests that Polly will find a better man to fall in love with, but in the meantime, in the woman who takes such pleasure in the masculine work that the men do not have the wit or the stamina for, Jewett has created a voice for her own dissatisfaction with the Victorian definitions of "true womanhood," and she has thus broadened the terms on which spinsterhood might be chosen.[21] Like the barberry bush and her farm, Polly, too, has "taken on a great splendor."

In a manner similar to Polly Finch's, Nan Prince's epiphany causes her to reject "the business of housekeeping and what is called a woman's natural work" (137) in favor of a career as a country doctor. Though she must often struggle in solitary silence with self-doubt, loneliness, and restlessness, and though she must frequently return to the green world for reaffirmation of her vocation, she finally finds strength to "live alone and work alone" (137) because she is true to her own nature, whose instincts are "all against" (320) marriage. Her rejection of the weak and envious George Gerry is not without pain, for she does have a dim sense of the "strange power" (299) of romantic love, but it is abundantly clear even to George that she can "get on capitally well without him . . ." (298). Her decision is blessed by an ecstatic vision at the end of the novel. Back at her grandmother's farm, Nan stands at the shore of the river, looks across the river to the hills, and sees the eagles flying high above the water. The wind, sunshine, and trees surround her, "and suddenly she reached her hands upwards in an ecstasy of life and strength and gladness. 'O God,' she said, 'I thank thee for my future'" (351). God and nature thus consecrate her into a purposeful New England celibacy.

A Country Doctor, however, unlike "A White Heron" or "Farmer Finch," contains portraits of two old spinsters, both of whom Jewett offers as warnings of what the future single life might be if a woman does not truly choose spinsterhood and does not "take hold" with a useful purpose in life. Anna Prince, Nan's aunt, is her double, the mirror in whom she can see her other, lonely self, grown older. Nan and Miss Prince at first delight each other, for each feels enriched and added to by the other's gifts. The affinity between them is captured in their exit from church on the first Sunday of Nan's visit; they walk down the aisle together "as if they had been married..." (231). But the irony in the image becomes clear when Nan recognizes that there is an important difference between herself and her namesake: the two women may share strength of will, determination, and "iron-like firmness of structure," but the elder Miss Prince has no "high aims or any especial and fruitful single-heartedness . . ." (236). Instead, she has spent her life regretting the petty misunderstanding that had cost her a lover, and her gifts have been used not even to create but to defend "a comparatively unimportant and commonplace existence" (237). A severe woman, "old and gray and alone in the world" (208), she can only urge upon Nan what she considers "the best happiness of . . . life" (320)—marrying George—but it is precisely Nan's equation of an "unimportant and commonplace existence" with marriage that causes her to seek "the best happiness of life" elsewhere. Nan does possess a "fruitful single-heartedness." When she rejects both George Gerry and the example of Anna Prince's "fettering and disappointing" (206) spinsterhood, she does so for the sake of a work that is her very life.

Jewett's other warning to Nan is contained in the picture of Miss Eunice Fraley, an aptly named spinster still living at home with an imperious mother who treats her as if she were sixteen instead of nearly sixty. Miss Fraley, too has long since lost a suitor, and her life has been "blighted because it lacked its mate, and was but half a life in itself . . ." (304). The childish Miss Fraley looks at Nan "as a caged bird at a window might watch a lark's flight . . ." (271–72), but when Nan defends her career to Miss Fraley's mother, Eunice lacks the courage to take flight with Nan's imagination. She grows "smaller and thinner than ever" (278) and wants to hide in the sugar bowl. A woman who would so diminish herself that she shrinks into oblivion, she is a "hindered little house-plant" to Nan's "slender, wild thing, that has sprung up fearlessly under the great sky, with only the sunshine and the wind and summer rain to teach it . . ." (303). If Miss Prince is fettered by her lack of purpose, Miss Fraley is imprisoned by her timidity; in their willingness to settle for half-lives and in their failure to grow up, neither are models of spinsterhood for Nan.

In Sylvy, Polly Finch, and Nan Prince, Jewett posits a productive future for young single women. Neither spiritually impoverished nor childish,[22] these three young women together make clear that once New England spinsters find their truest selves in nature, they are able to repudiate the traditional, patriarchal restrictions on women and to resist the domesticating promptings of their mothers or aunts. Their independence is not confined within small houses, but is given flight, like the birds with whom they are frequently compared.[23] Their work outside, not their place at the hearth, gives meaning to their lives. Their rejection of men is in no sense a repudiation of love but a ratification of their own autonomy. Able to imagine themselves as something other than wives or pinched old maids, they bravely create the contours of a mature single adulthood.

Once spinsterhood is elected, however, Jewett asserts that the process of growth is not ended. The freedom and solitude which mark the younger women as "outlaws" cannot be allowed to dissolve into dull contentment nor be exaggerated into an absolute self-sufficiency. Neither can marriage or men or "woman's proper place" be newly and falsely romanticized during middle or old age. Instead, the spinster's union with nature, her solitariness and liberty, must blossom into human fruitfulness, especially in a sharing community of women. The home which nurtures the adventurous self must invite new life and new friends. But the temptation to surrender to a stereotypical spinsterhood or to turn to the traditional path of wifehood exists throughout Jewett's works. Again, however, her healthy adult single women grow and change in ways that enlarge their lives.

Three elderly Jewett spinsters—Aunt Hannah of "An Every-Day Girl," Temperance Dent of "Miss Tempy's Watchers," and Betsey Lane of "The Flight of Betsey Lane"—can be seen as measures of how expansive the mature spinster life can become however narrow the space in which it is lived. Hannah and Tempy both become almost larger than life in the sense that they apparently have the power simply to appear—in person or in spirit—when they are needed by people. Their freedom to so appear is linked to their union with nature. Aunt Hannah hears the birds singing one morning and knows instinctively that she must visit the Flemings. Indeed, Mary Fleming remarks that "she sort of flies down out of the air" just when people want her.[24] Aunt Hannah "knows everything" (181) from herb teas, to the disappointments inherent in many marriages ("the worst always comes on the women" [182]), to the troubles of confused daughters. A good "witch" (181), she can swiftly clarify for Mary Fleming how young girls should shape their futures. "Have ambition then," she tells her, "an' make your gift serve you and other folks . . ." (182).

Miss Tempy Dent has done just as Aunt Hannah lived and advised. She, too, "always sensed things" that people needed, whether it was helping at marriages or funerals, rug-hooking, cleaning, tailoring, or simply "talkin' over things. . . ."[25] Her closeness to nature is evident in the way she could coax fruit from an old quince tree: "she'd go out in the spring and tend to it, and look at it so pleasant, and kind of expect the old thorny thing into bloomin' " (224). On the night of her wake, her presence permeates the house. Sister Binson feels "as if the air was full of her, kind of" (221), and, indeed, just as Aunt Hannah "flies down out of the air," Tempy's spirit does for her two women watchers what she had done for the quince tree: she expects them into blooming with a new understanding of each other.

Betsey Lane, too, serves her sisters, but she does so by exercising her spinster freedom to roam, temporarily leaving the Byfleet Poor-house "for the good o' the rest."[26] Betsey Lane "had always hoped to see something of the world before she died . . ." (181), and when she receives a gift of a hundred dollars, her mind "roved so high and so far" (192) that she makes up her mind to visit the Centennial exhibition in Philadelphia, then to report on it to the other women. Like the bird perched on the poor-house windowsill who "flitted away toward the blue sky" (189), she takes flight on an early June morning. Her excursion confirms her belief that "there was an amazing world outside the boundaries of Byfleet" (208) and recalls Sylvy's view from the pine tree. Understanding that "what's for the good o' one's for the good of all" (217), she returns home, meets her two closest friends in the woods, and immediately shares with them her gifts and, more importantly, her experiences and stories. As they walk together "triumphant . . . across the wide green fields" (218) in a scene resonant with overtones of Helen Denis' benediction at the end of *Deephaven*, it is clear that Betsey Lane's flight is the journey of a brave and adventurous woman. Aunt Hannah, Tempy Dent, and Betsey Lane are free, practical, loving women who throughout their lives put their gifts of nature and grace at the service of their communities. Single, old, and childless as they may be, their lives have been full and their spirits live on in the women who have listened to them.

The growth into wholeness and integrity can be thwarted, however, when single women settle into comfortable or mean-spirited spinsterhoods that are no longer fully connected with other human beings. In three short stories—"Miss Sydney's Flowers," "A Garden Story," and "A Guest at Home"—it is "the transfiguring power of friendship" that both renews and enlarges the lives of three old spinsters.

The aristocratic Miss Sydney, a "good woman in a negative kind of way," is reserved, aloof, and unfailingly polite, but more interested in fictional characters than in living people.[27] This changes when people passing by her home notice the plants and flowers in her newly visible greenhouse; gradually she begins to see the pleasures that her plants give others, and she herself starts to feel a "kindness and charity and helpfulness" (157). Her transformation is encouraged by Bessie Thorne, a young girl who visits with Miss Sydney, shares her girlish confidences, and invites the old spinster to participate in charitable activities. Under Bessie's influence, Miss Sydney's beneficence eventually extends to women in her own neighborhood, until finally she puts aside her sense of being "old and useless and friendless" (173). The garden of her heart finally holds blossoms for both herself and the community.

Ann Dunning's garden story is similar. Miss Dunning is a woman who generously shares the flowers from her "most old-fashioned" garden, but there is a kind of ruthlessness in the way she routs the weeds and an aloof self-sufficiency in the way she insists upon doing tasks herself.[28] There is also a slight sense of futility about her work, for "many patient hours were spent in the hot sunshine that nobody took note of but the flowers themselves" (106). Miss Dunning, however, takes in a little girl during "country week" and Peggy McAllister not only notices her efforts in the garden but also soon wins her heart while liberating Miss Dunning from the order she had imposed both on her garden and her life. Peggy implores her to let poppies, marigolds, and petunias sprout at will in the yard, and, like Betsey Thorne, she persuades Miss Dunning to share her flowers with the children in a Boston hospital. When Miss Dunning adopts Peggy, she discovers her full nurturing power. Miss Dunning and Miss Sydney both become as bountiful as the flowers they cherish.

Aunt Harriet, the half-paralyzed old maid whose "warped and twisted" temper makes her "suspicious and cross," softens under the influence of Annie Hollis in "A Guest at Home."[29] Though as a child Annie had "always hated" (56) Aunt Harriet, the two finally claim each other as friends. Aunt Harriet reveals her precious keepsakes to Annie, and the artistic Annie shares with the old woman some new stitches that enable her to sew pieces that seem to reach "the highest summit of art and beauty" (57). When the young woman connects the older one with her own talent and energy and gives her an outlet for her creativity, she also reconnects her to other human beings. Aunt Harriet, too, finally resists the stunted pattern her life had settled into, and grows instead into a newer, healthier spinsterhood.

If Miss Sydney, Aunt Harriet, and Ann Dunning must resist the temptation to retreat into emotionally limited, almost severe adulthoods, Esther Jaffrey of "A Village Shop" is a Jewett spinster who must exorcise her own sense of woman's proper place in order to grow into a free, adult woman. Miss Jaffrey is left to open a shop in the family mansion in order to continue support of a scholarly but unproductive brother who is utterly oblivious to the lengths to which the spinster must go to keep their home together. Part of her pain is her realization that she has the traits of character that have made the Jaffrey name great. "If she had been the son how she could work and win her way . . . ," she thinks to herself, but because "she was only a woman" and would not dare to "lead public opinion in unfeminine directions," she resigns herself to suitable woman's work.[30] After a successful start, however, the shop nearly fails and the Jaffreys are on the point of starvation; they are then offered rescue by a turn of events which include Leonard's marriage and his appointment as town librarian. Miss Jaffrey, who had revered her brother almost beyond reason, is appalled at his apparent betrayal of her. Finally realizing that "she had abased her pride and starved and forbidden the hopes of her own life for *this*" (283), she nonetheless resolutely retains her fierce independence and dignity. When Leonard suggests that she should close the shop and be supported by him, she responds, "*Never!*" (290). As pale and old as she has become, "her heart felt curiously light. At that moment the shop-bell tinkled impatiently, and Miss Jaffrey went in, stately as a princess, to wait upon an early customer" (290). Miss Jaffrey's resounding "*Never!*" is a proclamation that she will never again be defined by any man, including her own brother. She enters the shop as a princess, not because she carries the false pretensions of a faded gentility,[31] but because she has at last liberated herself from the notion that women were born to follow and to serve men. The talents that a productive spinsterhood could have long ago set free are at least not so starved as to be dead. The enlightened Miss Jaffrey sets about at last to create her own life.

When Jewett's young women turn away from their suitors, they each sense a wide world open to their activity. For several Jewett spinsters, however, middle or old age can cause them to look with nostalgia on a lost opportunity or to actively seek a marriage, but they invariably learn that they have missed very little and that Mrs. Patton's advice ("you're better off as ye be, dears") is sound. Horatia Dane ("A Lost Lover") discovers that her lost lover is alive and well but is a drunk and a tramp; the middle-aged Ann Floyd ("Marsh Rosemary") marries a young man only to be abandoned; Sister Wisby ("The Courting of Sister Wisby") finally marries the Deacon but only after a period of living together and even then, she leaves her money to his daughter. Eliza Peck and Joanna Todd, however, are two women rejected by men. Miss Peck responds with Yankee good humor and achieves self-knowledge and a fuller spinsterhood. Joanna Todd responds with a mad, self-punishing, absolute isolation. She is Jewett's proof that "for intense, self-centred, smouldering volcanoes of humanity, New England cannot be matched the world over."[32]

Miss Peck has lived happily in a farm house built on a Vermont hillside, but she occasionally feels the burden of solitariness with its "creepy dread and sense of defenselessness. . . ."[33] She is therefore happy for the opportunity to become temporary housekeeper for the Reverend William Elbury. Even though she discovers that he is "romantic, ease-loving, self-absorbed, and self-admiring" (182), he is generous with his library, and his shared love of literature attracts Miss Peck: "It was all a new world to the good woman . . . and if ever a mind waked up with joy to its possession of the world of books, it was hers" (189). When the Reverend Elbury remarks that "his books were hers now" (189) and begins referring to the two of them as "we," Miss Peck gets the notion that he may ask her to marry him. As excited as Miss Peck gets by the prospect of marriage, she is not desperate for love. Rather, the minister stands for "a widened life, a suggestion of added good and growth, a larger circle of human interests . . ." (189). When he comes home one day with a young bride from the city, Miss Peck hides her shock, acquaints the girl with her new life, and returns to her farm, where she happily takes over the care of her favorite nephew. She laughs at herself for not having "proper ideas of what gettin' promoted is" (204), and remarks that she has no regrets, even if she did just miss making a fool of herself. She counts herself happy to be back in her own house where she can visit with women friends, where there is a view out the windows, and where one can have "a good honest look at a yellow sunset" (206). Loving nature, finding community with other women, becoming a mother-figure to a child, Miss Peck has not been promoted into marriage, but she has been promoted into a valued tradition of New England spinsterhood. She learns to keep her own house.

Joanna Todd, however, is a woman unable to reconcile her own bitter experiences with what she thought life had promised her. She had understood her happiness to be completely bound up in "marryin', an' havin' a real home and somebody to look to."[34] But when she is jilted, "she acted just like a bird when its nest is spoilt" (104), and goes off to live her life on the appropriately named Shell-heap Island, "a dreadful small place to make a world of" (105). Her grim hermitage is motivated by a conviction that she has committed so "unpardonable" a sin against God that she "can't expect ever to be forgiven" (121). Besieged by the overpowering demands of marriage and theology, Joanna cannot forgive herself for having failed either one. She wants only to be left alone. The spinster narrator of *The Country of the Pointed Firs* understands that the searing pain of Joanna's living suicide is simply the exterior expression of many women's interior pain, but she also knows that Joanna Todd is a tragic spinster. With less resources than Esther Jaffrey or Eliza Peck or even Anna Prince or Eunice Fraley, she cannot find solace in home or friends or nature or work. The boundaries of her imagination shrunk to prison bars, her spinsterhood turned grotesque, it is herself she crushes like so many broken shells.

In Joanna Todd, Jewett recognizes that single women who let their lives be determined by false promises from man or God could wreak havoc on themselves and never experience the freedom of a Betsey Lane or the renewed joy of an Ann Dunning. But Jewett also recognizes that single women who finally make their way in a patriarchal world can also waste their gifts and blight the lives of others as well as themselves. Prudence Fellows of "The Growtown 'Bugle,'" for example, lives "a daily contracting life" and does her tasks "listlessly," partly because her environment is not large enough to accommodate her skills.[35] Having all the business sense and intelligence of a Polly Finch, she would like to live in a place "where there was a bustlin' drive 'mongst the menfolks, and buildin's a puttin' up, and all them things" (125). When she invests (by mail) in the Western village of Growtown, Kansas, she manages to outsmart speculators at their own game, but she shares her newfound wealth and energy not with her local community whose needs she can see but with the people of her unseen, adopted town whose gratitude will enhance her reputation. Her stinginess and meanness keep in check her intention to "do well" by Lizzie Peck, an impoverished little neighbor girl with a sickly, struggling mother. Prudence Fellows fails to act on her behalf, and Lizzie Peck starves to death. Jewett's story does end on a hint that Miss Fellows may yet be partially redeemed. So shocked by the news of Lizzie's death that she faints, Miss Fellows "never had felt so poor in her life as when she came to herself again" (131). If Prudence Fellows finally admits her own poverty of spirit, she may grow into a single woman marked by true generosity, but in the image of the woman who "comes to herself" very late in life, Jewett leaves a picture of distorted and empty spinsterhood.

The growth into mature and adult spinsterhood that Helen Denis and Kate Lancaster seemed to be sensing about themselves is realized most fully perhaps in the friendship between Mrs. Todd and the narrator of *Pointed Firs*. The depth of their friendship is captured, significantly, in the coral pin of Joanna Todd's that Mrs. Todd gives as a farewell present to her friend. Mutually acknowledging the "remote and islanded" places in themselves given over "to endless regret or secret happiness" (132), the two women know that in their matelessness they must appeal to each other to heal the private pain and to celebrate the secret joy. Yet, in another sense, these two mateless women are appealing to each other and to other women precisely because they know that behind their "able and warm-hearted" (211) public faces, they mysteriously and powerfully possess themselves. When, like Abby Pendexter and Aunt Cynthy Dallet and countless other spinster women, they intimately share moments "of ceremony and deep feeling,"[36] when, for example, they hold each other's hands all the way home from William's wedding, it is because they bring to each other an integrity born of reverence for nature, their homes, their friends, their possessions, their talents. When they separate, they know to what they will return.

The spinsters in Sarah Orne Jewett, then, are not simply diminished women preparing tea in cottages or reading the *Atlantic Monthly* in mansions. They are not trivial, not slight, not even always proper or pious. Rather, they are complex women set apart from the conventional by their willingness to explore how they might live in the world as free women. In the course of their literal and psychic journeys away from their homes to nature, to their friends, and back again, they discover and rediscover the work that is theirs to do and the people who are theirs to love. They come to know, in Doris Grumbach's words, "disappointments, despairs, rare intense joys."[37] They face the omnipresent aloneness of the human condition. For most, the promises of their girlhoods are fulfilled, and the significance of their full-grown spinsterhood is that they know themselves as happy, transfigured women. For others, regretting forever the wedded bliss they did not find, or surrendering helplessly to an eccentric isolation, their singleness serves only to reveal what they "yearned for and were refused, what they imagined and did not realize" (93). Jewett's honesty as a writer is that she gives voice to the Joanna Todds as well as the Kate Lancasters. She does "tell all the truth" through her spinsters. None of them, anymore than Jewett herself, is "merely a New England old maid."

Notes

1. Granville Hicks, *The Great Tradition: An Interpretation of American Literature Since the Civil War* (1933; rpt. Chicago: Quadrangle Paperbacks, 1969), pp. 104–05. All further references to the work appear in the text.

2. *A Room of One's Own* (1929; rpt. New York: Harcourt, 1957).

3. See especially Josephine Donovan, "A Woman's Vision of Transcendence: A New Interpretation of the Works of Sarah Orne Jewett," *Massachusetts Review*, 21 (Summer 1980), 365–80; and *Sarah Orne Jewett* (New York: Ungar, 1980).

4. The qualities of spinsterhood are captured by Alison Lurie in her essay "No One Asked Me to Write a Novel," *New York Times Book Review*, 6 June 1982, p. 13: "I knew all about Old Maids from the Victorian and Edwardian children's books that were my favorite reading. Old Maids wore spectacles and old-fashioned clothes and lived in cottages with gardens, where they entertained children and Old Maids to tea. They were always odd in some way: absent-minded or timid or rude or fussy. Sometimes they taught school, but most of their time was devoted to making wonderful walnut cakes and blackberry jam and dandelion wine, to telling tales and painting watercolors, to embroidery and knitting and crocheting, and to growing prize cabbages and roses. Occasionally they shared their cottage with another Old Maid, but mostly they lived alone, often with a cat. Sometimes the cat was their familiar, and they were really witches. You could tell which ones were witches . . . because there was always something wrong with them: They had six fingers on one hand, or their feet were on backward, and so on."

5. *Deephaven and Other Stories*, ed. Richard Cary (New Haven: College and University Press, 1966), p. 55. All further references to this work appear in the text.

6. *Letters of Sarah Orne Jewett*, ed. Annie Fields (Boston: Houghton Mifflin, 1911), p. 126.

7. Willa Cather, *Not Under Forty* (1936; rpt. New York: Knopf, 1953), p. 85. See also John Eldridge Frost, *Sarah Orne Jewett* (Kittery Point: Gundalow Club, 1960), p. 39: "Friendship was to take the first place in her life, with writing next to it." Jewett, of course, shared a lifelong relationship with Annie Fields.

8. In "Sarah Orne Jewett, The Apostle of New England," in *Appreciation of Sarah Orne Jewett: 29 Interpretive Essays*, ed. Richard Cary (Waterville: Colby College Press, 1973), p. 76, Esther Forbes writes of Jewett: "The process of mating, which for the average fiction writer holds center stage, is always in retrospect or in the wings. For better or worse she has left this side of human endeavor to others."

See also Clarice Short, "Studies in Gentleness," *Western Humanities Review*, 11 (1957); rpt. in *Appreciation of Sarah Orne Jewett*, pp. 128–34.

9. See Lillian Faderman, *Surpassing the Love of Men: Romantic Friendship and Love between Women from the Renaissance to the Present* (New York: Wm. Morrow, 1981), pp. 74–75.

10. *Archetypal Patterns in Women's Fiction* (Bloomington: Indiana Univ. Press, 1981), pp. 16–24.

11. See Julia Bader, "The Dissolving Vision: Realism in Jewett, Freeman, and Gilman," in *American Realism: New Essays*, ed. Eric J. Sundquist (Baltimore: Johns Hopkins Univ. Press, 1982), p. 183, in which she argues that "when the eye takes in a beloved scene, and the heart extends into a female community, . . . the world appears real and substantial in Jewett's fiction."

12. See Nina Auerbach, "Old Maids and the Wish for Wings," in *Woman and the Demon: The Life of a Victorian Myth* (Cambridge: Harvard Univ. Press, 1982), pp. 109–49. Auerbach identifies the spinster as a heroic character whose mobility, strength, intellect, and independence transcend and threaten the boundaries of the Victorian family.

13. "Natural Resources," in *The Dream of a Common Language: Poems 1974–1977* (New York: Norton, 1978), p. 66.

14. See Robert L. Horn, "The Power of Jewett's Deephaven," *Colby Library Quarterly*, 9 (1972); rpt. in *Appreciation of Sarah Orne Jewett*, pp. 293–94; and Ann Douglas Wood, "The Literature of Impoverishment: The Women Local Colorists in America 1865–1914," *Women's Studies*, 1 (1972), 21–22.

15. Perhaps the most important article on women's friendships in the nineteenth century is Carrol Smith-Rosenberg's "The Female World of Love and Ritual: Relations Between Women in Nineteenth Century America," *Signs: A Journal of Women in Culture and Society*, 1 (1975), 1–29. See also the chapter on "Sisterhood" in Nancy Cott's *The Bonds of Womanhood: 'Woman's Sphere' in New England, 1780–1835* (New Haven: Yale Univ. Press, 1977), pp. 160–97.

16. *A White Heron and Other Stories* (Boston: Houghton Mifflin, 1886), p. 12; hereafter cited in the text.

17. *A Country Doctor* (Boston: Houghton Mifflin, 1884), p. 44; hereafter cited in the text.

18. "Farmer Finch," in *A White Heron and Other Stories*, p. 64; hereafter cited in the text.

19. See Ellen Morgan, "The Atypical Woman: Nan Prince in the Literary Transition to Feminism," *Kate Chopin Newsletter*, 2 (Fall 1976), 33–37; and Malinda Snow, " 'That One Talent': The Vocation as Theme in Sarah Orne Jewett's *A Country Doctor*," *Colby Library Quarterly*, 16 (1980), 138–47.

20. See Annis Pratt, "Women and Nature in Modern Fiction," *Contemporary Literature*, 13 (Fall 1972), 478–80, and *Archetypal Patterns in Women's Fiction*, p. 19. See also Richard Brenzo, "Free Heron or Dead Sparrow: Sylvy's Choice in Sarah Orne Jewett's 'A White Heron,'" *Colby Library Quarterly*, 14 (1978), 36–41; and Theodore R. Hovet, "American's 'Lonely Country Child': The Theme of Separation in Sarah Orne Jewett's 'A White Heron,'" *Colby Library Quarterly*, 14 (1978), 166–71.

21. Donovan, *Sarah Orne Jewett*, pp. 53–54.

22. See Eugene Hillhouse Pool, "The Child in Sarah Orne Jewett," *Colby Library Quarterly*, 7 (1967); rpt. in *Appreciation of Sarah Orne Jewett*, pp. 223–28.

23. See Ellen Moers, *Literary Women: The Great Writers* (Garden City, N.Y.:

Doubleday-Anchor, 1977), pp. 369–82 for a discussion of bird metaphors in women's fiction.

24. "An Every-Day Girl," in *The Uncollected Short Stories of Sarah Orne Jewett*, ed. Richard Cary (Waterville: Colby College Press, 1971), p. 185; hereafter cited in the text.

25. "Miss Tempy's Watchers," in *The King of Folly Island and Other People* (Boston: Houghton Mifflin, 1888), p. 225; hereafter cited in the text.

26. "The Flight of Betsey Lane," in *A Native of Winby and Other Tales* (Boston: Houghton Mifflin, 1893), p. 218; hereafter cited in the text.

27. "Miss Sydney's Flowers," in *Old Friends and New* (Boston: Houghton, Osgood, 1879), p. 145; hereafter cited in the text.

28. "A Garden Story," in *The Uncollected Short Stories of Sarah Orne Jewett*, p. 106; hereafter cited in the text.

29. In *The Uncollected Short Stories of Sarah Orne Jewett*, pp. 53, 57.

30. "A Village Shop," in *The King of Folly Island and Other People*, p. 232; hereafter cited in the text.

31. In *Sarah Orne Jewett* (New York: Twayne, 1962), p. 105, Richard Cary reads this ending as evidence of Miss Jaffrey's inability to reconcile herself to even indirect dependence upon a social inferior. Her "insistence upon self" is a failure of an outmoded aristocracy. Yet this reading does not seem to capture the triumph of Esther Jaffrey's resounding *"Never!"*

32. Jewett, *A Country Doctor*, p. 100.

33. "Miss Peck's Promotion," in *The King of Folly Island and Other People*, p. 168; hereafter cited in the text.

34. *The Country of the Pointed Firs* (Boston: Houghton Mifflin, 1896), p. 104; hereafter cited in the text.

35. In *The Uncollected Short Stories of Sarah Orne Jewett*, pp. 125, 124; hereafter cited in the text.

36. "Aunt Cynthy Dallett," in *The Queen's Twin and Other Stories* (Boston: Houghton Mifflin, 1899), p. 216.

37. *Chamber Music* (New York: E. P. Dutton, 1978), p. 211; hereafter cited in the text.

Jewett's Witches   Elizabeth Ammons[*]

"She stood in the centre of a braided rug," the narrator says of Almira Todd early in *The Country of the Pointed Firs* (1896), "and its rings of black and gray seemed to circle about her feet in the dim light."[1] We have already been told that Mrs. Todd's herb plot, where she "trod heavily upon thyme" (the pun is perfect), includes rare vegetation that "might once have belonged to sacred and mystic rites, and have some occult knowledge handed with them down the centuries" (4). Now, we are wryly assured, this woman healer brews in her "small caldron"

*This essay was written especially for this volume and is included here by permission of the author.

only ordinary compounds for people who come "at night as if by stealth, bringing their own ancient-looking vials to be filled" (4–5). They receive "whispered directions" or, in special cases, "muttered long chapters of directions" delivered "with an air of secrecy and importance" all the way down the front walk (5). Should we wonder that intimacy grows between the narrator and this "sibyl" under the "spell" of some "herb of the night," which sends out its odor "late in the evening, after the dew had fallen, and the moon was high . . ." (10, 9)?

Linking witchcraft and female healing was not new for Jewett when she wrote *The Country of the Pointed Firs*. A dozen years earlier she had begun her novel about a young woman's decision to become a physician, *A Country Doctor* (1884), with foreboding images drawn from witch and ghost lore. As the novel opens, a haggard young woman stumbles with her child, who will become the physician, into a grave-yard where "a legion of ghosts . . . were chasing her and flocking around her and oppressing her from every side."[2] Meanwhile the baby's grand-mother, who has begun this black November night at her spinning wheel (a recurrent symbol in Jewett), recalls with two other crones the equally pitch-black night when this wandering daughter was born. The old woman remembers her daughter's "queer" great-great-aunt who would have been " 'hung for a witch if she'd lived in them old Salem days,' " and then another character thinks of " 'her gre't grandsir Thacker; you can see she's made out o' the same stuff. You might ha' burnt him to the stake, and he 'd stick to it he liked it better 'n hanging and al'ays meant to die that way' " (15, 27). For good reason, *A Country Doctor* opens by imaging the mother of the book's female physician as a witch. In Jewett woman's power as a healer and her connection to the spirit-world, traditionally the province of witchcraft, correspond: witches and healing go together. That conviction, as I explain in this essay, was basic to her lifelong interest in the relation between women and the occult.

I

Sarah Orne Jewett believed in the spirit-world. Richard Cary, who mentions her attending a séance and writing Whittier a fourteen-page letter about it, points out that the occult plays a significant role in a number of her stories.[3] Josephine Donovan explains that Jewett studied Swedenborgianism with Theophilus Parsons, a Harvard law professor, and found " 'a sense of it under everything else.' "[4] Certainly, Jewett considered extrasensory communication possible between the living and the dead. In a letter to Annie Fields in 1889 she tells of visiting an old friend, now bewildered by age, who keeps talking about her dead sister until, as Jewett exits, the old woman says "with strange emphasis, 'I have seen Betsey [the sister], she came one night and stood beside my bed; it shocked me a good deal, but I saw her, and one of my brothers came with her.' As she told me this," Jewett tells Annie Fields, "I believed it was the truth, and no delusion."[5] In a later letter to Mrs. Fields Jewett speaks of her own encounter with the dead in 1894 upon the passing of her dear friend Celia Thaxter: "What is a very strange thing, I can see her face,—you know I never could call up faces easily, and never before, that I remember, have I been able to see how a person looked who has died, but again and again I seem to see her. That takes me a strange step out of myself. All this new idea of Tesla's: must it not, like everything else, have its spiritual side, and yet where imagination stops and consciousness of the unseen begins, who can settle that even to one's self?"[6] Upon her sister's death she wrote to Horace E. Scudder in 1897 that "one always seems to begin a new life in company with the soul that disappears into 'the world of light,'—that goes away only to come nearer to one's heart than ever before. It all seems like a transfiguration of the old way of loving, and of friendship too."[7]

Jewett believed in extrasensory communication with the living as well as the dead. She wrote to a friend in 1898 upon visiting Rheims, "I feel a little as if I had almost seen you there. Whether a little wind that blew against you when you were there, is still flickering among the pillars of the cathedral or not, who can say! but I think we went together and I found something of you at every turn."[8] Jewett did not fear death. On the occasion of former President Grant's death in 1885 she wrote to Annie Fields her regret that "with all his clear sight he was no visionary or seer of spiritual things"; yet, she reflects: "Now he knows all, the step is taken, and the mysterious moment of death proves to be a moment of waking. How one longs to take it for one's self!"[9]

Jewett's attraction to the occult—her fascination with death and her belief in extrasensory communication—was not peculiar in nineteenth-century America. In upstate New York on the night of March 31, 1848, Margaret and Kate Fox, sisters approaching puberty, inaugurated a national love-affair with the spirit world that was to last almost until the turn of the century. To the astonishment of their parents, their neighbors, and, finally, their paying audiences, they established contact with the dead, who rapped replies to the girls's questions. The consequent rage for mesmerism, séances, and even serious research which the sisters kicked off (literally, as it turned out: after long careers as spiritualists the two women admitted that the rappings had all along been the result of an odd ability to crack their toe-joints) answered specific needs. In a period of high infant mortality, combined for the first time in history with an expectation of high maternal emotional investment in the very young,[10] the promise of communication with the dead probably helped many women survive agonizing bereavements. Likewise, after the Civil

War there existed intense need among thousands of grieving families for reassurance from "the other side" about their slain sons, husbands, and fathers, most of whom had died far from home and family.[11]

Behind these particular needs stood a general anxiety. Interest in spiritualism in the nineteenth century often reflected a growing desire to affirm the existence of an afterlife and of extramaterial reality, especially moral, in an era that saw biology and geology eroding traditional sureties. As Martha Banta explains in *Henry James and the Occult* (James was born in 1843, Jewett in 1849), one important motive for psychical research in the second half of the nineteenth century was the "attempt to revive . . . lost faith in a morally-guided supernatural structure by logically, scientifically testing the presence of extra-human manifestations in this world."[12] As science took over, nineteenth-century America saw spiritualism change from a minor phenomenon associated mainly with religious eccentrics, people preoccupied with the devil and demonology, into a popular and frequently highly secular fascination with psychic power both for itself and as a link to the transcendent.

A product of her century, Sarah Orne Jewett found in the occult valuable material for fiction. She respected the scientific perspective: her beloved father, a physician, had learned a great deal from science. But even when it came to her father's career, as *A Country Doctor* makes explicit, the inexplicable interested Jewett most. The unanalyzable and mysterious in human consciousness—extracorporeal as well as embodied— spoke to her most acutely. In particular she seems to have believed that there existed a type of therapeutic female psychic energy which could be communicated telepathically and which could operate both to bond individuals and to create a spiritual community—or occult sisterhood— among women in general. A key pattern in Jewett is the initiation of one woman, usually younger and sometimes a girl, into the powerful, extrasensory, and usually ultraterrestrial female knowledge possessed by another. This initiation typically involves friendship with a witch. Less interested in mesmerism and séances (at least in her fiction) than in witches, Sarah Orne Jewett channeled the general nineteenth-century fascination with the occult into a very specific question. What are the extraordinary powers available to women who maintain rather than forsake woman's ancient identification with the occult? What, in other words, is the living power of the witch?

To be sure, some of Jewett's fiction about the supernatural is quite conventional. "The Gray Man" (1886) imagines Death as a kind but unnerving stranger whose failure to smile marks him off irrevocably from the human community. In "Miss Tempy's Watchers" (1888), a simple but moving story, the invisible spirit of dead Miss Tempy brings together the two women who watch over her corpse through the night. The story explicitly argues for death as part of nature—" 'Tis as natural as bein' born or livin' on"[13]—and articulates Jewett's idea that the soul lingers with the corpse before departing. " 'I do believe,' " one of the watchers observes, " 'they kind of wake up a day or two after they die, and it's then they go.' "[14] These two stories, however, are unusual in Jewett, who more frequently turned the occult to less ordinary ends.

"In Dark New England Days" (1880), for example, is a bitter tale. When two spinsters are robbed of their inheritance and the thief is acquitted for lack of material evidence, one of them confronts the man: " 'Curse your right hand, then!' cried Hannah Knowles, growing tall and thin like a white flame drawing upward. 'Curse your right hand, yours and all your folks' that follow you! May I live to see the day!' "[15] The curse works. But it also rebounds on its author. Although Hannah and her sister have their revenge, they pay for it by placing themselves (and being placed by the community) outside the pale. Perceived as witches, complete with a devil in residence, " 'a kind o' black shadder, a cobweb kind o' a man-shape that followed 'em about the house an' made a third to them' " (clearly this shadow is the ghost of their father, an evil man who made his money " 'o' slave ships, an' all kinds o' devil's gold was mixed in' "),[16] they seem wraiths rather than women. Hannah had cause to curse her enemy. Nevertheless the negative power of the witch is crippling, this story says, for all parties. If the thief is punished for his crime (the last image in the story shows him scuttling one-armed across an empty field like some furtive insect), the two sisters have suffered horribly too. It is as if their tyrannical father never let them out of his grip.

Jewett's fondness for Elizabeth Stuart Phelps' ghost story, "Kentucky's Ghost," published in the *Atlantic* in 1868, fits in here.[17] Like Jewett's "In Dark New England Days," "Kentucky's Ghost" is a tale of revenge; but in Phelps, instead of a witch, it is the ghost of a stowaway that metes out punishment, luring to his death the sadistic officer who killed the boy. What makes Jewett's attraction to the piece interesting (other than the fact that it is a very good story) is Phelps' anger. Implicit in her simple ghost story is a fantasy of violent revenge on masculine authority, symbolized by the icy death of the officer on this ship ironically named the *Madonna*. The similar fantasy of efficacious female fury in "In Dark New England Days" shows a side of Jewett which should not be forgotten.

Anger, however, was not Jewett's usual mode. Pity, humor, paradox, celebration were; and she was finally more interested in the mystery of positive than of negative female energy. She made the witch as guide and healer rather than as destroyer the subject of her five most challenging fictional narratives drawing on the occult, "Lady Ferry" (1879),

"The Courting of Sister Wisby" (1887), *The Country of the Pointed Firs* (1896), "The Foreigner" (1900), and "The Green Bowl" (1901).

II

When "Lady Ferry" was rejected for publication by the *Atlantic*, Jewett, undaunted, brought it out herself in her anthology *Old Friends and New* (1879). She obviously felt strongly about seeing the story survive.

The tale opens by observing that we fear death but also find fearful the thought of not dying: leaving this life or remaining in it forever are equally scary ideas. Then the narrative treats in detail a figurative death, a little girl's first parting from her mother. That experience contains the same dilemma, of course, that Jewett has already sketched: to leave mother or to stay with her forever are equally terrifying prospects.

Separated from her parents who have set out on a long sea voyage, the child Marcia (who as a grown woman narrates "Lady Ferry"), is sent to live in a secluded old house in the country with her elderly cousin Agnes, a gray, grave, strong, sweet woman who manages the role of both mother and father. "She put her arms around me as kindly as my mother would have done, and kissed me twice in my father's fashion."[18] Marcia feels "safe and comfortable with her: it was the same feeling which one learns to have toward God more and more, as one grows older" (184). It then develops that this caretaker has an Other: Lady Ferry, who is neither androgynous nor God-like, but female and witchlike.

Lady Ferry cannot drown, does not age, and periodically shows up in Salem. She is tall, thin, bent, and hooded. Her skin is "pale and withered," her cheeks are "wrinkled in fine lines, like the crossings of a cobweb," and her eyes are colorless (179–80, 192, 203). Sharing the night with bats, she goes out only after dark, and she has been every-where, has no known birthplace, and inhabits the cold north gable of the house (193–97). She at one point wears a dress that seems to have frost on it and rustles like dead rushes and dry grasses, at another a faded maroon brocade with tiny flowers that look like "wicked little faces" (192, 203). Rumor has it that these "unearthly" clothes came out of the trunk of a Mistress Haverford "who was hung for a witch" (197).

Associated with the dark of the moon, Lady Ferry vividly brings to mind the witch of the waning moon, the classic fairy-tale witch-as-old-hag. As one modern authority on the traditional, folk, earth-religion of witchcraft explains, the hag is the last of three distinct images of women embodied by the witch in folk tradition (these distinctions prove very interesting to think about in Jewett):

[The] great symbol for the Goddess is the moon, whose three aspects reflect the three states in women's lives and whose cycles of waxing and waning coincide with women's menstrual cycles. As the new moon or crescent, she is Maiden, the Virgin . . . belonging to herself alone, not bound to any man. She is the wild child, lady of the woods, huntress, free and untamed—Artemis, Kore, Aradia, Nimue. White is her color. As the full moon, she is the mature woman, the sexual being, the mother and nurturer, giver of life, fertility, grain, offspring, potency, joy—Tana, Demeter, Diana, Ceres, Mari. Her colors are the red of blood and the green of growth. As waning or dark moon, she is the old woman, past menopause, the hag or crone that is ripe with wisdom, patroness of secrets, prophecy, divination, inspiration, power—Hecate, Ceridwen, Kali, Anna. Her color is the black of the night.[19]

These three images correspond remarkably to figures in Jewett. The virgin of the new moon, "belonging to herself alone, not bound to any man"—a "wild child" of the woods whose color is white—powerfully evokes Jewett's Sylvia (Latin for "woods") of "A White Heron" (1886), the untamed child whose task is to tend a cow and whose passion is to protect a white heron, which she does by climbing the tallest tree in the forest. All three (cow, bird, and tree) are standard symbols of the witch's fecund manifestation as Mother Earth: "She is mare, cow, cat, owl, crane, flower, tree, apple, seed, lion, sow, stone, woman."[20] The mature woman of the full moon, mother and nurturer, sower and harvester, finds her parallel of course in Jewett's large, robust Mrs. Todd, cutter of simples (certain proof of witchcraft) by moonlight.[21] The last figure—her "color is the black of the night" and her moon is waning, dying—suggests Jewett's Lady Ferry, whose chief occupation is to walk in the garden at night or to place the chairs in her gloomy room in a circle, symbol of the witch, in preparation for the funeral she constantly awaits, her own.

Also, these three stages of moon and woman (waxing, full, waning/ youth, maturity, old age) apply perfectly to the three women—Marcia, Agnes, Lady Ferry—who inhabit one dwelling in Jewett's haunting tale of female maturation and loss, "Lady Ferry." Indeed, Lady Ferry is so classic a witch of the waning moon, she even scares the neighborhood lout, a "worthless fellow" who tells of seeing Lady Ferry on the road late one night:

> "I was near scared to death. She looked fearful tall—towered way up above me. Her face was all lit up with blue light, and her feet didn't touch the ground. She wasn't taking steps, she wasn't walking, but movin' along like a sail-boat before the wind. I dodged behind some little birches, and I was scared she'd see me; but she went right out o' sight up the road. She ain't mortal." (218–19)

This immortal becomes Marcia's surrogate mother. Gaunt, childless (as far as we know), ancient and endlessly grieving, she delivers the motherless child to health.

For Marcia, separation from her mother brought the "pain of my

first real loneliness . . . into my heart" (182). She grieved at the thought
of parting—"I was very sorry, and at once thought I should be miserable
without my mother" (177)—and the leave-taking was agony: "We had
been together all my life, and now it was to be long months before she
could possibly see my face again, and perhaps she was leaving me
forever" (181). This intense pain abates only when Marcia meets Lady
Ferry. The forlorn child walks in the garden, filled with thoughts of her
mother: "Suddenly I had a consciousness that she was thinking of me,
and she seemed so close to me, that it would not be strange if she could
hear what I said. And I called her twice softly; but the sound of my un-
answered voice frightened me. . . . I was so terribly far away from the
mother whom I had called" (191). Despairing, the child turns to rush
away, only to catch "sight of a person in the path just before me. It was
such a relief to see some one, that I was not frightened when I saw that
it must be Lady Ferry" (191). Thoughts of the lost mother, in this
beautifully structured scene, propel the child directly into the arms of
the witch.

Jewett forces us to see Lady Ferry simultaneously as hag (the profusion of story-book imagery already cited) and as mother (the substi-
tution in the garden described above). But instead of treating the figures
as opposites, flip-sides of each other (the usual arrangement of mother
and witch), Jewett synthesizes them. Shriveled Lady Ferry, whose sweet
smile and melodic voice keep her from utterly terrifying the child (203),
takes the place of Marcia's mother. She helps bind the wound of the
child's loneliness—her presence helps the child survive her fear of being
motherless—at the same time that Lady Ferry, as witch, *is* the "mother"
Marcia fears: the mother who is involved in death not life. Jewett's
story with its ghostly, ancient, death-focused witch at the center confronts the child's (our) need to look at mother death, or mother dead—
the two amount to the same thing in "Lady Ferry"—and live through the
experience.

This idea literally materializes when Marcia visits the ancient
woman's rooms. When "the open space where Lady Ferry had left room
for her coffin began to be a horror to the child," as of course it must,
Lady Ferry intuits the little girl's terror of the invisible waiting casket
and glides into the next room where she "opened a drawer containing
some old jewelry; there were also some queer Chinese carvings, yellow
with age,—just the things a child would enjoy. I looked at them delightedly" (205). Deftly, Lady Ferry has replaced the cavity of death
with a container (not unlike the womb) overflowing with gifts. The
narrator exclaims: "I soon felt more at ease, and chattered to Lady Ferry
of my own possessions, and some coveted treasures of my mother's,
which were to be mine when I grew older" (205). Not only is Marcia's
passage to womanhood foreseen here: the "coveted treasures" of her
mother, the girl acknowledges, will be hers in time. But the terror of

mortality itself is met. In one stroke Lady Ferry's coffin becomes mother's jewels, the witch's barrenness becomes mother's bounty, death becomes life. As her name suggests, this spectral surrogate mother is indeed a ferry, a connector between points. She connects the living and the dead. In "seeing" this woman, the child "sees" death. In receiving from her "a tiny silver box with a gold one inside, in which I found a bit of fine sponge, dark brown with age, and still giving a faint, musty perfume and spiciness" (207), she receives a sort of tiny, precious coffin-womb—perfect symbol of the Dark Mother—which, given the moral contour of this story, is ultimately not frightening but sacred. In kissing Lady Ferry for the gift (207), the child kisses the flesh of the mother she most feared, the death-mother/dead-mother.

At the deepest level (deep in the night, in fact) Marcia's various mothers finally fuse. The child runs from the witch to the bed of Agnes. Gazing at the sleeping matron she wonders, in her "blessed sense of security, if she were ever afraid of any thing, and why I myself had been afraid of Lady Ferry" (220). Cradled by Agnes, Marcia is carried back to the witch: in looking at the one woman, she overcomes her fear of the other, as if the two are one and belong together, or as if in looking at Agnes she can see through to Lady Ferry. As she puts it herself a little later, "Under the best-loved and most beautiful face we know, there is hidden a skull as ghastly as that from which we turn aside with a shudder in the anatomist's cabinet" (221). That skull under the mother's face—Lady Ferry behind Agnes and mother—is what this story asks us to see and no longer fear.

Early in "Lady Ferry" the narrator reflects on her preternaturally deep understanding of life as a child and discloses, "I have known since that my mother's childhood was much like mine" (181). The statement invites us to generalize Marcia's experience. We can see it as hers, as her mother's, perhaps as all women's. The story invites us to think of Lady Ferry—surrogate mother, death-mother, witch of the dark moon—as the potent healer of all of us.

III

Most Jewett witches, in contrast to Lady Ferry, are not ghastly. Witches of the full rather than of the waning moon, they are venerable and warm. Their strength comes from the living earth; they inhabit the light of day as well as the shadows. Specifically they assert the whole-someness of female medicine in an era that witnessed the final pro-fessionalization (masculinization) of medicine.[22] Jewett's organic sor-cerers register her attachment to an earlier, older definition of human healing as something mysterious and empathic rather than scientific and analytical. In their knowledge of herbs, her women minister to the mind as well as the body, the spirit as well as the flesh. In harmony with nature, they are true witch-doctors. First appearing almost a decade after the publication of "Lady Ferry," her earthy herbalists epitomize the naturally engendered supernatural power available to women who embrace rather than discard our sinister heritage. As such they function— Mrs. Goodsoe, Mrs. Todd, Mrs. Patton—much like their ghostly forebear Lady Ferry. Each serves as the healing spiritual guide for a younger, wandering, "motherless" woman.

Jewett's first version of the type is the herbalist Mrs. Goodsoe (as Cary points out, "good soul")[23] in "The Courting of Sister Wisby" (1887). Precursor of Almira Todd, Mrs. Goodsoe declares at one point: "'Seems to me sometimes, when I get thinkin,' as if I'd lived a thousand years!'"[24] Maybe she has. Thin and small, with wrinkled brown skin and twinkling eyes, she looks like one of the dried weeds she busily gathers (264), and her knowledge of the therapeutic and healing powers of vegetable life has been passed down among women in her family immemorially. She scorns the herb-ignorant young male doctors of her day—"'Book-fools I call 'em, them young men'" (254)—and ministers rate no higher: "'I'd as soon hear a surveyor's book read out, figgers an' all, as try to get any simple truth out o' most sermons'" (358). Healer and sacred minister herself, Mrs. Goodsoe looks down on both classes of men.

Before telling her amusing story of Sister Wisby's trial marriage, a tale that takes great pleasure in female contempt for sexual convention, Mrs. Goodsoe spins a modern parable. She tells how a woman submerged in death comes back to life in the arms of a mother. She recalls an Irish fiddler named Jim Heron (the name echoes Jewett's sacramental use of the bird the year before in her tale of female rite-of-passage, "The White Heron") who, like Mrs. Goodsoe's maternal great-grandmother, had "the gift" (261). A "parochial Orpheus" (260), he can journey to the underworld and bring to life with his blood-colored fiddle the witch, the sorrow of women. "'He set by the window playin','" Mrs. Goodsoe says, "'as if there was a bewitched human creatur' in that old red fiddle of his. He could make it sound just like a woman's voice tellin' somethin' over and over, as if folks could help her out o' her sorrows if she could only make 'em understand'" (260). When a young woman's husband and three small children die, only the fiddle can help. Catatonic, the woman hears the voice from the underworld: "'Her face changed in a minute, and she come right over an' got into my mother's lap,—she was a little woman,—an' laid her head down, and there she cried herself into a blessed sleep'" (262). This anecdote is a paradigm of psychic healing in Jewett.

Symbolically, the rescued woman in "The Courting of Sister Wisby," like the little girl in "Lady Ferry," lives through the terror, in effect, of her own death. In the mother losing her children and in the child losing her mother we see two ends of the same experience: the loss of part, and what seems an inseparable part, of female self. Each figure survives the mutilation because of the healing power of maternal energy, positive and negative. In the arms of Agnes, Marcia accepts her death-mother, Lady Ferry. In the arms of Mrs. Goodsoe's mother, the devastated young woman in "The Courting of Sister Wisby" plunges herself without restraint into the ancient death-knowledge of the witch, the "voice" from the underworld, and sleeps. In each case, surrogate mothers, earthly and unearthly, life-giving and death-owning, help the younger female figure live through her terrifying loss.

While Mrs. Goodsoe tells her tale, she gathers mullein, an herb associated with weaning; it is used to help decrease milk production, thus easing the trauma of rupture between mother and child.[25] As she talks, Mrs. Goodsoe and the narrator harvest the plant. Jewett shows them "kneeling side by side" on the fertile earth, "as if in penitence for the march of progress" (255–56).

Mrs. Goodsoe gathers mullein because it is the wrong time of year to gather the "favorite" herb of Almira Todd in *The Country of the Pointed Firs*, pennyroyal (211). Pennyroyal is even today strongly associated with the female reproductive system. It is used in childbirth ("the standard birthing tea is a mixture of pennyroyal, cohosh" and other herbs)[26] because it especially aids the uterus in expelling the placenta. Thus involved in the healthy delivery of new life, pennyroyal also, because it causes uterine contractions and stimulates menstrual flow, is associated with miscarriage and abortion, the end of new life. A strong and even dangerous herb (taken internally or just as an extracted oil, it can kill),[27] pennyroyal is the perfect symbol for Jewett's potent midwife of the spirit, Almira Todd, whose last name rhymes with god and whose first name brings to mind the Latin word *alma*, soul (recall Mrs. "Goodsoe"), as well perhaps as the legendary upstate New York town Elmira, named to commemorate the bond between a mother and her daughter; the mother called her little girl so often and loudly that the townspeople in 1828 changed the name of their town from Newtowne to Elmira.[28] Almira Todd appears in *The Country of the Pointed Firs* as a kind of Demeter, who also called long and loud for her daughter, to the narrator's Persephone. Jewett's modern-day earth mother, a supernaturally attuned and yet ultra-earthbound Demeter, makes the world bloom for her disinterred "daughter" up from the city.

Mother-daughter love between Mrs. Blackett and her daughter, Mrs. Todd, and between Mrs. Todd and her figurative daughter, the narrator, animates *The Country of the Pointed Firs*;[29] and the most important job Mrs. Todd has as the narrator's maternal guide is, like Lady Ferry and Mrs. Goodsoe before her, to mediate between the realms of life and death. Figure of daylight—we first meet Almira Todd, "ardent lover of herbs" (3), crushing plants underfoot in her sunlit garden—she is equally a figure of darkness. She likes to fix her " 'darlin' ' " boarder surprise meals of mushrooms, succulents of the night, and refuses to tell the secrets of certain herbs, such as the "simple which grew in a certain slug-haunted corner of the garden, whose use she could never be betrayed into telling me, though I saw her cutting the tops by moonlight once, as if it were a charm, and not a medicine, like the great fading bloodroot leaves" (17). Explicitly compared to Antigone, defier of patriarchy, and called a sibyl (78, 10), Mrs. Todd is directly linked to the world of witch-craft: she cuts herbs by moonlight for charms, dispenses secret con-coctions after sundown, stands majestically encircled by the black and gray braids of her homespun rug, and offers the narrator an exotic herb tea that seems "part of a spell and incantation" created by an "en-chantress" (47). In Almira Todd, Jewett craftily mixes classical, folk, and fairy-tale imagery to yield a new female figure, a new witch, mistress of both day and night, life and death—an awesome maternal figure whose first social action in *The Country of the Pointed Firs* is to attend a funeral and whose last is to include the narrator in her family reunion.

Historically, Jewett's book bridges two eras. *The Country of the Pointed Firs* appeared at the end of a century in which institutionalized religion in America underwent increasing feminization. As Barbara Welter explains in *Dimity Convictions*, as early as the first half of the nineteenth century, in protestant America "two ideas gained popularity which showed an appreciation for the values of femaleness—the first was the idea of the Father-Mother God and the second was the concept of the female Saviour." This feminization of the spiritual world probably served utilitarian ends. "The giving over of religion to women, in its content and its membership, provided a repository for . . . female values [such as piety, patience, nurturance, self-sacrifice] during the period when the business of building a nation did not immediately require them."[30] Clearly, Jewett's interest in a feminized spirit-world follows these well-established, nineteenth-century trends. Also, however, it anticipates a large twentieth-century project: the feminist task of reconstructing, or if need be inventing, a resolutely female spiritual context that can re-claim the energy of degraded symbols and images such as the witch or Medea (to whom Jewett compares Mrs. Todd in the stories "A Dunnet Shepherdess" and "William's Wedding"[31]: Medea in Euripides is just another witch, of course, coming out of the exotic East under the pro-tection of Hecate, goddess of the moon, witches, and the underworld). The modern challenge was to redefine images that had been negatively construed, or dismissed—discarded as "primitive," not relevant to sophisti-cated belief-systems (the sibyl for example).[32]

A fellow thinker on some of these issues was William James, whose work Jewett admired. Six years after *The Country of the Pointed Firs* came out she read *The Varieties of Religious Experience* (1902) and wrote to Annie Fields: "I long to have you get to the chapter in Dr.

James's book that I have been reading to-day: 'The Value of Saintliness.'
I 'find' it most particularly fine, and penetrating."[33] James' project in
Varieties resembles Jewett's in *The Country of the Pointed Firs*. Writing
at a time when the scientific enterprise was on the ascendancy, James
looks seriously at the psychic experience of religious "fanatics" (mystics,
saints, martyrs) and finds considerable value in their antimaterial perspectives. Specifically, in the chapter Jewett praises to Annie Fields, he
identifies modern, "Nietzschian" antagonism to saintliness as the sick
antipathy of the ultramasculine to the feminine. He charges that "the
carnivorous-minded 'strong man,' the adult male and cannibal, can see
nothing but mouldiness and morbidness in the saint's gentleness and
self-severity, and regards him with pure loathing," and concludes: "The
whole feud revolves essentially upon two pivots: Shall the seen world or
the unseen world be our chief sphere of adaptation? and must our means
of adaptation in this seen world be aggressiveness or non-resistance?"
James asks: "Is the saint's type or the strong-man's type the more
ideal?"[34] No wonder Jewett liked James' chapter; it is in many ways a
gloss on *The Country of the Pointed Firs*, which presents a quiet,
matricentric world as ideal.

Indeed, change the pronouns, and William James' profile of a saint
describes Jewett's white witch, Almira Todd. James' saint is serene,
attentive to "the smallest details of this world," and abounding "in impulses to help"; moreover, this "help is inward as well as outward, for
his sympathy reaches souls as well as bodies, and kindles unsuspected
faculties therein." Unpretentious, the saint displays "felicity, purity,
charity, patience, [and] self-severity."[35] James argues that this person is
actually of the most, not the least, social utility because the saint is already adapted for utopia, for the millennium. (The thought applies
equally to Jewett's Mrs. Todd, of course.) Echoing discursively what
Jewett expresses pictorially, James says of the truly great saints: "Their
sense of mystery in things, their passion, their goodness, irradiate about
them and enlarge their outlines while they soften them." In Jewett's final
view of "able and warm-hearted" Mrs. Todd, she walks along a footpath:
"her distant figure looked mateless and appealing, with something about
it that was strangely self-possessed and mysterious" (211). Bending to
touch the earth, her spiritual as well as literal home, she disappears:
"Now and then she stooped to pick something,—it might have been her
favorite pennyroyal,—and at last I lost sight of her as she slowly crossed
an open space on one of the higher points of land, and disappeared again
behind a dark clump of juniper and the pointed firs" (211). Amid pennyroyal, Jewett's witch (James' saint) descends into the empowering earth.

The narrator's summer with this mysterious herb-woman inducts her
into reality preceding recorded time. She remembers as she leaves Dunnet
Landing "those long hours when nothing happened except the growth
of herbs and the course of the sun" (208) and hates to separate from

Mrs. Todd. As she watches Jewett's gatherer of herbs dispense her strange powders and potions, the narrator encounters the occult: "It may not have been only the common ails of humanity with which she tried to cope; it seemed sometimes as if love and hate and jealousy and adverse winds at sea might also find their proper remedies among the curious wild-looking plants in Mrs. Todd's garden" (5). Truly a witch-doctor, Almira Todd represents the disappearing but not unrecoverable psychic power of woman, in league with the earth, as healer.[36]

For both James and Jewett—and the idea was not original with them—otherworldliness might finally be very this-worldly. As Howard Kerr points out in *Mediums, and Spirit-Rappers, and Roaring Radicals*, spiritualism in nineteenth-century America not only affirmed the soul's immortality in an era of increasing skepticism, but also quickened millennialism. Kerr explains: people "no longer needed to depend on church and clergy and scripture for proof of the soul's immortality"; therefore social reformers could argue that "spirits wanted to make themselves felt in earthly affairs and would, in fact, lead mankind to social regeneration. Residents of some of the utopian communities of the time took up spiritualism; advocates of socialism, abolition, women's rights, and free love received angelic sanction for their programs; there were even a few plans for the reorganization of society along spirit-dictated lines."[37] The link Kerr makes between spiritualism and social reform bears emphasis in relation to Jewett. She was not a social reformer; but neither was she the utterly apolitical, detached conservative that too many critics have painted her. The imagined world of mother-rule and female solidarity in *The Country of the Pointed Firs* represents an astutely political statement. Its serenity points up, as any utopia might, the imperfections of the man-made world we, like the narrator, start from; and certainly one distinguishing feature of Jewett's fictive experiment in social reform at Dunnet Landing is the ability of women there to relate telepathically. As one critic points out in a close and illuminating study of technique in the book, at the center of *The Country of the Pointed Firs* are "women who are able to read nature, the physical world, and the minds of other people."[38] At the center of Jewett's most famous book, in other words, are women at home in the occult.

After the publication of *The Country of the Pointed Firs*, Jewett remained intrigued with Mrs. Todd's power and in 1900 published another story about the New England herbalist, this one explicitly a tale of the supernatural, called "The Foreigner." It recounts Almira Todd's initiation into an extended community of witches.

The tale opens with the narrator remarking that Mrs. Todd has never told her a ghost story. It is a classically Jewettesque night: cold and spooky. Wind and rain gust—"Folks used to say these gales only blew when somebody's a-dyin', or the devil was a-comin' for his own' "[39]—and

just as Mrs. Todd begins to oblige her guest with a tale of the supernatural, "wet twigs outside blew against the window panes and made a
noise like a distressed creature trying to get in. I started with sudden
fear, and so did the cat [standard appendage of the witch and practically
a major character in this story] but Mrs. Todd knitted away and did not
even look over her shoulder" (313).

Jewett's preoccupied herb-woman proceeds to describe Eliza, a
woman from Jamaica who came to Dunnet Landing many years before.
The mysterious foreigner, toward whom Mrs. Todd developed keen
"sisterly" feelings (320), possessed no known Christian last name, walked
out of church in the middle of a service, decorated her New England
parlor like a tropical bower, and reveled in the flesh (she loved to sing
and dance and made no secret of her passionate attachment to the sea
captain who brought her North). This woman, who names Almira Todd
her heir, resembles the young Lady Ferry, who also liked to dance and
to surround herself with rich, sumptuous possessions, according to a
dream of Marcia's which, we are told in "Lady Ferry," was so vivid that
she took it "for a vision and a reality" (214). But even more strongly,
this erotic woman from Jamaica calls to mind the witch locked at the
top of the house in Charlotte Brontë's *Jane Eyre*—with the difference that
here the figure is integrated into, rather than cast out of, female consciousness.

The Foreigner bonds with Mrs. Todd. " 'She taught me a sight o'
things about herbs I never knew before nor since; she was well acquainted
with the virtues o' plants' " (314). Specifically Eliza teaches her northern
sister about mushrooms, plants of the night (315); and though it un-
nerves other people, it does not frighten Jewett's herb-woman to know
that Eliza " 'act[s] awful secret about some things too, an' used to work
charms for herself' " (314). In the Foreigner Jewett's witch discovers a
soulmate. When the southern woman dies, the herbalist of the North
listens to the night wind play the dead woman's guitar (clearly an echo
of the witch-in-the-fiddle in "The Courting of Sister Wisby"); and when
the woman from Jamaica lies in her coffin, shunned by everyone else,
Almira Todd kisses the dead flesh—an action that vividly recalls Marcia's
kissing ghastly Lady Ferry, who also traveled from strange distant lands
to haunt New England.

Before Almira Todd can conclude her tale of the occult—her tale
of how she acquired wisdom from the underworld, land of wild music
and dance and death (the Foreigner's husband and children died in
Jamaica before she was led North)—she must ritually prepare herself.
Sitting before the hearth, she listens "to the wind, and sat for a moment
in deferential silence, as if she waited for the wind to speak first. The
cat suddenly lifted her head with quick excitement and gleaming eyes,
and her mistress was leaning forward toward the fire with an arm laid
on either knee, as if they were consulting the glowing coals for some

augury." Jewett says: "Mrs. Todd looked like an old prophetess as she sat there with the firelight shining on her strong face. . . . The woman with the cat was as unconscious and as mysterious as any sibyl" (321). Mrs. Todd can now disclose the heart of her story.

On the night of the Foreigner's death, Almira Todd reveals, her mother led her from this life. The woman who gave life bore it away. The experience, though terrifying initially, becomes restorative and buoying. Mother-death succors. In her last words to the Foreigner (a true bene/diction) Mrs. Todd replies to the dying woman's question, " 'You saw her, did n't you?' ": " *Yes, dear, I did; you ain't never goin' to feel strange an' lonesome no more* " (323). The appearance of this ghost, the mother who brings death, climaxes the story: it bonds the two herb-women at the moment of death much as the shared maternal presence of Mrs. Todd's perfectly named mother, Mrs. Blackett of Green Island, has united them in life. (Jewett expresses in that name and place the essential paradox of her herbal witches—their use of the power of darkness to support life.) The network of mothers and daughters in this story—Mrs. Blackett mothers the Foreigner as well as her daughter, Almira Todd; the ghost-mother of the Foreigner reveals herself to Almira Todd as well as to her own dying daughter, Eliza—unites all four women in a web of maternal, filial, and sororal support at once mundane (fleshly and vegetal) and transcendent, nonmaterial. In this story we learn that the source of Almira Todd's remarkable spiritual wisdom is both the earth, mother of us all, and other women, living and dead. She participates in a sisterhood transcending time and place.

IV

Jewett's last story about the occult, "The Green Bowl" (1901), is aggressively modern. It carries the question of the transmission of super-natural wisdom and power among women squarely into the twentieth century and asserts that the ancient mystery, the power of the witch, is completely compatible with woman's life in efficient, bicycle-mounted, modern America. The witch is not an archaism, a curiosity, a subject for nostalgia or sentimentality. She remains a living, potent reality.

The story opens with two very independent young women shocking their elders by describing how they travel about the countryside on their own. Of course, " 'One must wear a shirt-waist and a corduroy skirt and jacket,' " Katie Montague counsels the astonished older women in the room, and " 'Yes, one needs a good golf cape in case of rain.' "[40] But thus equipped, there is nothing to it. Find a companion, a light buggy, and a decent country road, and you are off for days or weeks. One such trip with Frances Kent into a deep, dark woods where the two young adventurers lose their way and are given a mysterious green bowl by a wizened old woman comprises this night's narrative.

"The Green Bowl" has all the essentials of fairy tale. Because someone has taken the sign-boards down, the two women lose their way on
a black, rainy, autumn night and head deeper and deeper into an unknown woods inhabited, they later discover, by a solitary old woman
(with cat) who can tell fortunes in an ancient green bowl (color of
plants) that was carried out of the mysterious East generations ago.
They meet this woman after spending the night in an empty church
where they are forced to use " 'a few leaves of a tattered hymn-book for
kindling' " (348). The next day, led like children by the old woman to
her cozy house, in which, significantly, the only artificially added color
is green, the three women spend the morning picking beans together.
That is, they spend the morning harvesting green fruits of the earth.

Because she trusts the young women, old Mrs. Patton reveals her
"gift" for fortune-telling, inherited from a dead aunt. It is a source of
strength for this old woman, who says proudly: " 'One of our ministers
went so far as to say 'twas a gift that would lead me and other folks
straight to the pit if I continued its exercise, but I made bold to say it
had heretofore seemed to lead the other way if I wasn't mistaken' "
(354). What she needs, however, is a psychic *companion* (the word
is always italicized, which gives it sinister resonance but also, I think,
calls attention to its essential communal meaning, its derivation from
the Latin words meaning "with" and "bread"). The old woman's bowl
is one of two, and for the magic to work the bowls must be owned by
companion fortune-tellers. Katie is chosen. The old woman takes her
into the bedroom, chamber of birth, love, sleep, and death, where behind
the closed door she initiates the younger woman into the "principles of
magic" contained in the round, green, translucent bowl. And " 'now I
am Mrs. Patton's *companion*,' as she calls it,' " Katie tells her stylish
urban auditors (355).

With great aplomb, "The Green Bowl," coming at the end of Jewett's
career, transforms the traditional fairy-tale plot of innocents lost in deep,
witch-infested woods into a celebration of female psychic power. The
journey into the unknown becomes in this story a trip into a new world
of female relationship which crosses generation and class lines to unite
women in shared power rather than weakness. The witch is not the
enemy of woman, her immobilizer, but her sister and mother—her companion. Most important, psychic power is corporate. It goes away if only
one bowl is possessed. The solitary bowl of this title, archetypal in its
evocation of femaleness (the circle, the container), is really one of two
bowls. One visualizes them next to each other, and the initial suggestion
of womb becomes, almost magically, breasts—as only women can "see"
them, from the inside out. The power of women, like the power of these
two ancient light-transmitting, green bowls, comes from community.

Jewett was serious about witches. From "Lady Ferry" through "The
Green Bowl" she examined the power of female psychic energy and con-

cluded, time after time, that it heals, strengthens, and links women. Even the most modern, citified woman, *The Country of the Pointed Firs* and "The Green Bowl" insist, can establish contact with her heritage; the witch is alive. The woman from the underworld—the witch in the blood-red fiddle—is mother and sister. The experience of death, cold and dreadful in "The Gray Man" where Death is male, can mean, as "Lady Ferry" tells us figuratively and "The Foreigner" says literally, a return to the endless maternal scheme of things, to the profound ecstatically potent realm of the mother witch. In an era that saw science, and particularly modern medicine, claiming for itself woman's ancient role as seer and healer, Jewett refused to give up the witch.

But Jewett could also revel in the witch, as she reveals in her exuberant self-portrait in "An October Ride" (1880). The sketch shows the author wild and sensuous on her favorite mare, Sheila. She relishes the horse's pride and willfulness, declaring that she "should not like her half so well if she were tamer and entirely and stupidly reliable; I glory in her good spirits."[41] Riding this mare on a dark stormy October night, month of the witch of course, Jewett feels "as if I had suddenly grown a pair of wings when she fairly flies over the ground and the wind whistles in my ears" (93). Rider and beast sail through the night: "there was no moon to light me home. Sheila took the strip of smooth turf just at the side of the road for her own highway, she tossed her head again and again until I had my hand full of her thin, silky mane, and she gave quick pulls at her bit and hurried little jumps ahead as if she expected me already to pull the reins tight and steady her for a hard gallop" (95). The erotic energy of this ride is as obvious as the sexual content of Jewett's later joke about Sheila's appetite for upright churchmen. Jewett and mare move through a stand of mullein which looks like rigid Scotch Covenanters worshiping in secret: "But one ancient worthy, very late on his way to the meeting, happened to stand in our way, and Sheila bit his dry head off, which was a great pity" (106). Jewett's night-mare gleefully wipes out phallic, Protestant obstacles. The rider may end up in a deserted parsonage musing about the Protestant God and a kindly old minister's ministry; but Sheila waits in the shed. It is on the mare that Jewett rides home.

Notes

1. Sarah Orne Jewett, *The Country of the Pointed Firs* (Boston: Houghton Mifflin, 1896), p. 10. References in the text are to this edition, which includes only the pieces the author collected into *The Country of the Pointed Firs*, as opposed to the later, larger collection under the same title made by Willa Cather in 1925. Happily Jewett's original is now available in a 1981 Norton paperback edited by Mary Ellen Chase.

2. Sarah Orne Jewett, *A Country Doctor* (Boston: Houghton Mifflin, 1884), p. 4; hereafter cited in the text.

3. Richard Cary, *Sarah Orne Jewett* (New York: Twayne, 1962), pp. 40–41; Richard Cary, ed., *The Uncollected Short Stories of Sarah Orne Jewett* (Waterville: Colby College Press, 1971), p. xvii.

4. Josephine Donovan, *Sarah Orne Jewett* (New York: Ungar, 1980), p. 17.

5. Annie Fields, ed., *Letters of Sarah Orne Jewett* (Boston: Houghton Mifflin, 1911), p. 49.

6. *Letters*, pp. 110–11. Nikola Tesla (1856–1943) was a pioneer in the field of electrical engineering. Son of a minister and himself interested in metaphysics, he wrote and lectured on such topics as the transmission of electrical current without wires, magnetic energy fields, and alternating current of very high frequency.

7. Richard Cary, ed., *Sarah Orne Jewett Letters* (Waterville: Colby College Press, 1967), p. 105.

8. Fields, *Letters*, p. 155.

9. Fields, *Letters*, p. 29.

10. For superb presentation of this changed concept of mothering, see Kathryn Kish Sklar, "Victorian Women and Domestic Life: Mary Todd Lincoln, Elizabeth Cady Stanton, and Harriet Beecher Stowe," *The Public and the Private Lincoln: Contemporary Perspectives*, ed. Cullom Davis et al. (Carbondale: Southern Illinois Univ. Press, 1979), pp. 20–37.

11. See, for example, Jay Martin, "Ghostly Rentals, Ghostly Purchases: Haunted Imaginations in James, Twain, and Bellamy," in *The Haunted Dusk: American Supernatural Fiction, 1820–1920*, ed. Howard Kerr, John W. Crowley, and Charles L. Crow (Athens: Univ. of Georgia Press, 1983), p. 124.

12. Martha Banta, *Henry James and the Occult* (Bloomington: Indiana Univ. Press, 1972), p. 18.

13. Sarah Orne Jewett, "Miss Tempy's Watchers," *Tales of New England* (Boston: Houghton Mifflin, 1894), p. 21.

14. "Miss Tempy's Watchers," p. 19.

15. Sarah Orne Jewett, "In Dark New England Days," *Strangers and Wayfarers* (Boston: Houghton Mifflin, 1890), p. 240.

16. "In Dark New England Days," p. 254.

17. For mention of Jewett's attraction to this story, see Donovan, *Sarah Orne Jewett*, p. 9.

18. Sarah Orne Jewett, "Lady Ferry," *Old Friends and New* (Boston: Houghton Mifflin, 1893), pp. 183–84; hereafter cited in the text.

19. Starhawk, "Witchcraft and Women's Culture," *Womanspirit Rising*, ed. Carol P. Christ and Judith Plaskow (New York: Harper and Row, 1979), p. 263.

20. Starhawk, "Witchcraft," p. 263.

21. *The Country of the Pointed Firs*, p. 17; Starhawk, "Witchcraft," p. 259.

22. For discussion of this process, see Linda Gordon, *Woman's Body, Woman's Right: A Social History of Birth Control in America* (New York: Viking, 1976).

23. Cary, *Sarah Orne Jewett*, p. 83.

24. Sarah Orne Jewett, "The Courting of Sister Wisby," *Tales of New England*, p. 275; hereafter cited in the text.

25. Emrika Padus, *Woman's Encyclopedia of Health and Natural Healing* (Emmaus: Rodale Press, 1981), p. 305.

26. Padus, p. 292.

27. Padus, pp. 299, 296.

28. George R. Stewart, *American Place-Names* (New York: Oxford Univ. Press, 1970), p. 152.

29. For an excellent discussion of this theme from a psychological point of view, see Marjorie Pryse's introduction to the 1981 Norton paperback edition of Jewett's book.

30. Barbara Welter, "The Feminization of American Religion: 1800–1860," *Dimity Convictions* (Athens: Ohio Univ. Press, 1976), pp. 87, 102.

31. Sarah Orne Jewett, "A Dunnet Shepherdess," *The Best Stories of Sarah Orne Jewett*, ed. Willa Cather (Boston: Houghton Mifflin, 1925), p. 206; and "William's Wedding," p. 290.

32. This project remains vital, of course, even as I write almost a century after the publication of Jewett's *The Country of the Pointed Firs*. For recent examples see the opening portions of Mary Daly's *Gyn/Ecology: The Metaethics of Radical Feminism* (Boston: Beacon Press, 1978) or Christine Downing's *The Goddess: Mythological Images of the Feminine* (New York: Crossroad Press, 1981). For a more secular variant, see Carol Gilligan, *In a Different Voice: Psychological Theory and Women's Development* (Cambridge: Harvard Univ. Press, 1982), which reinterprets in a positive light traditionally denigrated feminine modes of perception and judgment.

33. Fields, *Letters*, p. 90. This letter is dated 1892 in Fields; it had to have been written at least a decade later, however, since James' work was not published until 1902. It is well-known that Fields' collection of letters contains such errors; probably they occur because she was trying to reconstruct chronology from memory at many points.

34. William James, *The Varieties of Religious Experience* (New York: Longmans, Green, 1902), pp. 373–74.

35. James, pp. 369–70.

36. I discuss *The Country of the Pointed Firs* in more detail, and with special attention to form, in "Going in Circles: The Female Geography of Jewett's *Country of the Pointed Firs*," *Studies in the Literary Imagination*, 16 (Fall 1983), 83–92.

37. Howard Kerr, *Mediums, and Spirit-Rappers, and Roaring Radicals: Spiritualism in American Literature, 1850–1900* (Urbana: Univ. of Illinois Press, 1972), p. 11.

38. Marcia McClintock Folsom, " 'Tact is a Kind of Mind-Reading': Empathic Style in Sarah Orne Jewett's *The Country of the Pointed Firs*," *Colby Library Quarterly*, 18 (1982), 66–78.

39. Sarah Orne Jewett, "The Foreigner," *Uncollected Stories*, ed. Cary, p. 308; hereafter cited in the text. For a perceptive discussion of this story, see Marjorie Pryse, "Women 'At Sea': Feminist Realism in Sarah Orne Jewett's 'The Foreigner,' " *American Literary Realism*, 15 (1982), 244–52.

40. Sarah Orne Jewett, "The Green Bowl," *Uncollected Stories*, ed. Cary, p. 345; hereafter cited in the text.

41. Sarah Orne Jewett, "An October Ride," *Country By-Ways* (Boston: Houghton Mifflin, 1881), p. 93; hereafter cited in the text.

"Where Every Prospect Pleases":
Sarah Orne Jewett, South Berwick, and the Importance of Place   Rebecca Wall Nail*

The importance of setting in Sarah Orne Jewett's work has been recognized from the earliest days of her career. Although William Dean Howells at first urged her to rely less on character and setting, he admired the "Bits of New England landscape" in *Deephaven* (1877) and later spoke of her "incomparable sketches of New England" and their unique realism.[1] Horace Scudder, another of Jewett's early editors, saw "a most unconscious tribute to Miss Jewett's art" in the comments of those who mistook *Deephaven* for nonfiction.[2] Henry James respected Jewett's portrayal of setting enough to protest when he believed she had marred her work by straying into the past,[3] and George Washington Cable wrote to praise the realistic skill with which she depicted the repressed emotions of New England life, the nature that was always nearby, and the beauty whose portrayal required both delicacy and an unsentimental eye.[4] Later readers like Arthur Hobson Quinn, Mary Ellen Chase, and Margaret Farrand Thorp have agreed, and F. O. Matthiessen has even suggested that Jewett's growing skill in the depiction of setting is a major part of her development as a writer.[5]

Most critics have also agreed that Jewett's depiction of her best fictional settings is closely tied to her familiarity with her home and her love for it. She lived from birth to death in South Berwick, Maine, and her father's fondness for the region gave her from the first, says Matthiessen, "what many strive unsuccessfully ever to gain, an almost complete knowledge of her environment."[6] *Country By-Ways* (1881), an early collection of sketches closely tied to the Berwick setting, was dedicated to her father, "who taught me many lessons and showed me many things as we went together along the country by-ways."[7] The Berwick region became the material for much of her best work, and both she and her friends were aware of its influence. William Dean Howells, for example, wrote after a visit that her house and garden had surprised him greatly, precisely because they provided a perfect setting for her and her art, when literature more often grew in spite of its surroundings.[8] Jewett's fondness for Berwick was shown in a lengthy article she wrote about it (in 1894) for the *New England Magazine*[9] and in the major effort she devoted to her one historical novel, *The Tory Lover* (1901). Set in Revolutionary Berwick, the book fulfilled her lifelong ambition "to do what I could about keeping some of the old Berwick flowers in bloom."[10]

Although *The Tory Lover* is Jewett's only fictional work set openly

*This essay was written especially for this volume and is included here by permission of the author.

in Berwick, many of her most vivid settings clearly belong to the same region. She admitted that Deephaven had "a likeness to be traced" to a real town[11] and once wrote to Howells that *Deephaven* and *The Tory Lover* "together hold all my knowledge . . . and all my dreams about my dear Berwick and York and Wells—the people I know and have heard about: the very dust of thought and association that made me!"[12] The illustrations that depict Deephaven in the 1894 edition were prepared, with her approval, from real scenes in Berwick and surrounding places.[13] Dunnet Landing (scene of *The Country of the Pointed Firs*) was placed in an adjacent area, "somewhere 'along shore' between the region of Tenants Harbor and Boothbay, or . . . farther to the eastward."[14] Much of the rest of Jewett's work is set in anonymous spots closely resembling Deephaven, Dunnet Landing, or South Berwick itself.

In spite of her obvious affection for it, however, the fictional world Jewett creates is not a paradise, and there is considerable evidence to suggest that its imperfections reflect deficiencies she saw in the real South Berwick. One of her continual themes is that the dullest-seeming place can provide much to interest a properly tuned mind, that life can be challenging and stimulating wherever one may be. Her summary of this theme for "Looking Back on Girlhood," an autobiographical sketch published in 1892, hints that Berwick's richness could be seen only with carefully focused eyes: "The quiet village life, the dull routine of farming or mill life, early became interesting to me. I was taught to find everything that an imaginative child could ask, in the simple scenes close at hand."[15] Berwick was interesting, but only when looked at properly.

A diary preserved in the Houghton Library's Sarah Orne Jewett Collection suggests that this lesson of contentment may have been harder to learn than Jewett later admitted, and that perhaps she repeated the idea so often to share the fruit of hard-won emotional growth. The diary covers the period from May 1871 to December 1879, when Jewett was in her twenties and was depicting Berwick and its environs in *Deephaven* (1877). Several of the diary's passages show that she was not contented staying at home during this time and bitterly missed her friends and activities when she came back from visits in Boston and other cities. At one point, in an entry for 1872, she declares that she would be miserable in Berwick if it were not for her home and family, though she knows she ought to be content with the duty God has given her.[16] On the whole her discontent does not go much beyond that normal to a young person who has not left home, but it does suggest that Jewett was more ambivalent toward her world when she was writing *Deephaven* than remarks she made later (as in the 1893 *Deephaven* preface) might suggest.

Several comments in her published letters indicate that this discontent lingered even as Jewett's love and understanding of Berwick deepened. In 1876 she wrote to Anna Laurens Dawes that she wished to spend more time with her friends, and that "when I was growing up" separation from them had been a major sorrow to her. "I think village life makes one very narrow if one is not careful," she went on, but "I dont [sic] mean by this, that I am not fond of Berwick: there never was such a place in the world!"[17] To Whittier in 1882 Jewett complained that, although her home meant more to her each year, being forced to stay inside and having few social distractions in the long country winters contributed to her bad health and gave her too much time to worry about it. "I like to be where the outside life helps me to forget myself," she said, and so she was planning a trip to Boston.[18]

Another letter, probably also written in the 1880s, carries beneath its praise of Berwick a complaint that the modern reader, less familiar with hymns than Jewett and her correspondent, may miss: "I am always delighting in reading the old Berwick, picturesque as it was, under the cover of the new life which seems to you so dull and unrewarding. . . . 'Where every prospect pleases,' etc., ought to be your hymn for Berwick, the which I don't suggest unmercifully, but rather compassionately, and with a plaintive feeling at heart."[19] The line Jewett quotes is from the missionary hymn "From Greenland's Icy Mountains," and the next line, implied by the "etc." she adds, is "And only man is vile."[20] Her insistence that she does not speak "unmercifully" shows that she intends the implication that although Berwick is beautiful and picturesque, its human and social setting is inadequate. Hence she has "a plaintive feeling at heart," a feeling of ambivalence toward a place she both loves and rejects. The same dichotomy appears again, rather charmingly expressed, in a letter written a decade later. With an apology to Dr. Johnson, Jewett says, " 'Sir, when you have seen one snow field you have seen all snow fields. Sir I like to look upon men. Let us walk down Charles Street!' "[21] Her love for Berwick makes her go on to praise the beauty of even its winters, but her preference for Boston, especially in winter, is clear.

Jewett may also have felt less thoroughly rooted in Berwick than most of her critics have assumed. In spite of their prominence in the area, the Jewetts were not an old-line Berwick family and Sarah was actually the first of her family born there. When she summarized and praised the town's history in "Looking Back on Girlhood" she felt it necessary to "keep in mind the truth that I have no inheritance from the ancient worth and dignity of Berwick. . . . My own people are comparatively late comers."[22] Jewett's grandfather moved to South Berwick around 1839, and her father brought his family there only about a year before Jewett's birth in 1849.[23] When Jewett was growing up she and her family were still recent arrivals, and traditional communities are slow to accept newcomers fully. When she wrote "Looking Back on Girlhood" (1892) the Jewetts had been established in Berwick for over a half-century, but her need to disclaim an inheritance from Berwick's past suggests a continuing sense of newness beneath Jewett's affectionate sense of belonging.

Ambivalence, however, is by no means rejection. After 1880 Jewett was increasingly involved in the urban life of Boston's Brahmin aristocracy, a group to which she is frequently said to have belonged.[24] Like the earlier Berwick upper class described in her historical sketch of the town, she associated with Boston's "people of refinement and cultivation" as an equal,[25] and she seems to have been quite at home in the Boston social and intellectual milieu. Even on Beacon Hill, however, she habitually introduced herself as "a country person."[26] She had resented Berwick's limitations as a young woman, and she continued to need a larger and more varied society, but although it could not meet all her needs South Berwick was still her home.

Jewett was by no means the only person in her lifetime who found rural New England inadequate, and the conditions of country life as she must have seen them may have been another reason for her ambivalence. Even Howard Mumford Jones, who vigorously disputes the idea of an overall debility in the New England culture of the period, admits that "in this half-century [1865–1915] New England agriculture steadily declined."[27] More specific data appear in John Donald Black's study of New England's rural economy. Black points out that the years between 1870 and 1920 saw many farms revert to pasture and then to woodland as a large number of families deserted agricultural life. Many young people left the farms to seek more secure employment, and birth rates declined. In northern New England, however, these setbacks occurred about thirty years after their beginning in the southern part of the region. Black's data suggest some remaining vitality in the agriculture of Jewett's own area during much of her life, since the amount of land from which crops were harvested in York County reached its peak in 1890. They also show, however, that as early as 1830 Maine's population had leveled off, and that between 1870 and 1920, in an era of great national growth, most of York County either lost population or gained only very slightly.[28] What Jewett probably observed in her lifetime (1849–1909) was a pervasive but not precipitous falling-off in agricultural activity. From 1890 to 1910 South Berwick itself was losing population,[29] and in New Hampshire, which lay immediately south and west, the reversion to woodland had already begun in 1880.[30] This agricultural decay came on top of the decline in shipping and shipbuilding which dated in the Berwick (and Deephaven) area to the Embargo of 1807 and farther east, in the region where Dunnet Landing belongs, to the post–Civil War displacement of sail by steam.[31] As late as 1894 Jewett could maintain that Berwick's "common stock of prosperity" had never been better,[32] but her portrait of country life shows her awareness not only of economic decline but also of the hardships that drove her rural neighbors from their land.

The economic hardships she observed and the social inadequacy she experienced combined with Jewett's love for her home to give her an understanding of rural life that went far deeper than simple celebration or rejection. "Country versus City" is indeed, as Richard Cary has suggested,[33] one of her major themes, but the country does not always win out and Jewett is no single-minded rural apologist. Instead, as several critics have recognized, the city-country theme becomes in Jewett's work more dialogue than opposition,[34] and the characters who choose between them face loss as well as gain no matter what their decision.

Jewett's awareness of the grim reality of country life is apparent even in *Deephaven* (1877). Robert Horn has argued that the book presents a stark picture of rural degeneration and decay,[35] and the placid beauty the village offers to visitors is clearly a poor compensation for the poverty, deprivation, loneliness, and degeneracy experienced by the natives. As a decayed port Deephaven is an extension of urban life becoming rural again, so that its very existence undercuts the stereotype of the rural village as the scene of primal bucolic bliss. Further disparagement of the myth comes from many parts of the book, but two passages are particularly clear about rural hardship. A description of life on the isolated hill-farms of the township provides an early view of the bleakness and thwarted ambition Hamlin Garland would find in other rural scenes in *Main Travelled Roads*:

> Some of the more enterprising young people went away to work in shops and factories; but the custom was by no means universal, and the people had a hungry, discouraged look. It is all very well to say that they knew nothing better . . . there was too often a look of disappointment in their faces, and sooner or later we heard or guessed many stories: that this young man had wished for an education, but there had been no money to spare for books or schooling; and that one had meant to learn a trade, but there must be some one to help his father with the farm work, and there was no money to hire a man to work in his place if he went away. (133)

Even more vivid is the depiction of stark rural failure in "In Shadow," the story of a young farm couple's defeat and death. A combination of the depression of the ship-building industry, poor health, and nearly worthless land has thwarted all the effort they can exert, and the scenes of the farmer's funeral, following that of his wife by a few months, complete a grim story of rural hardship and failure with stark images that convey the heartlessness of nature and the desolation that can easily overtake rural life:

> the thistles which the man who is dead had fought so many years will march in next summer and take unmolested possession.
> I think today of that fireless, empty, forsaken house, where the winter sun shines in and creeps slowly along the floor; the bitter cold is in and around the house, and the snow has sifted in at every crack; out-

side it is untrodden by any living creature's footstep. The wind blows and rushes and shakes the loose window sashes in their frames, while the padlock knocks—knocks against the door. (149)

The only hope for a better life in these scenes lies in emigration to the city. The "more enterprising young people" have left the hill farms for industrial jobs, and the defeated family's eldest son is "getting ahead" by working "in a box shop in Boston," sending money and presents home (141–42). The same point is made even more clearly in a comic episode in which the narrator's friend, a young Brahmin lady, is mistaken for the daughter of the keeper of the Deephaven Lighthouse and offered help in going to Boston to work as a sales clerk. The reader's knowledge of Kate's true social and economic status makes the proposal ludicrous, but the unchallenged assumption is that if she actually were a country girl like her would-be helper she would certainly prefer to live in the city, where life is less lonely and one can earn money to send home.

Many of the works Jewett wrote after *Deephaven* continue the city-country dialogue, often depicting rural hardships but also emphasizing rural advantages. Some characters achieve a compromise that preserves the country's values while easing its drudgery and isolation. Such a possibility is the explicit theme of "A Guest at Home" (1882), in which city-educated Annie Hollis comes home to her parents' farm determined to share the city advantages she has gained. She believes that "God would not have made it her home unless she could help them more, and they could help her more, than anybody else"[36]—a sentence that seems almost a restatement of Jewett's own musings, in her diary for 1872, about life in Berwick as her duty. With a good deal of effort and determination Annie succeeds in making rural life easier and more fulfilling for the whole family, and Jewett affirms that one can make the best of farm life "without much money to spend" (58). The new joys and comforts belong, however, almost completely to the city, with even the enjoyment of nature shaped by painting lessons Annie has had there. The farm work becomes lighter partially because Annie hires a neighbor girl to help, suggesting that money is indeed needed to lighten rural burdens, and Jewett evades the issue of whether even Annie can have enough spirit to undertake to battle rural drudgery all her life by marrying a farmer. The fact that country life becomes pleasant with such massive infusions of energy and urban knowledge cannot really offset the sketch's bleak picture of the more typical rural existence, in which Annie's parents have "begun to feel like horses in a treadmill" (58).

A much later story, "A Born Farmer" (1901), shows a rural family shaping a different compromise between country and city. An inheritance allows them to leave their farm, where there are "no great possibilities" for the young people,[37] but, although the son adapts to the city quickly, the rest of the family grows increasingly unhappy. At the story's end husband, wife, and daughter have all returned, ostensibly for a visit, but actually to live under "the starlit sky and the dim familiar shapes of the old Maine hills" (344). In one sense, then, the story celebrates the superiority of country life to the city,[38] but this implication is strongly qualified by the son's decision to remain in the city and the fact that the inheritance, by ending the "dreadful anxious times" suffered in trying to pay off the mortgage, has cushioned rural life for the whole family. Where only the severest industry and toil kept them afloat before, there is now plenty of money, and work becomes "a perfect delight" (336–39).

Most rural people, however, cannot import city habits, or use wealth to eliminate drudgery, or alternate between city and country as Jewett herself did. In order to gain the city's wider opportunities they must abandon rural advantages as well as rural hopelessness. But "It is a serious thing," as the narrator of "A Born Farmer" says, "to pull up a human plant by the roots" (340). For Jewett, with her own love for South Berwick, place is closely linked to personality and the self. In *Deephaven* the pitiful Miss Chauncey dies as a result of attempting to return to her ruined home, and the Widow Jim is defined by a description of her parlor, which like her is plain and limited to "an exact sufficiency" but also has "a certain dignity" (62). In *A Marsh Island* (1885) Israel Owen and his daughter Doris have "a passion" for their farm which is shared by Dan Lester, the appropriate suitor; but Dick Dale, the outsider, continually sees the farm as a "picturesque bit of country," and eventually realizes for himself that it would be wrong to "take Doris away from her own world."[39] This closeness of place to personality gives place a moral impact, as when the heroine of "The Growtown 'Bugle'" allows her neighbors to starve while her attention is focused on a Kansas town, or Mercy Bascom of "Fair Day" (1888) decides to end a quarrel after returning to the place where she has a "comfortable feeling of relationship to her surroundings."[40] To be out of one's proper place, mentally or physically, may be to have one's values disarranged, and the return may be a return to moral clarity.

If place is this basic to character, then those who leave their native places risk a loss deeper than homesickness. In Jewett's sketches the rural people (French Canadians and Irishmen as well as Americans) who emigrate to the city usually do find the wider opportunities they seek, but Jewett also puts a strong emphasis on the pain of emigration. Perhaps the most explicit description of this price paid for a larger chance comes when Mike Bogan of "The Luck of the Bogans" (1889), the first of the Irish stories, cuts a square of Irish sod to carry with him to the new land: "The golden stories of life in America turned to paltry tinsel, and a love and pride of the old country, never forgotten by her sons and daughters, burned with fierce flame on the inmost altar of his heart."[41] However hard life may be in Ireland or on an isolated farm, love of place is a deep and abiding emotion, and the decision to leave one's place cannot be easy.

In Jewett's later work this depiction of the meaning place has for human beings becomes a theme in its own right. "Aunt Cynthy Dallett" (1896) is about the relation among love of place, independence, and love of family; "Where's Nora?" shows Ireland rejoicing for her child's success; and "A Spring Sunday" (1904) explores the effect of place on memory. More significant, however, are the discussion of place in *Pointed Firs* (1896) and the extension of that discussion in "William's Wedding" (1910). *The Tory Lover* (1901) too involves a lengthy examination of the subject, and in its case the theme of place provides a unity that is otherwise lacking.

The relation of persons to places is a submerged theme throughout *The Country of the Pointed Firs* (1896). The book's first chapter is entitled "The Return," and amid its description of Dunnet Landing the narrator says that "When one really knows a village like this and its surroundings, it is like becoming acquainted with a single person. The process of falling in love at first sight is as final as it is swift in such a case, but the growth of true friendship may be a lifelong affair." She goes on to explain her reason for coming: "After a first brief visit . . . in the course of a yachting cruise, a lover of Dunnet Landing returned. . . ."[42] The narrator has been to the Landing before and, experiencing "love at first sight," has become its "lover." Now, however, she has returned to stay long enough to begin "the growth of true friendship," to know the Landing as she might know a person.

Finding lodgings with Mrs. Todd, the unnamed narrator settles in to study her village. Before the third chapter ends Mrs. Todd's house is referred to as "home" (19), and in the fourth sketch the new lodger, untroubled by the *Deephaven* narrator's feeling of intruding in a similar situation, has attended a village funeral. Considering the deceased "an acquaintance and neighbor" (19), she regrets leaving before the burial procession and reminding herself and her new friends "that I did not really belong to Dunnet Landing" (21). Though she feels momentarily estranged at this point, she has already settled into her new place and applied some of the most intimate place-related words, like "home" and "neighbor," to her surroundings.

In order to know both Mrs. Todd and the "surroundings" of Dunnet Landing better, the narrator goes to Mrs. Todd's home on Green Island. She finds that the house there is both a "beacon" (37) and "rooted" (40), a guide planted firmly in place, and she learns how vital this place is to Mrs. Todd and her family. Later when she hears the story of "poor Joanna," who fled to Shell-heap Island after disappointment in love spoiled her "nest," her own place, the narrator visits the "dreadful small place to make a world of" that became Joanna's home in order to know her better (62). While there she realizes that place is a metaphor for human individuality: "In the life of each of us . . . there is a place remote and islanded" (75). The Bowden reunion sequence that follows is held at the "old Bowden house," which is like "a motherly brown hen" awaiting the family whose place it is (88).

When the narrator later visits Elijah Tilley, who keeps his home exactly as it is was when his wife was alive, she learns that a place may enshrine and preserve personality and memory, but that when a place no longer changes it becomes stagnant and unwholesome. (Tilley's devotion, however touching, is hardly healthy, and Mrs. Todd's remark that she prefers not to visit the house with Sarah Tilley gone seems to indicate disapproval.) The episode also gives a clue to the narrator's acceptance in Dunnet Landing. His wife, Tilley says, would have been pleased to meet "somebody new that took such an int'rest" (106). The narrator's desire to know the village apparently makes the village willing to return the act of friendship.

The book ends with a lengthy description of place and with Dunnet Landing's gradual blending back into its surroundings as the narrator's boat pulls away. She has formed many human attachments, but she has also come to know the place: "Once I had not even known where to go for a walk; now there were many delightful things to be done and done again, as if I were in London" (157–58).

Since she has already remarked that forming a friendship with a place one loves "may be a lifelong affair" (13), the narrator's return to the Landing in later Dunnet sketches is not surprising. In one of them, "William's Wedding" (1910), place becomes a major theme. The narrator comes back because she is "homesick,"[43] again identifying the Landing as home, and she comes seeking to retrieve her own identity in a place that can make her "feel solid and definite again, instead of a poor, incoherent being" (147). At first, however, she tries to ignore the change inherent in Dunnet's being a real place rather than Arcadia. Hoping to begin rural life where she left off, she is surprised by both Johnny Bowden's growth and the visible effects of winter. To impress upon her the lesson that the Landing is not a paradise immune to time, Mrs. Todd immediately asks about the fashion in bonnets, and later when the narrator has received a wordless but "just rebuke" the question is repeated (153). This failure to accept Dunnet Landing as a real, changing place rather than an embodied daydream is paralleled by the narrator's initial failure, when Mrs. Todd begins to detail the land-ownership arrangements so vital to rural life, to take her usual interest. "I couldn't stop for details," she says, and so when Mrs. Todd repeats the requested central information her attitude is "not without scorn" (149). Because the narrator is thus out of touch with Dunnet Landing and the interest that gives her acceptance there, she has "an odd feeling of strangeness," and Mrs. Todd's house is like "a cold new shell" (149) instead of the cozy "larger body, or . . . double shell" it had become in her earlier visit (53). The weather, silent and gray, parallels her feelings.

Finally, however, on her second morning back, the narrator has managed to rid herself of the "ditsractions and artifices" of her other world and wakes to bright spring weather and "the familiar feeling of interest and ease" (149–51). Although in her absence she has "lost instead of gained" in interest and understanding (152), she is finally ready to resume the empathy of her earlier visit, and so she is able to divine Maria Harris' feelings about William Blackett's marriage and earn Mrs. Todd's "how you do understand poor human natur'!" (155). Reinstated in her Dunnet status, she participates with Mrs. Todd, William, and Esther in the wedding cake and wine that are "like a true sacrament" (156), and she and Mrs. Todd appear in a muted final scene that expresses the narrator's spiritual acceptance in Dunnet Landing: "We went home together up the hill, and Mrs. Todd said nothing more; but we held each other's hands all the way" (157). In spite of her temporary estrangement, the narrator's "friendship" with Dunnet Landing has stood the test of separation, and her right in the place she has adopted is secure.

Seen in light of this interest in place, *The Tory Lover* (1901) becomes in one sense the culmination of Jewett's career rather than an unfortunate anticlimax. The only one of Jewett's longer works to be set openly in a real place, the novel depicts her native area at the time of the Revolution and gives a sympathetic picture of the difficulty many people of the time had in deciding to follow or reject the Patriot cause. Herself the descendent of both Tories and Patriots,[44] Jewett is unusually willing to depict fairly the reasoning and suffering of the two sides. *The Tory Lover* becomes a novel about the choice of one's own place, and about the difficulty with which place-related affections came to center on the new country rather than the old.

Many characters have already made their choice as the novel begins. John Paul Jones, born in the British Isles, has joined the Patriot cause so thoroughly that he can say, as he attacks a town, "Come after me. . . . I am at home here!" and suffer no apparent pangs at the incongruity.[45] Madam Wallingford, the hero's mother, although a child of the New World, has also made her choice. She cannot accept the Patriot oath that would secure her house and lands, and when her American-born son Roger tells her he must fight for his country, she says "All your country, boy! . . . not alone this willful portion of our heritage. Can you forget that you are English born?" (89).

Mary Hamilton, the story's heroine, is an ardent Patriot, but although her choice is made she still feels the attraction of England, the old home. In arguing her party's case she says, "we are English folk, and are robbed of our rights" (312). Leaving New England to help Madam Wallingford search for Roger is difficult for Mary; it is "a great change" to leave "this dear landscape and . . . home" (267), but she discovers that the English landscape also has claims on her: "she was in England at last, and the very heart of the mother country seemed to welcome her. . . . The fields and hedges, the bright foxglove and green ivy, the larks and blackbirds and quiet robins, the soft air against her cheeks,—each called up some far-inherited memory, some instinct of old relationship. All her elders in Berwick still called England home, and her thrilled heart had come to know the reason" (319). For a moment Mary is "half afraid that she had misunderstood everything in blaming old England so much" (320), but thoughts of New England scenes and her accustomed friends and surroundings bring her back to her usual loyalties.

What is for Mary a momentary doubt is a choice of major proportions for Roger Wallingford. Influenced by Loyalist guardians, the young man has been slow to declare his mind. As the book begins he still opposes the war, but says that "since there is a war . . . my place is with my countrymen" (37), suggesting that it is friendship and personal honor, more than love of country, that motivate him. His psychological conflict reaches its crisis as the *Ranger* is about to make its first attack on the English coast: "These were the shores of England, and he was bound to do them harm. He was not the first man who found it hard to fight against the old familiar flag which a few months earlier had been his own" (211). Remembering a lengthy stay in England, Roger regrets finding himself "the accomplice" of France. But then his inherited thoughts of England are replaced by his own thoughts; "he had come to fight for the colonies. . . . The lieutenant looked down at the solid deck planks where he stood,—they had grown out of the honest ground of his own neighborhood; he had come to love his duty, after all, and even to love his ship" (211–12). Built from Berwick lumber and manned with Berwick men, the *Ranger* becomes for Roger a visible extension of his true home, the place where he belongs, and the sight of the ship cancels out the pull of England's shores. When he later needs to identify himself secretly in a letter he calls himself "Roger W——, of Piscataqua, in New England" (384), substituting the homeland he has chosen for the surname inherited from his English forefathers. His final speech concludes with a declaration of loyalty to his country, and the book ends as he and Mary step ashore at home.

Place thus supplies a unifying theme for *The Tory Lover*, and in this sense the historical novel not only has a certain coherence but also follows naturally from *Pointed Firs* and the concern with place in Jewett's other works. Jewett herself faced the choice of the place she would belong, whether to South Berwick, the beloved but limited country town, or to Boston, the cosmopolitan city. Unlike most who made this choice she was able to find a compromise, but her experience made her aware of the importance place has for human beings, and her remarks to Cather that her sketches began "when an old house and an old woman came together in her brain with a click"[46] suggests that she used this insight in the creation of her fiction. The skillfully depicted interaction of setting and character that provides much of the interest of Jewett's work is thus more than a technique; it is, instead, the matrix from which her art begins.

Notes

1. "The Editors," letter to Sarah Orne Jewett, 5 Mar. 1871, and William Dean Howells to Sarah Orne Jewett, 11 Mar. 1871, both in the William Dean Howells Collection, Houghton Library, Harvard University. Also Howells, "Recent Literature," *Atlantic Monthly*, 39 (1877), 759, and "Recollections of an *Atlantic* Editorship," *Atlantic Monthly*, 100 (1907), 599.

2. "Miss Jewett," *Atlantic Monthly*, 73 (1894), 130–33; rpt. in *Appreciation of Sarah Orne Jewett*, ed. Richard Cary (Waterville: Colby College Press, 1973), p. 17.

3. 5 Oct. 1901, *Selected Letters of Henry James*, ed. Leon Edel (New York: Farrar, Strauss and Cudahy, 1955), pp. 202–03.

4. Letter to Sarah Orne Jewett, 29 Nov. 1888, Sarah Orne Jewett Collection, Houghton.

5. Quinn, *American Fiction*, Students' Edition (New York: Appleton-Century, 1936), pp. 329–30; Chase, "Sarah Orne Jewett as a Social Historian," in *The World of Dunnet Landing*, ed. David Bonnell Green (Lincoln: Univ. of Nebraska Press, 1962), pp. 365-72, rpt. in *Appreciation*, pp. 184–86; Thorp, *Sarah Orne Jewett*, Minnesota Pamphlets on American Writers, No. 61 (Minneapolis: Univ. of Minn. Press, 1966), p. 7; and Matthiessen, *Sarah Orne Jewett* (Boston: Houghton Mifflin, 1929), pp. 98–99.

6. Matthiessen, *Sarah Orne Jewett*, p. 51.

7. (Boston: Houghton Mifflin, 1894), p. iii.

8. Letter to Sarah Orne Jewett, 15 Sept. 1903, Sarah Orne Jewett Collection, Houghton.

9. "The Old Town of Berwick," *New England Magazine*, 16 (1894), 585–609; rpt. by Old Berwick Historical Society, South Berwick, Maine (1967).

10. "To William Dean Howells," 12 July 1901, letter 122, *Sarah Orne Jewett Letters*, ed. Richard Cary (Waterville: Colby College Press, 1967), p. 143.

11. Preface to the 1877 edition, *Deephaven and Other Stories*, ed. Richard Cary (New Haven, Conn.: College and University Press, 1966), p. 29.

12. Quoted in Matthiessen, *Sarah Orne Jewett*, p. 120.

13. Babette Ann Boleman, "Deephaven and the Woodburys," *Colophon*, 3 (Sept., 1939), 21–22.

14. "To Mary E. Mulholland," 23 Jan. 1899, letter 96, *Letters*, ed. Cary, p. 116.

15. *Youth's Companion*, 65 (7 Jan. 1892), 5–6; rpt. in *The Uncollected Short Stories of Sarah Orne Jewett*, ed. Richard Cary (Waterville: Colby College Press, 1971), p. 7.

16. 14 Jan. [1872], MS diary May 1871–Dec. 1879, Sarah Orne Jewett Collection, Houghton. Josephine Donovan has also used Jewett's diary and has reached conclusions similar to my own. See *Sarah Orne Jewett* (New York: Ungar, 1980), pp. 25 et passim.

17. 11 Dec. 1876, letter 10, in C. Carroll Hollis, "Letters of Sarah Orne Jewett to Anna Laurens Dawes," *Colby Library Quarterly*, 8 (1968), 116–17.

18. 21 Feb. 1882, in Richard Cary, ed., " 'Yours Always Lovingly': Sarah Orne Jewett to John Greenleaf Whittier," *Essex Institute Historical Collections*, 107 (1971), 418.

19. [Letter to Annie Fields?], Monday morning, *Letters of Sarah Orne Jewett*, ed. Annie Fields (Boston: Houghton Mifflin, 1911), p. 33.

20. Reginald Heber, "From Greenland's icy mountains," in *Favorite Hymns in Their Original Form*, ed. William Leonard Gage (New York: A. S. Barnes, 1874), p. 27.

21. "To Arthur Stedman," 25 Feb. 1895, in David Bonnell Green, "Sarah Orne Jewett's 'A Dark Night,'" *PBSA*, 53 (1959), 331–32.

22. "Looking Back on Girlhood," p. 4.

23. John Eldridge Frost, *Sarah Orne Jewett* (Kittery Point: Gundalow Club, 1960), pp. 2–3.

24. See, for example, Fred Lewis Pattee, *History of American Literature Since 1870* (New York: Century, 1915), p. 235.

25. "The Old Town of Berwick," p. 600.

26. Cary, ed., *Letters*, p. 3.

27. *The Age of Energy: Varieties of American Experience, 1865–1915* (New York: Viking Press, 1970), p. 57.

28. John D. Black, *The Rural Economy of New England: A Regional Study* (Cambridge: Harvard Univ. Press, 1950), pp. 20–21, 71–73, 155.

29. U.S. Dept. of Commerce, Bureau of the Census, *Population*, Vol. 2 of *Thirteenth Census of the United States* (Washington, D.C.: Government Printing Office, 1913), p. 806.

30. Black, *Rural Economy*, p. 153.

31. The York customs district, which included Berwick, reached its highest shipping tonnage in 1810, but the Wiscasset and Waldoboro districts, roughly equivalent to the Tenants Harbor–Boothbay location Jewett suggested for Dunnet Landing, reached their highs in 1860. See William Hutchinson Rowe, *The Maritime History of Maine* (New York: W. W. Norton, 1948), p. 317. (The high figure for York in 1850 appears to be a misprint, as it does not agree with the total.)

32. "The Old Town of Berwick," pp. 603–04.

33. *Sarah Orne Jewett* (New York: Twayne, 1962), p. 44.

34. See Cary, *Jewett*, p. 151; Donovan, *Sarah Orne Jewett*, pp. 25–28, et passim; Sister Mary Williams, "The Pastoral in New England Local Color," Diss. Stanford 1971, pp. 154–55; Randall R. Mawer, "Setting as Symbol in Jewett's *A Marsh Island*," *Colby Library Quarterly*, 12 (1976), 86; Mary Kraus, "Sarah Orne Jewett and Temporal Continuity," *Colby Library Quarterly*, 15 (1979), 169–70; and Paul John Eakin, "Sarah Orne Jewett and the Meaning of Country Life," *American Literature*, 38 (1967), 508–31, rpt. in *Appreciation*, p. 212.

35. "The Power of Jewett's *Deephaven*," *Colby Library Quarterly*, 9 (1972), 617–31; rpt. in *Appreciation*, pp. 284–96.

36. *Uncollected Short Stories*, p. 57. Donovan (*Sarah Orne Jewett*, pp. 25–26) sees a strong autobiographical element in this sketch.

37. *Uncollected Short Stories*, p. 339.

38. See Cary, "Introduction," *Uncollected Short Stories*, p. viii.

39. 4th ed. (Boston: Houghton Mifflin, 1886), pp. 148, 12, 205.

40. "Fair Day," *Strangers and Wayfarers* (Boston: Houghton Mifflin, 1890), pp. 131–32.

41. *Strangers*, pp. 84–85.

42. (Garden City: Doubleday, 1956), p. 13.

43. *Pointed Firs and Other Stories*, p. 148.

44. "Looking Back on Girlhood," p. 5.

45. (Boston: Houghton Mifflin, 1901), p. 217.

46. Willa Cather, "Preface," *Pointed Firs and Other Stories*, p. 9.

The Literary Rubrics of Sarah Orne Jewett

Richard Cary*

The reputation of Sarah Orne Jewett is in bad straits. Since her death in 1909 she has been shabbily served in all three of the retrospective categories: F. O. Matthiessen's biography is gravely derelict in quotidian detail, in literary evolvement and appraisal; Annie Fields's volume of collected letters is malformed and undocumented; and Clara and Carl Weber's bibliography is a construct flawed by imprecision and omission. These books have reigned unquestioned as the standards of scholarship on Jewett's life and works from as long ago as 1911 until as recently as 1978 when Gwen and James Nagel ably rectified and updated the Webers' section on secondary studies. It is deplorable that only in short analytical and interpretive essays can one find saving grace, pointedly those by Charles Miner Thompson, Edward M. Chapman, A. M. Buchan, Warner Berthoff, Hyatt Waggoner, and Paul John Eakin. It is deplorable because, in the eighth decennium after her death, Sarah Orne Jewett still stands paramount among prose expositors of the Maine scene, its people, and their ways. That may sound a prodigal judgment until one tries calling up any single novel about Maine that can be placed beside *The Country of the Pointed Firs* as a full-fledged peer. Few will disavow Jewett's text as the acme of its kind.

The object of this essay is to identify the main routes Jewett followed and the touchstones she picked up along the way to this enviable high station. Mindfully skirting the quicksands of psychobiography, I propose herewith that the most potent influence on her sensibility was hereditarian, and that its mate and abettor was her community, natural and human. From this improportionable mix of race and place she derived elements of amplitude and balance that fetched her through ignorance to excellence. The compelling force of family flowed principally from three patriarchs, all hallowed by the impressionable juvenile.

*This essay was written especially for this volume and is included here by permission of the author.

There was her paternal grandfather (Theodore Furber Jewett), sea captain in the West Indies trade, shipbuilder, and to her, breathlessly, "a citizen of the whole geography." Through him she first learned of sailors and shipmasters and up-country woodsmen. Appetite aroused, she began "to linger about the busy country stores, and listen to the graphic talk"; to "the greetings of old friends"; to the "minute details of neighborhood affairs"; and to the "delightful jokes and Munchausen-like reports"[1] of beached seamen and lumberjacks at ease.

There was her maternal grandfather (Dr. William Perry), an irrepressible bravo who in his late eighties raced spirited horses along the Hampton oceanfront, performed surgery until ninety-two, and lived to ninety-eight. Jewett fondly acknowledged that "[He was] always showing me where good work had been done, and insisting upon my recognition of the moral qualities of achievement."[2] A man of adamantine resolve, he helped her shake off the mists of adolescence and pay "proper attention" to her talent. "I look upon that generation as the one to which I really belong," she told Sarah Wyman Whitman, "I who was brought up with grandfathers and grand-uncles and aunts for my playmates."[3]

And then there was her father (Dr. Theodore Herman Jewett), hub of the wheel. As a child, she accompanied him on his daily round of farms, fishing shacks, and factory hovels, during which he familiarized her with indigenous flora and fauna, and regaled her with extracts from his readings in religion, science, legendry, and literature. Despite some skittish resistance to his gentle indoctrination on her part, love of the land and of good books took hold. The intriguing particularities of men, women, and children she met along his line of march inscribed themselves on the deepest filaments of her being. "The best of my education was received in my father's buggy and the places to which it carried me,"[4] she wrote in maturity. "I had no consciousness of watching or listening . . . [but now], as I write my sketches of country life, I remember again and again the wise things he said and the sights he made me see. . . . I owe a great deal to his patience with a heedless little girl."[5] Patently, her involvement in the sights, sounds, and smells of her province, in the look and talk of her people, was not premeditated or professional. She never walked about, finically alert, notebook at the ready, like Hawthorne[6]; nor, like Emerson, did she keep exhaustive journals. She absorbed impressions as spontaneously as she inhaled. Appraising "the surroundings which have affected the course of my works as a writer," she paid rich tribute to her revered mentors, "those who taught me to observe, and to know the deep pleasure of simple things; and to be interested in the lives of people about me."[7]

Before quitting the field of speculative genetics, a glance at Jewett's paternal grandmother is obligatory. "My father had inherited . . . from his mother's French ancestry, that peculiarly French trait, called *gaieté de coeur*,"[8] which to Jewett connoted kindness of heart and outgoing charm. If, as Samuel Butler allowed, a chicken is only an egg's way of making another egg, it follows that the *gaieté de coeur* in Jewett's pedigree induced in her the urge to perpetuate her beloved Arcadian world of laconic farmers, mettlesome widows, and bronzed sea captains long after that world had succumbed to the onslaught of machines, iron rails, and corporate boards. It was her one unbounded passion. Averting the folly and fustian of a Quixote, she fostered these ghosts of a vanished culture with affection and rue.

Jewett's first serious impulsion to write came at age fourteen, after reading Harriet Beecher Stowe's *The Pearl of Orr's Island*. At the outset she finds it "clear and perfectly original and strong," captivated by its "exquisite flavor and reality of delight." Upon further reflection, Jewett exclaims: "Alas, that she couldn't finish it in the same noble key of simplicity and harmony," and puts it down as "an incomplete piece of work" with "a divine touch here and there."[9] Jewett is distressed by Stowe's studied manipulation of plot, tone, diction, and by the synthetic rusticity of settings, characters, and dialect. Growingly certain that she is capable of "a more true and sympathetic rendering," she draws immense comfort and confidence from the fact that "I have grown more and more fond of the old-fashioned countryfolks. I have always known their ways and I like to be with them."[10] She adopts as her ensign "a noble saying of Plato that the best thing that can be done for the people of a state is to make them acquainted with one another."[11] This view of the function of literature as communication and consociation she repeats verbatim in at least four contexts. In 1892, at the verge of her final productive decade, she recapitulates with thanksgiving the propitious convergence of discovery and self-discovery. "I began my work in life, most happy in finding that I was to write of those country characters and rural landscapes to which I myself belonged."[12]

The benign populism broached in Plato's dictum is by no means her sole guide. She perceives and descants upon numerous ramifications of the literary act: on artistic conscience, on the virtues of interchange between writer and reader, on the necessity for conceptional serenity; on the texture of realism; choice and use of subject matter, delineation of character, transfiguration of background, the patterns and hazards of plot, primacy of viewpoint, congruent tone, and how to coordinate optimum effects. Regrettably, she never encompassed in one treatise her philosophy of composition, as did Poe, or her formularies on the art of fiction, as did Henry James. One must sieve through her entire literary residue in order to retrieve opportune nuggets she dispensed in letters to eager apprentice authors (including Willa Cather), in prefaces to books, in newspaper and magazine interviews, in scattered reviews of her work, and in reports of conversations. Snippets reclaimed in this process range from ardent abstractions to solid tips on techniques. Assembled under pertinent headings they provide both a syllabus of

Jewett's literary code and a tool useful in gauging the breach between her intent and her attainment. Each rubric is less a lodestar by which she steers a fixed course than it is a beacon glinting off and on, as the occasion entails.

Jewett's lineal and communal grounding conferred on her a self-assurance which precluded any need to invent artful or eccentric criteria to write by. Given her instincts and formative experience, her sequestered region and rooted neighbors, the stunning upheavals of a rowdy new era sparked this predictable reaction from her: "When I was, perhaps, fifteen, the first 'city boarders' began to make their appearance near Berwick; and the way they misconstrued the country people and made game of their peculiarities fired me with indignation. I determined to teach the world that country people were not the awkward, ignorant set those persons seemed to think. I wanted the world to know their grand, simple lives; and so far as I had a mission, when I first began to write, I think that was it."[13] Simplicity—not mummery, not embroidery—simplicity and probity would carry her through.

Loyal, protective, and evangelical as these sentiments are, Jewett did not immediately put them into play. Like most amateurs she floundered in waters too muddy or too deep before striking off on a clear stream. Her first two publications, tremulously concealed under a pen name, bear faint allegiance to her brave manifesto. "Jenny Garrow's Lovers" (1868), a short story which surfaced in an eclectic Boston weekly, is overplotted, overwrought melodrama devoid of skill or promise; "Mr. Bruce" (1869), in the *Atlantic Monthly*, a rompish fling at urban social comedy obviously beyond her aptitude. Neither has anything to do with the "grand, simple lives" of her constituents. After an interlude of stories for children and primly superficial poems, she unfurls "The Shore House" (1873), unmistakable signal that her resolve to become the prose laureate of Maine life was not just a puerile daydream. Henceforward her father's curt admonition, "Don't try to write *about* people and things, tell them as they are,"[14] occupies highest priority in her mind. From the tumbling flood of her reading she plucks a maxim by Flaubert, "*Écrire la vie ordinaire comme on écrit l'histoire*,"[15] and tacks it prominently at the front of her writing desk. To these cautionary mandates she annexes another pair of bolsters. First, tradition: "I think we must know what good work is, before we can do good work on our own."[16] Second, diligence: "There must be a solid foundation of drill and accuracy and certainty and *justesse* of touch."[17] Dedication to both she fully avouches in habitual references to literary classics, ancient and modern, in her diurnal correspondence, and in the rigorously revised drafts among her manuscripts.

The major motif in Jewett's literary praxis is this consonance of simplicity, veracity, Puritan ethic, and pedagogic zeal. However, running companionably alongside it is an obverse strain of mysticism set in motion by Socrates and pursued by a legion of latter-day epigones. Central to this concept is *ekstasis*, the involuntary displacement of human capacities by a resistless supernatural agent. In *Ion* Plato ascribes to his mentor the presumption that "They [the good epic poets] are seized with the Bacchic transport and are possessed . . . for not by art do they utter these [admirable poems], but by the power divine . . . the deity has bereft them of their senses, and uses them as ministers." Creativity, thereby, is totally dependent on afflatus. The artist is a mere intervener, God's conduit in the propagation of beauty. Eager acquiescence outstrips intellection as the prime desideratum.

Of *Uncle Tom's Cabin* Mrs. Stowe annunciated: "God wrote it." Not quite so gaudily, Jewett said to one of her editors, "I don't wish to ignore such a great gift as this, God has given me," confiding that this inexplicable boon "frightens me more than it pleases me."[18] To a newspaperwoman she pictures herself diffidently "a penholder" who does not write her stories, "they take possession of her and guide her pen."[19] A troubled neophyte, Laura E. Bellamy, receives assurance by mail that "The great messages and discoveries of literature come to us, they *write us*, and we do not control them in a certain sense."[20] Pleased yet perplexed by this cosmic enigma, Jewett bares its operation to her closest confidante Annie Fields: "day before yesterday the plan of the story comes into my mind, and in half an hour I have put all the little words and ways into their places and can read it off to myself like print. Who does it? for I grow more and more sure that I don't!"[21] When Rose Lamb, as intermediary for another struggling novice, entreats advice about rudiments, Jewett proposes incessant toil backed by intense perusal of selections from Maupassant, Anne Thackeray, Mary Wilkins Freeman, and Daudet. Toward the end, however, she reverts to *"that something which does itself"*[22] as the ineffable element which imparts magic to storytelling. In the course of a fervid outpouring to her *Atlantic Monthly* editor, Horace E. Scudder, she remarks morosely, "I lose my best manner by studying hard and growing older and wiser!"[23] Inspiration rather than perspiration reigns here, even though at loggerheads with her sterner edicts on heedful anaylsis of models and unflagging exertion over the work in progress.

Concordant with Jewett's gossamer theory of aesthetics is another Socratic doctrine, divulged in Plato's *Phaedo*. All knowledge is inherently recollection, says the Athenian master, then proceeds to elucidate and define.

> when we perceive something, either by the help of sight, or hearing, or some other sense, from that perception we are able to obtain a notion of some other thing like or unlike which is associated with it but has been forgotten. . . . But if the knowledge which is acquired before birth was lost by us at birth, and if afterward by the use of the senses we recovered what we previously knew, will not the process

we call learning be a recovery of the knowledge which is natural to us, and may not this be rightly termed recollection?

Although no adversion to this source has yet turned up in Jewett's writings, her faith in the doctrine springs to light along several points of her transit with Willa Cather. During an interview in 1921 Cather released this forethought on *O Pioneers!*: "I decided not to 'write' at all—simply to give myself up to the pleasure of recapturing in memory people and places I had believed forgotten. This was what my friend Sarah Orne Jewett had advised me to do."[24]

Over and over again in sketch and story Jewett symbolically re-vives her isolate world of dispassioned people, with a mode of life and a setting that are inexpungeably a part of her psychic history. She re-animates a diversity of persons: young Elisha, ablaze with enterprise, in "By the Morning Boat"; the pathetic Dobin sisters in "The Dulham Ladies"; rude, shrewd, contemptible Mrs. Persis Flagg in "The Guests of Mrs. Timms"; Captain Littlepage, once a prince among men, now cracked and garrulous, in *The Country of the Pointed Firs*; bright and decisive Polly Finch, who covets the appellation "Farmer"; "Miss Dan'el Gunn ("An Autumn Holiday") and Elijah Tilley (*The Country of the Pointed Firs*), bereaved sex-befuddled dotards. All play out their private dramas with ingrained reserve, rectitude, compassion, abnega-tion, gnomic humor, meanness, and intransigent pride. They function, grow old, and die within sound of the omnipresent ocean with its punc-tuation of islands and lighthouses, along stands of regal evergreens, in trim white cottages or failing farmhouses, amid kaleidoscopes of familiar birds and flowers. Jewett, like Wordsworth, remembered "a time when meadow, grove, and stream, / The earth, and every common sight, / To me did seem / Appareled in celestial light, / The glory and the freshness of a dream." She did not record, she recalled, imbuing the past with tinctures of her own disposition.

In this area Jewett leaves no room for quibble. Her discrete per-ceptions float inert in a solution of memory and intuition, waiting a pulse of recognition to incite them to viable union. Cather furnishes two more comments substantiating Jewett's accord with Socrates' thesis. From a packet of her late friend's letters Cather singles out this apothegm on the incubative nature of literature "whether little or great": "The thing that teases the mind over and over for years, and at last gets itself put down rightly on paper."[25] In the second instance, Cather recounts the time "She once laughingly told me that her head was full of dear old houses and dear old women, and that when an old house and an old woman came together in her brain with a click, she knew that a story was under way."[26]

Applicable here is Henry James' tribute to the English novelist who produced a certifiable portrait of junior French Protestant life on the basis of a momentary glance "as she ascended a staircase, passed an open door where . . . some of the young Protestants were seated at table round a finished meal." This single "direct personal impression" "made a picture" which, combined with her previous knowledge and experience, she converted into "a concrete image and produced a reality." Given an inch, she took an ell. "The power to guess the unseen from the seen, to trace the implication of things, to judge the whole piece by the pattern, the condition of feeling life in general so completely that you are well on your way to knowing any particular corner of it."[27] Jewett's short story, "The Quest of Mr. Teaby," germinated from just such a fleeting glimpse of "the funny old man in the linen duster whom I caught sight of at Chapel Station."[28]

Along that track it may be asked if Jewett does violence to truth, admits and adapts her impressions too subjectively. V. L. Parrington scores her unawareness of the economic and social stresses that elbowed her peerless world into obsolescence. One need only read "The Gray Mills of Farley," "River Driftwood," or "The Failure of David Barry" to find refutation. She was in fact thoroughly cognizant of what she calls "the destroying left hand of progress."[29] Law of temperament and love of retrospection induced her to veil its ferocity. People, not historic forces, engrossed her. Concluding that "impressions *are* experience," James counsels new authors, "Write from experience and experience only." As if in point-blank response, Jewett said, "I have only written about what I knew and felt,"[30] secure in the virtue of her stance. And— leaving out her tales of the South, *The Story of the Normans*, and *The Tory Lover*—that is precisely what she did after her initial sophomoric fumblings.

When Jewett's early regional sketches began turning up at the *Atlantic* offices, Howells called for longer stories and Scudder suggested more "invention," to which she retorted, in July 1873, "they are bright and real and have an individuality,"[31] displaying an acuity of self-knowledge rare in one so young and with so brief an apprenticeship. Helplessly awash in Walter Scott's "big bow-wow" manner, proved in her disastrous last novel *The Tory Lover*, she excelled as "a gem-cutter," Lowell's phrase.[32] "I am certain I could not write one of the usual magazine stories,"[33] as for instance "a good big Harper's story" by Charles Craddock. "[S.O.J.'s] French ancestry comes to the fore, and makes her nibble all round her stories like a mouse. They used to be as long as yardsticks, they are now as long as spools, and they will soon be the size of old-fashioned peppermints, and have neither beginning or end, but shape and flavor may still be left them."[34] She instructs Scudder: "Those sketches I sent you . . . were experiments,"[35] and a quarter century thereafter (1896) reiterates to Rose Lamb, "Story-writing is always experimental."[36] She moves along the outer fringes of convention in matters of form, dialogue, and tone, most markedly in her hybrid sketch-stories ("An Autumn Holiday," "The Courting of Sister Wisby," "The Landscape Chamber") wherein she commingles without check the actuating precepts of the personal essay, the narrative, the character vignette, and the memoir. "One must have one's own methods," she maintains, leaning as ever toward the ideal. "We must be ourselves, but we must be our best selves,"[37] she writes Cather, who later testifies, "She was content to be slight if she could be true."[38]

Jewett disdained both permutations of literary realism that confronted her era: the raucous naturalism exemplified by Frank Norris, and the verisimilitudes of lower-level local-colorists who dodged the ordinary in favor of idiosyncrasy, purveying garish "atmosphere," brummagen dialects, and blatant stereotypes. She is assailed, often unduly, for tilting toward "the more smiling aspects of existence," as Howells described his own predilection. Sex is absent from her pages, as is largely violence, and she recoils from grotesques interposed for mere shock value. One time she berates John Thaxter for presenting an unpleasant half-witted man who is "quite too horrible, and carries a kind of disgust. . . . I don't think the story needs such a proof."[39] Nevertheless, she is far from being all nostalgia and cotton candy at the fair. Her work does contain a quantum of the uglier traits: greed, cowardice, spite, callosity, fraudulence; intermittent flashes of squalor, sadism, and aberration crop up in her domain. There is lunacy in "Lady Ferry" and "A Sorrowful Guest"; degradation in "Marsh Rosemary," "The Dulham Ladies," and "In Dark New England Days"; a ghastly circus and an abject funeral overhang *Deephaven*; and social dissension agitates "The Town Poor," *A Country Doctor*, and a fair stock of others.

She makes her point in each of these cases without recourse to the eye-gouging minutiae of modernist fiction, operating admittedly at one remove from the actual. Having savored fully the limitations imposed on artists by foreshortened background and percipience, she sagely deposes to Willa Cather: "You can write about life, but never write life itself."[40] In addition, the new scatter-shot manner intrudes upon her a compulsion to distort. This she resists. "The trouble with most realism," she complains to Thomas Bailey Aldrich, "is that it isn't seen from any point of view at all, and so its shadows fall in every direction and it fails of being art."[41] Instead, she harps on the superiority of "imaginative" and "selective" realism[42] over uncurbed documentation in prose fiction. In other words, she speaks out again for individuality, for her faith in people unfazed by the bombardment of confused images from a furiously motile world. Thus she brings back to life Dunnet Landing, Marsh Island, Miss Sydney and her flowers, William Blackett. In the end, who is prepared to denounce her homemade brand of muted realism as less "real" than that of an angry Zola, a cryptic Borges, or a macho Hemingway?

Jewett's rationale on the subject of setting stems from two convictions: (1) inborn affinity with one's immediate locale, and (2) firm footing in the world at large. The first she spells out unconditionally in her synopsis of childhood days in rural, coastal, southern Maine: "I believe that we should know our native towns much better than most of us do, and never let ourselves be strangers at home." And, in tune with Thoreau: "One may travel at home in the most literal sense, and be always learning history, geography, botany, or biography—whatever one chooses." Here too she revels in the "rides and drives and tramps and voyages within the borders of my native town. There is always something fresh, something to be traced or discovered, something particularly to be remembered."[43] Moreover, she treasures the feeling that "every bush and tree seem like my cousins,"[44] and is wont to talk about being "neighborly" with a toad, "very intimate," with a poppy, "first cousin" to a caterpillar, and "own sister to a giddy-minded bobolink." The epitome of this kind of assimilation is realized in "A White Heron," brilliantly refracted through the eyes and mind of a hypersensitive child.

Jewett's extraordinary ability to coalesce symptomatic details of the land with human emotion and aspiration is abundantly evident throughout her work. Two examples here bespeak the turn of her mystic transitions, streaming inward to the silent, secret self or outward to grander, resplendent goals. In the closing paragraph of "The Hiltons' Holiday" the excitation of a long day in town surrenders to the elemental poetry of nature and the sanctuary of home, which then suffuse with peace the hearts of the repleted family.

> It was evening again, the frogs were piping in the lower meadows, and in the woods, higher up the great hill, a little owl began to hoot. The sea air, salt and heavy, was blowing in over the country at the end of the hot bright day. A lamp was lighted in the house, the happy children were talking together, and supper was waiting. The father and mother lingered for a moment outside and looked down over the shadowy fields; then they went in, without speaking. The great day was over, and they shut the door.

By contrast to this regressive modality Jewett invests nature with expansionary illusions, intimations of boundless potential for the human spirit. In chapter 7 of *The Country of the Pointed Firs* the nameless narrator's gaze overleaps the endmost islands to other more distant seas and invisible horizons.

> We were standing where there was a fine view of the harbor and its long stretches of shore all covered by the great army of the pointed firs, darkly cloaked and standing as if they waited to embark. As we looked far seaward among the outer islands, the trees seemed to march seaward still, going steadily over the heights and down to the water's edge.

As the indispensable adjunct to domestic propinquity, Jewett recommends being "away from one's neighborhood long enough to see it quite or almost from the outside."⁴⁵ Though not a cosmopolite, she was well-traveled in Boston, New York, Cincinnati, Philadelphia, Washington, D.C., Virginia, Wisconsin, Florida; had taken four trips to Europe during which she toured England, France, Italy, Norway, Belgium, Switzerland, Greece, Turkey; and cruised among the Caribbean ports. Her numerous letters from these locations brim with depictions of divers people seen and heard on "countless drives and excursions," of customs quaint or exotic by Maine measure, of colors and songs and flowers and forests, of prisons and chalets, of bursting seasons, of small boats and cluttered trains, of weatherworn herders, bathers, towers historic and mysterious, of protean skyscapes. The gain to Jewett in distended vista and freshened insight is quickly perceived. It is no wonder, then, that having advised Cather to "find your own quiet centre of life, and write from that to the world,"⁴⁶ she also cautions her, "You must know the world before you can know the village."⁴⁷ With amicable candor and the warrant of a lifetime of fecund maturation she comes tersely to the point: "I want you to be surer of your backgrounds,—you have your Nebraska life,—a child's Virginia.... These are uncommon equipment, but you don't see them yet quite enough from the outside,—you stand right in the middle of each of them when you write, without having the standpoint of the looker-on."⁴⁸ To amplify perspective and enrich the particular through the general—this Jewett learned to do after *Deephaven*, and this Cather in time learned to do. With a symmetry not unlike systolic-diastolic action, they both found access to and explored the human heart.

In respect of plot Jewett shows her steel in the first skirmish. When in 1873 Scudder presses her for "a more positive story," meaning denser plot, she rebuffs him out of hand. "I have no dramatic talent. The story would have no plot.... It seems to me I can furnish the theatre, and show you the actors, and the scenery, and the audience, but there never is any play!"⁴⁹ Not for her the Aristotelian imperative of beginning, middle, end. No formalistic clamps pinch her storytelling, which in her eyes is homologous to "a watercolor sketch."⁵⁰ Observation, imagination, experience, and inspiration must be allowed to flow without constraint and merge into a channel naturally carved by their contending energies. She chides John Thaxter for chasing down blind alleys of intrigue and improbability. "I wish that you would try something that does not aim so much at incidents. Take a simpler history of life," some desultory walk along a country road, a funny horse trade, a wagon come to pieces, a hoaxed husband standing off his jeering wife. "Don't write a 'story' but just *tell the thing*!"⁵¹ she exhorts him in an echo of her father's indelible behest.

Disposed to the humanist over the cartoonist view of her people,

Jewett repudiates "the caricatured Yankee of fiction, striped trousers, bell-crowned hat, and all, driving his steady horses along the shady roads." Despite antithetic emphasis on the spirit of the past by provincial folk and upon the dynamics of the present by municipal dwellers, no dissimilarity in essence really obtains. "Human nature is the same the world over," she insists; city and country "influences must ever produce much the same effects upon character."[52] In "A Landless Farmer" she professes the truism that "the great plays of life" hidden away in "gray old New England farmhouses . . . the comedies and tragedies, with their lovers and conspirators and clowns; their Juliets and Ophelias, Shylocks and King Lears, are acted over and over and over again." Pushing this a pace farther, Jewett in *A Country Doctor* has a much-traveled urban friend tell the titular character: "I tell you, Leslie, that for intense, self-centered, smouldering volcanoes of humanity, New England cannot be matched the world over."[53] Incontestably to her, rustic or townsman, princeling or peasant, all are progeny of the same universal nucleus.

Jewett empathizes with her characters of whatever station, at whatever pole of emotion, treating each evenhandedly, soliciting neither pathos nor ridicule. Ann Floyd, the lonely spinster in "Marsh Rosemary," succumbs to the flattery of a handsome, shiftless hanger-on, many years younger than herself. With unblinking realization of her folly, she marries him, confident that she can hold together their May-December union by fierce volition alone. In short order he decamps. Ensuing discoveries lead to utter collapse of her hopes and she is more than ever a prisoner of desolation. Jewett bares her misadventure without probing for tears or pausing to preach. "Who can laugh at my Marsh Rosemary, or who can cry, for that matter?" she ponders as Ann sinks into the darkness of her final grief.

With unaccustomed asperity Jewett decries George Eliot's turgidity in *Middlemarch*: "She draws her characters so that they stand alive before you and know what they have in their pockets and then goes on for three pages analyzing them & their motives."[54] It can be asserted without qualm that in the main Jewett avoids the twin traps of photography and psychography, inviting recognition by the reader through salient attributes, self-revelatory speech and actions instead. The widow Almira Todd, herbalist *sans pareil* and director of her own destiny in *The Country of the Pointed Firs*, must be acclaimed the supreme exemplar of that subtle art in Jewett's fictive community.

Of all Jewett's rubrics regarding characterization none is more visceral than the self-verified scripture she passes on to Annie Fields in 1890: any person unreconciled with "the attraction of rural surroundings" is truly destitute; the intrinsic persuasions of life amid natural influences cannot be effaced by sophisticated scorn or disgruntled malignity. Citing Madame Bovary as a hapless paradigm, Jewett writes:

"She is such a lesson to dwellers in country towns, who drift out of relation to their surroundings, not only social, but the very companionships of nature, unknown to them."[55] This friction of country-city values Jewett plumbs in the theme of "A White Heron." Eight-year-old Sylvia, removed from a crowded manufacturing town to her grandmother's farm, takes avidly to nature's lure. Although enamored of the young hunter-taxidermist who comes by seeking the heron, she withstands his blandishments and never reveals the bird's whereabouts. The victory of her tenacious idealism over his exploitative materialism is the foregone victory of country over city. Henry Stroud in "A New Parishioner" and The Honorable Joseph K. Laneway in "A Native of Winby" exemplify the disruption or destruction of youthful values after long exposure to metropolitan mores. In her heart, Jewett was an Emersonian transcendentalist.

The montage of rules mustered above constitutes the pith of Jewett's meager pronouncements on the craft of fiction. Clearly incompatible in several couplings, each directive is purely optional, contingent upon its singular fitness in her quickening design. She was palpably unruffled by logical discrepancy. Upon an armature formed by the crossbars of heredity and community she fleshed out these guidelines—the personal and the generic, the intuitive and the empirical, the manifest and the latent—that subsumed her active life in art. It was a happy confluence of discernment and determination. Jewett's scope is regional but her aim is worldwide. "You must write to the human heart, the great consciousness that all humanity goes to make up,"[56] she tells Cather.

Jewett's literary record is a triumph of individuation. "What the books are, she herself preeminently was,"[57] said Mark Howe. She reached uniqueness by unsealing and sorting out the bountiful riches within and around her, reaping the best of nurture and nature. And she achieved her highest desire: to transcribe and commemorate her dream of a paradise regained.

In her review of Jewett's *A Country Doctor*, Th. Bentzon, French novelist and good friend of Jewett, adjudged no doubt reluctantly that George Eliot possessed "all the gifts of genius," Miss Jewett only "the gentle seduction of talent."[58] To which may be subjoined, "Ah, but how affectional a talent, and how consummate a seductress."

Notes

1. Sarah Orne Jewett, "Looking Back on Girlhood," *Youth's Companion*, 65 (7 Jan. 1892), 5.

2. Frances Perry Dudley, *The Mid-Century in Exeter* (Exeter: News-Letter Press, 1943), p. 16.

3. Annie Fields, ed., *Letters of Sarah Orne Jewett* (Boston: Houghton Mifflin, 1911), p. 111.

4. La Salle Corbell Pickett, *Across My Path: Memories of People I Have Known* (New York: Brentano's, 1916), p. 143.

5. Jewett, "Looking Back on Girlhood," p. 6.

6. In a letter to Mrs. Fields Jewett disparaged "a volume of Hawthorne's younger journals, a conscious effort after material . . . ; but these last lack any reality or imagination . . . far-fetched and oddly feeble and sophomorish" (Fields, *Letters*, pp. 72–73).

7. Jewett, "Looking Back on Girlhood," p. 5.

8. Jewett, "Looking Back on Girlhood," p. 6.

9. Fields, *Letters*, p. 47; to Annie Fields, 5 July [1889].

10. Richard Cary, ed., *Sarah Orne Jewett Letters* (Waterville: Colby College Press, 1967), pp 35–36; to Ida Agassiz Higginson, 2 June 1877.

11. Preface to *Deephaven* (Boston: Houghton Mifflin, 1894), p. 3.

12. Jewett, "Looking Back on Girlhood," p. 6.

13. Cary, *Letters*, p. 16; undated clipping from the *Boston Journal*.

14. Jewett, "Looking Back on Girlhood," p. 6; see also Cary, *Letters*, p. 90.

15. Fields, *Letters*, p. 165; to Annie Fields, Saturday night [1899].

16. Fields, *Letters*, pp. 118–19; to Rose Lamb, Monday, 11 [May] 1896.

17. John Eldridge Frost, *Sarah Orne Jewett* (Kittery Point: The Gundalow Club, 1960), p. 144; letter to Emma Claflin Ellis, 2 Oct. 1888.

18. Cary, *Letters*, p. 30; to Horace E. Scudder, 13 July 1873.

19. Annie C. Muirhead, "Habits of Authors: How Some New England Story Writers Work," *Boston Evening Transcript*, 19 Nov. 1899, p. 15.

20. Cary, *Letters*, p. 52; 31 Aug. 1885.

21. Fields, *Letters*, p. 52.

22. Fields, *Letters*, p. 118; Monday, 11 [May] 1896.

23. Cary, *Letters*, p. 29; 13 July 1873.

24. Latrobe Carroll, "Willa Sibert Cather," *Bookman*, 53 (May 1921), 214.

25. Willa Cather, ed., *The Best Stories of Sarah Orne Jewett* (Boston: Houghton Mifflin, 1925), I, ix.

26. Cather, p. xvi.

27. Henry James in "The Art of Fiction." The English novelist, not identified in that essay, is Anne Thackeray Ritchie; the book, *The Story of Elizabeth*.

28. Fields, *Letters*, p. 57.

29. Jewett, "River Driftwood," in *Country By-Ways* (Boston: Houghton Mifflin, 1881), p. 17. In *The Country of the Pointed Firs* (Chapter 7) the narrator reflects during a conversation with Captain Littlefield: "I was familiar with the subject of the decadence of shipping interests in all its affecting branches."

30. Walter Blackburn Harte, "A Rural World," *Boston Sunday Journal*, (4 Feb. 1894), p. 18.

31. Cary, *Letters*, p. 29.

32. Francis Otto Matthiessen, *Sarah Orne Jewett* (Boston: Houghton Mifflin, 1929), p. 89.

33. Cary, *Letters*, p. 30; to Horace E. Scudder, 13 July 1873.

34. Fields, *Letters*, p. 81; to Annie Fields, 12 Oct. 1890.

35. Cary, *Letters*, p. 29; 13 July 1873.

36. Fields, *Letters*, p. 118.

37. Fields, pp. 249–50; 13 Dec. [1908]. Cather recounts that after hardy discouragements "I had the good fortune to meet Sarah Orne Jewett, who had read all of my early stories and had very clear and definite opinions about them and about where my work fell short. She said, 'Write it as it is, don't try to make it like this or that. You can't do it in anybody else's way—you will have to make a way of your own. If the way happens to be new, don't let it frighten you. Don't try to write the kind of short story that this or that magazine wants—write the truth, and let them take it or leave it'" (in Bernice Slote, ed., *The Kingdom of Art: Willa Cather's First Principles and Critical Statements, 1893–1896* [Lincoln: Univ. of Nebraska Press, 1966], p. 449).

38. Willa Cather, *Not Under Forty* (New York: Alfred A. Knopf, 1936), p. 89. In a volume of Emerson's essays Jewett underlined this statement: "I value qualities more and magnitudes less."

39. Cary, *Letters*, p. 140; 3 May [1901].

40. Fields, *Letters*, p. 249; 13 Dec. [1908].

41. Fields, *Letters*, p. 79; [ca. Dec. 1900].

42. Cary, *Letters*, p. 91, to Andress S. Floyd, 22 Nov. 1894; Fields, *Letters*, p. 113, to A. O. Huntington, 15 Apr. 1895; Cary, *Letters*, p. 141, n. 1, to Annie Fields, spring 1901.

43. Jewett, "Looking Back on Girlhood," p. 5. Charles Miner Thompson, "The Art of Miss Jewett," *Atlantic Monthly*, 94 (Oct. 1904), 497: "I always think of her as one who, hearing New England accused of being a bleak land without beauty, passes confidently over the snow, and by the gray rock, and past the dark fir trees, to a southern bank, and there, brushing away the decayed leaves, triumphantly shows to the fault-finder a spray of the trailing arbutus."

44. Samuel T. Pickard, *Life and Letters of John Greenleaf Whittier* (Boston: Houghton Mifflin, 1895), II, 718.

45. Fields, *Letters*, pp. 196–97; to Charles Miner Thompson, 12 Oct. 1904.

46. Fields, p. 249; 13 Dec. [1908]. See also the preface to Willa Cather, *Alexander's Bridge* (Boston: Houghton Mifflin, 1922), p. vii.

47. Cather, *Not Under Forty*, p. 88.

48. Fields, *Letters*, p. 248; 13 Dec. [1908].

49. Cary, *Letters*, p. 29.

50. Fields, *Letters*, p. 118; to Rose Lamb, Monday, 11 [May] 1896. She commonly alluded to her finest novel as "my Pointed firs sketches."

51. Cary, *Letters*, pp. 119–20, 129; 11 June [1899] and [Nov.–Dec., 1899].

52. Jewett, preface to *Deephaven*, pp. 3, 6.

53. Dr. Ferris in *A Country Doctor* (Boston: Houghton Mifflin, 1884), pp. 99–100.

54. John Paul Eakin, "Sarah Orne Jewett and the Meaning of Country Life," *American Literature*, 38 (Jan. 1967), 509; letter to Annie Fields, n.d., in the Sarah Orne Jewett Collection, Houghton Library, Harvard.

55. Fields, *Letters*, pp. 82–83.

56. Fields, *Letters*, p. 249, 13 Dec. [1908].

57. Mark A. DeWolfe Howe, "Sarah Orne Jewett," *Atlantic Monthly*, 104 (Aug. 1909), 281.

58. Richard Cary, "Miss Jewett and Madame Blanc," *Colby Library Quarterly*, 7 (1967), 471.

Sarah Orne Jewett's Critical Theory: Notes toward a Feminine Literary Mode

Josephine Donovan*

Two central problems of the scholarship on Sarah Orne Jewett have been whether she is a realist and how to explain the "plotless" structure of her short stories and such longer works as *Deephaven* and *The Country of the Pointed Firs*. An examination of Jewett's critical theory sheds considerable light on these problems, even though Jewett never formally articulated her critical ideas; they are found scattered through her correspondence, mainly in the form of advice to such younger writers as Willa Cather, John Thaxter, and Andress S. Floyd. Comments she made on works she was reading and on her own work appear primarily in letters to Annie Adams Fields. Early letters to editors and early diary notations, still unpublished, are further sources of her critical theory.[1]

One of the central elements in Jewett's literary credo was that the artist should transmit reality with as little interference and doctoring up as possible. This idea, at the heart of the realist doctrine of *mimesis*, Jewett apparently learned from her father. On numerous occasions when giving counsel to other writers she stated: "My dear father used to say to me very often, 'Tell things *just as they are!*' . . . The great messages and discoveries of literature come to us, they *write us*, and we do not control them in a certain sense."[2] One of two aphorisms of Flaubert she had tacked up on her secretary read: "Écrire la vie ordinaire comme on écrit l'histoire."[3] The artist's job is to "write" ordinary life as if writing history. Similar to her father's injunction the implication in Flaubert's statement is that the writer neutrally or objectively recounts events with minimal comment, arrangement, or literary artifice.

Jewett reacted strongly against any writing that seemed to be pretentiously "arty"—that is, that revealed a self-conscious effort on the part of the author to be "literary," to use established literary devices and forms. She once convicted Nathaniel Hawthorne of just this failing in his *American Notebooks* (1868), deploring the author's "conscious effort after material." The sketches, she said, "lack any reality or imagination, rootless little things that could never open seed in their turn . . . so 'delicate' in their fancy as to be far-fetched and oddly feeble and sophomorish" (Fields, *Letters*, 73).

By contrast Jewett prefers Charles W. Brewster's *Rambles About Portsmouth* (first series, 1859; second series, 1869), a completely unliterary collection of sketches which she finds "a mine of wealth." As an example she notes a "description of the marketwomen coming down the river,—their quaintness and picturesqueness at once seems to be so

*This essay was written especially for this volume and is included here by permission of the author.

great, and the mere hints of description so full of flavor, that it all gave me much keener pleasure than anything I found in the other much more famous book [by Hawthorne]." She recognizes that such a view is "high literary treason" but predicts that Brewster's work will outlive Hawthorne's because of the veracity of its realism. "Such genuine books always live, they get filled so full of life" (Fields, *Letters*, 72). The artist must not only transmit reality as faithfully as possible, but the images that are selected must "in their turn" "open seed." This thesis, issued in 1890, became during the 1890s Jewett's central artistic theory.

On various occasions Jewett enjoined younger writers against self-consciously following established literary norms. She told John Thaxter not to "write a 'story' but just *tell the thing!*" (Cary, *Letters*, 120). In other words, the artist should try to eliminate the artificial construct, "story," from mind in order to directly transmit the reality in question. Implicit in this thesis is the idea that form follows function (that is, content and purpose), rather than the other way around.

Similar counsel to that given Thaxter was offered to Willa Cather. In a newspaper interview published in 1913 after Jewett's death Cather recalled that Jewett had advised, "Don't try to write the kind of short story that this or that magazine wants—write the truth, and let them take it or leave it": "Write it as it is, don't try to make it like this or that. You can't do it in anybody else's way—you will have to make a way of your own. If the way happens to be new, don't let that frighten you."[4] "Story-writing," Jewett once noted, "is always experimental . . . and that *something which does itself* is the vitality of it" (Fields, *Letters*, 118).

Jewett, therefore, proposes a theory of the artist as one who is a relatively passive transmitter of "things as they are," who ideally imposes as little artifice as possible upon the material, and who does not consciously follow literary precedents but evolves formal devices appropriate to her own purpose.

Such a theory may be particularly congenial to the female talent. In her second preface to *Pilgrimage* (1938) Dorothy Richardson, a pioneer of literary modernism (and in particular of the anti-authorial "stream of consciousness" technique), explained that she had proposed in her fiction to produce "a feminine equivalent of the current masculine realism." What she particularly disliked in the masculine style, according to Leon Edel, was the presence of the male author intruding upon the subject matter: "Bang, bang, bang," she wrote, "on they go, these men's books, like an L. C. C. tram, yet unable to make you forget them, the authors, for a moment." She also deplored what she saw as the "self-satisfied, complacent, know-all condescendingness" of the masculine narrator in Conrad and James.[5]

Margaret Fuller suggested decades earlier that women are more inclined toward the kind of process Jewett advocates than toward the rigidly controlling authorial process that Richardson condemns in "masculine realism." "[Woman] excels . . . in . . . a simple breathing out of what she receives, that has the singleness of life, rather than the selecting and energizing of art."[6]

A considerable body of contemporary theory has recently developed that suggests that women's historical experience may have inclined them toward "a mode of thinking" that is, as Carol Gilligan recently put it, "contextual and inductive rather than formal and abstract."[7] Kathryn Allen Rabuzzi, in *The Sacred and the Feminine: Towards a Theology of Housework* (1982), has proposed that out of their housebound experience women have developed a "mode of being" that is quite different from the masculine mode of questing, conquering, and imposing one's will. The feminine mode is one of waiting; it involves a kind of passive responsiveness to the environment: "Responding in this way . . . is markedly different from imposing your own will. . . . The passivity so induced is that of a light object thrown into the water; it is not the object that determines its direction, but the movement of the water.[8] Such a response contrasts to the "assertive striving more typical of the masculine temporal mode, questing."[9]

Rabuzzi suggests that traditional literary modes have been evolved to convey the typical masculine activity of the quest. Yet, "both history and story, traditionally so full of quests as to be virtually synonymous with them, may not be formally appropriate to express traditional feminine experience. In fact, both forms may so consistently have obscured women's experiences in the waiting mode as to have rendered women largely invisible not just to men, but to themselves.[10] Jewett fashioned a formal structure that expresses the kind of serendipitously passive mode that Rabuzzi sees as characteristic of the feminine experience. Jewett's critical theory—both her notion of the passive artist and her concept of "imaginative realism"—provided the rationale for the formal structure she developed in her fiction.

Jewett did not, of course, view the artist as a completely passive machine that simply records surrounding reality. Her injunctions about the noninterfering artist must be seen as relative statements; the artist must be comparatively restrained in the transposition of the material. But Jewett was aware that the material is filtered through a selecting mind. Indeed, a second major component of her critical theory is that the artist must develop a point of view, an authentic vision, a clear sustaining design or telos.

One of the more pointed criticisms that Jewett made in this regard was of Harriet Beecher Stowe's novel *The Pearl of Orr's Island* (1862), a work that she had much admired in her youth.[11] As an adult, however, she found the work lacked integrity, an overall design. "Alas, that she could n't finish it in the same noble key of simplicity and harmony. . . . [The result is] a divine touch here and there in an incomplete piece of work" (Fields, *Letters*, 47). Here Jewett is expressing an Aristotelian precept, that of *dianoia*, or unity of thought: a work of art must evince a consistency, an underlying unity.[12] A work like the *Pearl*, which Stowe had composed on and off over a period of a decade, provides a profusion of somewhat haphazardly related events that are not properly integrated.

Jewett believed that the author must develop a personal point of view, an authentic perspective through which the material is selected and according to which it is weighed and arranged. "The trouble with most realism," Jewett complained in an 1890 letter to Thomas Bailey Aldrich, "is that it is n't seen from any point of view at all, and so its shadows fall in every direction and it fails of being art" (Fields, *Letters*, 79). Jewett explicitly rejected the naturalist theory offered by Emile Zola, who carried the notion of artistic objectivity much further than Jewett found acceptable. In *Le Roman expérimental* (1880) Zola urged an analogy between the writer and the scientist; each retains objective neutrality toward his or her "experimental" matter. Jewett rejected the lack of moral perspective that such a thesis seemed to entail. Speaking with enthusiasm in 1889 of Thackeray's *Vanity Fair* (one of her favorite works) Jewett noted how "full [it is] of splendid scorn for meanness and wickedness, which the Zola school seems to lack" (Fields, *Letters*, 55–56). Many of Jewett's early works are, indeed, imbued with strong moral messages, despite her early self-remonstrance to follow Charles Lamb's advice not to be too preachy. In her 1872 diary she resolved to confine herself to "silent scripture" in future work.[13]

It was not, however, just a moral perspective, but a personal viewpoint gleaned from experience that she believed a writer must bring to the material. In much-cited counsel she told the novice Willa Cather that she must first see the "world" before she could describe the "parish."[14] In 1908 she urged Cather to step back in order to develop perspective on her material. "You don't see [it] yet quite enough from the outside,—you stand right in the middle . . . without having the standpoint of the looker-on . . ." (Fields, *Letters*, 248). It takes time for such a process to occur: "The thing that teases the mind over and over for years, and at last gets itself put down rightly on paper—whether little or great, it belongs to Literature."[15]

Yet the process is essentially one that happens to the artist, rather than the artist consciously arranging it:

> Good heavens! What a wonderful kind of chemistry it is that evolves all the details of a story and writes them presently in one flash of time! For two weeks I have been noticing a certain string of things and having hints of character, etc., and day before yesterday the plan of the story comes into my mind, and in half an hour I have put all the little words and ways into their places and can read it off to myself like print. Who does it? For I grow more and more sure that I don't! (Fields, *Letters*, 51–52)

The process is nevertheless personal, and the product is imbued with the personality of the creator: "It is, after all, Miss Thackeray herself in *Old Kensington* who gives the book its charm" (Cary, *Letters*, 52)[16]. And, she concluded in advice given to Rose Lamb: "one must have one's own method: it is the personal contribution that makes true value in any form of art or work of any sort" (Fields, *Letters*, 118).

The reality that Jewett was interested in was, of course, life "in its *everyday* aspects" (Cary, *Letters*, 51–52). "A dull little village," she found, "is just the place to find the real drama of life."[17] But the reason such commonplace material had interest was because there she found intuitions of a transcendent order.[18] In this theoretical perception, a third major aspect of her theory, she came close to symbolist literary poetics.

Shortly before she published her masterwork, *The Country of the Pointed Firs* (1896), Jewett used the phrase "imaginative realism" to explain her artistic ideal to another aspiring writer, Andress S. Floyd (Cary, *Letters*, 91). Although she does not elaborate in the letter, written in 1894, it is clear from other comments what the concept means. In her 1871 diary Jewett wrote:

> Father said this one day "A story should be managed so that it should *suggest* interesting things to the *reader* instead of the author's doing all the thinking for him, and setting it before him in black and white. The best compliment is for the reader to say 'Why didn't he put in "this" or "that." ' "[19]

The implications of this statement lead away from realist doctrine and point in the direction of symbolism, especially as it developed in late nineteenth-century France. Symbolist poet Stéphane Mallarmé, for example, urged that the poet's job was to "suggest" rather than to "name."[20] The other statement of Flaubert's that Jewett had before her when she wrote offered counsel similar to her father's. "Ce n'est pas de faire rire, ni de faire pleurer, ni de vous mettre à fureur, mais d'agir à la façon de la nature, c'est à dire de faire rêver" (Fields, *Letters*, 165)[21]. The writer's job is to make one dream; that is, to make one aware of another realm, a transcendent realm by means of images drawn from earthly, everyday reality. This is what Jewett meant by "imaginative realism."

Jewett's symbolist inclinations may have been encouraged by her readings in Emmanuel Swedenborg, in particular his theosophical doctrine of correspondences. This theory, so fundamental to symbolist poetics,[22] claimed a correlation between the "microcosm" and the "macrocosm;" that is, between this world "here below" and a realm beyond. Jewett had been introduced to Swedenborgianism by a youthful mentor, Theophilus Parsons, a Harvard professor. She once stated that she felt "a sense of it under everything else" (Fields, *Letters*, 21–22).

Especially in her later work Jewett was interested in depicting intuitions of a realm beyond this, but she never erred in the direction of a didactic Swedenborgianism (as did Elizabeth Stuart Phelps in *Beyond the Gates* [1883] and *The Gates Between* [1886]). The narrative of Captain Littlepage in *The Country of the Pointed Firs* about the Arctic limbo with its "fog-shaped" shades is a good example of the kind of intimations Jewett sought. The land "between this world and the next" described in the narrative is at such a remove, and the narrators' reliability so dubious, that its reality remains problematic. Thus, Jewett allows for only a suggestion of things beyond.

When her friend poet Celia Thaxter died, Jewett wondered "where imagination stops and consciousness of the unseen begins, who can settle that even to one's self?" (Fields, *Letters*, 110–11). It was not a literal "heaven" that concerned her, but the hints of such transcendence that are intuited within this world—and the moral effects that such intuitions have upon people. She once noted that she found "something transfiguring in the best of friendship" (Fields, *Letters*, 126). Her real concern was with this kind of transcendence, and in this sense she was more of a humanist than a symbolist, for she remained primarily concerned with the moral dimension of human experiences of the transcendent.

Yet Jewett wished to go beyond the limits of realism. In an early comment on Jane Austen's meticulous attention to detail Jewett complained, "all the reasoning is done for you and all the thinking. . . . It seems to me like hearing somebody talk on and on and on, while you have no part in the conversation and merely listen" (Cary, *Letters*, 21). Later, in complimenting her friend Sarah Wyman Whitman on her interpretation of "Martha's Lady" (1897), Jewett noted, "You bring something to the reading of a story that [it] would go very lame without. . . . It is," she asserted, "those unwritable things that the story holds in its heart, if it has any, that make the true soul of it, and these must be understood, and yet how many a story goes lame for lack of that understanding" (Fields, *Letters*, 112). Jewett, therefore, extended her conception of authorial restraint to the point where she allowed the reader a creative role in the process. The author should not attempt to exert complete control over the reader's thoughts, but rather attempt to communicate images that "open seed" in the reader's mind, that allow the reader to intuit meanings beyond the literal. Jewett's theory thus provides for the feminine realism that Richardson envisaged—one in which the author is a relatively passive transmitter who delegates, as it were, some of her authority and control to the reader.

Jewett's "plotless" structure is appropriate to this purpose. It is an essentially feminine literary mode expressing a contextual, inductive sensitivity, one that "gives in" to the events in question, rather than imposing upon them an artificial, prefabricated "plot."

Jewett was not unaware, however, of the dangers of an inductive, associative and relatively undirected narrative style. In "Miss Debby's

Neighbors" (1883) she offers a complaint that the narrator's method "of going around Robin Hood's barn between the beginning of her story and its end can hardly be followed at all. . . ."[23] An earlier American woman writer, Caroline Kirkland, once apologized for having used a similarly feminine, gossipy style in A New Home—Who'll Follow? (1839): "This going back to take up dropped stitches, is not the orthodox way of telling one's story; and if I thought I could do any better, I would certainly go back and begin at the very beginning; but I feel conscious that the truly feminine sin of talking 'about it and about it,' the unconquerable partiality for wandering wordiness would cleave to me still. . . ."[24] At its worst a "feminine" style of undirected meandering lacks the controlling design—the unity of thought—necessary to significant art, as Jewett herself noted. But this is not the case with Kirkland's work, despite her fears. Nor is it the case with Jewett's.

As a young writer Jewett worried about her tendency toward plotlessness. In an early letter to her editor, Horace Scudder, she noted,

> I don't believe I could write a long story. . . . In the first place, I have no dramatic talent. The story would have no plot. I should have to fill it out with descriptions of character and meditations. It seems to me I can furnish the theatre, and show you the actors, and the scenery, and the audience, but there never is any play! I could write you entertaining letters perhaps, from some desirable house where I was in most charming company, but I couldn't make a story about it. (Cary, Letters, 29).

By the end of her career, as indicated in her advice to John Thaxter, Jewett had come to the conclusion, however, that the compulsion to "make a story" like stories done in the past interferred with the genuine artistic process. By then she knew that the form she had developed did not require a conventional plot. This was because the conventional plot followed the typical masculine activity of questing. As Rabuzzi notes, "it is plot that strongly militates against story as an appropriate vehicle for traditional women's experience." "By and large," she urges, "most women have known a nonstoried existence. . . ." Jewett needed a form appropriate to that existence.[25]

Rabuzzi's basic contention is that the traditional female experience, that of being confined to the domestic sphere and charged with the repetitive labor of housework, created a sense of time that was markedly different than the characteristically Western (and masculine) linear, historical time of the quest—the basis for traditional "story." Rather, the housewife's time was closer to the sacred time of myth, what Mircea Eliade called "illo tempore," or Henri Bergson, "la durée." It is the "timeless" time of cyclic ritual, the time of the "eternal return" (Eliade). The woman's experience appears, therefore, static, and in a mode of waiting. It is not progressive, or oriented toward events happening sequentially or climactically, as in the traditional masculine story plot. The feminine experience most essentially becomes that of the sacredness of space, of time frozen into stasis.[26]

If we consider Jewett's characteristic plot patterns we will see that they are reflective of such an experience: they are designed to reveal the sacredness that is inherent in the everyday, and they express a static, or, at most, a cyclical sense of movement. An early story, "Beyond the Toll-Gate," which appears in *Play Days* (1878), clearly establishes this pattern: a young girl ventures out of her house, beyond her domestic confines only to discover two kindly older women who treat her with beneficence; she returns home then with this knowledge. It is a cyclical plot in which the central figure returns home, having learned of the existence of benign female space.

One of the primary plot patterns in Jewett's works is that of a relatively sophisticated urban woman, usually a Jewett persona, traveling to the country where she experiences an epiphany—where she learns something—before returning to her urban home. The rural realm came to symbolize for Jewett the world of the traditional woman, a world of timeless ritual, of time frozen into space. In Jewett's historical circumstances it was a world of the mothers' generation, for, as I explore in *New England Local Color Literature*,[27] the daughters' generation—of which Jewett was a member—in the latter part of the nineteenth century was moving away from the traditional realm. Jewett herself, as a professional woman anchored at least part of the year in the sophisticated Boston circle of Annie Fields, necessarily came to feel a certain distance from the rural matriarchal world, but it remained the place where she experienced spiritual regeneration, and it remained the spiritual fount of her art.

This typical Jewett plot pattern was established in her earliest work. *Deephaven* (1877) is structured upon the visit of two urban girls to a coastal town in Maine one summer. An early sketch included in that work, "My Lady Brandon and the Widow Jim" (probably written in 1873) establishes the archetypal structure that Jewett was to use over and over. The story opens with a meandering meditation by the I-narrator (Helen Denis—a Jewett persona) about her friend, Kate Lancaster; her great-aunt, Miss Brandon; and about "gentlewomen of the old school."[28] None of this is irrelevant to the story that follows or to *Deephaven*, if one considers that the work is about the girls' maturation. The various people they meet serve as examples of figures whom life has harrowed. From these exempla the girls gain wisdom; they achieve a measure of spiritual growth. In this story they meet a Mrs. Patton, "the Widow Jim," who in the divagitating fashion of feminine oral history tells her story. The story ends with the revelation by another neighbor, Mrs. Dockum, that Mrs. Patton had been the victim of wife abuse. The girls also discover that country people are more in tune with the transcendent realm than urban (this is especially developed in the sketch, "Cunner-Fishing"), and that single nature-women, such as Mrs. Bonny, are often towers of spiritual strength. These ideas became central to Jewett's picture of the rural world.

Another work that follows a plot structure similar to *Deephaven* is "A Bit of Shore Life" (1879) in which a Jewett persona journeys "up-country" where she encounters again various exempla from whom she gains wisdom before returning home. Once again the main people she meets are women. Similarly, in "An Autumn Holiday" (1881) a young woman wanders through the fields, meandering in her journey as the narrative meanders to describe the rural setting in some detail. Finally, she reaches an isolated home where two sisters sit spinning. They begin reminiscing—again a kind of gossipy oral history commences—finally focusing on the story of the addled transvestite sea captain. While the story is highly comic, as many of Jewett's are, there is nevertheless a moral message implied—that of wonder at human diversity—and a piece of wisdom gleaned—that of the tenuous nature of gender identity, an early Jewett concern.

A similar structure obtains in "The Courting of Sister Wisby" (1887) where the urban narrator-persona, again wandering in the country, encounters Mrs. Goodsoe, an herbalist out gathering "mulleins." A lengthy conversation ensues in which the two women show themselves to be of different generations. Mrs. Goodsoe is of the older matriarchal generation: she sustains the women's culture of herb-medicine that she learned from her mother. She is opposed to technological progress and to rapid transportation systems. People should remain rooted in their home realms. Hers is the voice of the traditional woman, where the younger urban woman argues that some modern advances, such as opportunities for travel, may be to the good. The story about Sister Wisby is finally told, another in the genre of comic humanism, and another that depicts a powerful country woman.

In some early pieces Jewett did not even bother with the rudiments of plot seen in these stories. "An October Ride" (1881) and "A Winter Drive" (1881) involve excursions by the woman narrator into nature where she experiences meditational epiphanies, but where nothing per se happens—again a static or cyclical pattern. Similarly, "The Landscape Chamber" (1887) describes the travels of a young horsewoman and the dismal exempla she encounters on her circular journey. In "The King of Folly Island" (1888) the persona is a man, but the plot structure is the same.

The Country of the Pointed Firs (1896) relies on an homologous structure. The Jewett persona comes to the country from the city seeking, it appears, spiritual regeneration and artistic inspiration. In the course of her stay she discovers a land of timeless rituals, a land that seems to have escaped the processes of historical progress: it seems a place where time has frozen into space. The farther up country one goes the closer one comes to a transcendent realm: indeed, the land between the living and the dead that is described in Littlepage's story is located in the Arctic.

Mrs. Todd, the central personnage, is, like Mrs. Goodsoe, a matriarch rooted in her world, the transmitter of the matrilineal traditions of herbal lore. The people the narrator meets or whom she learns about, such as Joanna, serve as exempla of diverse human experience and provide her with moral wisdom—sometimes about the human condition, often more specifically about women's situation. Here, as throughout Jewett's works, the narrator-persona remains a kind of passive recorder, rather than an active participant in events—though in *Pointed Firs* she evinces a strong desire to do so and briefly participates in the ceremonials at the Bowden family reunion. Nevertheless, she is fundamentally cut off from this world, and must return in the end to her urban, modern world.

The layers of narrative in these Jewett works suggests the remove the modern (late nineteenth-century) woman is from the transcending matriarchal realm. The meandering series of conversations serve the symbolic purpose of illustrating the psychological distance the urban woman is from the gynocentric world of the traditional woman—the mother—and of the sacred female space that is her world.

In "The Foreigner" (1900), for example, a late sequel to *Pointed Firs*, the story is structured similarly to the Joanna episode in the earlier work: Mrs. Todd, the narrator, and a visitor are sitting around a Franklin stove gossiping. Gradually in the process of reminiscing the central story, told by Mrs. Todd, emerges. It concerns a moment in which the transcendent literally erupts into the everyday: "the foreigner's" dead mother appears at her daughter's death-bed to carry her "home." This was probably Jewett's most literal depiction of a transcendent, salvific mother. It remains at a considerable remove from the everyday, urban, modern world of the narrator, buried, as it is, within layers of narrative.

Several stories involve cyclical transits within the rural world. "A Late Supper" (1878), a humorous early story, entails an inadvertent trip taken by Catherine Spring. When unexpected guests arrive for dinner she runs to a neighbor's farm for cream. On the way back her way is blocked by a train. As she steps aboard to cross over, the train starts up. She must travel to the next stop and back before she can return home for supper. On the way, however, she encounters some women who provide her with a means out of financial difficulties she had been experiencing. Thus, the plot concerns a housebound woman whose circular journey serendipitously results in a change of fortune; it is a stroke of the miraculous in the everyday.

Other stories that follow a similarly eventless cyclical pattern include "The Hiltons' Holiday" (1893), "The Flight of Betsey Lane" (1893), and "The Guests of Mrs. Timms" (1894). Betsey Lane travels all the way to Philadelphia in her adventure, but she returns home to her community in the end. Nothing has really changed, except that like other Jewett travelers her moral horizons have been broadened.

One of the most static of Jewett's stories is one of her most brilliant: "Miss Tempy's Watchers" (1888). The entire story takes place indoors one evening, in the home of a dead woman. It consists in the conversation of two woman in attendance at the wake. Through the conversation the women achieve spiritual growth and experience a connection with the transcendent through the effect of Tempy's spirit (not her literal spirit in the sense of a ghost, but the spirit of charity in which she lived her life).

Occasionally a character who is not a Jewett persona comes to the rural world from the city. In this pattern the rural world remains the emotional and spiritual centrum. The structure is evident, comically, in "Miss Esther's Guest" (1893), and more seriously in "A White Heron" (1886) and "Martha's Lady" (1897). "A White Heron" involves the repudiation of an urban intruder, so that the rural world remains intact. The only events in the story are, again, a matter of moral growth. The young girl learns more about her rural environment in her ascent up the tree, and it is that knowledge that provides her with the resolve to protect the life of the white heron that the ornithologist seeks to kill. The story thus is a static one of the preservation of a female sanctuary. As a reverse Cinderella story "A White Heron" connects imagistically to the Grimm version of the fairy tale, for, in the Cinderella story a white bird emerges from the grave of the girl's mother; in "A White Heron" the white bird similarly comes to symbolize the world of the mothers.[29]

"Martha's Lady" is another static story that takes place in a waiting mode. After forty years an urban woman, to whom a rural servant woman has been devotedly attached, returns "home" to Martha. The reunion of the women constitutes the story's only event, but it too is a kind of revelation of the sacred; it reveals the matriarchal transcendence that emerges out of the female experience of patience and resignation—what Rabuzzi calls the traditional woman's "*via negativa.*"[30]

Jewett's "imaginative realism" thus came close to symbolism in that it attempted to suggest a world beyond the literal world of the realists, but it remained a moral humanism in that it retained roots in the everyday world of human experience. The plot structure that she developed was uniquely appropriate for the transmission of her vision. It entailed cyclical journeys of spiritual growth; in her most significant works, these moral and sometimes physical journeys are undertaken by alienated urban "daughters" seeking to reconnect with and preserve the matriarchal world of traditional rural "mothers," a realm of timeless ritual. It was an escape from the masculine time of history into transcending feminine space.

Notes

1. This article focuses on those aspects of Jewett's theory that are relevant to interpretive problems. A more extensive discussion of her critical theory may be found in Josephine Donovan, *Sarah Orne Jewett* (New York: Ungar, 1980), chap. 6, "Criticism and Influence," and in Donovan, *New England Local Color Literature: A Women's Tradition* (New York: Ungar, 1983), chap. 7. See also Richard Cary, "Jewett on Writing Short Shories," *Colby Library Quarterly*, 6 (1964), 425–40, and "Jewett's Literary Canons," *Colby Library Quarterly*, 7 (1965), 82–87.

2. Richard Cary, ed., *Sarah Orne Jewett Letters* (Waterville: Colby College Press, 1967), p. 52; hereafter cited in the text.

3. Annie Fields, ed., *Letters of Sarah Orne Jewett* (Boston: Houghton Mifflin, 1911), p. 165; hereafter cited in the text.

4. Willa Cather, "Willa Cather Talks of Work," *Philadelphia Record*, 9 Aug. 1913; rpt. in *The Kingdom of Art: Willa Cather's First Principles and Critical Statements, 1893–1896*, ed. Bernice Slote (Lincoln: Univ. of Nebraska, 1966), p. 449.

5. The Richardson comments are cited in Leon Edel, *The Psychological Novel, 1900–1950* (London: Rupert Hart-Davis, 1955), p. 74.

6. Margaret Fuller, *Woman in the Nineteenth Century* (New York: Norton, 1971), p. 115.

7. Carol Gilligan, "Woman's Place in Man's Life Cycle," *Harvard Educational Review*, 49, No. 4 (1979), 442. In her *In A Different Voice: Psychological Theory and Women's Development* (Cambridge: Harvard Univ. Press, 1982), p. 19, Gilligan changed the term "inductive" to "narrative." In a recent article, "Maternal Thinking," *Feminist Studies*, 6 (1980), 342–67, Sara Ruddick has contrasted maternal thinking with scientific (masculine) thought patterns; the former expresses respect and "humility" before the contextual environment, while the latter impose control. A similar contrast is drawn by Evelyn Fox Keller in an article, "Feminism and Science," *Signs*, 7 (1982), 589–602. Keller cites a woman scientist's attitude as an example of a feminine mode; that scientist urges "letting the material speak to you" rather than "imposing" "an answer" upon it (p. 599). Contemporary psychologists have also detected a feminine tendency to "see" and respect the context of an event, rather than lifting the phenomenon out of context and rearranging it according to a prior paradigm (Joanna Rohrbach, *Women, Psychology's Puzzle* [New York: Basic, 1979], p. 71). All of these studies tend to suggest a feminine *episteme* that respects the environmental context, that hesitates before wrenching and reshaping that environment. Such a sensitivity seems to be present in Jewett's theory of the artist who does little to reshape reality. For a further discussion of this direction in modern feminist thought see my forthcoming *A History of Feminist Theory*, chap. 7.

8. Kathryn Allen Rabuzzi, *The Sacred and the Feminine: Towards A Theology of Housework* (New York: Seabury, 1982), p. 153.

9. Rabuzzi, p. 153.

10. Rabuzzi, p. 153.

11. Jewett vascillated about this novel. In a later unpublished letter she recanted her criticism, saying: "I take back [my belief] that the last half of the book was not so good. . . . I still think that she wrote it, most of it at her very best height . . ."

(Sarah Orne Jewett to Annie Adams Fields, n.d., Houghton MS bMS 1743.1 [117] 14; cited by permission of the Houghton Library, Harvard University).

12. On other Aristotelian precepts in Jewett's criticism see Donovan, *Sarah Orne Jewett*, pp. 123–26.

13. Manuscript diary 1871–79, entry for 13 July 1872, Houghton MS Am 1743.1 (341); cited by permission of the Houghton Library, Harvard University.

14. This advice is cited variously by Cather herself. See her 1922 preface to *Alexander's Bridge* and also her essay, "Miss Jewett," in *Not Under Forty*, (New York: Knopf, 1953), p. 88.

15. As cited in Cather's 1925 preface to *The Best Short Stories of Sarah Orne Jewett*.

16. Jewett is citing an unnamed literary critic in her comment on Thackeray.

17. LaSalle Corbell Pickett, *Across My Path: Memories of People I Have Known* (New York: Brentano's, 1916), p. 145.

18. While Jewett admired Wordsworth and shared many of his critical ideas— especially the essentially democratic ideal of poetry found in the preface to the second edition of *Lyrical Ballads* (see Donovan, *Sarah Orne Jewett*, pp. 133–34), her concept of nature and of the rural world as a source of spiritual knowledge is different from his. A thorough comparison of the two perceptions would require another article; suffice to note here that Wordsworth's "intimations of immorality" are rooted within the poet's soul, where for Jewett such intimations come from beyond the self. Wordsworth and the romantics pose a heroically egocentric artist that contrasts quite markedly with Jewett's view. For a further discussion of Jewett's ideas about transcendence, see Josephine Donovan, "A Woman's Vision of Transcendence: A New Interpretation of the Works of Sarah Orne Jewett," *Massachusetts Review*, 21, No. 2 (1980), 365–80.

19. Manuscript diary 1871–79, Houghton MS Am 1743.1 (341), inside front cover. Cited by permission of the Houghton Library, Harvard University.

20. The complete phrase is: "*Nommer* un objet, c'est supprimer . . . le suggérer, voilà le rêve" (Mallarmé, *Oeuvres Complètes* [Paris: Pléiade, 1945], p. 869).

21. The version given here is more complete than Jewett's; it comes from F. O. Matthiessen, *Sarah Orne Jewett* (Boston: Houghton Mifflin, 1929), p. 67.

22. See William York Tindall, *The Literary Symbol* (Bloomington: Indiana Univ. Press, 1955), pp. 53 ff.

23. Jewett, "Miss Debby's Neighbors," *The Mate of the Daylight, and Friends Ashore* (Boston: Houghton Mifflin, 1884), p. 191.

24. Caroline Kirkland [Mrs. Mary Clavers], *A New Home—Who'll Follow? Or, Glimpses of Western Life* (1839; rpt. New York: Garrett Press, 1969), p. 140.

25. Rabuzzi, pp. 163, 173.

26. See especially Rabuzzi, pp. 143–51. I have paraphrased and condensed her thesis somewhat, but I trust I have remained faithful to it. Another recent article that draws somewhat similar distinctions is Julia Kristera, "Women's Time," *Signs*, 7, No. 1 (1981), 13–35.

The transformation of time into space is another formal and thematic concern of the modernists that seems to express a fundamentally feminine sensibility. On this direction see Joseph Frank, "Spatial Form in Modern Literature," *Sewanee Review*, 13, No. 2 (Apr.–June 1945), 221–40; No. 3 (July–Sept. 1945), 433–56, and No. 4 (Oct.–Dec. 1945), 643–61, and Nathan A. Scott, Jr., *The Broken Center, Studies in the Theological Horizon of Modern Literature* (New Haven: Yale Univ. Press, 1966), chap. 2, "Mimesis and Time in Modern Literature."

Probably their "feminine" tendencies are due to the fact that the modernists were rebelling against a rigidly patriarchal literary tradition. In any event, Jewett anticipated some of their directions.

27. See especially Donovan, *New England Local Color Literature*, pp. 99–138.

28. Jewett, *Deephaven and Other Stories*, ed. Richard Cary (New Haven: College & University Press, 1966), p. 56.

29. This thesis is developed more extensively in Donovan, *New England Local Color Literature*, pp. 107–10.

30. Rabuzzi, p. 181.

Two Lost Stories by Sarah Orne Jewett: "A Player Queen" and "Three Friends"

Philip B. Eppard*

Our knowledge of the extent of Sarah Orne Jewett's publishing activities is still incomplete. American short story writers in the late nineteenth century had an extremely large number of outlets for the products of their pens. Although Jewett naturally favored the high prestige monthlies such as the *Atlantic* and *Harper's,* she was clearly not above submitting her work to lesser publications. Here are two such stories, "A Player Queen" and "Three Friends," recently discovered in obscure and short-lived periodicals. Although the stories are not major works, they are not without some interest for the ways in which they show Jewett handling certain familiar themes in her fiction.

Of these two stories, "A Player Queen" is the more important and the more interesting because in it Jewett attempted to portray a bit of the life of the theater. The evidence which can be gleaned from her letters suggests that she labored for quite a while on the story.[1] Jewett mentioned the story in a letter to Annie Fields which probably dates from late in 1887: "And a story which has been lagging a good while is beginning to write itself. Its name is 'A Player Queen,' and it hopes to be liked."[2] In attempting to write about theatrical characters, however, Jewett was aware that her subject matter may have been beyond her. She sent the completed story to her friend Thomas Bailey Aldrich, editor of the *Atlantic Monthly,* on 6 November 1887 with the following words of reservation:

> I send you this sketch with many fears that you will think I have tried something quite beyond me. It is the sort of thing that *you* could do beautifully! and perhaps the other S. Jewett would be better fitted than

*This essay was written especially for this volume and is included here by permission of the author.

I.[3] I loved it very much in the beginning and then put it away to cool and now as I have worked over it it seems to have cooled too much.[4]

Having sent this kind of a cover letter with her manuscript Jewett was probably not surprised to receive a tenderly phrased rejection note from Aldrich. " 'The Player Queen' is charming and clever, but I always like to have from you the kind of story which nobody else can tell. This is not quite one of those."[5] Jewett swiftly sent a note of concurrence to Aldrich, saying, "I proudly agree with your decision. *The Player Queen* must come back to be mended in her ways."[6]

It is impossible to tell exactly what mending, if any, was done to the story. Even a story of marginal quality by Sarah Orne Jewett was a very marketable commodity in 1887, and a rejection by her most preferred forum did not cause Jewett to give up on a story in which she had invested much time and energy. It is not known whether the story made the rounds of the editorial offices of the other leading monthlies, but it ultimately appeared in *America*, a new weekly published in Chicago which had debuted on 5 April 1888. Founded by the journalist Slason Thompson, *America* was a general literary and political journal whose primary editorial position was opposition to liberal immigration laws. Its list of contributors included several prominent literary names. The magazine survived only a little over three years, however, and "A Player Queen," published in the issue of 28 July 1888, was Jewett's only contribution.[7]

In one sense "A Player Queen" is a fairly conventional love story involving two pairs of lovers who are actors and actresses. If it were only a love story of the stage, however, it would not be of much greater interest than many other such stories by nameless authors published in the Sunday newspapers of the day. Jewett has made the theatrical love story into a classic confrontation between the city and the country in which the beneficient influences of country life and the simple kindnesses of a country woman awaken the stage performers' sense of themselves and their lives. The plot is simple. Four members of Bill Sharp's Comedy Company have a day off during a run at "one of the smaller Boston theatres." They go off for a ride, their destination being "a first class hotel out beyond Cambridge where the Harvard men bestowed their patronage." They lose their way, however, and after passing through miles of woods and country come upon an old country tavern, once on the main road to Boston but now bypassed and neglected. The proprietor is a typically warmhearted Jewett country woman, Mrs. Fleck. The travelers are made welcome, a dinner is prepared, and they revel in the simple pleasures of the country environment. The result is that the younger pair of lovers, Vicky Dean and Postern, agree to marry. The effect on Jack Sprague is to remind him of his own country origins which he abandoned for the theater, and the story ends with the suggestion that he and Nelly Hall, the "Queen" of the story's title, will some day return to such a setting as husband and wife.

The best scene in the story is perhaps the initial confrontation between the stage players and Mrs. Fleck. When Nelly Hall announces to Mrs. Fleck that "We are strangers in the country," the elderly woman assumes that they are foreigners. Nelly plays along with her, says that they are from Scotland, and identifies herself as Lady Macbeth and Jack Sprague as Mr. Macduff. Mrs. Fleck, who is hard of hearing, refers to Nelly as Miss Mackby and Jack as Mr. Duffy, adding, "I had a cousin who married with a Duffy, but they lived down New Bedford way, somewheres." But the humor is not all at the expense of the poor country woman. In describing the tavern's garden, Jewett says, "There was a smell of herbs in the air—of fresh sage and thyme—because the leading gentleman had walked straight across the herb-bed."

Despite certain charming features, however, Aldrich and Jewett were right to have reservations about the story. Jewett was a cosmopolitan woman, and the world of the theater was not totally terra incognita for her. Still she lacked the kind of intimate knowledge of it which she could bring to a description of rural scenes and characters. The theatrical characters appear rather wooden and artificial. Furthermore, Nelly Hall does not seem to possess the prominence in the story which the title would seem to indicate. The image of the rootless theatrical troupe foregoing the pleasures of champagne and hotel fare and succumbing to the delights of elder wine and homemade cherry pie has a certain pathos, but without fully realized characters it loses some of its force. In the short story "Law Lane," Jewett observes that the great themes of life—"love and prosperity, death and loss and misfortune"—"weave themselves over and over again, never mind whether the ploughman or the wit of the clubs plays the part of hero."[8] "A Player Queen" demonstrates that Jewett was better at telling the story of the "ploughman" than that of the "wit of the clubs."

In "A Player Queen," Jewett was working on what she clearly considered to be an important story. The fact that she submitted it to the *Atlantic* is evidence of the stature she felt or hoped that it deserved. "Three Friends," by comparison, is a much more modest effort. This story was published in *Good Cheer*, which described itself as "A Monthly Paper Devoted to the Interests of Home and Family." It was published in Greenfield, Massachusetts, and edited by Kate Upson Clark from 1882 to 1887. It seems to have passed out of existence in 1888. Mary E. Wilkins contributed a few pieces to *Good Cheer*, but "Three Friends" appears to be Jewett's only contribution.[9] The editor got maximum mileage out of this one contribution, however. It was billed as "A Story in Three Parts," and therefore she was able to feature Jewett on the front page of three issues, from January to March 1886.

The story is narrated in the first person by Elizabeth Prime and revolves around her friendship with Mary Dean and Hannah Fennel. All three are "country girls from different states" living "in the fourth story of a city boarding-house." The narrator and Mary Dean have been close friends for a few years when Hannah Fennel comes to their boardinghouse. After several months, Hannah becomes a welcome member of their circle although there always seems to be an air of mystery about her. She reveals nothing about her past and is often heard crying herself to sleep at night. During the course of an extended summer vacation spent at an abandoned farmhouse adjacent to Elizabeth's homestead, a farm now operated by her brother Tom, the source of Hannah's mystery is revealed. She has rejected a lover who has now tracked her down to her vacation farm. He explains that although she loved him, she refused his proposal of marriage because her own father "was a rascal" and she felt that "it would be a sin to link an honest name to such shame as belonged to hers." Once the two are reunited, however, Hannah is persuaded to relent and marry him. The narrator and Mary Dean are happy for their friend and content to return to their city boardinghouse together.

"Three Friends" is indeed as slight as this brief summary would indicate. The audience it was aimed at seems to have been the adolescent girl who, like the three friends, has left the country for work in the city. Consequently there is a moderate dose of didacticism in the story. In the first part Jewett warns, "Single women who are busy all day in a great city are apt to live very uncomfortable lives,—to have to pay much more than they can afford for very little real comfort or a decent sort of home." The narrator confesses that she and Mary Dean had "fallen into a silly way of living on tea and crackers at one time" nearly ruining their health. Their experience in opening themselves up to Hannah is an object lesson for young women already established in the city, a lesson which Jewett drives home clearly in the story's penultimate paragraph: "There is a great deal we can do for some younger girls whom we have learned to know in the city, who don't understand any better how to take care of themselves and their money than we did at first, and we mean to lend them a helping hand and perhaps start a little friendly society or club among the girls who live in our fashion."

The story's greater interest, however, lies in the picture Jewett draws of female friendship. When Elizabeth Prime describes how she first became friends with Mary Dean, she says, "We felt almost like lovers, we had been so lonesome." Their friendship is described in terms suggestive of Jewett's own friendship with Annie Fields. "We had a pleasant room and a good many books, and somehow we used to feel disappointed when anything called either of us away for an evening, we liked so much to be quiet and to carry out our own plans." At the story's end, Hannah is happily married, but Elizabeth and Mary seem destined for a permanent kind of "Boston marriage." The narrator speculates on forsaking the city for the country some day, but Mary Dean is definitely in her plans.

> Dear Hannah! She did look very happy the day she was married. I don't know whether Mary Dean and I shall ever forsake our life together in our sky-parlor, but I have often thought I should like to go back to the little old Ford house where we spent last summer, and end my days. I told my brother Tom in the last letter I wrote, to be sure and keep it in good repair for Mary Dean and me.

This theme of female friendship is also closely related to the story's function as an instructional device for the country girl who has moved to the city. The formation of close friendships with other young women like that between Elizabeth and Mary is presented as a model defense against the alien urban environment.

In her letter to Thomas Bailey Aldrich acknowledging his adverse judgment on "A Player Queen," Jewett wrote, "I can only say that my head is buzzing full of stories and I am only afraid that there won't be winter enough to write them in."[10] Jewett was clearly in a productive period, and the two stories reprinted for the first time here are reflective of just how productive a writer she was in the 1880s. Although they are not Jewett at her best, it is important to have recovered these stories. They broaden our understanding of Jewett as a professional author and supplement our knowledge of two subjects important in her fiction: the confrontation of urban and rural values and the nature and value of friendships between women.

A PLAYER QUEEN.[11]
By Sarah Orne Jewett.

One hot evening in July three illustrious members of Bill Sharp's Comedy Company were waiting, ready to go on, in the flies of one of the smaller Boston theatres. There was a long scene going forward between Young Postern and Vicky Dean, whose immensely popular song of "Starlight Hannah" was presently to be sung, and encored at least three times, before any other event could take place. The three persons, who played the parts of dramatic father, mother, and deceived husband, were waiting in the flies until the scene between the lovers was over; it was much cooler there than in the green-room, which was more stuffy and tiresome than usual. Nelly Hall, the leading lady, was apt to be dilatory in her preparations, and often had to be summoned impatiently, but to-night she had already been waiting four or five minutes. She had seated herself in a gorgeous gilt chair of state, which was to be used in the next piece as the throne in a burlesque of "Hamlet"; the two young men were crouching on the dusty floor at her side. Jack Sprague, whom his admirers called the most stylish man on the American stage, was absurd enough in his elderly-gentleman makeup; at this short range his high, bald forehead was easily distinguished from his veritable smooth skin.

"What a life it is!" sighed the slender Queen in the gilt chair. "I wish that Billy had put on the "Lady of Lyons" instead of that "Hamlet" nonsense. I don't half know my lines. I keep saying the real thing and getting in earnest. If Billy hadn't written this burlesque himself, he would have sworn at any body who offered it to him. The house always gets as empty as a rainy Sunday church before we are through the first act, and then he scolds us all around, and says we don't take trouble with our parts."

This was an old grievance; the young men assented gloomily. "Give me tragedy forever," said Old Postern, who was really the younger of the two brothers. Young Postern himself was playing the lover with Vicky. "Give me tragedy forever!" he repeated, more decidedly. "I could play 'Macbeth' two years on a stretch—."

"Oh no, you couldn't," answered the Queen, quickly, with a twinkle in her pretty eyes. "Think of the audience!"

"Nelly, what shall we do tomorrow?" asked Jack Sprague, hastily, for Old Postern was not fond of a joke; he was but a dull player, poor lad, and yet the company would have sadly missed him from its ranks.

"I haven't had a week-day to myself for so long that I have forgotten what I can do," answers the girl, eagerly. "Then you aren't going off by yourselves?" in a pleased tone. "We'll sleep as late as we can, of course; it isn't often we get a Sunday-morning nap in the middle of the week. Suppose we go on the water somewhere?"

"Count me out then," responded Jack Sprague, good-humoredly. "I'm no sailor. See here, it's pretty in the country now, let's go out somewhere for a good long drive and have a high, old dinner and come home by moonlight. I forget how green grass looks in anything but small samples."

"It's my birthday," exclaimed the Queen, rising to her feet excitedly. "I'll ask Vicky Dean; it must be my ball."

"It was your birthday only a month ago," said Old Postern, with amazement; and Nelly denied the charge unblushingly.

"Then I won't have Vicky," she insisted at last, and her companions laughed aloud.

"Old Postern doesn't care about your birthdays; he is all for truth," urged Jack Sprague, seriously, as the prompter walked by. "Let her have her birthdays, old boy, and you and Vicky be young together;" and Postern blushed a lively crimson through his make-up.

"Perhaps Vicky wont go," he said, ruefully. Postern was very cheerful-looking and absurdly red-cheeked and boyish when one reflected upon his tragic bent. He had very little to say, and there was generally more or less hopelessness about his remarks. "You know she never will leave her family when we are here. She spends so much time on the road that she hasn't a word for anybody while the company is in Boston."

The hopeless passion of Old Postern for Vicky Dean was recognized by all their associates, for the little actress sang and danced and painted her pale cheeks all for her father's sake. He had been an actor, and was now an invalid, from the fall of a stage balcony and perhaps a little carelessness as to his fashion of life. Vicky liked to tell everybody that he had played with Booth, but nobody ever asked her about his part. Postern expressed great pride and admiration in the stage lore and experience of his inevitable father-in-law, but he was jealous of Dean, too, Vicky's papa being his only rival.

Vicky and her lover drew but small salaries. It was good of Nelly, the Queen, to arrange a day's pleasuring; but everybody knew that Nelly was the kindest heart in the world.

There was a droll cadence and a cheerful swing in Vicky's gay tune, which had already been sung twice. The audience would beg for it again, and the heavy gallery boots kept time, while even the players themselves could feel the delight of it, familiar as "Starlight Hannah" had become. They were pleased that hard-working little Vicky had made a hit, but it was plain that her voice was getting sharp now, and they gaily made their entrance at this auspicious moment.

They were obliged to glower with rage at once, and they did it handsomely. Nelly was full of spirit; the silly play ceased to weary the overheated audience. The Comedy Company had long ago paid tribute with Nelly's nickname, and the Queen ruled her small and penniless court with great sympathy and decision. Nobody was half satisfied with her salary, and every one said that Nelly deserved to go to England, where people knew genius when they saw it. Yet the Comedy Company thought very well of itself as a troupe; there was nothing on the road that could equal it in ability. Nelly was its star, the large-lettered person of the posters and programmes, but her honest admirers were beginning to wonder why she did not have the recognition she deserved. Now and then an envious voice said that she did not put her whole heart into her playing as she used; and on such an evening as this, when she was in good spirits, she was sure to be told that she made somebody think of old times. It could not be even dreamed that our Queen was in danger of criticism, or that she reigned timidly.

An actor's holiday often means a long morning's sleep, and these were tired young folk, but for all that it was hardly noon when the four comedians set forth. Billy Sharp had made an excellent bargain in underletting the theatre for a grand mass meeting of certain labor societies, and was no doubt glad to have an evening to himself. No rehearsal or mockery of it in the morning; no footlights at night to make one's eyes smart and one's head grow dizzy with the flicker; no tyrannical, fickle audience to scorn or applaud; no dust and clatter of scene shifting; no hurry in the dressing room; no supes; no nervous weariness when the play was done, and no extravagant supper ordered in excitement and regretted directly it was served. An off day that was not a Sunday, and our four friends in a decent hired carryall with a willing pair of horses bound country-ward.

Jack Sprague was the leader of the excursion. He had been once at a first-class hotel out beyond Cambridge where the Harvard men bestowed their patronage. Jack had been asked to join a party made by Museum men, and two or three guests from the Irving Company the winter before. He had often spoken of this grand occasion to his companions, and was sure that he knew the way. "If they give you half as good a dinner as I had that day," Jack said, "you'll wish you could go there to live."

Beside Jack on the front seat was Nelly, radiant with pleasure. She wore a very wide-brimmed Gainsborough hat and her best long gloves, and a dress which Jack had once noticed with approval. There was something not exactly conspicuous, but for all that uncommon, in the aspect of these pleasure makers, though they had dressed most carefully for the parts of picnicing ladies and gentlemen. They could not forget the Public, their requiring task-master, and when some young vagrant gave a saucy cheer, as they drove along, Jack Sprague snapped his whip at them magnificently. Our friends were so possessed with the idea of themselves and the Comedy Company that it was easy to fancy that everybody else knew them too.

"Dear me!" yawned Nelly, as they went their rural way, "I haven't been up so early in the morning this summer. What makes it seem so much earlier out here than it does in town? Let me drive, or I shall go to sleep. Did you say that we should have a good dinner, my lord?"

To which my lord responded with enthusiasm.

"Are you and Vicky enjoying everything?" the Queen inquired, presently, without turning her head or giving a hint of looking round at the pair on the back seat. "I wish that you would give me my little red silk shawl, if it is perfectly convenient," and then she glanced over her shoulder at Vicky, who was blushing a little, and looked very pretty.

"We are your Majesty's servants," says Postern, gallantly. "Sprague, are we on the right road? This is uncommon rural."

The little red shawl had become familiar on many a provincial stage. It always lighted up well, and took on the color of a live cardinal flower, but it never had been more admired than now, against a daylight background of green. The Queen looked paler than she did in the evening, but some wild flowers beguiled the pleasure-makers, and they clambered down from the high carriage, and ran among the bushes like children to fill their hands with white ox-eye daisies. The two girls pinned them on in stage fashion of breast knots, and garlanded not only their own headgear but the young men's beside. There was a pretty bit of woodland, and they deeply regretted that the holiday had not been planned with a view to picnicing in this very spot. The horses browsed by the wayside; they were much more used to being hurried along dusty suburban roads, and hardly knew what to make of this bit of horse-heaven a dozen miles from town.

"We're getting deeper and deeper into the country," insisted Postern. "You ought to have taken that turn to the left; we're bearing to the north'ard all the time since we left Cambridge, and there's no end to this Forest of Arden, that I can see."

"Oh, my dinner," pleaded the Queen; I wish I had eaten my breakfast, bad as it was. I was up in time. I fibbed about that, for I was waiting at the window an hour before I saw the horses turn round the corner."

And Jack Sprague, quite crestfallen, stopped the amiable horses at last, and tried to consider the error of his ways. He had a desperate moment of fear that he had spoiled the holiday. Should they go on or turn back, he asked, after he had patiently submitted to much derision.

"Oh, go on!" exclaimed Vicky Dean, who thought this was the loveliest of drives. "We shall come to some village or other, and there is sure to be a hotel. Let's go on!"

But even Vicky's high courage began to give out half an hour later, for they saw no steeples and went still through a bushy woodland country, and only passed a small, unpromising farmstead now and then in the half-cleared sandy fields. There was a shout of joy when at last they struck a more traveled road, and saw in the distance some high roofs and chimneys. It looked like a very small village, but it was certainly a village. The Queen insisted that they had been taken up by a whirlwind and set down unharmed very far inland. "I always wondered how they did it so easily in Shakespeare," she laughed. "A seaport in Bohemia this minute and somewhere else the next; wishing—carpets and big birds, and all those things used to be true, you know."

"I wish they were true now," whispered Jack Sprague, unexpectedly, with an unusual shine in his eyes; and Nelly was filled with joy, and blushed as she seldom blushed nowadays. Lovers had been very plentiful in her short life, and it had been easy to disdain them, but Jack Sprague!—

"Look, look!" cries the Queen, forgetting her pleasant reverie. "Here is the very place; an old-fashioned country tavern with a sign like ours in the scenery! Oh stop here, do stop, and see if they will take us in!"

Old Postern groaned and tried to remonstrate, and Jack warned everybody of complete disappointment, but turned the horses toward the grass-grown tavern yard. A hulking boy came out of the tumble-down stables, and the next moment a quaint old woman appeared in the side doorway. She wore large, blinking gold spectacles, and was singularly long-waisted, but short of stature, as if she were cut off at her knees.

She was a good study of makeup, and here was an event at last—the drive had been a trifle dull and uncertain.

"Doesn't it seem like England?" whispered the Queen, authoritatively, and everybody assented, though not one of the four had ever crossed the sea.

Jack Sprague leaped from the carriage and stood before the door, hat in hand, after a great bow. "Is this a public house, and can you afford us entertainment, madam?" says he.

"Well, sir," answers the old woman, with a pleased smile at this charming politeness, "I don't know as I ought to call it so now; we used to do a gre't business; this was the main road into Boston, and lots o' folks used to put up here over night and go into town early. An' as it happens to-day, I'm left sole alone, except Tobias there, and I'm not provided as I should be, but he can do for your team and I can give you some kind of a bite, if it's so that you don't want to go farther."

There was but a moment's hesitation at the end of this almost breathless speech, and then Nelly Hall decided the question by getting out of the carryall and approaching the friendly old dame with a beaming face. She and Sprague, you remember, always took the part of first lady and gentleman. She dropped the landlady a charming courtesy, and stood before her with all her wilting posies and the famous red shawl about her shoulders.

"We are only too glad to have what you may please to give!" she said. "We are strangers in the country."

"French folks, be you, dear?" inquired Mrs. Fleck, who loved a little adventure, and was only by force of habit a humdrum person.

"From Scotland," said the Queen, unblushingly. "I am Lady Macbeth, and this"—she couldn't call Jack her husband—"this is Mr. Macduff; this," as Vicky approached, "is my sister Ophelia, and Mr. Smith." There was a thrill of laughter in the very air, and Nelly herself shook for a moment, and almost spoiled the little scene.

"Come in, all of you," cried the hostess, hospitably. "Way from Scotland; I want to know! You're Miss Mackby, be you?" She didn't hear very well, good soul. "And Mr. Duffy, this one? I had a cousin who married with a Duffy, but they lived down New Bedford way, somewheres. Come right in. We don't keep no book now. I don't know's I ought to say we keep tavern at all," and she led them across the wide, arched entry to a cool room that looked out into the garden.

There they seated themselves, right centre and left centre, as if waiting for the curtain to rise. Postern thought it unmentionably slow. He whispered something about dried-apple pies to the Queen, who spoke of cider in a more cheerful tone; but Sprague depressed her again with a suggestion of wilted crackers. This solitary, old, gone-to-seed hostelry was a poor exchange for the gay, townish hotel which he had in mind. His mouth had been fairly watering all the way for the chilled champagne, with which he meant to treat his companions. The four members of the Comedy Company were beyond asking for any delicacies, however; it was honest hunger that assailed them.

The old hostess reappeared presently, like a busy ant. "You'll have to wait the longer, 'less some one of you comes right out into the garden with me and helps me pick a mess of peas," she said, with a persuasive briskness. "I aint going to make company of you. I know by your looks how hungry you be, and p'raps one o' you won't mind helping 'till Tobias is free of his hosses. They was warm, too."

The four members of the Comedy Company rose together from their chairs and insisted upon going to the garden. There was something motherly and delightful about Mrs. Fleck, and the disused inn parlor was stuffy. Nelly, the Queen, went first, and talked with the inn's mistress all the way down the garden walk. The red shawl showed bravely above the pea-vines.

There was not much paint left on the gambrel-roofed house, but on the side next the garden grew woodbines and grapevines, and morning-glories were blooming yet about the kitchen windows, though the day was at high noon. There was a smell of herbs in the air—of fresh sage and thyme—because the leading gentleman had walked straight across the herb-bed. The old garden was full of bees; the roses were hardly out of bloom in the shade of the trees, and the hot sun made the pea-vines a very pale blue green. "Why can't we have dinner out of doors," asked Nelly Hall. "There was that table and the benches under the cherry trees as we came out."

Mrs. Fleck was greatly amused at this proposal. "Why, yes, honey," she answered, as if the Queen were a willful child; "if so be you'd rather than have things fixed decent in the dining-room. I let that old kitchen table stay out all weathers. I do my ironin' on it in hot mornin's. But I aint goin' to put on a good table-cloth that I had in mind fer ye. Bless you! we've got peas enough a'ready—'many hands makes light work,' says the proverb—but, my sakes! aint some o' you be'n pickin' small an' big ones an' leaves all together!"

"Now," said the Queen, as they all went toward the house. "Dear sister Ophelia and Mr. Smith, will you be kind enough to take yourselves off for a long walk. I can't have you in my way. Mr. Duffy must play about the house because he may be wanted about setting the table. For me, I shall help to cook the dinner."

There were mild protests, but the Queen had her way, and Vicky gave a grateful glance to her friend as she disappeared toward the orchard shade, out beyond the bee hives. Jack Sprague lounged into the old house. Perhaps he went to sleep on a wide, prickly haircloth sofa in the best room; at any rate, he lay there listening to the pleasant country-sounds out in the garden, and to the tones of Nelly's voice as she went and came in the old kitchen.

It seemed strangely silent and lonely, that old house, which had been the shelter of so many people. What tender hearts and hard hearts, what good and bad errand–runners had slept and walked within its walls! A feeling of unrest still lingered to vex the most leisurely traveler, but the rural peace and isolation had almost quelled it, and nature was having its way. Seeds of the wild field flowers sprouted closer together every year in the garden, and when this pleasant old hostess was gone the sun and rain and the field flowers would have their way. The four members of the Comedy Company were vexed with themselves because they were not more provoked at having lost their way. Jack Sprague had resigned himself to the absence of champagne, and they were all soothed by the silence and more amused with the old tavern than any one would believe. Hard-worked, late o' nights, uncomplaining young majesty, servants these, who thought no ill of making an audience laugh when your own heart ached; who fitted not so badly into the pinchbeck trappings of state and even royalty. Alas! there are spangles worn or torn off the robes of other high gentlefolk beside those of the stage, and happy are they who can bring good-humored smiles to the faces of this anxious world.

"Where are they all three?" and Nelly comes bustling to the door in a great gingham apron and rings a big bell with both hands. Jack Sprague comes out of the dark parlor looking flushed and sleepy, and years younger, like a hungry boy, and then Postern and Vicky appear from under the far apple trees, quite coy and shame-faced with delight, the two of them. Nelly knows in an instant that Postern has asked Vicky to marry him, and has not been refused, either. She has been telling him for weeks that he ought to do it, and leave the stage by and by and settle down. Postern will never make an actor.

They come to the table in the garden where the Queen stands triumphant before her little feast. This is the quickest-fingered and quickest-footed creature that ever was, and not only have the old flag-bottomed chairs been brought out from the dining-room, and the brightest old crockery hunted out of every cupboard, but she has put nosegays at every plate and made the dinner a picture of gayety. And she will have it that Mrs. Fleck sits down with them at the garden table and takes the seat at the head, though Mrs. Fleck wonders who is to serve them, and is a little worried and self-conscious. Nelly's kind heart is brimming over with a great wish that everybody should have the best of good times. She has often spent her last cent in hot theatre suppers, under flaring gas-lights; she has known the hard side of life so well that she seizes every chance for gayety. Nobody else would have thought to sprinkle little flowers and fine maple leaves all over the white table-cloth; and having stolen enough mouthfuls of dinner by the way to quell her hunger, she sits down meekly, and takes all the praise she can get.

"'Twas Mis' Mackby did it all," insists Mrs. Fleck, with a pleased smile, and then they began to eat their luncheon like school children.

There was but a small piece of cold roasted lamb—a very small piece, indeed—but Nelly had made an omelet, such as her old Italian friend Signor Floretti, used to make; he who played accompaniments while she sang her childish songs many years ago. Nelly's mother was an actress before her, and the Signor was an old music teacher, who lived in the same New York boarding house. There never was such an omelet put upon a table. Mrs. Fleck would often try to copy it afterward, and never succeed in giving it just quite the same taste. And then there were the green peas, and Nelly had made salad of the potatoes with a pinch of herbs and a bit of yellow cream and vinegar. There was good country bread and butter, and—there was elder wine! Jack Sprague's eyes had brightened at the sight of the old decanter with its thick-stalked, round-bowled wine glasses. They listened to Mrs. Fleck's long story of how she made it, and how she always depended upon currants in old times, and upon cider, but now for long and tedious reasons she had none of either. The happy company ate and drank and were merry, and pledged each other in the wine, and were thankful, though it certainly was a little too sweet. They would have Mrs. Fleck take a whole glass, though she said it would be sure to go to her head.

And then Nelly commanded the two cavaliers to clear the table, and to do it carefully, too, and not pile up the plates as they went to the kitchen, because if they did wrong in any way they should have no cherry pie.

What a cherry pie it was—large and deep, and baked in a square dish! What a triumph of engineering to cut it into five equal portions; but the Queen did that, and everybody had a fair share of juice. Mrs. Fleck was more than thankful that she had baked it yesterday, and of such immense size; but she had a foreboding, and the tall cherry-tree stood in the shade of the house and bore more than common fruit that year.

"But where is Tobias?" asked somebody. "Is he eating hay with the horses?"

"He's mortal bashful," responds Mrs. Fleck. "I gave him some bread and sweet-cake and my yaller pitcher full o' milk. 'Twill keep him till I can further attend." At which everybody shouted with delight. The elder wine was stronger than it tasted.

What an afternoon of delight! The very bees came about the table to get their share of the cherry pie, or went waddling about the table-cloth, after a visit to the glasses; there was a bewildering flicker of shadows moving to and fro on the table from the cherry leaves overhead. Nelly could not be urged to have another bite of anything, though she declared herself to have been hungry enough to have eaten the paste-board fowls belonging to the Comedy Company when she first sat down. Mrs. Fleck was almost tearful in her sentimental enjoyment of this unexpected occasion. She could not hear exactly what Nelly said about the Comedy Company; in truth she could hardly follow the quick, merry speech of her companions. She felt certain that they were foreigners; but it was all a little confused, except that they had come out for a frolic and were successful in finding one. "No, you brought your good time with you," she said aloud, in a little pause, while somebody was urging somebody else to sing. Vicky Dean protested that she would not and could not sing "Starlight Hannah" then or there. She would rather forget it this one day in a whole, long month. They all joined in a pretty chorus presently, and Mrs. Fleck thought this the best of all, until Vicky and Postern sang the air of a stage dance, and Jack and the Queen took the steps of it to and fro on the green grass.

"Perhaps you sing yourself, Mrs. Fleck?" says Jack Sprague, gallantly, as they take their seats again, for he had heard the widow join in the refrain tremulously as she beat time with her cloth-slippered foot.

"I used to have a pretty tuneful voice when I was young," she answers. "I always was the one to sing trible in the singing seats." Whether it was the elder wine or the good company, who can tell? but when the guests urged Mrs. Fleck to sing a song, she cleared her voice directly and began, " 'Mid pleasures and palaces"—that dear old tune which touches every heart of us as we grow older. It touched the hearts of the four companions of the Comedy Troupe. Perhaps it was not a fortunate selection, for neither of them had any home but lodgings. Jack Sprague, after his eyes and Nelly's had met with a dear surprise of conscious prophecy—Jack Sprague strolled off a little way down the garden, and then, coming hastily back, struck into the last refrain with a then, coming hastily back, struck into the last refrain with a friendly friendly tenor, and helped the old lady along on the high notes, just as her voice began to break a little.

" 'Tis hard to be growin'. old," she said, by way of gentle apology, when she had ended. "My heart is as young as ever it was when I get among young folks, but I declare my voice is a-goin'."

And everyone said it was a sweet voice still, and what a dear old song it was after all; and Nelly sang "Hunting Tower" charmingly, and afterward some delicious Italian street songs, taught her by the omelet-making Signor. Jack Sprague liked them, and that was the reason why they were sung.

Postern was a well-known athlete in the company, and after the songs began to fail he kindly did amazing things on the grass plot with his own arms and legs and a sturdy old clothes-pole, and frightened both Mrs. Fleck and Vicky in a delightful way. The afternoon shadows of the old house covered most of the garden, and still they sat there and amused themselves cheerfully. At last they gravely agreed that they must go away—they must go back to town. "There would be nothing for our supper," whispers Nelly. "May we come again some day, Mrs. Fleck?" she added, aloud.

They wandered through the quaint old house while Tobias harnessed the horses. Nelly held a little prim blue-and-white crockery pitcher, which she had fallen in love with on a high shelf and filled with flowers for the table. "'Taint worth five cents, darlin', but I wish you'd keep it to remember me by," urged Mrs. Fleck. They said good-bye over and over again. Jack Sprague tipped Tobias like a lord, and nearly took his dwindling wits away. And Mrs. Fleck must have $5, too, though she insisted that 50 cents a dinner was her usual charge, and that by good rights she ought to pay them for such a pleasure-making. Jack Sprague apologized for such generosity to the Queen. "We should have spent twice as much at the other place, you know, and she looked as if she didn't know what money was." Poor young spendthrift! Mrs. Fleck was a forehanded old soul, and they were just keeping themselves meanly fed and covered with fast-fading theatre splendors.

"To think that I and my mother before me have spent our lives behind the footlights!" said Nelly, wistfully, as they drove away, "and here that quiet old place has been going on and the garden growing and blooming every year. Did you hear the old lady say that she wished we could come out some Sunday and hear the new minister?" and they all laughed.

But the queen did not confess that she had asked Mrs. Fleck whether, if some time she should be ill or tired out, she might not come to the old tavern to stay a long time and get rested. Mrs. Fleck had taken the red silk shawl into her motherly arms for answer, and stroked the Queen's head kindly before she said a word.

Vicky Dean and Mr. Postern sat together on the back seat of the carryall, and, as usual, were seldom heard to speak, but all agreed that it was a wonderfully beautiful evening.

"Think of my poor mother and me!" the Queen repeated. "Think of us, Jack Sprague!" she commanded her loyal subject gently.

For Nelly, having played many a part on many a stage, had now put her whole heart into this carefully-studied scene of housekeeping. She hoped that Jack would like it best of all her rôles. Did he, too, think sometimes how good it would be if they had a home together? Alas! theirs was a life of change and hurry and weariness behind the foot-lights, and her woman's heart was unsatisfied. She would always play the part of Herself for the leading gentleman if the Fates proved kind.

The leading gentleman was also busy with his thoughts. He had a look of cities and of fashionable life, but his own mother had been a simple country woman for all that, and had grieved, provokingly, when Jack felt a vocation for the stage. She had been dead a long time now, it seemed to him, as he thought of her. Perhaps he and Nelly would go some time to the old farm-house on its green hillside; he never sup-posed before that Nelly would like that sort of thing. Jack Sprague lighted a cigar, but it went out; and he wished that he had either worked hard enough to be a first-rate actor or had let it all alone in the beginning. The Player Queen began to feel chilly in the damp evening air; she drew the red silk shawl closer and closer, then she moved a bit nearer to Jack, and put her warm thin little hand into his: "Why, I almost forgot that you used to be a country lout yourself, Mr. Duffy," said she.

THREE FRIENDS.[12]

A STORY IN THREE PARTS.   PART I.

By Sarah Orne Jewett

We have never grown tired yet, Mary Dean and Hannah Fennel and I, of talking over past times and the way in which we came to live together and be so fond of each other—three country girls from different states, in the fourth story of a city boarding-house. I am a teacher in a primary school, and Hannah used to keep accounts in a circulating library, and Mary Dean is in a fancy goods store—one of the first sales-women. My name is Elizabeth Prime—they always call me Lizzie at home but the girls always say Betsey, and I must confess that I have grown to like to hear them, but it took me a good while to get used to the sound at first. I always hated my Aunt Betsey Prime when I was a little girl, though I believe now that she was as good a woman as she knew how to be, being made in the likeness of a round-topped slate tombstone, without the least understanding of anything in the way of a joke. She kept house for my brother and me after father and mother died, and ran the farm and brought us up to know how to use our hands and to be thrifty and self-supporting. I didn't half know how to thank her for it, and I am afraid I never really did seem grateful. She had two or three thousand dollars of her own—that she had pinched herself to save—and when she died we found she had left everything, even her clothes, to the foreign Missionary society. The boys and I were dreadfully put out, but poor soul, the only pleasure she ever had, I believe, was in thinking about her donation, and in one way we were just as well off without her poor gains. The farm belonged to my oldest brother Tom, and there was a charge on it to pay for Dan's learning his trade and my getting an education to teach; then we always were to have a right to go back to the old place if we were tired out, or sick or in trouble, if we would help Tom according to our ability. Tom is as large-hearted a man as ever was, but I never liked his wife over well—that is, I never could make her seem one of our folks. One of the children looks and acts just like me when I was her age, and there's another just like Tom himself when he was a boy. It seems as if we were starting out in life over again, and I like to have a visit to the old place every summer for Tom's sake if for nothing else, but of course I don't feel bound to the farm as if my father and mother were still alive.

Mary Dean has much the same homeless feeling, or had until we made a little home together. Her own mother is dead and her father is married again to a woman who almost turned the older children out-of-doors. He is a weak sort of man, it always seemed to me, but Mary does every kind thing for them that she can think of, and even sends them their flour and sugar, besides little things that she knows her father likes. I used to think she was foolish, but I have learned better, for it makes her so happy; and, to be sure, her father isn't always able to work now and the other children are none of them able to help much yet. But Mary was sure to have left home soon enough to take care of herself; that woman needn't have pushed her out as she did, a sickly child, even if there were so many hungry mouths to feed and hardly anything to put into them.

Mary and I have been friends for ten years; ours was a boarding-house acquaintance to begin with, but I had just come to the city from a country school-room and felt very lonely and strange, and Mary, who had been living there a year already, came and spoke to me that first evening and we were friends right away. She says that she doesn't understand now what made her take the first step, for she never liked to be forward with strangers and hardly knew anybody in the house to speak to. We always like to think of these first days, we were both so happy and surprised at finding each other out. We felt almost like lovers, we had been so lonesome. The school was hard for me, coming straight from old fashions of teaching to new ones, and it was so good to have somebody to tell my troubles to when I got home at night. I used to be kept hours after school closed getting my reports right and straightening out what I had to do. If we had been younger we might have cared less about each other, but we had lived long enough to need a real friend and helper, not a playmate.

So we went on together for two or three years, and sometimes I took Mary home to Tom's with me to spend a vacation, while I became as interested in her family affairs as if they were mine. We had a pleasant room and a good many books, and somehow we used to feel disappointed when anything called either of us away for an evening, we liked so much to be quiet and to carry out our own plans. But first one of us and then the other noticed a plain-looking girl a few years older than we, who sat at the end of the boarding-house table, a sad-faced, kind-looking sort of person, and presently we found out that her name was Fennel and that she had a room above ours.

We used to say sometimes that she was just like one of ourselves if we had not met each other and had lived on alone. At last, after we had begun to say good-night and good-morning whenever we had the chance, Mary came hurrying home one evening and put down some library books on the table, and told me that she had some news.

I was tired, for school had been very hard and the weather was growing warm, and I am afraid I didn't show much interest.

"You know Miss Fennel?" said Mary, eagerly, "I found her in Fenby's library this noon, and had such a nice talk with her. She promised to come down this evening after she gets back. It is her free evening and she seemed so pleased. She has been here four months,—can you believe it?"

I gave a little groan, and Mary was disappointed because I was tired and cross, but after supper when Hannah Fennel came shyly to our doors, my heart warmed toward her, and we had a nice evening together. The end of a month found us a family of three instead of two, for somehow Hannah seemed to belong to us, and took the room next ours, and we had a bed that turned up against the wall in the day time and was hidden by a curtain, so we used to make a parlor of our room and were very fine and comfortable.

We never could exactly understand Hannah Fennel, for all we liked her so much. She had more fun than any of us, for though Mary and I used to have an evening now and then when we felt very cheerful and laughed and teased each other, Hannah had a bit of fun ready for any time of day, a quick word or two that would keep us merry until we saw her again; such a droll sense of humor, such a way of seeing the funny side of a thing, that it did us all good. Yet she used to cry herself to sleep night after night, and often looked so sad and old that it made our hearts ache to see her, especially after we found out she was younger than either of us instead of five or six years older as we supposed.

We never liked to ask her what troubled her, and with all her sorrow she brought so much happiness into our lives that we did not know how to thank her. It was Hannah who knew what to do when I had a school-headache, and who was always ready to go to a concert or for a walk with Mary Dean, who seemed to carry half our cares and troubles but never to hint at any of her own.

Single women who are busy all day in a great city are apt to live very uncomfortable lives,—to have to pay much more than they can afford for very little real comfort or a decent sort of home. We had tried a great many experiments and made some mistakes, but I believe that we really spent less money on our clothes and our living expenses and had a better return than any three girls we knew. Hannah was a capital manager, and had "head" as Mary Dean was always saying. We had fallen into a silly way of living on tea and crackers at one time, and nearly ruined our health, I must confess, for our first boarding mistress, a kind, careful, country-bred woman, had died some years after we had been together, and the house was turned into a lodging house, so we used to get most of our meals for ourselves in our room. Hannah would have no such nonsense, and we used to have a regular dinner at a boarding-house near by and cook our breakfasts and suppers, but good ones they were! She was so sensible and kept us so well and hearty, and made us get a good, brisk walk every day. Once I couldn't help saying to her that she was too good and kind to us, and I didn't see how her own family could get on without her. I was sorry the minute I had spoken, for she almost burst out crying; I saw her cheeks flush scarlet and I turned away and tried to talk carelessly about something else, but she went into her own room and dressed herself to go out. It was Sunday afternoon, and she didn't come back until after dark. Then we both tried to appear as if nothing had happened, but I was very sorry because I had spoken the natural thought of my heart, it seemed in some strange way to give her such a wound.

PART II.

I had the long school vacation, of course, but Mary Dean had only a fortnight every summer, and sometimes less than that if the firm that employed her was unusually busy. Hannah was never sure of more than a week's holiday, but I used to spend a good part of my resting time in town—after I made a visit or two. We had very good air and were living in a quiet part of the city; two of our windows overlooked the river, and we had a drive now and then by ourselves, or some short excursion. I used to find little time for sewing or reading while I was hard at work teaching, and I really loved the long, quiet summer days, while the girls were away and nobody tapped at my door or asked me a question all day long. Once or twice I went down to the seashore for a few days to visit the mother of a little scholar whom I was very fond of. But this last summer it happened that instead of Mary and I going off in different directions and leaving Hannah alone, as often happened, we suddenly found that we had a great deal of spare time on our hands and must make some new arrangement.

The library where Hannah was writing, was in the same building where Mary Dean's business was, and it came to pass that the owners of the property decided to make extensive repairs. The girls came home the same evening in a great state of excitement, to tell me that they were each given the choice of an extra holiday of two months and possibly a little longer, or of employment on half-wages. Both the store and the library were to be removed for the time being, but it was always a very dull time in mid-summer and they could probably well be spared. Indeed they had both asked not long before for a longer vacation than usual, as Hannah, "the Captain," as we called her, had decided that Mary needed it after several years' steady work, and Mary, who held the same opinion, agreed only upon the promise that Hannah, who was looking pale and thin, would follow the example.

So here we were, the owners of two whole idle months, and at first we hardly knew what to do with them. Hannah insisted that we should both go away, and I insisted that she must go with us, and that we must find some plan that we could carry out together. I was filled with wonder even then that Hannah said nothing of any plans of her own. She never had a letter and never spoke of her past life. And yet whoever knew her could not help loving her, and I was sure that somewhere or other at least one houseful of friends was keeping her in fond remembrance. I was more and more puzzled to know what strange fate had outwardly severed her from all her old associations and the affection of her early friends.

I have forgotten exactly how it came about that we made up our minds to spend that whole vacation in a little, old-fashioned farm-house near my old home. Some neighbors of my father and mother who were old people when I left the farm had died only a year or two before and my brother Tom had bought their few acres to add to his property. I don't know what made me think of taking the house, which had been standing empty, but, to make my story short, we did go there, we three girls together, and were as happy as heart could wish. Tom was good enough to give us the rent and as many vegetables as we wanted off the farm, but Hannah and Mary wouldn't hear to our plundering anybody when we had plenty of money, by living carefully, to pay our own way. So we used to go foraging among the neighbors and buy some pears here and some early beets or corn in the next place; and Tom's wife always had the butter-money and egg-money, so we used to put something in her pocket every week, and she was more friendly than I ever knew her to be. I was so thankful to have Tom's boy and girl to myself a little, and I do believe that they enjoyed having us in the Ford house as much as we did being there. We felt all the time as if we were on a picnic, and I have wished a great many times that people who want to be right out in the country, and who haven't much money to spend on their holidays, would remember the little deserted farmhouses that stand near the by-ways and lanes all over New England; that are good shelter enough for a few weeks in summer, and have a real gift of restfulness and lovely human associations within their gray walls.

Somehow I never could look at the white lilac tree that old Mrs. Ford was so fond of, or at the few flowers that were left in the turf where her little garden used to be, without tears coming into my eyes as I thought of her. There were a few blossoms of London-pride and sweet-williams and some sprigs of ambrosia, and behind the house was her hop-vine and two or three currant bushes, and before we left, the yellow sweet apples were dropping from their boughs, that I used to tease her for when I was a little girl.

Mary and I used to wonder a great deal about Hannah—perhaps because there was more time to do it in. We used to walk a great deal together, because of course I had to go to see all the people I used to know, and sometimes the neighbors used to ask us all to come and drink tea, after haying time was over, but Hannah always seemed to dislike going about. She was so happy and so much brighter than usual that it did our hearts good, but we used to say that she behaved as if she thought we were safe at last from somebody or something that had made her afraid. I asked two or three scholars of mine to come and spend a week. Poor little city-bred things they were, that never had rolled in the grass; and I don't believe they had a word to say about anybody except Hannah after they went home, she was so good to them and knew so well how to please them.

Perhaps one reason why we talked more about this dear, silent friend of ours was this: we had grown a little better used to the fact that we did not know anything about her, until just before we came away from town, the very day before, when I was packing my trunk and the other girls were out doing some last shopping. The little errand boy from the circulating library came running over to bring a letter for Hannah which the proprietor thought she might be glad to have before she left the city. I never had seen a letter of hers before; they must all have come to the library, so I couldn't help stealing a look at this as it lay on the table. The address was in a man's hand-writing and the postmark was not very far from my own home, just over the boundary of the next State. When Hannah came in and saw it, she flushed quickly and I thought her very glad, too, as she caught up the letter and went into her own room and stood close by the window and read it. The daylight was almost gone but she read the letter twice through. That night it was very late before she put out her light, and in the morning I could see the tear-marks under her eyes where she must have lain awake and cried. Just as we were on our way to the station, I saw a young man spring forward from the sidewalk as if he wished to stop us; of course I told the girls, for he seemed to recognize one of them and to be very eager to speak to her, but Hannah seemed really alarmed, and said, "No! no! go on, or we shall lose the train."

PART III.

It was true that we were in some danger of being late, so I said nothing more as I had lost sight of the stranger, at any rate, in the crowd that was passing a street corner.

You may be sure that Mary Dean and I talked this over together more than once. My sister-in-law, Tom's wife, managed to find out that we really knew nothing about Hannah's past history, and made me very angry one day by saying that she wondered how we dared to be such friends with her, and to take her to live with us. This seemed so silly; the idea of once doubting Hannah—Hannah, who was so much more sensible and careful than either of us—who was as straight-forward and honest-hearted and kind as the day was long. She seemed above any sort of suspicion. Yet it was strange that something held us back from questioning her, and made Mary Dean, who was quick-spoken and careless as a child about most things, always on her guard against hurting Hannah's feelings by anything that seemed like curiosity. If she had a secret to keep, we liked her and trusted her none the less.

But one day I was sitting alone in our little house, feeling very sorry, as I sat at my sewing, that our time was so nearly spent, and yet not a little glad to think about my school and how glad I should be to see the children. Everything was still except the rustle of the leaves and the chirping of the cricket in the long grass under the apple trees, and I started at the sound of footsteps coming up the path that led from the road. Whose face should I see but the young man's I had noticed in the street the day we left town.

He asked me if Miss Fennel lived there and I said yes. Then I remembered her avoidance of him, though whether she also had seen him I could not tell, and I looked him straight in the eyes, and said: "You must tell me first if you have come to trouble her. I know nothing about her affairs or her friends, but I know her well and love her dearly, and I am not going to let anybody trouble her in any way."

"Nobody in this world cares half so much for her as I do," and the minute the stranger spoke I knew he told me the truth.

"If she has never told you her history, I will.—There is not a better soul alive, but her father was a rascal, and her mother died of a broken heart, and though I have loved Hannah ever since I can remember, when her poor mother was gone she told me that she never would consent to marry me—it would be a sin to link an honest name to such shame as belonged to hers."

"Poor girl," said I. "What an awful weight she has had to carry, and never a soul to speak to! We should have cared for her all the more."

"She made me promise that I would not try to find her or to write to her for three years, and I kept my promise," the lover said. "I wish I hadn't, too, for I dare say she only thought I would forget that I ever cared anything about her. I wrote her early in the summer, when my time was out, and she wrote such a pitiful letter, to tell me we must give each other up. But when I found she still loved me, I started right off to find her, though I didn't know any address except the city. I saw her in the street—"

"Yes," I said eagerly, "I saw you that day, but she would not stop."

"Then I lost track of her, of course, and I didn't know what to do. I supposed they would know at the place where she worked; but they had mislaid her address in the confusion of moving, and it took me a long time to get it, and then I found that we had been near together all summer. I own a place over in Stratton now. I always thought it would be better to strike root in a new place, for Hannah's sake. And I am going to marry her whether she says yes, or says no!"

"I would if I were you," said I. "You go across this next field and into the orchard beyond, and there you'll find her. I see her dress from here." I was so glad to think it was the blue gingham dress that she looked so pretty in; and away Hannah's lover went, straight toward that bit of dark blue. I must say, I wished I were one of the robins in the apple trees for a little while, to listen to what was said. My heart beat as fast as it could, and I did not feel like sitting still and sewing any longer. I went up the lane to where the young man's horse stood and fed him with white clover and then ran back to the house and began to get ready for the best kind of a company tea. Once or twice I was afraid that Hannah would say no, but one look at her face was enough to relieve me of any such fears, as they came across the field together.

She came and put her arms round me and kissed me when she came in; and I couldn't help crying a little. "It isn't right, I'm afraid," says Hannah, looking at me with her appealing eyes, "but Jim would have it so;" and you never saw anything like the nod of Jim's head, nor the beaming happiness of him. "I told your friend here what your misery had been," he said as gently as could be, as if he were so afraid of hurting her feelings, and Hannah gave me such a frightened look, so I went and kissed her again.

"I'm sure I don't know what Mary Dean and I shall ever do without you," I whispered to her. "You have made us a real home and been such a help;" while Hannah said we never should know what it had been to her, alone in the world as she felt, to have us treat her like a sister.

So that winter Mary Dean and I were alone together again and happy enough too, though we missed our old companion every day. Still, we like to have her letters and are going to spend all the time we can get with her this summer, though of course, Mary cannot expect very long holidays, and I cannot leave her alone in town all through my long vacation.

There is a great deal we can do for some younger girls whom we have learned to know in the city, who don't understand any better how to take care of themselves and their money than we did at first, and we mean to lend them a helping hand and perhaps start a little friendly society or club among the girls who live in our fashion.

Hannah seems to be very happy. I always liked "Jim" as she calls him, from the first moment I saw him. I think she still worries about the sins of the fathers being visited upon the children, and sometimes thinks she may have done wrong to marry; but I believe she does good enough in this world to make up for the harm her father did. She never forgets it, I can see that, and she looks older by ten years than she really is, but her husband cares enough about her to make her grow younger and younger now. Dear Hannah! She did look very happy the day she was married. I don't know whether Mary Dean and I shall ever forsake our life together in our sky-parlor, but I have often thought I should like to go back to the little old Ford house where we spent last summer, and end my days. I told my brother Tom in the last letter I wrote, to be sure and keep it in good repair for Mary Dean and me.

Notes

1. An incomplete manuscript draft of the story is in the Jewett papers at Harvard's Houghton Library.

2. Annie Fields, ed., *Letters of Sarah Orne Jewett* (Boston: Houghton Mifflin, 1911), p. 42. In this crazy quilt edition of letters, this quotation is located as part of a letter obviously misdated 1889. I could not turn up this passage in Jewett's letters to Fields preserved at the Houghton Library.

3. The other S. Jewett was the actress Sara Jewett (1847–99) with whom Sarah Orne Jewett was sometimes confused. One of the most beautiful and famous actresses of her day, Sara Jewett was forced to retire from the stage for health reasons in 1883.

4. Jewett to Aldrich, 6 Nov. [1887], Thomas Bailey Aldrich Papers, Houghton Library, Harvard University. Quoted by permission of the Houghton Library.

5. Aldrich to Jewett, 25 Nov. 1887, Sarah Orne Jewett Papers, Houghton Library, Harvard University. Quoted by permission of the Houghton Library.

6. Jewett to Aldrich, 25 Nov. 1887, Thomas Bailey Aldrich Papers, Houghton Library, Harvard University. Quoted by permission of the Houghton Library.

7. There is a brief sketch of *America* in Frank Luther Mott, *A History of American Magazines 1885–1905* (Cambridge, Mass.: Harvard Univ. Press, Belknap Press, 1957), pp. 60–61.

8. *The King of Folly Island and Other People* (Boston: Houghton Mifflin, 1888), p. 134.

9. No single complete file of *Good Cheer* exists, but a full run can be assembled from the holdings of the Library of Congress, the Boston Public Library, and Harvard University. The last issue was apparently Mar. 1888.

10. Jewett to Aldrich, 25 Nov. 1887, Thomas Bailey Aldrich Papers, Houghton Library, Harvard University. Quoted by permission of the Houghton Library.

11. *America*, 1 (28 July 1888), 6–8.

12. *Good Cheer*, 4 (Jan. 1886), 1–2; 4 (Feb. 1886), 1–2; 4 (Mar. 1886), 1–2.

INDEX

DATE DUE
